On Competition

The Harvard Business Review Book Series

On Competition

Updated and Expanded Edition

Michael E. Porter

A Harvard Business Review Book

The *Harvard Business Review* articles in this collection are available as individual reprints. Discounts apply to quantity purchases. For information and ordering contact Customer Service, Harvard Business School Publishing, Boston, MA 02163. Telephone: (617) 783-7500, 8 a.m. to 6 p.m. Eastern Time, Monday through Friday. Fax: (617) 783-7555, 24 hours a day. E-mail: custserve@hbsp.harvard.edu.

Library of Congress Cataloging-in-Publication Data

Porter, Michael E., 1947–
    On competition / Michael E. Porter
        p.   cm. — (The Harvard business review book series)
    Includes index.
    ISBN 978-1-4221-2696-7
    1. Competition, International.   2. Comparative advantage (International trade)   3. Industrial policy.   4. Environmental policy.   5. Social policy.   I. Title.
    HF1414.P67   2008
    382'.1042—dc22   2008022292

The paper used in this publication meets the requirements of the American National Standard for Permanence of Paper for Printed Library Materials Z39.48-1984.

To John H. McArthur,
former Dean of Harvard Business School

Contents

Part V   **Strategy and Leadership**

Introduction

COMPETITION IS ONE OF SOCIETY'S MOST powerful forces for making things better in many fields of human endeavor. The study of competition and the creation of value, in their full richness, have preoccupied me for several decades. Competition is pervasive, whether it involves companies contesting markets, countries coping with globalization, or social organizations responding to societal needs. Every organization needs a strategy in order to deliver superior value to its customers.

This is truer today than ever before, as competition has intensified dramatically over the last several decades in almost all domains. It has spread across geography, so that nations must compete to maintain their existing prosperity, much less enhance it. Competition has also spread to all sectors of society, including fields like the arts, education, health care, and philanthropy, where there are growing needs but scarce resources.

Today organizations in all spheres must compete to deliver value. Value is the ability to meet or exceed the needs of customers, and do so efficiently. Companies have to deliver value to their customers, and countries have to deliver value as business locations. This is now just as true for a hospital delivering health care, or a foundation making charitable contributions, as it is for a company producing a product or service. Delivering social value—high social benefits per dollar expended—is fast becoming the imperative for any organization that seeks to advance the public good.

I would like to thank Joan Magretta for her assistance in writing the Introduction, as well as her important role in a number of the articles in this collection. Thomas Stewart and Andrea Ovans also provided helpful comments on the Introduction. Thanks as well to Lyn Pohl and Hannah Ginley for their expert help in preparing the manuscript. Of course, without the terrific work of my coauthors this collection would not have been possible.

In understanding competition and value creation, my aim is to capture the complexity of what actually happens on the ground. While trained as an economist and steeped in the discipline of economic reasoning, I have sought both to advance theory and make that theory operational for practitioners. My goal has been to develop rigorous and useful frameworks that effectively bridge the gap between theory and practice.

This book brings together in one place the full range of concepts and tools I have developed to understand competition and value creation. This includes both my newer work and the original foundations on which it is built. The articles here examine competition at multiple levels and in different settings, but with a common framework that connects them all.[1]

This expanded edition has five parts. Part I, "Competition and Strategy: Core Concepts," lays out the core concepts of competitive strategy for companies, first at the level of a single industry and then for multi-business or diversified companies. The drivers of industry competition, the ways in which companies gain and sustain competitive advantage, and the principles of developing a distinctive strategy are at the core of competition. A sophisticated understanding of how to be competitive in a particular business provides the foundation on which other corporate choices are built; diversification, for example, cannot be approached sensibly without linking it directly to competition in individual businesses. Also, the principles in Part I are as relevant for nonprofits as for companies.[2]

Part II, "The Competitiveness of Locations," addresses the role of location in competition. As competition has spread and intensified, interest in the competitiveness of nations, states, and cities has exploded. As technology has allowed companies to become more global in their activities and as capital moves more freely across borders, many theorists claim that location diminishes in importance. The articles in Part II, however, challenge this notion. In them, I show how the prosperity of both companies and entire countries is dependent on the local environment in which competition takes place. Traditionally, the competitiveness of a region or a nation has been seen primarily as an issue for governments seeking to promote investment and job creation. The new model of competitiveness reveals unfamiliar roles for companies in shaping their competitive context; the need for a new type of relationship between business, government, and other local institutions; and entirely new ways of thinking about government policy. Understanding the influence of location on competition, together with the ideas in Part I, is also essential to setting global strategy for companies.[3]

Part III, "Competitive Solutions to Societal Problems," draws on the frameworks in Parts I and II to address important societal issues. The environment, urban poverty and income inequality, and health care, among others, are normally seen as social problems. However, each of them is inextricably bound up with economics and, more specifically, with competition. I am increasingly convinced that lasting, self-sustaining solutions to these problems lie in our ability to apply effectively the deepest lessons of competition. There are huge win-win opportunities for both society and for companies if we approach issues such as the environment, disadvantaged communities, and health-care delivery in the right way. Creating positive-sum competition in these arenas will foster innovation that produces enormous value for society.[4]

Part IV, "Strategy, Philanthropy, and Corporate Social Responsibility," applies strategy principles to philanthropy and giving by both social organizations and corporations. In a world of scarce public resources and rising aspirations to address social needs, the need for philanthropy to deliver value is urgent. The social sector must justify the enormous resources being devoted to giving, many of which are tax subsidized and thus supported by all citizens. The act of giving can no longer be seen as beneficial for its own sake. Instead, giving must achieve true social impact.

The corporate sector is being asked to participate in social issues as never before, often under the banner of corporate social responsibility. How and where corporations should engage social issues, and how they should invest their philanthropic giving, is a pressing issue for every corporate leader. The key to doing this well is understanding that social issues and economic issues are not mutually exclusive but can be mutually reinforcing, as highlighted in Part III. Thus, social considerations can and should become part of a company's strategy, not a separate agenda.

Part V, "Strategy and Leadership," recognizes that leadership is needed to achieve superior value creation. For any organization, developing a strategy is an act of leadership, and strategy represents perhaps the most powerful tool available to leaders to get all the individuals in the organization aligned around a common purpose and direction. As crucial as leadership is, we still know surprisingly little about the role of leaders, especially the leaders of large complex organizations such as those that populate the *Fortune* 100 or *Fortune* 500. Such organizations are too large and complex for any leader to fully understand all of the businesses, manage the many thousands of employees, or make even a small fraction of all the decisions. In such organizations, the roles of leaders are subtle and indirect, and we have begun to explore these roles in recent work.

Competition and Strategy: Core Concepts

The collection begins with "The Five Competitive Forces That Shape Strategy" (2008), a new and updated version of the article that has helped to shape business practice and academic thinking since it first appeared in 1979. The performance of any company in a particular business can be divided into two parts: the first attributable to the industry and the second to a company's relative profitability in its industry. I am often asked where to start if one wants to understand my work. Even for those who feel they are familiar with "the five forces," this article is the essential entry point. This updated version has allowed me to further develop the implications of industry analysis for strategists and investors.

Many mistakes in strategy proceed from a fundamental misconception of what competition is and how it works. Competition is often defined too narrowly, as if it occurred only between direct rivals. This article presents a framework, grounded in economic theory, for assessing competition in any industry. It offers a systematic way to assess any industry's structure, and how it might change.[5] The five-forces framework concentrates on the first part; that is, explaining the large and sustained differences in the average profitability of industries and the implications for strategy. The five-forces diagnostics, consisting of the bargaining power of buyers, the bargaining power of suppliers, the threat of new entry, the threat of substitutes, and the intensity of rivalry, allows the long-term profitability of any industry to be understood, as well as how companies can influence industry competition in their favor.

"What Is Strategy?" addresses the second part of the profitability equation: why some companies are able to outperform their rivals. I first tackled the subject of positioning, or the creation of an advantaged approach to competing in an industry, in my book *Competitive Strategy* (1980), introducing the concept of generic strategies.[6] The book *Competitive Advantage* (1985) took the thinking one step further through introducing the notion of the value chain. "What Is Strategy?" first published in 1996, takes the concept of positioning a big step further. A company achieves superior profitability in its industry by attaining either higher prices or lower costs than rivals. In this article, I show how these price or cost differences between competitors arise from two different sources: operational effectiveness (that is, whether a company has attained best practice) and strategic positioning. Competing on achieving best practices is what I call "competition to be the best." All companies must continually improve operational effectiveness in their activities; however, this is a competition that is hard to win. Profitability differences most often arise from having a distinctive strategic position, or what I call "competition to be unique." Competing to be unique is ultimately more sustainable that competing to be the best, and this article explains why.

"What Is Strategy?" presents the underlying theory of strategic positioning. Strategy differences rest on differences in activities in the value chain, such as the way companies go about logistics, order processing, product design, assembly, training, and so on. A strategy is sustainable because of trade-offs, or choices that firms make to offer certain types of value but sacrifice others and fit, or tying choices in the value chain together. Competitive advantage depends on offering a unique value proposition delivered by a tailored value chain, involving trade-offs different from those of rivals, and where there is fit among numerous activities that become mutually reinforcing.

The first two articles in Part I provide the core analytical frameworks for developing strategy at the level of any individual business: industry structure and competitive positioning. The next two articles in Part I—"How Information Gives You Competitive Advantage" and "Strategy and the Internet" examine the ubiquitous role of information technology in modern competition. These articles apply and extend the core frameworks and show how they can be used to understand any innovation.

"How Information Gives You Competitive Advantage" (1985) provides an overall framework for the role of information technology in competition. In it, Victor Millar and I suggest that information technology plays a role in both industry structure and competitive positioning. The five-forces framework provides the structure for analyzing the industry effect, while the value chain provides the structure for examining the competitive advantage effect in a rapidly evolving field. This article remains relevant many years after it was written because it exposes the underlying concepts rather than documenting current trends. For that reason, the article continues to provide an approach to understanding the competitive significance of each new generation of information system.

How often have we heard the claim, "The Internet changes everything"? The article "Strategy and the Internet" (2001) addresses the role of the Internet in competition—exploring both what changes and what does not, and how any organization can evaluate the impact of the Internet on its competitiveness. Once again, industry structure analysis is shown to be a powerful source of strategic insight for organizations struggling to make sense of a powerful force for change. While many argued that the Internet would render strategy obsolete, the opposite has been true. The article shows why the Internet has tended to weaken industry profitability without providing proprietary advantages, thus making strategy more important than ever.

By extension, this article tackles the question of how to think strategically about any technological discontinuity. Most work on innovation presumes that it will be disruptive and that incumbents will be the casualties. The tools of industry structure help managers predict whether an industry can remain profitable as it is impacted by a new technology. The logic of competitive advantage shows when incumbents may be able to harness new technology better than newcomers, and helps any firm (new or established) think about the profitable positions it can occupy if the industry is transformed. In the twenty-first century, we can expect a steady stream of technological innovations that will reshape prevailing industry economics. That is the inevitable thrust of the intensifying competitiveness that we see all around us. My observation has been that too often companies, to their detriment, suspend strategic thinking when they find themselves confronted with major technological change.

The first four articles in Part I address strategy in a single business, or what I call *competitive strategy*. Competition in an individual industry is the core level of strategy, because it is at this level that industry profitability is determined and competitive advantage is either won or lost. However, many firms diversify into multiple industries. The article "From Competitive Advantage to Corporate Strategy" (1987) addresses strategy at the other important level—the overall strategy of a corporation diversified into more than one business. I call this *corporate strategy*.

Many accounts treat diversification as a distinct question, separate from competitive strategy at the business level. This false dichotomy, however, starts to explain the dismal performance of most companies in diversifying, a result I first documented in this article. Bad things often happen to companies that separate their thinking about diversification from the realities of competing in their various businesses.

"From Competitive Advantage to Corporate Strategy" argues that while corporate strategy involves different questions from competitive strategy, the two must be intimately connected. From an industry perspective, corporate strategy is concerned with the choice of what industries a company should occupy and how it should enter them. From a competitive advantage standpoint, the central question at the corporate level is how the competitive advantages of each business unit are enhanced (rather than undermined) by other units in the corporation. This article explores these questions once again, making use of the concepts of industry structure and the value chain. It shows how the notion of activities can be used to understand the strategic logic of diversification, and how corporate strategy must be linked to organization structure and operating practices in order to achieve the fruits of diversification.

Companies have not lost their taste for diversification since this article was first published, and the diversification track record remains problematic. Discredited portfolio models of diversification have been supplanted by notions of core competencies and critical resources in the diversification rationales of many companies. However, these ideas are simplistic, and diversification outcomes continue to suffer. Experience has shown that diversification that is not closely tied to sustainable competitive advantage at the business-unit level is more likely to destroy economic value than create it.

The Competitiveness of Locations

The core concepts of competitive and corporate strategy provide the foundation for examining any competitive situation. Today, that often means competition across borders. Firms compete across geographic locations with national, regional, and global strategies. At the same time, countries and regions must compete with other locations to provide a hospitable business environment. For both companies and countries, addressing competition across locations requires two new sets of ideas. The first concerns the role of location in competition. As firms compete across borders, they gain the ability to locate activities anywhere. How location affects competitive advantage is essential to firms but also crucial to guide policy for economic development. The second new issue raised by international competition is the way firms can gain competitive advantage by spreading and coordinating activities in the value chain across borders in regional or global networks. The value chain is being spread across borders as never before as barriers to trade and investment have fallen and new countries have become cost-effective locations for outsourcing.

Part II begins with the issue of location. In "The Competitive Advantage of Nations" (1990), I develop a new theory of the competitiveness of nations, states, and other geographic areas. Most treatments of competitiveness have concentrated either on macroeconomic policies (such as government budget deficits, monetary policy, opening of markets, and privatization) or on comparative advantages due to endowments of inputs such as labor, natural resources, and capital. My article takes a very different approach, arguing that the competitiveness of locations is primarily rooted in the nature of the business environment they offer firms. Access to labor, capital, and natural resources no longer determines prosperity, because these have become widely accessible. Rather, competitiveness arises from the productivity with which firms in a location can *use* inputs to produce valuable goods and services. The productivity and prosperity possible in a given location depend not on what industries its firms compete in, but on how they compete. Traditional distinctions between high tech and low tech, or between manufacturing and services, have little relevance in an economy in which manufacturing and services have blurred and virtually all industries can employ advanced technologies and high skill levels to achieve high levels of productivity.

In "The Competitive Advantage of Nations," I show how the roots of productivity lie in the national and regional environment for competition. The article introduces the diamond theory of competitiveness that involves four primary facets: factor conditions, demand conditions, the context for strategy and rivalry, and related and supporting industries. Government policies can influence all four parts of the diamond positively or negatively. "The Competitive Advantage of Nations" explores these sources of competitiveness, how they change, and the implications for governments and companies. Diamond theory is not only a tool for managers but also a microeconomically based approach to economic development for governments.[7]

"Clusters and Competition: New Agendas for Companies, Governments, and Institutions" (1998) explores one of the most important ideas in my overall competitiveness theory—the concept of clusters. Clusters are geographic concentrations of firms, suppliers, related industries, and specialized institutions that occur in a particular field in a nation, state, or city. Examples of clusters are Wall Street in financial services, Hollywood in entertainment, and Southern Germany in automobiles. This article pulls together my learning about clusters both from research and practice in terms of cluster theory, the role of clusters in competition, and implications of clusters for government policy, company behavior, and institutions such as universities and trade associations. Clusters are a prominent feature on the landscape of every advanced economy, and cluster formation is an essential ingredient of economic development. Clusters offer a new way to think about economies and economic development; raise new roles for business, government, and other institutions; and provide new ways to structure business-government and business-university relationships. Many hundreds of cluster initiatives have sprung up in all parts of the world, and this article summarizes some of the learning gleaned from both advanced and developing economies.

The final article in Part II, "Competing Across Locations: Enhancing Competitive Advantage Through a Global Strategy" (1999), brings together the two aspects of competing across borders—location and global networks. The concept of activities and the value chain, so important to understanding competitive advantage in general terms, provides the basic framework for international strategy as well. When competing across borders, firms can spread activities to multiple locations to harness their locational advantages, while coordinating among dispersed activities to harness network advantages.

"Competing Across Locations" develops the implications of this framework for global strategy in a particular business. Global strategy taps the innovation and productivity advantages of locating headquarters or "home-base" activities in some cluster locations while spreading other activities to source low cost inputs and gain access to foreign markets. Coordination transforms this array of dispersed activities into a global network. Earlier thinking about global strategy, which focused only on globalness, was clearly too simple. Location still matters, and this article aims to take global-strategy thinking to the next level. It also makes clear that global strategy is just a special case of the more general issue of competing across geography. The same framework can be applied to inform the thinking of a local producer striving to become national.

Competitive Solutions to Societal Problems

A deep understanding of competition and value creation offers powerful insights into a wide variety of societal problems. Part III begins with an article on the environment, "Green and Competitive: Ending the Stalemate" (1995), written with Claas van der Linde. Environmental improvement is often seen as being at odds with economic competitiveness because dealing with environmental standards can impose costs on business. This view, however, derives from a static and oversimplified view of competition. Drawing on my work on competitiveness, "Green and Competitive" suggests that "environment versus competitiveness" is a false dichotomy.

In the new thinking, competitiveness arises from increasing productivity in the use of resources. Productivity improvements must be never-ending. Seen in this light, virtually all forms of corporate pollution are manifestations of economic waste; for example, resources used inefficiently, energy wasted, or valuable raw materials discarded. Improving environmental performance through better technology and methods, then, will often increase productivity and offset or partially offset the cost of making such improvements, an idea that has come to be known in the environmental community as the *Porter Hypothesis*.[8] This implies that environmental regulation should focus on raising environmental performance standards without specifying means, reducing unnecessary transactions costs of the regulation itself, and facilitating product and process innovation.[9] This article, once intensely controversial, is now quite widely accepted, especially in the practitioner community. Corporations should see environmental improvement not as a regulatory nuisance but as an essential part of improving productivity and competitiveness.

"The Competitive Advantage of the Inner City" (1995) addresses the economic distress of America's urban core neighborhoods. Urban poverty has been seen primarily as a social problem, and proposed solutions have focused on meeting the pressing human needs of inner-city residents. But the problem is equally an economic one. No community can be truly healthy without a healthy economy. Without accessible jobs and opportunities for income and wealth creation, social investment will be insufficient to achieve lasting benefits. While there have been numerous efforts at inner-city economic development, too many have tried to defy the laws of the marketplace. Based on the presumption that inner cities face many competitive disadvantages as business locations, "economic" development has often consisted largely of creating nonprofits and relocating government buildings. Alternatively, large subsidies have been used in attempts to distort companies' location choices.

Rather than concentrate on competitive disadvantages, "The Competitive Advantage of the Inner City" turns the question on its head. In it, I argue that only by focusing on the inherent competitive advantages of inner-city locations will economic development be sustainable. I apply my broader work on competitiveness to inner cities, outlining the advantages of inner cities that have given rise to many thousands of successful inner-city-based companies in major cities all across the country. An economic development approach that builds on these advantages, while tackling frontally the competitive disadvantages of inner cities as a business location, offers a much better model for addressing our most distressed communities. There is nothing inevitable about the decline of cities if we shift our focus from reducing poverty to creating jobs, income, and wealth. The thesis of this article gave rise to a nonprofit, the Initiative for a Competitive Inner city (ICIC), which has extended the research on inner-city economies and helped put the ideas into practice.[10] I have also applied this thinking to address the challenges of economic development in rural areas.[11]

Health care is another pressing social concern facing the United States and every nation. In the United States, high costs and the large number of people without health insurance have triggered a national debate on how best to restructure the system. In "Redefining Competition in Health Care" (2004), Elizabeth Teisberg and I argue that the wrong kinds of competition have made a mess of the American health-care system. In contrast, the right kind of competition, focused on creating value for patients, will provide a sustainable solution. Value is defined as patient health outcomes per dollar spent. Only through continued innovation focused on improving value in the delivery of care can the cost of health care be controlled without rationing care or eroding its quality. In fact, the only way to truly reduce the cost of health care is to improve its quality, because good health is inherently less expensive than poor health.

The article explores why health-care competition has become zero-sum, with system participants dividing value instead of increasing it. Competition takes place at the wrong level and over the wrong things. There is rampant cost shifting and the accumulation of bargaining power to extract more revenue or capture patients from other actors. Fixing the system will require that the locus of competition shifts from "Who pays?" to "Who provides the best value?" We lay out a vision for what positive-sum competition in health care would look like. This vision has subsequently been extensively elaborated in our book *Redefining Health Care* (2006), which shows how health-care delivery can be transformed and how each system actor can create value in terms of patient health.

The articles in Part III represent the beginnings of a new integration of economic and social policy. Traditionally, economic policy and social policy have been seen as distinct and often conflicting. Economic policy concerns itself with creating wealth by providing incentives, encouraging savings and investment, and minimizing government intervention. Social policy has concentrated on providing for public education and other human needs, aiding disadvantaged groups, protecting citizens through various forms of regulation, and, recently, preserving the environment. Social policy has relied heavily on intervention in markets, subsidies, and redistribution.

Social policymakers tend to see the market as the problem and consequently attempt to modify its outcomes. Economic policy makers tend to see government intervention as the problem. Social advocacy groups often view business as the problem. Businesses see social concerns as outside their realm of interest and often view social organizations as special interests. Businesses point to a strong economy, unshackled by counterproductive intrusions, as the best social program.

These old dichotomies are false ones and represent an increasingly obsolete perspective. Social and economic goals are not inherently conflicting in the long run. A productive and growing economy requires educated, safe, healthy, decently housed workers who are motivated by a sense of opportunity. Economic competitiveness can be enhanced by better environmental performance, because corporate pollution results from unproductive use of resources. The only real conflict lies in means. Efforts to advance social goals via redistribution, subsidies, and market distortion usually fail and, in the process, inflict steep economic costs, as illustrated in my articles on the environment and inner-city economic development. Similarly, efforts to boost profits at the expense of worker training, safety, and a sense of well-being will also fail in the long run.

The articles in this section set forth a new approach based on harmonizing and pursuing simultaneously economic and social goals. This can be done through a central focus on competition, innovation, and value—working through the market rather than against it. Social programs must prepare individuals to succeed in the market system, not insulate them from it. Efforts to address social issues, such as pollution and the high costs of health care, must harness innovation and competition to address underlying causes, rather than attempt to shift the costs onto some other group within society.

The articles in Part III illustrate these principles, using as examples health care, the environment, and urban poverty. The same principles, however, can be applied to many social issues, including social security, education, or housing.

Strategy, Philanthropy, and Corporate Social Responsibility

To address social problems, society has moved away from a reliance solely on government. Today, philanthropy involving foundations, corporations, and countless NGOs is deploying hundreds of billions of dollars to address some of society's most intractable challenges, often in collaboration with government. The value generated by this enormous investment of scarce resources is of growing concern.

Part IV begins with the question of how to create value through philanthropy. Most philanthropy focuses on the act of giving, with the presumption is that giving does good. However, in "Philanthropy's New Agenda: Creating Value" (1999), Mark Kramer and I make the case that much philanthropic giving delivers limited social benefit, and certainly much less social benefit than is possible. The huge and growing resources being deployed by philanthropists, and especially by foundations, heighten the lost opportunity for society.

This article, which has proved controversial, makes the case that foundations create little value by giving money alone. To truly create value, foundations need a conscious strategy to do more than dole out grants to worthy causes. The article provides a framework for how foundations can add value through the selection of grantees, providing assistance to grantees in expanding and increasing their social impact, and investing systematically to advance the state of practice in fields where the foundation can become truly expert. All of this requires that foundations make clear strategic choices to define the fields in which they will operate, and the activities through which they will be distinctive in catalyzing social impact.

In "The Competitive Advantage of Corporate Philanthropy" (2002), we apply these general principles of philanthropy to giving by corporations. Corporations, more than almost any other institution in society, have powerful assets with which to create value in addressing social issues. However, the ability of corporations to create social value comes only from selecting those social issues where there is a clear connection to their business, giving them the skills, resources, and relationships to make a difference. The article offers tools that companies can use to make their giving more strategic, by finding those areas where there is a win-win opportunity to improve social performance while enhancing the long-term competitive context for their business.

The final article of Part IV, "Strategy and Society: The Link Between Competitive Advantage and Corporate Social Responsibility" (2006), tackles the broad question of the relationship between corporations and the society in which they operate. Companies are being scrutinized and held accountable for social impacts as never before, but many companies have treated corporate social responsibility defensively and worried more about image than social impact. However, company competitiveness and social progress are not separate and conflicting, but interdependent, as discussed previously. This article provides a framework for understanding the points of intersection between a company and the communities in which it operates, which will guide how the company can make social responsibility integral to strategy. Many companies can integrate a social dimension into their strategy, which can make the strategy more sustainable.

Taken as a group, the articles in Part III and Part IV show how strategy principles are fundamental to social progress, not just economic progress. Thinking in terms of value will separate those organizations that will truly make a difference from those satisfied with the act of giving to worthy causes.

Strategy and Leadership

Part V introduces an emerging body of work on the role of leadership. No company, country, or social organization can create maximum value without effective leadership. Yet we still know little about this subtle topic, especially in large, complex organizations.

In "Seven Surprises for New CEOs" (2004), Nitin Nohria, Jay Lorsch, and I examine the underlying nature of leadership in complex business organizations by distinguishing how the role of CEOs differs from other senior managerial roles in a corporation. We draw on the unique perspective gained from Harvard's New CEO Workshop, an intensive program to assist newly appointed CEOs in setting their agenda and making the personal transitions necessary. More than one hundred new CEOs of multibillion-dollar corporations have participated. The article describes the surprises about the job awaiting new CEOs, and the lessons these surprises hold for CEO effectiveness. Strategy proves to be an especially crucial tool for CEO success. This article is the first from a body of research on CEO leadership that is continuing.

Expanding Frontiers

As I hope is evident, all my work rests on a core set of ideas about competition and value creation and embodies a consistent perspective. Yet my ideas continually evolve and have broadened over time to encompass new dimensions. The *five forces* have become shorthand for the idea that industry structure defines the playing field on which competition unfolds. The *value chain* has become shorthand for an activity-based view of competitive advantage; that is, superior profitability can be traced to differences in activities that allow a company to lower costs or in its ability to charge higher prices. *Strategic positioning* versus *operational effectiveness* has become the essential distinction in understanding the nature of strategy and how it is different from other managerial agendas. The *diamond* and *clusters* have become shorthand for the way location affects competition. This set of core frameworks cuts across all my work, including the work on social issues. My understanding of each one, and of the connections among them, is continually being deepened and extended.

As I explored one question in trying to understand competition and strategy, the next question was suggested, and the next. Thinking about competition and strategy in a single industry, for example, led me to an interest in the influence of diversification on industry competition. My early work on positioning provided the impetus for the activity-based view of the firm, which provided a framework for thinking about value creation. As I struggled with how strategy was different from all the other things managers did, I began to see the distinction between strategy and operational effectiveness. Thinking about activities led me to puzzle over the influence of globalization or spreading activities across geography, which in turn raised the question of how location mattered. A focus on location led to the source of competitiveness of nations and regions, and the role of government in competition, not just companies. As I looked more closely at countries and communities, I was drawn to explore how competition and the principles of value creation, properly understood and channeled, could be put into service to address a number of society's most pressing challenges, from environmental sustainability to urban poverty to quality health care. As more of society's resources were deployed through foundations and other philanthropic organizations, I turned my attention to how such organizations could be more effective.

Over time, I have been led to explore new units of analysis. My initial work stressed the *industry* at a time when the firm as the unit of analysis was dominant. As I understood that competitive advantage did not arise from the firm as a whole, my subsequent work stressed the *activity*. When focus in management thinking was almost exclusively on what went on inside firms, I added consideration of the *geographic location*. When industrial policy concentrated on the industry or the country, I highlighted the role of the *cluster*. In health care, while the dominant focus was on the insurance, hospital, or clinics, our work identified the *medical condition* and the *cycle of care* as the essential value-creation units.

As each new question arose and each new set of ideas developed, I have been led to re-examine what came before. The activity-based view of the firm caused me to refine and extend my earlier thinking about generic strategies. The distinction I now make between operational effectiveness and strategy ("What Is Strategy?") both builds on earlier work and informs it. The new theory has deepened my understanding of positioning and linked it more tightly to activities. Through this new work, I was also able to extend the activity view of the firm through the concepts of trade-offs and fit.

The distinction between operational effectiveness and positioning also sheds new light on a wide variety of other issues. Financial market pressures, for example, can be desirable motivators of operational improvement, but often lead companies to compromise their unique strategic positions by pursuing growth in segments where they lack any real advantage. Another example of the distinction is in evaluating the role of information technology in competition. Much of the new information technology is being directed at improving best practice—operational effectiveness—rather than enabling unique positioning. The lurking danger with the new generation of IT tools, however, is that too many companies will apply them in the same way. This will have the unwitting effect of homogenizing competition, limiting customer choice, and triggering mutually destructive rivalry.

The research on location has opened up important new connections as well. The most obvious one is an enriched conception of global strategy. Locational factors clearly play a role in industry structure and competitive advantage, and influence feasible forms of competing. The state of the diamond and the depth of the cluster can raise or lower barriers to entry into an industry, shift the power of customers and suppliers, and set the mix and threat of substitutes. Locational factors also influence the forms of rivalry that take place in a national economy, which can range from imitation and price competition in developing economies to innovation and differentiation in advanced ones. In developing economies, locational deficiencies create difficulties in attempting to enter attractive industries and in avoiding destructive price rivalry. At the same time, government intervention and a shortage of capital often suspend competitive forces and preserve monopolies.

Location also strongly influences competitive advantage and the types of strategies firms can choose and successfully implement. The state of local infrastructure, the skills of local employees, and other diamond conditions contribute directly to operational effectiveness. Diamond conditions such as local demand sophistication, unique skill pools, and the local presence of related industries can also shape the types and variety of strategic positions chosen, in terms of customer segments or product varieties. The business environment at a location not only influences the choice of strategy, but also the ability to carry out strategies. At the level of activities, it is also evident that access to many of the resources, capabilities, and skills that contribute significantly to a firm's uniqueness depends on the nature of the local environment.

Location also bears on corporate strategy. Diamond conditions influence the types of corporate value added that truly affect competitive advantage. In developing countries, value is created by a corporate parent's ability to provide capital access and to introduce professional management. This helps explain the prevalence of conglomerate groups in many emerging economies. In more advanced economies, portfolio management adds little value, and other approaches to diversification are needed. Conditions in the diamond, such as in logistical system and supplier industries, affect the kind of synergies that are feasible.

Many readers have noted an apparent contradiction between my work on strategy and my ideas on location. The industry-structure framework shows how powerful buyers and suppliers and intense rivalry can depress profitability, while diamond theory suggests that local rivalry, demanding customers, and sophisticated local suppliers foster competitiveness by stimulating and supporting high productivity and rapid innovation. How can these perspectives be reconciled? First, we must distinguish between an industry in a single location and the industry globally. The presence of a favorable diamond in one location, including intense local rivalry, allows firms based there to achieve collectively a higher level of productivity and also to progress faster than firms based in other locations. Profitability in the local market may be lower, but the global profitability of firms based there will be superior. Another way of making the same point is to recognize that diamond conditions will affect the ability of firms based in one location to gain a competitive advantage, on average, over firms based elsewhere. However, average industry profitability globally will be dependent on average industry structure globally.

The work on location addresses the determinants of productivity and highlights the importance of dynamic improvement to competitiveness. The industry-structure and activity frameworks provide the intellectual framework to understand the firm and its markets. My early investigations were more cross-sectional (for example, answering such question as why some industries are more profitable than others at a given time or why one rival is more profitable than another). These were the logical first questions.

My more recent work on operational effectiveness and positioning, however, begins to bridge positioning, location, and dynamic improvement. It stresses the necessity of continual improvement in operational effectiveness but emphasizes the need for continuity in strategy. Both operational effectiveness and strategy are influenced by location.

A deeper understanding of competition and value creation, enriched by work on location, has opened up a whole new frontier for exploring the connection between competition and social issues. Economic competitiveness and social progress can be harmonized and improved together. Social organization can make huge strides in performance by embracing the principles of value creation. Competition can stimulate rapid progress in the social sector if it is channeled toward value.

Finally, the effort to understand the connection between competition and social issues led me to a major focus on the philanthropic sector. How to deploy the rapidly growing resources flowing to this sector in ways that deliver greater value to society is an urgent priority as the limits of government in solving all of society's problems are recognized.

New connections remain to be discovered, and my learning about competition and value creation is unlikely to stop anytime soon. Any number of shifts in the business environment and technology are emerging, which will find their way into theory and practice. One is the evolving relationship between firms and capital markets, now that most capital is invested by large, often activist, institutions rather than long-term individual holders. Another development is the fusion of economic and social strategy, in which social goals (e.g., environmental stewardship) are addressed in a market framework. However, these trends, and others, will not themselves hold the key to value creation. Instead, it will come from the ability to see an organization and its context holistically. Strategic thinking will be rarer and more precious than ever.

Whatever the future holds, one thing is certain. As competition continues to evolve, it will be both unsettling and the source of much of our prosperity. If this collection could convey only one message, I would want it to be a sense of the staggering power of competition to make things better—both for companies and for society.

NOTES

1. For a comprehensive bibliography of my work in all of these areas, including presentations and interviews, see the Web site of the Institute for Strategy and Competitiveness (http://isc.hbs.edu).

2. Other *Harvard Business Review* articles in this area include Michael Porter and Kathryn Rudie Harrigan, "End Game Strategies for Declining Industries," *Harvard Business Review*, July–August 1983.

3. Other *Harvard Business Review* articles in this area include "Capital Disadvantage: America's Failing Capital Investment System," *Harvard Business Review*, September–October 1992; and Michael E. Porter with T.M. Hout and E. Rudden, "How Global Companies Win Out," *Harvard Business Review*, September–October 1982.

4. Other *Harvard Business Review* articles in this area include Michael E. Porter and Forest L. Reinhardt, "A Strategic Approach to Climate," *Harvard Business Review*, October 2007; and Michael E. Porter with Elizabeth O. Teisberg and Gregory B. Brown, "Making Competition in Health Care Work," *Harvard Business Review*, July–August 1994.

5. The original article became the lead chapter of my book *Competitive Strategy: Techniques for Analyzing Industries and Competitors* (New York: Free Press, 1980).

6. For my earlier work on positioning, see *Competitive Strategy*, chapter 2, and *Competitive Advantage: Creating and Sustaining Superior Performance* (New York: Free Press, 1985).

7. These ideas are developed in more detail in my book, *The Competitive Advantage of Nations* (New York: The Free Press, 1990; republished with a new introduction, 1998).

8. The Porter Hypothesis was first put forward in a short article "America's Green Strategy," *Scientific American* (April 1991), 168.

9. A companion article develops the theory and implications for regulation in more detail for the academic reader. See "Towards a New Conception of the Environment-Competitiveness Relationship," *Journal of Economic Perspectives*, 9, no. 4 (Autumn 1995): 97–118.

10. For further information and citations, see http://www.icic.org and http://isc.hbs.edu.

11. "Competitiveness in Rural U.S. Regions: Learning and Research Agenda," Economic Development Administration, February 2004.

Part I Competition and Strategy: Core Concepts

CHAPTER 1

The Five Competitive Forces That Shape Strategy

Michael E. Porter

IN ESSENCE, THE JOB OF THE STRATEGIST is to understand and cope with competition. Often, however, managers define competition too narrowly, as if it occurred only among today's direct competitors. Yet competition for profits goes beyond established industry rivals to include four other competitive forces as well: customers, suppliers, potential entrants, and substitute products. The extended rivalry that results from all five forces defines an industry's structure and shapes the nature of competitive interaction within an industry.

As different from one another as industries might appear on the surface, the underlying drivers of profitability are the same. The global auto industry, for instance, appears to have nothing in common with the worldwide market for art masterpieces or the heavily regulated health-care delivery industry in Europe. But to understand industry competition and profitability in each of those three cases, one must analyze the industry's underlying structure in terms of the five forces. (See figure 1.1.)

If the forces are intense, as they are in such industries as airlines, textiles, and hotels, almost no company earns attractive returns on investment. If the forces are benign, as they are in industries such as software, soft drinks, and toiletries, many companies are profitable. Industry structure drives competition and profitability, not whether an industry produces a product or service, is emerging or mature, high tech or low tech, regulated or unregulated. While a myriad of factors can affect industry profitability in the short run—including the weather and the

January 2008

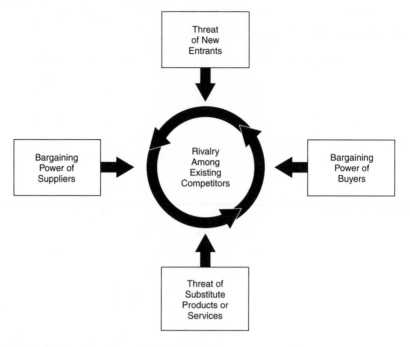

Figure 1.1   The Five Forces That Shape Industry Competition

business cycle—industry structure, manifested in the competitive forces, sets industry profitability in the medium and long run. (See figure 1.2.)

Understanding the competitive forces, and their underlying causes, reveals the roots of an industry's current profitability while providing a framework for anticipating and influencing competition (and profitability) over time. A healthy industry structure should be as much a competitive concern to strategists as their company's own position. Understanding industry structure is also essential to effective strategic positioning. As we will see, defending against the competitive forces and shaping them in a company's favor are crucial to strategy. (See the inserts "Industry Analysis in Practice" and "Typical Steps in Industry Analysis.")

Forces That Shape Competition

The configuration of the five forces differs by industry. In the market for commercial aircraft, fierce rivalry between dominant producers Airbus and Boeing and the bargaining power of the airlines that place

Industry Analysis in Practice

Good industry analysis looks rigorously at the structural underpinnings of profitability. A first step is to understand the appropriate time horizon. One of the essential tasks in industry analysis is to distinguish temporary or cyclical changes from structural changes. A good guideline for the appropriate time horizon is the full business cycle for the particular industry. For most industries, a three-to-five-year horizon is appropriate, although in some industries with long lead times, such as mining, the appropriate horizon might be a decade or more. It is average profitability over this period, not profitability in any particular year, that should be the focus of analysis.

The point of industry analysis is not to declare the industry attractive or unattractive but to understand the underpinnings of competition and the root causes of profitability. As much as possible, analysts should look at industry structure quantitatively, rather than be satisfied with lists of qualitative factors. Many elements of the five forces can be quantified: the percentage of the buyer's total cost accounted for by the industry's product (to understand buyer price sensitivity); the percentage of industry sales required to fill a plant or operate a logistical network of efficient scale (to help assess barriers to entry); the buyer's switching cost (determining the inducement an entrant or rival must offer customers).

The strength of the competitive forces affects prices, costs, and the investment required to compete; thus the forces are directly tied to the income statements and balance sheets of industry participants. Industry structure defines the gap between revenues and costs. For example, intense rivalry drives down prices or elevates the costs of marketing, R&D, or customer service, reducing margins. How much? Strong suppliers drive up input costs. How much? Buyer power lowers prices or elevates the costs of meeting buyers' demands, such as the requirement to hold more inventory or provide financing. How much? Low barriers to entry or close substitutes limit the level of sustainable prices. How much? It is these economic relationships that sharpen the strategist's understanding of industry competition.

Finally, good industry analysis does not just list pluses and minuses but sees an industry in overall, systemic terms. Which forces are underpinning (or constraining) today's profitability? How might shifts in one competitive force trigger reactions in others? Answering such questions is often the source of true strategic insights.

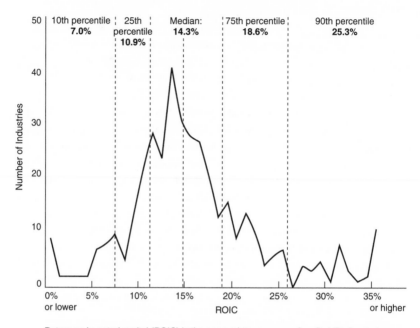

Return on invested capital (ROIC) is the appropriate measure of profitability for strategy formulation, not to mention for equity investors. Return on sales or the growth rate of profits fail to account for the capital required to compete in the industry. Here, we utilize earnings before interest and taxes divided by average invested capital less excess cash as the measure of ROIC. This measure controls for idiosyncratic differences in capital structure and tax rates across companies and industries.

Source: Standard & Poor's, Compustat, and author's calculations

Figure 1.2 Differences in Industry Profitability
The average return on invested capital varies markedly from industry to industry. Between 1992 and 2006, for example, average return on invested capital in U.S. industries ranged as low as zero or even negative to more than 50%. At the high end are industries like soft drinks and prepackaged software, which have been almost six times more profitable than the airline industry over the period.

huge orders for aircraft are strong, while the threat of entry, the threat of substitutes, and the power of suppliers are more benign. In the movie theater industry, the proliferation of substitute forms of entertainment and the power of the movie producers and distributors who supply movies, the critical input, are important.

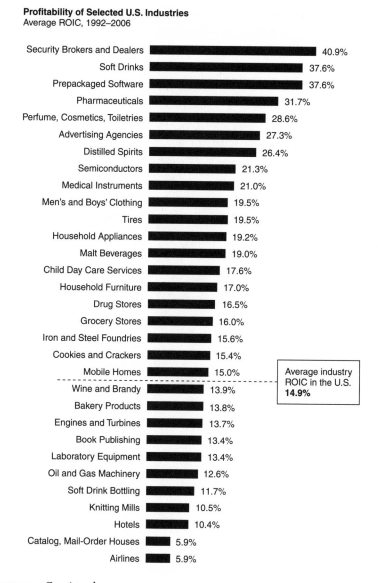

Profitability of Selected U.S. Industries
Average ROIC, 1992–2006

Security Brokers and Dealers	40.9%
Soft Drinks	37.6%
Prepackaged Software	37.6%
Pharmaceuticals	31.7%
Perfume, Cosmetics, Toiletries	28.6%
Advertising Agencies	27.3%
Distilled Spirits	26.4%
Semiconductors	21.3%
Medical Instruments	21.0%
Men's and Boys' Clothing	19.5%
Tires	19.5%
Household Appliances	19.2%
Malt Beverages	19.0%
Child Day Care Services	17.6%
Household Furniture	17.0%
Drug Stores	16.5%
Grocery Stores	16.0%
Iron and Steel Foundries	15.6%
Cookies and Crackers	15.4%
Mobile Homes	15.0%
Wine and Brandy	13.9%
Bakery Products	13.8%
Engines and Turbines	13.7%
Book Publishing	13.4%
Laboratory Equipment	13.4%
Oil and Gas Machinery	12.6%
Soft Drink Bottling	11.7%
Knitting Mills	10.5%
Hotels	10.4%
Catalog, Mail-Order Houses	5.9%
Airlines	5.9%

Average industry ROIC in the U.S. **14.9%**

Figure 1.2   Continued

The strongest competitive force or forces determine the profitability of an industry and become the most important to strategy formulation. The most salient force, however, is not always obvious.

For example, even though rivalry is often fierce in commodity industries, it may not be the factor limiting profitability. Low returns in the photographic film industry, for instance, are the result of a superior substitute product—as Kodak and Fuji, the world's leading producers of photographic film, learned with the advent of digital photography. In such a situation, coping with the substitute product becomes the number one strategic priority.

Industry structure grows out of a set of economic and technical characteristics that determine the strength of each competitive force. We will examine these drivers in the pages that follow, taking the perspective of an incumbent, or a company already present in the industry. The analysis can be readily extended to understand the challenges facing a potential entrant.

THREAT OF ENTRY

New entrants to an industry bring new capacity and a desire to gain market share that puts pressure on prices, costs, and the rate of investment necessary to compete. Particularly when new entrants are diversifying from other markets, they can leverage existing capabilities and cash flows to shake up competition, as Pepsi did when it entered the bottled water industry, Microsoft did when it began to offer internet browsers, and Apple did when it entered the music distribution business.

The threat of entry, therefore, puts a cap on the profit potential of an industry. When the threat is high, incumbents must hold down their prices or boost investment to deter new competitors. In specialty coffee retailing, for example, relatively low entry barriers mean that Starbucks must invest aggressively in modernizing stores and menus.

The threat of entry in an industry depends on the height of entry barriers that are present and on the reaction entrants can expect from incumbents. If entry barriers are low and newcomers expect little retaliation from the entrenched competitors, the threat of entry is high and industry profitability is moderated. It is the *threat* of entry, not whether entry actually occurs, that holds down profitability.

Typical Steps in Industry Analysis

Define the relevant industry:

- What products are in it? Which ones are part of another distinct industry?

- What is the geographic scope of competition?

Identify the participants and segment them into groups, if appropriate:

Who are

- the buyers and buyer groups?

- the suppliers and supplier groups?

- the competitors?

- the substitutes?

- the potential entrants?

Assess the underlying drivers of each competitive force to determine which forces are strong and which are weak and why.

Determine overall industry structure, and test the analysis for consistency:

- *Why* is the level of profitability what it is?

- Which are the *controlling* forces for profitability?

- Is the industry analysis consistent with actual long-run profitability?

- Are more-profitable players better positioned in relation to the five forces?

Analyze recent and likely future changes in each force, both positive and negative.

Identify aspects of industry structure that might be influenced by competitors, by new entrants, or by your company.

Barriers to entry. Entry barriers are advantages that incumbents have relative to new entrants. There are seven major sources:

1. *Supply-side economies of scale.* These economies arise when firms that produce at larger volumes enjoy lower costs per unit because they can spread fixed costs over more units, employ more efficient technology, or command better terms from suppliers. Supply-side scale economies deter entry by forcing the aspiring entrant either to come into the industry on a large scale, which requires dislodging entrenched competitors, or to accept a cost disadvantage.

   Scale economies can be found in virtually every activity in the value chain; which ones are most important varies by industry.[1] In microprocessors, incumbents such as Intel are protected by scale economies in research, chip fabrication, and consumer marketing. For lawn care companies like Scotts Miracle-Gro, the most important scale economies are found in the supply chain and media advertising. In small-package delivery, economies of scale arise in national logistical systems and information technology.

2. *Demand-side benefits of scale.* These benefits, also known as network effects, arise in industries where a buyer's willingness to pay for a company's product increases with the number of other buyers who also patronize the company. Buyers may trust larger companies more for a crucial product: Recall the old adage that no one ever got fired for buying from IBM (when it was the dominant computer maker). Buyers may also value being in a "network" with a larger number of fellow customers. For instance, online auction participants are attracted to eBay because it offers the most potential trading partners. Demand-side benefits of scale discourage entry by limiting the willingness of customers to buy from a newcomer and by reducing the price the newcomer can command until it builds up a large base of customers.

3. *Customer switching costs.* Switching costs are fixed costs that buyers face when they change suppliers. Such costs may arise because a buyer who switches vendors must, for example, alter product specifications, retrain employees to use a new product, or modify processes or information systems. The larger the switching costs, the harder it will be for an entrant to gain customers. Enterprise resource planning (ERP) software is an example of a product with very high switching costs. Once a company has installed SAP's ERP system, for example, the costs of moving to a new vendor are astronomical because of embedded data, the fact that internal processes have been adapted to SAP, major retraining needs, and the mission-critical nature of the applications.

4. *Capital requirements.* The need to invest large financial resources in order to compete can deter new entrants. Capital may be necessary not only for fixed facilities but also to extend customer credit, build inventories, and fund start-up losses. The barrier is particu-

larly great if the capital is required for unrecoverable and therefore harder-to-finance expenditures, such as up-front advertising or research and development. While major corporations have the financial resources to invade almost any industry, the huge capital requirements in certain fields limit the pool of likely entrants. Conversely, in such fields as tax preparation services or short-haul trucking, capital requirements are minimal and potential entrants plentiful.

It is important not to overstate the degree to which capital requirements alone deter entry. If industry returns are attractive and are expected to remain so, and if capital markets are efficient, investors will provide entrants with the funds they need. For aspiring air carriers, for instance, financing is available to purchase expensive aircraft because of their high resale value, one reason why there have been numerous new airlines in almost every region.

5. *Incumbency advantages independent of size.* No matter what their size, incumbents may have cost or quality advantages not available to potential rivals. These advantages can stem from such sources as proprietary technology, preferential access to the best raw material sources, preemption of the most favorable geographic locations, established brand identities, or cumulative experience that has allowed incumbents to learn how to produce more efficiently. Entrants try to bypass such advantages. Upstart discounters such as Target and Wal-Mart, for example, have located stores in freestanding sites rather than regional shopping centers where established department stores were well entrenched.

6. *Unequal access to distribution channels.* The new entrant must, of course, secure distribution of its product or service. A new food item, for example, must displace others from the supermarket shelf via price breaks, promotions, intense selling efforts, or some other means. The more limited the wholesale or retail channels are and the more that existing competitors have tied them up, the tougher entry into an industry will be. Sometimes access to distribution is so high a barrier that new entrants must bypass distribution channels altogether or create their own. Thus, upstart

low-cost airlines have avoided distribution through travel agents (who tend to favor established higher-fare carriers) and have encouraged passengers to book their own flights on the internet.

7. *Restrictive government policy.* Government policy can hinder or aid new entry directly, as well as amplify (or nullify) the other entry barriers. Government directly limits or even forecloses entry into industries through, for instance, licensing requirements and restrictions on foreign investment. Regulated industries like liquor retailing, taxi services, and airlines are visible examples. Government policy can heighten other entry barriers through such means as expansive patenting rules that protect proprietary technology from imitation or environmental or safety regulations that raise scale economies facing newcomers. Of course, government policies may also make entry easier—directly through subsidies, for instance, or indirectly by funding basic research and making it available to all firms, new and old, reducing scale economies.

Entry barriers should be assessed relative to the capabilities of potential entrants, which may be start-ups, foreign firms, or companies in related industries. And, as some of our examples illustrate, the strategist must be mindful of the creative ways newcomers might find to circumvent apparent barriers.

Expected retaliation. How potential entrants believe incumbents may react will also influence their decision to enter or stay out of an industry. If reaction is vigorous and protracted enough, the profit potential of participating in the industry can fall below the cost of capital. Incumbents often use public statements and responses to one entrant to send a message to other prospective entrants about their commitment to defending market share.

Newcomers are likely to fear expected retaliation if:

- Incumbents have previously responded vigorously to new entrants.

- Incumbents possess substantial resources to fight back, including excess cash and unused borrowing power, available productive capacity, or clout with distribution channels and customers.

- Incumbents seem likely to cut prices because they are committed to retaining market share at all costs or because the industry has high fixed costs, which create a strong motivation to drop prices to fill excess capacity.

- Industry growth is slow so newcomers can gain volume only by taking it from incumbents.

An analysis of barriers to entry and expected retaliation is obviously crucial for any company contemplating entry into a new industry. The challenge is to find ways to surmount the entry barriers without nullifying, through heavy investment, the profitability of participating in the industry.

THE POWER OF SUPPLIERS

Powerful suppliers capture more of the value for themselves by charging higher prices, limiting quality or services, or shifting costs to industry participants. Powerful suppliers, including suppliers of labor, can squeeze profitability out of an industry that is unable to pass on cost increases in its own prices. Microsoft, for instance, has contributed to the erosion of profitability among personal computer makers by raising prices on operating systems. PC makers, competing fiercely for customers who can easily switch among them, have limited freedom to raise their prices accordingly.

Companies depend on a wide range of different supplier groups for inputs. A supplier group is powerful if:

- It is more concentrated than the industry it sells to. Microsoft's near monopoly in operating systems, coupled with the fragmentation of PC assemblers, exemplifies this situation.

- The supplier group does not depend heavily on the industry for its revenues. Suppliers serving many industries will not hesitate to extract maximum profits from each one. If a particular industry accounts for a large portion of a supplier group's volume or profit, however, suppliers will want to protect the industry through reasonable pricing and assist in activities such as R&D and lobbying.

• Industry participants face switching costs in changing suppliers. For example, shifting suppliers is difficult if companies have invested heavily in specialized ancillary equipment or in learning how to operate a supplier's equipment (as with Bloomberg terminals used by financial professionals). Or firms may have located their production lines adjacent to a supplier's manufacturing facilities (as in the case of some beverage companies and container manufacturers). When switching costs are high, industry participants find it hard to play suppliers off against one another. (Note that suppliers may have switching costs as well. This limits their power.)

• Suppliers offer products that are differentiated. Pharmaceutical companies that offer patented drugs with distinctive medical benefits have more power over hospitals, health maintenance organizations, and other drug buyers, for example, than drug companies offering me-too or generic products.

• There is no substitute for what the supplier group provides. Pilots' unions, for example, exercise considerable supplier power over airlines partly because there is no good alternative to a well-trained pilot in the cockpit.

• The supplier group can credibly threaten to integrate forward into the industry. In that case, if industry participants make too much money relative to suppliers, they will induce suppliers to enter the market.

THE POWER OF BUYERS

Powerful customers—the flip side of powerful suppliers—can capture more value by forcing down prices, demanding better quality or more service (thereby driving up costs), and generally playing industry participants off against one another, all at the expense of industry profitability. Buyers are powerful if they have negotiating leverage relative to industry participants, especially if they are price sensitive, using their clout primarily to pressure price reductions.

As with suppliers, there may be distinct groups of customers who differ in bargaining power. A customer group has negotiating leverage if:

- There are few buyers, or each one purchases in volumes that are large relative to the size of a single vendor. Large-volume buyers are particularly powerful in industries with high fixed costs, such as telecommunications equipment, offshore drilling, and bulk chemicals. High fixed costs and low marginal costs amplify the pressure on rivals to keep capacity filled through discounting.

- The industry's products are standardized or undifferentiated. If buyers believe they can always find an equivalent product, they tend to play one vendor against another.

- Buyers face few switching costs in changing vendors.

- Buyers can credibly threaten to integrate backward and produce the industry's product themselves if vendors are too profitable. Producers of soft drinks and beer have long controlled the power of packaging manufacturers by threatening to make, and at times actually making, packaging materials themselves.

A buyer group is price sensitive if:

- The product it purchases from the industry represents a significant fraction of its cost structure or procurement budget. Here buyers are likely to shop around and bargain hard, as consumers do for home mortgages. Where the product sold by an industry is a small fraction of buyers' costs or expenditures, buyers are usually less price sensitive.

- The buyer group earns low profits, is strapped for cash, or is otherwise under pressure to trim its purchasing costs. Highly profitable or cash-rich customers, in contrast, are generally less price sensitive (that is, of course, if the item does not represent a large fraction of their costs).

- The quality of buyers' products or services is little affected by the industry's product. Where quality is very much affected by the industry's product, buyers are generally less price sensitive. When purchasing or renting production quality cameras, for instance, makers of major motion pictures opt for highly reliable equipment with the latest features. They pay limited attention to price.

• The industry's product has little effect on the buyer's other costs. Here, buyers focus on price. Conversely, where an industry's product or service can pay for itself many times over by improving performance or reducing labor, material, or other costs, buyers are usually more interested in quality than in price. Examples include products and services like tax accounting or well logging (which measures below-ground conditions of oil wells) that can save or even make the buyer money. Similarly, buyers tend not to be price sensitive in services such as investment banking, where poor performance can be costly and embarrassing.

Most sources of buyer power apply equally to consumers and to business-to-business customers. Like industrial customers, consumers tend to be more price sensitive if they are purchasing products that are undifferentiated, expensive relative to their incomes, and of a sort where product performance has limited consequences. The major difference with consumers is that their needs can be more intangible and harder to quantify.

Intermediate customers, or customers who purchase the product but are not the end user (such as assemblers or distribution channels), can be analyzed the same way as other buyers, with one important addition. Intermediate customers gain significant bargaining power when they can influence the purchasing decisions of customers downstream. Consumer electronics retailers, jewelry retailers, and agricultural-equipment distributors are examples of distribution channels that exert a strong influence on end customers.

Producers often attempt to diminish channel clout through exclusive arrangements with particular distributors or retailers or by marketing directly to end users. Component manufacturers seek to develop power over assemblers by creating preferences for their components with downstream customers. Such is the case with bicycle parts and with sweeteners. DuPont has created enormous clout by advertising its Stainmaster brand of carpet fibers not only to the carpet manufacturers that actually buy them but also to downstream consumers. Many consumers request Stainmaster carpet even though DuPont is not a carpet manufacturer.

THE THREAT OF SUBSTITUTES

A substitute performs the same or a similar function as an industry's product by a different means. Videoconferencing is a substitute for travel. Plastic is a substitute for aluminum. E-mail is a substitute for express mail. Sometimes, the threat of substitution is downstream or indirect, when a substitute replaces a buyer industry's product. For example, lawn-care products and services are threatened when multifamily homes in urban areas substitute for single-family homes in the suburbs. Software sold to agents is threatened when airline and travel websites substitute for travel agents.

Substitutes are always present, but they are easy to overlook because they may appear to be very different from the industry's product: To someone searching for a Father's Day gift, neckties and power tools may be substitutes. It is a substitute to do without, to purchase a used product rather than a new one, or to do it yourself (bring the service or product in-house).

When the threat of substitutes is high, industry profitability suffers. Substitute products or services limit an industry's profit potential by placing a ceiling on prices. If an industry does not distance itself from substitutes through product performance, marketing, or other means, it will suffer in terms of profitability—and often growth potential.

Substitutes not only limit profits in normal times, they also reduce the bonanza an industry can reap in good times. In emerging economies, for example, the surge in demand for wired telephone lines has been capped as many consumers opt to make a mobile telephone their first and only phone line.

The threat of a substitute is high if:

- It offers an attractive price-performance trade-off to the industry's product. The better the relative value of the substitute, the tighter is the lid on an industry's profit potential. For example, conventional providers of long-distance telephone service have suffered from the advent of inexpensive internet-based phone services such as Vonage and Skype. Similarly, video rental outlets are struggling with the emergence of cable and satellite video-on-demand services, online video rental services such as Netflix, and the rise of internet video sites like Google's YouTube.

• The buyer's cost of switching to the substitute is low. Switching from a proprietary, branded drug to a generic drug usually involves minimal costs, for example, which is why the shift to generics (and the fall in prices) is so substantial and rapid.

Strategists should be particularly alert to changes in other industries that may make them attractive substitutes when they were not before. Improvements in plastic materials, for example, allowed them to substitute for steel in many automobile components. In this way, technological changes or competitive discontinuities in seemingly unrelated businesses can have major impacts on industry profitability. Of course the substitution threat can also shift in favor of an industry, which bodes well for its future profitability and growth potential.

RIVALRY AMONG EXISTING COMPETITORS

Rivalry among existing competitors takes many familiar forms, including price discounting, new product introductions, advertising campaigns, and service improvements. High rivalry limits the profitability of an industry. The degree to which rivalry drives down an industry's profit potential depends, first, on the *intensity* with which companies compete and, second, on the *basis* on which they compete.

The intensity of rivalry is greatest if:

• Competitors are numerous or are roughly equal in size and power. In such situations, rivals find it hard to avoid poaching business. Without an industry leader, practices desirable for the industry as a whole go unenforced.

• Industry growth is slow. Slow growth precipitates fights for market share.

• Exit barriers are high. Exit barriers, the flip side of entry barriers, arise because of such things as highly specialized assets or management's devotion to a particular business. These barriers keep companies in the market even though they may be earning low or negative returns. Excess capacity remains in use, and the profitability of healthy competitors suffers as the sick ones hang on.

- Rivals are highly committed to the business and have aspirations for leadership, especially if they have goals that go beyond economic performance in the particular industry. High commitment to a business arises for a variety of reasons. For example, state-owned competitors may have goals that include employment or prestige. Units of larger companies may participate in an industry for image reasons or to offer a full line. Clashes of personality and ego have sometimes exaggerated rivalry to the detriment of profitability in fields such as the media and high technology.

- Firms cannot read each other's signals well because of lack of familiarity with one another, diverse approaches to competing, or differing goals.

The strength of rivalry reflects not just the intensity of competition but also the basis of competition. The *dimensions* on which competition takes place, and whether rivals converge to compete on the *same dimensions,* have a major influence on profitability.

Rivalry is especially destructive to profitability if it gravitates solely to price because price competition transfers profits directly from an industry to its customers. Price cuts are usually easy for competitors to see and match, making successive rounds of retaliation likely. Sustained price competition also trains customers to pay less attention to product features and service.

Price competition is most liable to occur if:

- Products or services of rivals are nearly identical and there are few switching costs for buyers. This encourages competitors to cut prices to win new customers. Years of airline price wars reflect these circumstances in that industry.

- Fixed costs are high and marginal costs are low. This creates intense pressure for competitors to cut prices below their average costs, even close to their marginal costs, to steal incremental customers while still making some contribution to covering fixed costs. Many basic-materials businesses, such as paper and aluminum, suffer from this problem, especially if demand is not growing. So do delivery companies with fixed networks of routes that must be served regardless of volume.

- Capacity must be expanded in large increments to be efficient. The need for large capacity expansions, as in the polyvinyl chloride business, disrupts the industry's supply-demand balance and often leads to long and recurring periods of overcapacity and price cutting.

- The product is perishable. Perishability creates a strong temptation to cut prices and sell a product while it still has value. More products and services are perishable than is commonly thought. Just as tomatoes are perishable because they rot, models of computers are perishable because they soon become obsolete, and information may be perishable if it diffuses rapidly or becomes outdated, thereby losing its value. Services such as hotel accommodations are perishable in the sense that unused capacity can never be recovered.

Competition on dimensions other than price—on product features, support services, delivery time, or brand image, for instance—is less likely to erode profitability because it improves customer value and can support higher prices. Also, rivalry focused on such dimensions can improve value relative to substitutes or raise the barriers facing new entrants. While nonprice rivalry sometimes escalates to levels that undermine industry profitability, this is less likely to occur than it is with price rivalry.

As important as the dimensions of rivalry is whether rivals compete on the *same* dimensions. When all or many competitors aim to meet the same needs or compete on the same attributes, the result is zero-sum competition. Here, one firm's gain is often another's loss, driving down profitability. While price competition runs a stronger risk than non-price competition of becoming zero sum, this may not happen if companies take care to segment their markets, targeting their low-price offerings to different customers.

Rivalry can be positive sum, or actually increase the average profitability of an industry, when each competitor aims to serve the needs of different customer segments, with different mixes of price, products, services, features, or brand identities. Such competition can not only support higher average profitability but also expand the industry, as the needs of more customer groups are better met. The opportunity for positive-sum competition will be greater in industries serving diverse customer groups. With a clear understanding of the structural underpinnings of rivalry, strategists can sometimes take steps to shift the nature of competition in a more positive direction.

Factors, Not Forces

Industry structure, as manifested in the strength of the five competitive forces, determines the industry's long-run profit potential because it determines how the economic value created by the industry is divided—how much is retained by companies in the industry versus bargained away by customers and suppliers, limited by substitutes, or constrained by potential new entrants. By considering all five forces, a strategist keeps overall structure in mind instead of gravitating to any one element. In addition, the strategist's attention remains focused on structural conditions rather than on fleeting factors.

Common Pitfalls

In conducting the analysis avoid the following common mistakes:

- Defining the industry too broadly or too narrowly.

- Making lists instead of engaging in rigorous analysis.

- Paying equal attention to all of the forces rather than digging deeply into the most important ones.

- Confusing effect (price sensitivity) with cause (buyer economics).

- Using static analysis that ignores industry trends.

- Confusing cyclical or transient changes with true structural changes.

- Using the framework to declare an industry attractive or unattractive rather than using it to guide strategic choices.

It is especially important to avoid the common pitfall of mistaking certain visible attributes of an industry for its underlying structure. Consider the following.

INDUSTRY GROWTH RATE

A common mistake is to assume that fast-growing industries are always attractive. Growth does tend to mute rivalry, because an expanding pie offers opportunities for all competitors. But fast growth can put suppliers in a powerful position, and high growth with low entry barriers will draw in entrants. Even without new entrants, a high growth rate will not guarantee profitability if customers are powerful or substitutes are attractive. Indeed, some fast-growth businesses, such as personal computers, have been among the least profitable industries in recent years. A narrow focus on growth is one of the major causes of bad strategy decisions.

TECHNOLOGY AND INNOVATION

Advanced technology or innovations are not by themselves enough to make an industry structurally attractive (or unattractive). Mundane, low-technology industries with price-insensitive buyers, high switching costs, or high entry barriers arising from scale economies are often far more profitable than sexy industries, such as software and internet technologies, that attract competitors.[2]

GOVERNMENT

Government is not best understood as a sixth force because government involvement is neither inherently good nor bad for industry profitability. The best way to understand the influence of government on competition is to analyze how specific government policies affect the five competitive forces. For instance, patents raise barriers to entry, boosting industry profit potential. Conversely, government policies favoring unions may raise supplier power and diminish profit potential. Bankruptcy rules that allow failing companies to reorganize rather than exit can lead to excess capacity and intense rivalry. Government operates at multiple levels and through many different policies, each of which will affect structure in different ways.

COMPLEMENTARY PRODUCTS AND SERVICES

Complements are products or services used together with an industry's product. Complements arise when the customer benefit of two products combined is greater than the sum of each product's value in isolation. Computer hardware and software, for instance, are valuable together and worthless when separated.

In recent years, strategy researchers have highlighted the role of complements, especially in high-technology industries where they are most obvious.[3] By no means, however, do complements appear only there. The value of a car, for example, is greater when the driver also has access to gasoline stations, roadside assistance, and auto insurance.

Complements can be important when they affect the overall demand for an industry's product. However, like government policy, complements are not a sixth force determining industry profitability since the presence of strong complements is not necessarily bad (or good) for industry profitability. Complements affect profitability through the way they influence the five forces.

The strategist must trace the positive or negative influence of complements on all five forces to ascertain their impact on profitability. The presence of complements can raise or lower barriers to entry. In application software, for example, barriers to entry were lowered when producers of complementary operating system software, notably Microsoft, provided tool sets making it easier to write applications. Conversely, the need to attract producers of complements can raise barriers to entry, as it does in video game hardware.

The presence of complements can also affect the threat of substitutes. For instance, the need for appropriate fueling stations makes it difficult for cars using alternative fuels to substitute for conventional vehicles. But complements can also make substitution easier. For example, Apple's iTunes hastened the substitution from CDs to digital music.

Complements can factor into industry rivalry either positively (as when they raise switching costs) or negatively (as when they neutralize product differentiation). Similar analyses can be done for buyer and supplier power. Sometimes companies compete by altering conditions in complementary industries in their favor, such as when videocassette-recorder producer JVC persuaded movie studios to favor its standard in issuing prerecorded tapes even though rival Sony's standard was probably superior from a technical standpoint.

Identifying complements is part of the analyst's work. As with government policies or important technologies, the strategic significance of complements will be best understood through the lens of the five forces.

Changes in Industry Structure

So far, we have discussed the competitive forces at a single point in time. Industry structure proves to be relatively stable, and industry profitability differences are remarkably persistent over time in practice. However, industry structure is constantly undergoing modest adjustment—and occasionally it can change abruptly.

Shifts in structure may emanate from outside an industry or from within. They can boost the industry's profit potential or reduce it. They may be caused by changes in technology, changes in customer needs, or other events. The five competitive forces provide a framework for identifying the most important industry developments and for anticipating their impact on industry attractiveness.

SHIFTING THREAT OF NEW ENTRY

Changes to any of the seven barriers described above can raise or lower the threat of new entry. The expiration of a patent, for instance, may unleash new entrants. On the day that Merck's patents for the cholesterol reducer Zocor expired, three pharmaceutical makers entered the market for the drug. Conversely, the proliferation of products in the ice cream industry has gradually filled up the limited freezer space in grocery stores, making it harder for new ice cream makers to gain access to distribution in North America and Europe.

Strategic decisions of leading competitors often have a major impact on the threat of entry. Starting in the 1970s, for example, retailers such as Wal-Mart, Kmart, and Toys "R" Us began to adopt new procurement, distribution, and inventory control technologies with large fixed costs, including automated distribution centers, bar coding, and point-of-sale terminals. These investments increased the economies of scale and made it more difficult for small retailers to enter the business (and for existing small players to survive).

CHANGING SUPPLIER OR BUYER POWER

As the factors underlying the power of suppliers and buyers change with time, their clout rises or declines. In the global appliance industry, for instance, competitors including Electrolux, General Electric, and Whirlpool have been squeezed by the consolidation of retail channels (the decline of appliance specialty stores, for instance, and the rise of big-box retailers like Best Buy and Home Depot in the United States). Another example is travel agents, who depend on airlines as a key supplier. When the internet allowed airlines to sell tickets directly to customers, this significantly increased their power to bargain down agents' commissions.

SHIFTING THREAT OF SUBSTITUTION

The most common reason substitutes become more or less threatening over time is that advances in technology create new substitutes or shift price-performance comparisons in one direction or the other. The earliest microwave ovens, for example, were large and priced above $2,000, making them poor substitutes for conventional ovens. With technological advances, they became serious substitutes. Flash computer memory has improved enough recently to become a meaningful substitute for low-capacity hard-disk drives. Trends in the availability or performance of complementary producers also shift the threat of substitutes.

NEW BASES OF RIVALRY

Rivalry often intensifies naturally over time. As an industry matures, growth slows. Competitors become more alike as industry conventions emerge, technology diffuses, and consumer tastes converge. Industry profitability falls, and weaker competitors are driven from the business. This story has played out in industry after industry; televisions, snowmobiles, and telecommunications equipment are just a few examples.

A trend toward intensifying price competition and other forms of rivalry, however, is by no means inevitable. For example, there has been enormous competitive activity in the U.S. casino industry in recent decades, but most of it has been positive-sum competition directed toward new niches and geographic segments (such as riverboats, trophy properties, Native American reservations, international expansion, and novel customer groups like families). Head-to-head rivalry that lowers prices or boosts the payouts to winners has been limited.

The nature of rivalry in an industry is altered by mergers and acquisitions that introduce new capabilities and ways of competing. Or, technological innovation can reshape rivalry. In the retail brokerage industry, the advent of the internet lowered marginal costs and reduced differentiation, triggering far more intense competition on commissions and fees than in the past.

In some industries, companies turn to mergers and consolidation not to improve cost and quality but to attempt to stop intense competition. Eliminating rivals is a risky strategy, however. The five competitive forces tell us that a profit windfall from removing today's competitors often attracts new competitors and backlash from customers and suppliers. In New York banking, for example, the 1980s and 1990s saw escalating consolidations of commercial and savings banks, including Manufacturers Hanover, Chemical, Chase, and Dime Savings. But today the retail-banking landscape of Manhattan is as diverse as ever, as new entrants such as Wachovia, Bank of America, and Washington Mutual have entered the market.

Implications for Strategy

Understanding the forces that shape industry competition is the starting point for developing strategy. Every company should already know what the average profitability of its industry is and how that has been changing over time. The five forces reveal *why* industry profitability is what it is. Only then can a company incorporate industry conditions into strategy.

The forces reveal the most significant aspects of the competitive environment. They also provide a baseline for sizing up a company's strengths and weaknesses: Where does the company stand versus buyers, suppliers, entrants, rivals, and substitutes? Most importantly, an understanding of industry structure guides managers toward fruitful possibilities for strategic action, which may include any or all of the following: positioning the company to better cope with the current competitive forces; anticipating and exploiting shifts in the forces; and shaping the balance of forces to create a new industry structure that is more favorable to the company. The best strategies exploit more than one of these possibilities.

POSITIONING THE COMPANY

Strategy can be viewed as building defenses against the competitive forces or finding a position in the industry where the forces are weakest. Consider, for instance, the position of Paccar in the market for heavy trucks. The heavy-truck industry is structurally challenging. Many buyers operate large fleets or are large leasing companies, with both the leverage and the motivation to drive down the price of one of their largest purchases. Most trucks are built to regulated standards and offer similar features, so price competition is rampant. Capital intensity causes rivalry to be fierce, especially during the recurring cyclical downturns. Unions exercise considerable supplier power. Though there are few direct substitutes for an 18-wheeler, truck buyers face important substitutes for their services, such as cargo delivery by rail.

In this setting, Paccar, a Bellevue, Washington–based company with about 20% of the North American heavy-truck market, has chosen to focus on one group of customers: owner-operators—drivers who own their trucks and contract directly with shippers or serve as subcontractors to larger trucking companies. Such small operators have limited clout as truck buyers. They are also less price sensitive because of their strong emotional ties to and economic dependence on the product. They take great pride in their trucks, in which they spend most of their time.

Paccar has invested heavily to develop an array of features with owner-operators in mind: luxurious sleeper cabins, plush leather seats, noise-insulated cabins, sleek exterior styling, and so on. At the company's extensive network of dealers, prospective buyers use software to select among thousands of options to put their personal signature on their trucks. These customized trucks are built to order, not to stock, and delivered in six to eight weeks. Paccar's trucks also have aerodynamic designs that reduce fuel consumption, and they maintain their resale value better than other trucks. Paccar's roadside assistance program and IT-supported system for distributing spare parts reduce the time a truck is out of service. All these are crucial considerations for an owner-operator. Customers pay Paccar a 10 percent premium, and its Kenworth and Peterbilt brands are considered status symbols at truck stops.

Paccar illustrates the principles of positioning a company within a given industry structure. The firm has found a portion of its industry where the competitive forces are weaker—where it can avoid buyer power and price-based rivalry. And it has tailored every single part of the value chain to cope well with the forces in its segment. As a result, Paccar has been profitable for 68 years straight and has earned a long-run return on equity above 20 percent.

In addition to revealing positioning opportunities within an existing industry, the five forces framework allows companies to rigorously analyze entry and exit. Both depend on answering the difficult question: "What is the potential of this business?" Exit is indicated when industry structure is poor or declining and the company has no prospect of a superior positioning. In considering entry into a new industry, creative strategists can use the framework to spot an industry with a good future before this good future is reflected in the prices of acquisition candidates. Five forces analysis may also reveal industries that are not necessarily attractive for the average entrant but in which a company has good reason to believe it can surmount entry barriers at lower cost than most firms or has a unique ability to cope with the industry's competitive forces.

EXPLOITING INDUSTRY CHANGE

Industry changes bring the opportunity to spot and claim promising new strategic positions if the strategist has a sophisticated understanding of the competitive forces and their underpinnings. Consider, for instance, the evolution of the music industry during the past decade. With the advent of the internet and the digital distribution of music, some analysts predicted the birth of thousands of music labels (that is, record companies that develop artists and bring their music to market). This, the analysts argued, would break a pattern that had held since Edison invented the phonograph: Between three and six major record companies had always dominated the industry. The internet would, they predicted, remove distribution as a barrier to entry, unleashing a flood of new players into the music industry.

A careful analysis, however, would have revealed that physical distribution was not the crucial barrier to entry. Rather, entry was barred by other benefits that large music labels enjoyed. Large labels could pool the risks of developing new artists over many bets, cushioning the impact of inevitable failures. Even more important, they had advantages in breaking through the clutter and getting their new artists heard. To do so, they could promise radio stations and record stores access to well-known artists in exchange for promotion of new artists. New labels would find this nearly impossible to match. The major labels stayed the course, and new music labels have been rare.

This is not to say that the music industry is structurally unchanged by digital distribution. Unauthorized downloading created an illegal but potent substitute. The labels tried for years to develop technical platforms for digital distribution themselves, but major companies hesitated to sell their music through a platform owned by a rival. Into this vacuum stepped Apple with its iTunes music store, launched in 2003 to support its iPod music player. By permitting the creation of a powerful new gatekeeper, the major labels allowed industry structure to shift against them. The number of major record companies has actually declined—from six in 1997 to four today—as companies struggled to cope with the digital phenomenon.

When industry structure is in flux, new and promising competitive positions may appear. Structural changes open up new needs and new ways to serve existing needs. Established leaders may overlook these or be constrained by past strategies from pursuing them. Smaller competitors in the industry can capitalize on such changes, or the void may well be filled by new entrants.

SHAPING INDUSTRY STRUCTURE

When a company exploits structural change, it is recognizing, and re-acting to, the inevitable. However, companies also have the ability to shape industry structure. A firm can lead its industry toward new ways of competing that alter the five forces for the better. In reshaping structure, a company wants its competitors to follow so that the entire industry will be transformed. While many industry participants may benefit in the process, the innovator can benefit most if it can shift competition in directions where it can excel.

An industry's structure can be reshaped in two ways: by redividing profitability in favor of incumbents or by expanding the overall profit pool. Redividing the industry pie aims to increase the share of profits to industry competitors instead of to suppliers, buyers, substitutes, and keeping out potential entrants. Expanding the profit pool involves increasing the overall pool of economic value generated by the industry in which rivals, buyers, and suppliers can all share.

Redividing profitability. To capture more profits for industry rivals, the starting point is to determine which force or forces are currently constraining industry profitability and address them. A company can potentially influence all of the competitive forces. The strategist's goal here is to reduce the share of profits that leak to suppliers, buyers, and substitutes or are sacrificed to deter entrants.

To neutralize supplier power, for example, a firm can standardize specifications for parts to make it easier to switch among suppliers. It can cultivate additional vendors, or alter technology to avoid a power-ful supplier group altogether. To counter customer power, companies may expand services that raise buyers' switching costs or find alternative means of reaching customers to neutralize powerful channels. To temper profit-eroding price rivalry, companies can invest more heavily in unique products, as pharmaceutical firms have done, or expand support services to customers. To scare off entrants, incumbents can elevate the fixed cost of competing—for instance, by escalating their R&D or marketing expenditures. To limit the threat of substitutes, companies can offer better value through new features or wider product accessibility. When soft-drink producers introduced vending machines and convenience store channels, for example, they dramatically improved the availability of soft drinks relative to other beverages.

Sysco, the largest food-service distributor in North America, offers a revealing example of how an industry leader can change the structure of an industry for the better. Food-service distributors purchase food and related items from farmers and food processors. They then warehouse and deliver these items to restaurants, hospitals, employer cafeterias, schools, and other food-service institutions. Given low barriers to entry, the food-service distribution industry has historically been highly fragmented, with numerous local competitors. While rivals try to cultivate customer relationships, buyers are price sensitive because food represents a large share of their costs. Buyers can also choose the substitute approaches of purchasing directly from manufacturers or using retail sources, avoiding distributors altogether. Suppliers wield bargaining power: They are often large companies with strong brand names that food preparers and consumers recognize. Average profitability in the industry has been modest.

Sysco recognized that, given its size and national reach, it might change this state of affairs. It led the move to introduce private-label distributor brands with specifications tailored to the food-service market, moderating supplier power. Sysco emphasized value-added services to buyers such as credit, menu planning, and inventory management to shift the basis of competition away from just price. These moves, together with stepped-up investments in information technology and regional distribution centers, substantially raised the bar for new entrants while making the substitutes less attractive. Not surprisingly, the industry has been consolidating, and industry profitability appears to be rising.

Industry leaders have a special responsibility for improving industry structure. Doing so often requires resources that only large players possess. Moreover, an improved industry structure is a public good because it benefits every firm in the industry, not just the company that initiated the improvement. Often, it is more in the interests of an industry leader than any other participant to invest for the common good because leaders will usually benefit the most. Indeed, improving the industry may be a leader's most profitable strategic opportunity, in part because attempts to gain further market share can trigger strong reactions from rivals, customers, and even suppliers.

There is a dark side to shaping industry structure that is equally important to understand. Ill-advised changes in competitive positioning and operating practices can *undermine* industry structure. Faced with pressures to gain market share or enamored with innovation for its own sake, managers may trigger new kinds of competition that no incumbent can win. When taking actions to improve their own company's competitive advantage, then, strategists should ask whether they are setting in motion dynamics that will undermine industry structure in the long run. In the early days of the personal computer industry, for instance, IBM tried to make up for its late entry by offering an open architecture that would set industry standards and attract complementary makers of application software and peripherals. In the process, it ceded ownership of the critical components of the PC—the operating system and the microprocessor—to Microsoft and Intel. By standardizing PCs, it encouraged price-based rivalry and shifted power to suppliers. Consequently, IBM became the temporarily dominant firm in an industry with an enduringly unattractive structure.

Expanding the profit pool. When overall demand grows, the industry's quality level rises, intrinsic costs are reduced, or waste is eliminated, the pie expands. The total pool of value available to competitors, suppliers, and buyers grows. The total profit pool expands, for example, when channels become more competitive or when an industry discovers latent buyers for its product that are not currently being served. When soft-drink producers rationalized their independent bottler networks to make them more efficient and effective, both the soft-drink companies and the bottlers benefited. Overall value can also expand when firms work collaboratively with suppliers to improve coordination and limit unnecessary costs incurred in the supply chain. This lowers the inherent cost structure of the industry, allowing higher profit, greater demand through lower prices, or both. Or, agreeing on quality standards can bring up industrywide quality and service levels, and hence prices, benefiting rivals, suppliers, and customers.

Expanding the overall profit pool creates win-win opportunities for multiple industry participants. It can also reduce the risk of destructive rivalry that arises when incumbents attempt to shift bargaining power or capture more market share. However, expanding the pie does not reduce the importance of industry structure. How the expanded pie is divided will ultimately be determined by the five forces. The most successful companies are those that expand the industry profit pool in ways that allow them to share disproportionately in the benefits.

DEFINING THE INDUSTRY

The five competitive forces also hold the key to defining the relevant industry (or industries) in which a company competes. Drawing industry boundaries correctly, around the arena in which competition actually takes place, will clarify the causes of profitability and the appropriate unit for setting strategy. A company needs a separate strategy for each distinct industry. Mistakes in industry definition made by competitors present opportunities for staking out superior strategic positions. (See the insert "Defining the Relevant Industry.")

Defining the Relevant Industry

Defining the industry in which competition actually takes place is important for good industry analysis, not to mention for developing strategy and setting business unit boundaries. Many strategy errors emanate from mistaking the relevant industry, defining it too broadly or too narrowly. Defining the industry too broadly obscures differences among products, customers, or geographic regions that are important to competition, strategic positioning, and profitability. Defining the industry too narrowly overlooks commonalities and linkages across related products or geographic markets that are crucial to competitive advantage.

Also, strategists must be sensitive to the possibility that industry boundaries can shift.

The boundaries of an industry consist of two primary dimensions. First is the *scope of products or services.* For example, is motor oil used in cars part of the same industry as motor oil used in heavy trucks and stationary engines, or are these different industries? The second dimension is *geographic scope.* Most industries are present in many parts of the world. However, is competition contained within each state, or is it national? Does competition take place within regions such as Europe or

North America, or is there a single global industry?

The five forces are the basic tool to resolve these questions. If industry structure for two products is the same or very similar (that is, if they have the same buyers, suppliers, barriers to entry, and so forth), then the products are best treated as being part of the same industry. If industry structure differs markedly, however, the two products may be best understood as separate industries.

In lubricants, the oil used in cars is similar or even identical to the oil used in trucks, but the similarity largely ends there. Automotive motor oil is sold to fragmented, generally unsophisticated customers through numerous and often powerful channels, using extensive advertising. Products are packaged in small containers and logistical costs are high, necessitating local production. Truck and power generation lubricants are sold to entirely different buyers in entirely different ways using a separate supply chain. Industry structure (buyer power, barriers to entry, and so forth) is substantially different. Automotive oil is thus a distinct industry from oil for truck and stationary engine uses. Industry profitability will differ in these two cases, and a lubricant company will need a separate strategy for competing in each area.

Differences in the five competitive forces also reveal the geographic scope of competition. If an industry has a similar structure in every country (rivals, buyers, and so on), the presumption is that competition is global, and the five forces analyzed from a global perspective will set average profitability. A single global strategy is needed. If an industry has quite different structures in different geographic regions, however, each region may well be a distinct industry. Otherwise, competition would have leveled the differences. The five forces analyzed for each region will set profitability there.

The extent of differences in the five forces for related products or across geographic areas is a matter of degree, making industry definition often a matter of judgment. A rule of thumb is that where the differences in any one force are large, and where the differences involve more than one force, distinct industries may well be present.

Fortunately, however, even if industry boundaries are drawn incorrectly, careful five forces analysis should reveal important competitive threats. A closely related product omitted from the industry definition will show up as a substitute, for example, or competitors overlooked as rivals will be recognized as potential entrants. At the same time, the five forces analysis should reveal major differences within overly broad industries that will indicate the need to adjust industry boundaries or strategies.

Competition and Value

The competitive forces reveal the drivers of industry competition. A company strategist who understands that competition extends well beyond existing rivals will detect wider competitive threats and be better equipped to address them. At the same time, thinking comprehensively about an industry's structure can uncover opportunities: differences in customers, suppliers, substitutes, potential entrants, and rivals that can become the basis for distinct strategies yielding superior performance. In a world of more open competition and relentless change, it is more important than ever to think structurally about competition.

Understanding industry structure is equally important for investors as for managers. The five competitive forces reveal whether an industry is truly attractive, and they help investors anticipate positive or negative shifts in industry structure before they are obvious. The five forces distinguish short-term blips from structural changes and allow investors to take advantage of undue pessimism or optimism. Those companies whose strategies have industry-transforming potential become far clearer. This deeper thinking about competition is a more powerful way to achieve genuine investment success than the financial projections and trend extrapolation that dominate today's investment analysis.

If both executives and investors looked at competition this way, capital markets would be a far more effective force for company success and economic prosperity. Executives and investors would both be focused on the same fundamentals that drive sustained profitability. The conversation between investors and executives would focus on the structural, not the transient. Imagine the improvement in company performance—and in the economy as a whole—if all the energy expended in "pleasing the Street" were redirected toward the factors that create true economic value.

NOTES

1. For a discussion of the value chain framework, see Michael E. Porter, *Competitive Advantage: Creating and Sustaining Superior Performance* (The Free Press, 1998).

2. For a discussion of how internet technology improves the attractiveness of some industries while eroding the profitability of others, see Michael E. Porter, "Strategy and the Internet" (HBR, March 2001).

3. See, for instance, Adam M. Brandenburger and Barry J. Nalebuff, *Co-opetition* (Currency Doubleday, 1996).

CHAPTER 2

What Is Strategy?

Michael E. Porter

Operational Effectiveness Is Not Strategy

For almost two decades, managers have been learning to play by a new set of rules. Companies must be flexible to respond rapidly to competitive and market changes. They must benchmark continuously to achieve best practice. They must outsource aggressively to gain efficiencies. And they must nurture a few core competencies in the race to stay ahead of rivals.

Positioning—once the heart of strategy—is rejected as too static for today's dynamic markets and changing technologies. According to the new dogma, rivals can quickly copy any market position, and competitive advantage is, at best, temporary.

But those beliefs are dangerous half-truths, and they are leading more and more companies down the path of mutually destructive competition. True, some barriers to competition are falling as regulation eases and markets become global. True, companies have properly invested energy in becoming leaner and more nimble. In many industries, however, what some call *hypercompetition* is a self-inflicted wound, not the inevitable outcome of a changing paradigm of competition.

The root of the problem is the failure to distinguish between operational effectiveness and strategy. The quest for productivity, quality, and speed has spawned a remarkable number of management tools and

This article has benefited greatly from the assistance of many individuals and companies. The author gives special thanks to Jan Rivkin, the coauthor of a related paper. Substantial research contributions have been made by Nicolaj Siggelkow, Dawn Sylvester, and Lucia Marshall. Tarun Khanna, Roger Martin, and Anita McGahan have provided especially extensive comments.

November–December 1996

techniques: total quality management, benchmarking, time-based competition, outsourcing, partnering, reengineering, change management. Although the resulting operational improvements have often been dramatic, many companies have been frustrated by their inability to translate those gains into sustainable profitability. And bit by bit, almost imperceptibly, management tools have taken the place of strategy. As managers push to improve on all fronts, they move farther away from viable competitive positions.

OPERATIONAL EFFECTIVENESS: NECESSARY BUT NOT SUFFICIENT

Operational effectiveness and strategy are both essential to superior performance, which, after all, is the primary goal of any enterprise. But they work in very different ways.

A company can outperform rivals only if it can establish a difference that it can preserve. It must deliver greater value to customers or create comparable value at a lower cost, or do both. The arithmetic of superior profitability then follows: delivering greater value allows a company to charge higher average unit prices; greater efficiency results in lower average unit costs.

Ultimately, all differences between companies in cost or price derive from the hundreds of activities required to create, produce, sell, and deliver their products or services, such as calling on customers, assembling final products, and training employees. Cost is generated by performing activities, and cost advantage arises from performing particular activities more efficiently than competitors. Similarly, differentiation arises from both the choice of activities and how they are performed. Activities, then, are the basic units of competitive advantage. Overall advantage or disadvantage results from all a company's activities, not only a few.[1]

Operational effectiveness (OE) means performing similar activities *better* than rivals perform them. Operational effectiveness includes but is not limited to efficiency. It refers to any number of practices that allow a company to better utilize its inputs by, for example, reducing defects in products or developing better products faster. In contrast, strategic positioning means performing *different* activities from rivals' or performing similar activities in *different ways*. (See Figure 2.1.)

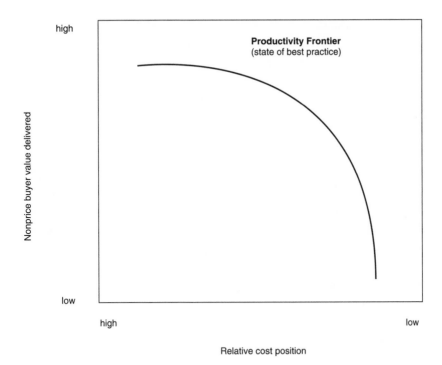

Figure 2.1   Operational Effectiveness Versus Strategic Positioning

Differences in operational effectiveness among companies are pervasive. Some companies are able to get more out of their inputs than others because they eliminate wasted effort, employ more advanced technology, motivate employees better, or have greater insight into managing particular activities or sets of activities. Such differences in operational effectiveness are an important source of differences in profitability among competitors because they directly affect relative cost positions and levels of differentiation.

Differences in operational effectiveness were at the heart of the Japanese challenge to Western companies in the 1980s. The Japanese were so far ahead of rivals in operational effectiveness that they could offer lower cost and superior quality at the same time. It is worth dwelling on this point, because so much recent thinking about competition depends on it. Imagine for a moment a *productivity frontier* that constitutes the sum of all existing best practices at any given time. Think of it as the maximum value that a company delivering a particular product or service can create at a given cost, using the best available technologies, skills, management techniques, and purchased inputs. The productivity frontier can apply to individual activities, to groups of linked activities such as order processing and manufacturing, and to an entire company's activities. When a company improves its operational effectiveness, it moves toward the frontier. Doing so may require capital investment, different personnel, or simply new ways of managing.

The productivity frontier is constantly shifting outward as new technologies and management approaches are developed and as new inputs become available. Laptop computers, mobile communications, the Internet, and software such as Lotus Notes, for example, have redefined the productivity frontier for sales-force operations and created rich possibilities for linking sales with such activities as order processing and after-sales support. Similarly, lean production, which involves a family of activities, has allowed substantial improvements in manufacturing productivity and asset utilization.

For at least the past decade, managers have been preoccupied with improving operational effectiveness. Through programs such as TQM, time-based competition, and benchmarking, they have changed how they perform activities in order to eliminate inefficiencies, improve customer satisfaction, and achieve best practice. Hoping to keep up with shifts in the productivity frontier, managers have embraced continuous improvement, empowerment, change management, and the so-called learning organization. The popularity of outsourcing and the virtual corporation reflect the growing recognition that it is difficult to perform all activities as productively as specialists.

As companies move to the frontier, they can often improve on multiple dimensions of performance at the same time. For example, manufacturers that adopted the Japanese practice of rapid changeovers in the 1980s were able to lower cost and improve differentiation simultaneously. What were once believed to be real trade-offs—between defects and costs, for example—turned out to be illusions created by poor operational effectiveness. Managers have learned to reject such false trade-offs.

Constant improvement in operational effectiveness is necessary to achieve superior profitability. However, it is not usually sufficient. Few companies have competed successfully on the basis of operational effectiveness over an extended period, and staying ahead of rivals gets harder every day. The most obvious reason for that is the rapid diffusion of best practices. Competitors can quickly imitate management techniques, new technologies, input improvements, and superior ways of meeting customers' needs. The most generic solutions—those that can be used in multiple settings—diffuse the fastest. Witness the proliferation of OE techniques accelerated by support from consultants.

OE competition shifts the productivity frontier outward, effectively raising the bar for everyone. But although such competition produces absolute improvement in operational effectiveness, it leads to relative improvement for no one. Consider the $5 billion-plus U.S. commercial-printing industry. The major players—R.R. Donnelley & Sons Company, Quebecor, World Color Press, and Big Flower Press—are competing head to head, serving all types of customers, offering the same array of printing technologies (gravure and web offset), investing heavily in the same new equipment, running their presses faster, and reducing crew sizes. But the resulting major productivity gains are being captured by customers and equipment suppliers, not retained in superior profitability. Even industry-leader Donnelley's profit margin, consistently higher than 7 percent in the 1980s, fell to less than 4.6 percent in 1995. This pattern is playing itself out in industry after industry. Even the Japanese, pioneers of the new competition, suffer from persistently low profits. (See the insert "Japanese Companies Rarely Have Strategies.")

Japanese Companies Rarely Have Strategies

The Japanese triggered a global revolution in operational effectiveness in the 1970s and 1980s, pioneering practices such as total quality management and continuous improvement. As a result, Japanese manufacturers enjoyed substantial cost and quality advantages for many years.

But Japanese companies rarely developed distinct strategic positions of the kind discussed in this article. Those that did—Sony, Canon, and Sega, for example—were the exception rather than the rule. Most Japanese companies imitate and emulate one another. All rivals offer most if not all product varieties, features, and services; they employ all channels and match one anothers' plant configurations.

The dangers of Japanese-style competition are now becoming easier to recognize. In the 1980s, with rivals operating far from the productivity frontier, it seemed possible to win on both cost and quality indefinitely. Japanese companies were all able to grow in an expanding domestic economy and by penetrating global markets. They appeared unstoppable. But as the gap in operational effectiveness narrows, Japanese companies are increasingly caught in a trap of their own making. If they are to escape the mutually destructive battles now ravaging their performance, Japanese companies will have to learn strategy.

To do so, they may have to overcome strong cultural barriers. Japan is notoriously consensus oriented, and companies have a strong tendency to mediate differences among individuals rather than accentuate them. Strategy, on the other hand, requires hard choices. The Japanese also have a deeply ingrained service tradition that predisposes them to go to great lengths to satisfy any need a customer expresses. Companies that compete in that way end up blurring their distinct positioning, becoming all things to all customers.

This discussion of Japan is drawn from the author's research with Hirotaka Takeuchi, with help from Mariko Sakakibara.

The second reason that improved operational effectiveness is insufficient—competitive convergence—is more subtle and insidious. The more benchmarking companies do, the more they look alike. The more that rivals outsource activities to efficient third parties, often the same ones, the more generic those activities become. As rivals imitate one another's improvements in quality, cycle times, or supplier partnerships, strategies converge and competition becomes a series of races down identical paths that no one can win. Competition based on operational effectiveness alone is mutually destructive, leading to wars of attrition that can be arrested only by limiting competition.

The recent wave of industry consolidation through mergers makes sense in the context of OE competition. Driven by performance pressures but lacking strategic vision, company after company has had no better idea than to buy up its rivals. The competitors left standing are often those that outlasted others, not companies with real advantage.

After a decade of impressive gains in operational effectiveness, many companies are facing diminishing returns. Continuous improvement has been etched on managers' brains. But its tools unwittingly draw companies toward imitation and homogeneity. Gradually, managers have let operational effectiveness supplant strategy. The result is zero-sum competition, static or declining prices, and pressures on costs that compromise companies' ability to invest in the business for the long term.

Strategy Rests on Unique Activities

Competitive strategy is about being different. It means deliberately choosing a different set of activities to deliver a unique mix of value. (See the insert "Finding New Positions: The Entrepreneurial Edge.")

Southwest Airlines Company, for example, offers short-haul, low-cost, point-to-point service between midsize cities and secondary airports in large cities. Southwest avoids large airports and does not fly great distances. Its customers include business travelers, families, and students. Southwest's frequent departures and low fares attract price-sensitive customers who otherwise would travel by bus or car, and convenience-oriented travelers who would choose a full-service airline on other routes.

Most managers describe strategic positioning in terms of their customers: "Southwest Airlines serves price- and convenience-sensitive travelers," for example. But the essence of strategy is in the activities—choosing to perform activities differently or to perform different activities than rivals. Otherwise, a strategy is nothing more than a marketing slogan that will not withstand competition.

A full-service airline is configured to get passengers from almost any point A to any point B. To reach a large number of destinations and serve passengers with connecting flights, full-service airlines employ a hub-and-spoke system centered on major airports. To attract passengers who desire more comfort, they offer first-class or business-class service. To accommodate passengers who must change planes, they coordinate schedules and check and transfer baggage. Because some passengers will be traveling for many hours, full-service airlines serve meals.

Southwest, in contrast, tailors all its activities to deliver low-cost, convenient service on its particular type of route. Through fast turn-arounds at the gate of only fifteen minutes, Southwest is able to keep planes flying longer hours than rivals and provide frequent departures with fewer aircraft. Southwest does not offer meals, assigned seats, interline baggage checking, or premium classes of service. Automated ticketing at the gate encourages customers to bypass travel agents, allowing Southwest to avoid their commissions. A standardized fleet of 737 aircraft boosts the efficiency of maintenance.

Southwest has staked out a unique and valuable strategic position based on a tailored set of activities. On the routes served by Southwest, a full service airline could never be as convenient or as low cost. (See Figure 2.2.)

Ikea, the global furniture retailer based in Sweden, also has a clear strategic positioning. Ikea targets young furniture buyers who want

---

Finding New Positions:
The Entrepreneurial Edge

Strategic competition can be thought of as the process of perceiving new positions that woo customers from established positions or draw new customers into the market. For example, superstores offering depth of merchandise in a single product category take market share from broad-line department stores offering a more limited selection in many categories. Mail-order catalogs pick off customers who crave convenience. In principle, incumbents and entrepreneurs face the same challenges in finding new strategic positions. In practice, new entrants often have the edge.

Strategic positionings are often not obvious, and finding them requires creativity and insight. New entrants often discover unique positions that have been available but simply overlooked by established competitors. Ikea, for example, recognized a customer group that had been ignored or served poorly. Circuit City Stores' entry into used cars, CarMax, is based on a new way of performing activities—extensive refurbishing of cars, product guarantees, no-haggle pricing, sophisticated use of in-house customer financing—that has long been open to incumbents.

New entrants can prosper by occupying a position that a competitor once held but has ceded through years of imitation and straddling. And entrants coming from other industries can create new positions because of distinctive activities drawn from their other businesses. CarMax borrows heavily from Circuit City's expertise in inventory management, credit, and other activities in consumer electronics retailing.

Most commonly, however, new positions open up because of change.

New customer groups or purchase occasions arise; new needs emerge as societies evolve; new distribution channels appear; new technologies are developed; new machinery or information systems become available. When such changes happen, new entrants, unencumbered by a long history in the industry, can often more easily perceive the potential for a new way of competing. Unlike incumbents, newcomers can be more flexible because they face no trade-offs with their existing activities.

style at low cost. What turns this marketing concept into a strategic positioning is the tailored set of activities that make it work. Like Southwest, Ikea has chosen to perform activities differently from its rivals.

Consider the typical furniture store. Showrooms display samples of the merchandise. One area might contain twenty-five sofas; another will display five dining tables. But those items represent only a fraction of the choices available to customers. Dozens of books displaying fabric swatches or wood samples or alternate styles offer customers thousands of product varieties to choose from. Salespeople often escort customers through the store, answering questions and helping them navigate this maze of choices. Once a customer makes a selection, the order is relayed to a third-party manufacturer. With luck, the furniture will be delivered to the customer's home within six to eight weeks. This is a value chain that maximizes customization and service but does so at high cost.

In contrast, Ikea serves customers who are happy to trade off service for cost. Instead of having a sales associate trail customers around the store, Ikea uses a self-service model based on clear, in-store displays. Rather than rely solely on third party manufacturers, Ikea designs its own low-cost, modular, ready-to-assemble furniture to fit its positioning. In huge stores, Ikea displays every product it sells in room-like

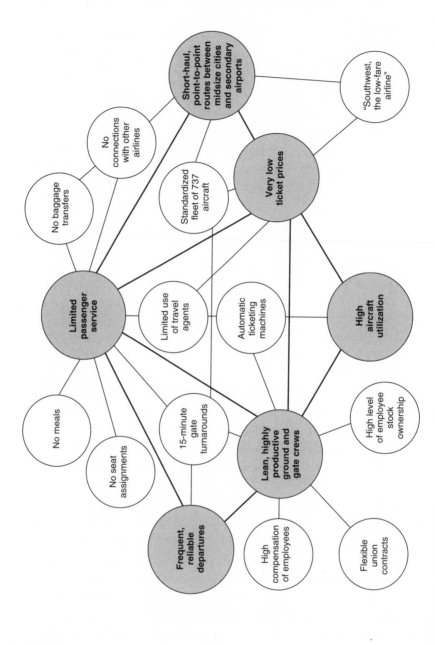

Figure 2.2 Southwest Airlines' Activity System

The nodes in the diagram contain the following text:

- Short-haul, point-to-point routes between midsize cities and secondary airports
- "Southwest, the low-fare airline"
- No connections with other airlines
- No baggage transfers
- Very low ticket prices
- Standardized fleet of 737 aircraft
- Limited passenger service
- Limited use of travel agents
- Automatic ticketing machines
- High aircraft utilization
- No meals
- 15-minute gate turnarounds
- Lean, highly productive ground and gate crews
- High level of employee stock ownership
- No seat assignments
- Frequent, reliable departures
- High compensation of employees
- Flexible union contracts

settings, so customers don't need a decorator to help them imagine how to put the pieces together. Adjacent to the furnished showrooms is a warehouse section with the products in boxes on pallets. Customers are expected to do their own pickup and delivery, and Ikea will even sell you a roof rack for your car that you can return for a refund on your next visit.

Although much of its low-cost position comes from having customers "do it themselves," Ikea offers a number of extra services that its competitors do not. In-store child care is one. Extended hours are another. Those services are uniquely aligned with the needs of its customers, who are young, not wealthy, likely to have children (but no nanny), and, because they work for a living, have a need to shop at odd hours. (See Figure 2.3.)

THE ORIGINS OF STRATEGIC POSITIONS

Strategic positions emerge from three distinct sources, which are not mutually exclusive and often overlap. First, positioning can be based on producing a subset of an industry's products or services. I call this *variety-based positioning* because it is based on the choice of product or service varieties rather than customer segments. Variety-based positioning makes economic sense when a company can best produce particular products or services using distinctive sets of activities.

Jiffy Lube International, for instance, specializes in automotive lubricants and does not offer other car repair or maintenance services. Its value chain produces faster service at a lower cost than broader line repair shops, a combination so attractive that many customers subdivide their purchases, buying oil changes from the focused competitor, Jiffy Lube, and going to rivals for other services.

The Vanguard Group, a leader in the mutual fund industry, is another example of variety-based positioning. Vanguard provides an array of common stock, bond, and money market funds that offer predictable performance and rock-bottom expenses. The company's investment approach deliberately sacrifices the possibility of extraordinary performance in any one year for good relative performance in every year. Vanguard is known, for example, for its index funds. It avoids making

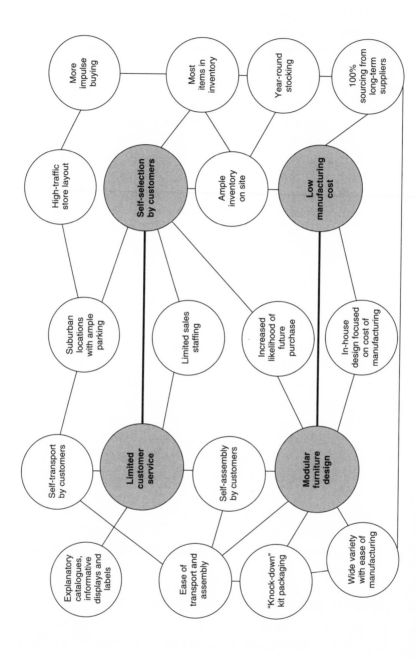

Figure 2.3 Mapping Activity Systems

Activity-system maps, such as this one for Ikea, show how a company's strategic position is contained in a set of tailored activities designed to deliver it. In companies with a clear strategic position, a number of higher-order strategic themes (in shaded circles) can be identified and implemented through clusters of tightly linked activities (in white circles).

bets on interest rates and steers clear of narrow stock groups. Fund managers keep trading levels low, which holds expenses down; in addition, the company discourages customers from rapid buying and selling because doing so drives up costs and can force a fund manager to trade in order to deploy new capital and raise cash for redemptions. Vanguard also takes a consistent low-cost approach to managing distribution, customer service, and marketing. Many investors include one or more Vanguard funds in their portfolio, while buying aggressively managed or specialized funds from competitors.

The people who use Vanguard or Jiffy Lube are responding to a superior value chain for a particular type of service. A variety-based positioning can serve a wide array of customers, but for most it will meet only a subset of their needs. (See Figure 2.4.)

A second basis for positioning is that of serving most or all the needs of a particular group of customers. I call this *needs-based positioning*, which comes closer to traditional thinking about targeting a segment of customers. It arises when there are groups of customers with differing needs, and when a tailored set of activities can serve those needs best. Some groups of customers are more price sensitive than others, demand different product features, and need varying amounts of information, support, and services. Ikea's customers are a good example of such a group. Ikea seeks to meet all the home furnishing needs of its target customers, not just a subset of them.

A variant of needs-based positioning arises when the same customer has different needs on different occasions or for different types of transactions. The same person, for example, may have different needs when traveling on business than when traveling for pleasure with the family. Buyers of cans—beverage companies, for example—will likely have different needs from their primary supplier than from their secondary source.

It is intuitive for most managers to conceive of their business in terms of the customers' needs they are meeting. But a critical element of needs-based positioning is not at all intuitive and is often overlooked. Differences in needs will not translate into meaningful positions unless the best set of activities to satisfy them *also* differs. If that were not the case, every competitor could meet those same needs, and there would be nothing unique or valuable about the positioning.

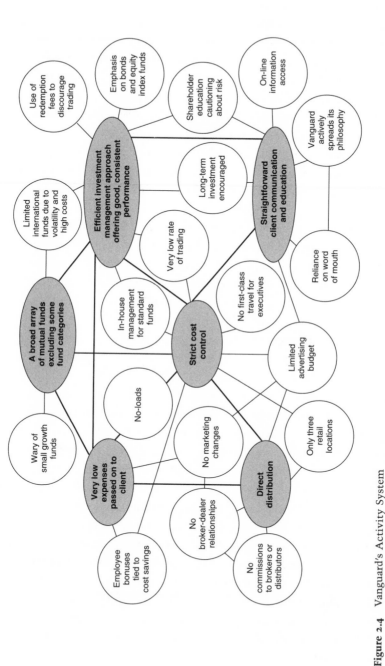

Figure 2.4 Vanguard's Activity System

Activity-system maps can be useful for examining and strengthening strategic fit. A set of basic questions should guide the process. First, is each activity consistent with the overall positioning—the varieties produced, the needs served, and the type of customers accessed? Ask those responsible for each activity to identify how other activities within the company improve or detract from their performance. Second, are there ways to strengthen how activities and groups of activities reinforce one another? Finally, could changes in one activity eliminate the need to perform others?

In private banking, for example, Bessemer Trust Company targets families with a minimum of $5 million in investable assets who want capital preservation combined with wealth accumulation. By assigning one sophisticated account officer for every 14 families, Bessemer has configured its activities for personalized service. Meetings, for example, are more likely to be held at a client's ranch or yacht than in the office. Bessemer offers a wide array of customized services, including investment management and estate administration, oversight of oil and gas investments, and accounting for racehorses and aircraft. Loans, a staple of most private banks, are rarely needed by Bessemer's clients and make up a tiny fraction of its client balances and income. Despite the most generous compensation of account officers and the highest personnel cost as a percentage of operating expenses, Bessemer's differentiation with its target families produces a return on equity estimated to be the highest of any private banking competitor.

Citibank's private bank, on the other hand, serves clients with minimum assets of about $250,000 who, in contrast to Bessemer's clients, want convenient access to loans—from jumbo mortgages to deal financing. Citibank's account managers are primarily lenders. When clients need other services, their account manager refers them to other Citibank specialists, each of whom handles prepackaged products. Citibank's system is less customized than Bessemer's and allows it to have a lower manager-to-client ratio of 1:125. Biannual office meetings are offered only for the largest clients. Both Bessemer and Citibank have tailored their activities to meet the needs of a different group of private banking customers. The same value chain cannot profitably meet the needs of both groups.

The third basis for positioning is that of segmenting customers who are accessible in different ways. Although their needs are similar to those of other customers, the best configuration of activities to reach them is different. I call this *access-based positioning*. Access can be a function of customer geography or customer scale—or of anything that requires a different set of activities to reach customers in the best way.

Segmenting by access is less common and less well understood than the other two bases. Carmike Cinemas, for example, operates movie theaters exclusively in cities and towns with populations under 200,000.

How does Carmike make money in markets that are not only small but also won't support big-city ticket prices? It does so through a set of activities that result in a lean cost structure. Carmike's small-town customers can be served through standardized, low-cost theater complexes requiring fewer screens and less sophisticated projection technology than big-city theaters. The company's proprietary information system and management process eliminate the need for local administrative staff beyond a single theater manager. Carmike also reaps advantages from centralized purchasing, lower rent and payroll costs (because of its locations), and rock-bottom corporate overhead of 2 percent (the industry average is 5 percent). Operating in small communities also allows Carmike to practice a highly personal form of marketing in which the theater manager knows patrons and promotes attendance through personal contacts. By being the dominant if not the only theater in its markets—the main competition is often the high school football team—Carmike is also able to get its pick of films and negotiate better terms with distributors.

Rural versus urban-based customers are one example of access driving differences in activities. Serving small rather than large customers or densely rather than sparsely situated customers are other examples in which the best way to configure marketing, order processing, logistics, and after-sale service activities to meet the similar needs of distinct groups will often differ.

Positioning is not only about carving out a niche. A position emerging from any of the sources can be broad or narrow. A focused competitor, such as Ikea, targets the special needs of a subset of customers and designs its activities accordingly. Focused competitors thrive on groups of customers who are overserved (and hence overpriced) by more broadly targeted competitors, or underserved (and hence underpriced). A broadly targeted competitor—for example, Vanguard or Delta Air Lines—serves a wide array of customers, performing a set of activities designed to meet their common needs. It ignores or meets only partially the more idiosyncratic needs of particular customer groups. (See the insert "The Connection with Generic Strategies.")

Whatever the basis—variety, needs, access, or some combination of the three—positioning requires a tailored set of activities because it is

The Connection with Generic Strategies

In *Competitive Strategy* (The Free Press, 1985), I introduced the concept of generic strategies—cost leadership, differentiation, and focus—to represent the alternative strategic positions in an industry. The generic strategies remain useful to characterize strategic positions at the simplest and broadest level. Vanguard, for instance, is an example of a cost leadership strategy, whereas Ikea, with its narrow customer group, is an example of cost-based focus. Neutrogena is a focused differentiator. The bases for positioning—varieties, needs, and access—carry the understanding of those generic strategies to a greater level of specificity. Ikea and Southwest are both cost-based focusers, for example, but Ikea's focus is based on the needs of a customer group, and Southwest's is based on offering a particular service variety.

The generic strategies framework introduced the need to choose in order to avoid becoming caught between what I then described as the inherent contradictions of different strategies. Trade-offs between the activities of incompatible positions explain those contradictions. Witness Continental Lite, which tried and failed to compete in two ways at once.

always a function of differences on the supply side; that is, of differences in activities. However, positioning is not always a function of differences on the demand, or customer, side. Variety and access positionings, in particular, do not rely on *any* customer differences. In practice, however, variety or access differences often accompany needs differences. The tastes—that is, the needs—of Carmike's small-town customers, for instance, run more toward comedies, Westerns, action films, and family entertainment. Carmike does not run any films rated NC-17.

Having defined positioning, we can now begin to answer the question, "What is strategy?" Strategy is the creation of a unique and valuable position, involving a different set of activities. If there were only one ideal position, there would be no need for strategy. Companies would face a simple imperative—win the race to discover and preempt it. The essence of strategic positioning is to choose activities that are different from rivals'. If the same set of activities were best to produce all varieties, meet all needs, and access all customers, companies could easily shift among them and operational effectiveness would determine performance.

A Sustainable Strategic Position Requires Trade-offs

Choosing a unique position, however, is not enough to guarantee a sustainable advantage. A valuable position will attract imitation by incumbents, who are likely to copy it in one of two ways.

First, a competitor can reposition itself to match the superior performer. J.C. Penney, for instance, has been repositioning itself from a Sears clone to a more upscale, fashion-oriented, soft-goods retailer. A second and far more common type of imitation is straddling. The straddler seeks to match the benefits of a successful position while maintaining its existing position. It grafts new features, services, or technologies onto the activities it already performs.

For those who argue that competitors can copy any market position, the airline industry is a perfect test case. It would seem that nearly any competitor could imitate any other airline's activities. Any airline can buy the same planes, lease the gates, and match the menus and ticketing and baggage handling services offered by other airlines.

Continental Airlines saw how well Southwest was doing and decided to straddle. While maintaining its position as a full-service airline, Continental also set out to match Southwest on a number of point-to-point routes. The airline dubbed the new service Continental Lite. It eliminated meals and first-class service, increased departure frequency, lowered fares, and shortened turnaround time at the gate. Because Continental remained a full-service airline on other routes, it continued to use travel agents and its mixed fleet of planes and to provide baggage checking and seat assignments.

But a strategic position is not sustainable unless there are trade-offs with other positions. Trade-offs occur when activities are incompatible. Simply put, a trade-off means that more of one thing necessitates less of another. An airline can choose to serve meals—adding cost and slowing turnaround time at the gate—or it can choose not to, but it cannot do both without bearing major inefficiencies.

Trade-offs create the need for choice and protect against repositioners and straddlers. Consider Neutrogena soap. Neutrogena Corporation's variety-based positioning is built on a "kind to the skin," residue-free soap formulated for pH balance. With a large detail force calling on dermatologists, Neutrogena's marketing strategy looks more like a drug company's than a soap maker's. It advertises in medical journals, sends direct mail to doctors, attends medical conferences, and performs research at its own Skincare Institute. To reinforce its positioning, Neutrogena originally focused its distribution on drugstores and avoided price promotions. Neutrogena uses a slow, more expensive manufacturing process to mold its fragile soap.

In choosing this position, Neutrogena said no to the deodorants and skin softeners that many customers desire in their soap. It gave up the large volume potential of selling through supermarkets and using price promotions. It sacrificed manufacturing efficiencies to achieve the soap's desired attributes. In its original positioning, Neutrogena made a whole raft of trade-offs like those, trade-offs that protected the company from imitators.

Trade-offs arise for three reasons. The first is inconsistencies in image or reputation. A company known for delivering one kind of value may lack credibility and confuse customers—or even undermine its reputation—if it delivers another kind of value or attempts to deliver two inconsistent things at the same time. For example, Ivory soap, with its position as a basic, inexpensive everyday soap would have a hard time reshaping its image to match Neutrogena's premium "medical" reputation. Efforts to create a new image typically cost tens or even hundreds of millions of dollars in a major industry—a powerful barrier to imitation.

Second, and more important, trade-offs arise from activities themselves. Different positions (with their tailored activities) require different product configurations, different equipment, different employee behavior, different skills, and different management systems. Many trade-offs reflect inflexibilities in machinery, people, or systems. The more Ikea has configured its activities to lower costs by having its customers do their own assembly and delivery, the less able it is to satisfy customers who require higher levels of service.

However, trade-offs can be even more basic. In general, value is destroyed if an activity is overdesigned or underdesigned for its use. For example, even if a given salesperson were capable of providing a high level of assistance to one customer and none to another, the salesperson's talent (and some of his or her cost) would be wasted on the second customer. Moreover, productivity can improve when variation of an activity is limited. By providing a high level of assistance all the time, the salesperson and the entire sales activity can often achieve efficiencies of learning and scale.

Finally, trade-offs arise from limits on internal coordination and control. By clearly choosing to compete in one way and not another, senior management makes organizational priorities clear. Companies that try to be all things to all customers, in contrast, risk confusion in the trenches as employees attempt to make day-to-day operating decisions without a clear framework.

Positioning trade-offs are pervasive in competition and essential to strategy. They create the need for choice and purposefully limit what a company offers. They deter straddling or repositioning, because competitors that engage in those approaches undermine their strategies and degrade the value of their existing activities.

Trade-offs ultimately grounded Continental Lite. The airline lost hundreds of millions of dollars, and the CEO lost his job. Its planes were delayed leaving congested hub cities or slowed at the gate by baggage transfers. Late flights and cancellations generated a thousand complaints a day. Continental Lite could not afford to compete on price and still pay standard travel-agent commissions, but neither could it do without agents for its full-service business. The airline compromised by cutting commissions for all Continental flights across the board. Similarly, it could not afford to offer the same frequent-flier benefits to travelers paying the much lower ticket prices for Lite service. It compromised again by lowering the rewards of Continental's entire frequent-flier program. The results: angry travel agents and full-service customers.

Continental tried to compete in two ways at once. In trying to be low cost on some routes and full service on others, Continental paid an enormous straddling penalty. If there were no trade-offs between the two positions, Continental could have succeeded. But the absence of trade-offs is a dangerous half-truth that managers must unlearn. Quality is not always free. Southwest's convenience, one kind of high quality, happens to be consistent with low costs because its frequent departures are facilitated by a number of low-cost practices—fast gate turnarounds and automated ticketing, for example. However, other dimensions of airline quality—an assigned seat, a meal, or baggage transfer—require costs to provide.

In general, false trade-offs between cost and quality occur primarily when there is redundant or wasted effort, poor control or accuracy, or weak coordination. Simultaneous improvement of cost and differentiation is possible only when a company begins far behind the productivity frontier or when the frontier shifts outward. At the frontier, where companies have achieved current best practice, the trade-off between cost and differentiation is very real indeed.

After a decade of enjoying productivity advantages, Honda Motor Company and Toyota Motor Corporation recently bumped up against the frontier. In 1995, faced with increasing customer resistance to higher automobile prices, Honda found that the only way to produce a less-expensive car was to skimp on features. In the United States, it replaced the rear disk brakes on the Civic with lower-cost drum brakes and used cheaper fabric for the back seat, hoping customers would not notice. Toyota tried to sell a version of its best-selling Corolla in Japan with unpainted bumpers and cheaper seats. In Toyota's case, customers rebelled, and the company quickly dropped the new model.

For the past decade, as managers have improved operational effectiveness greatly, they have internalized the idea that eliminating trade-offs is a good thing. But if there are no trade-offs companies will never achieve a sustainable advantage. They will have to run faster and faster just to stay in place.

As we return to the question, What is strategy? we see that trade-offs add a new dimension to the answer. Strategy is making trade-offs in competing. The essence of strategy is choosing what not to do. Without trade-offs, there would be no need for choice and thus no need for strategy. Any good idea could and would be quickly imitated. Again, performance would once again depend wholly on operational effectiveness.

Fit Drives Both Competitive Advantage and Sustainability

Positioning choices determine not only which activities a company will perform and how it will configure individual activities but also how activities relate to one another. While operational effectiveness is about achieving excellence in individual activities, or functions, strategy is about *combining* activities.

Southwest's rapid gate turnaround, which allows frequent departures and greater use of aircraft, is essential to its high-convenience, low-cost positioning. But how does Southwest achieve it? Part of the answer lies in the company's well-paid gate and ground crews, whose productivity in turn-arounds is enhanced by flexible union rules. But the bigger part of the answer lies in how Southwest performs other activities. With no meals, no seat assignment, and no interline baggage transfers, Southwest avoids having to perform activities that slow down other airlines. It selects airports and routes to avoid congestion that introduces delays. Southwest's strict limits on the type and length of routes make standardized aircraft possible: every aircraft Southwest turns is a Boeing 737.

What is Southwest's core competence? Its key success factors? The correct answer is that everything matters. Southwest's strategy involves a whole system of activities, not a collection of parts. Its competitive advantage comes from the way its activities fit and reinforce one another.

Fit locks out imitators by creating a chain that is as strong as its *strongest* link. As in most companies with good strategies, Southwest's activities complement one another in ways that create real economic value. One activity's cost, for example, is lowered because of the way other activities are performed. Similarly, one activity's value to customers can be enhanced by a company's other activities. That is the way strategic fit creates competitive advantage and superior profitability.

TYPES OF FIT

The importance of fit among functional policies is one of the oldest ideas in strategy. Gradually, however, it has been supplanted on the management agenda. Rather than seeing the company as a whole, managers have turned to "core" competencies, "critical" resources, and "key" success factors. In fact, fit is a far more central component of competitive advantage than most realize.

Fit is important because discrete activities often affect one another. A sophisticated sales force, for example, confers a greater advantage when the company's product embodies premium technology and its marketing approach emphasizes customer assistance and support. A production line with high levels of model variety is more valuable when combined with an inventory and order processing system that minimizes the need for stocking finished goods, a sales process equipped to explain and encourage customization, and an advertising theme that stresses the benefits of product variations that meet a customer's special needs. Such complementarities are pervasive in strategy. Although some fit among activities is generic and applies to many companies, the most valuable fit is strategy-specific because it enhances a position's uniqueness and amplifies trade-offs.[2]

There are three types of fit, although they are not mutually exclusive. First-order fit is *simple consistency* between each activity (function) and the overall strategy. Vanguard, for example, aligns all activities with its low-cost strategy. It minimizes portfolio turnover and does not need highly compensated money managers. The company distributes its funds directly, avoiding commissions to brokers. It also limits advertising, relying instead on public relations and word-of-mouth recommendations. Vanguard ties its employees' bonuses to cost savings.

Consistency ensures that the competitive advantages of activities cumulate and do not erode or cancel themselves out. It makes the strategy easier to communicate to customers, employees, and shareholders, and improves implementation through single-mindedness in the corporation.

Second-order fit occurs when *activities are reinforcing*. Neutrogena, for example, markets to upscale hotels eager to offer their guests a soap recommended by dermatologists. Hotels grant Neutrogena the privilege of using its customary packaging while requiring other soaps to feature the hotel's name. Once guests have tried Neutrogena in a luxury hotel, they are more likely to purchase it at the drugstore or ask their doctor about it. Thus Neutrogena's medical and hotel marketing activities reinforce one another, lowering total marketing costs.

In another example, Bic Corporation sells a narrow line of standard, low-priced pens to virtually all major customer markets (retail, commercial, promotional, and giveaway) through virtually all available channels. As with any variety-based positioning serving a broad group of customers, Bic emphasizes a common need (low price for an acceptable pen) and uses marketing approaches with a broad reach (a large sales force and heavy television advertising). Bic gains the benefits of consistency across nearly all activities, including product design that emphasizes ease of manufacturing, plants configured for low cost, aggressive purchasing to minimize material costs, and in-house parts production whenever the economics dictate.

Yet Bic goes beyond simple consistency because its activities are reinforcing. For example, the company uses point-of-sale displays and frequent packaging changes to stimulate impulse buying. To handle point-of-sale tasks, a company needs a large sales force. Bic's is the largest in its industry, and it handles point-of-sale activities better than its rivals do. Moreover, the combination of point-of-sale activity, heavy television advertising, and packaging changes yields far more impulse buying than any activity in isolation could.

Third-order fit goes beyond activity reinforcement to what I call *optimization of effort*. The Gap, a retailer of casual clothes, considers product availability in its stores a critical element of its strategy. The Gap could keep products either by holding store inventory or by restocking from warehouses. The Gap has optimized its effort across these activities by restocking its selection of basic clothing almost daily out of three warehouses, thereby minimizing the need to carry large in-store inventories. The emphasis is on restocking because The Gap's merchandising strategy sticks to basic items in relatively few colors. While comparable retailers achieve turns of three to four times per year, The Gap turns its inventory seven and a half times per year. Rapid restocking, moreover, reduces the cost of implementing The Gap's short model cycle, which is six to eight weeks long.[3]

Coordination and information exchange across activities to eliminate redundancy and minimize wasted effort are the most basic types of effort optimization. But there are higher levels as well. Product design choices, for example, can eliminate the need for after-sale service or make it possible for customers to perform service activities themselves. Similarly, coordination with suppliers or distribution channels can eliminate the need for some in-house activities, such as end-user training.

In all three types of fit, the whole matters more than any individual part. Competitive advantage grows out of the *entire system* of activities. The fit among activities substantially reduces cost or increases differentiation. Beyond that, the competitive value of individual activities—or the associated skills, competencies, or resources—cannot be decoupled from the system or the strategy. Thus in competitive companies it can be misleading to explain success by specifying individual strengths, core competencies, or critical resources. The list of strengths cuts across many functions, and one strength blends into others. It is more useful to think in terms of themes that pervade many activities, such as low cost, a particular notion of customer service, or a particular conception of the value delivered. These themes are embodied in nests of tightly linked activities.

FIT AND SUSTAINABILITY

Strategic fit among many activities is fundamental not only to competitive advantage but also to the sustainability of that advantage. It is harder for a rival to match an array of interlocked activities than it is merely to imitate a particular sales-force approach, match a process technology, or replicate a set of product features. Positions built on systems of activities are far more sustainable than those built on individual activities. (See Table 2.1.)

Consider this simple exercise. The probability that competitors can match any activity is often less than one. The probabilities then quickly compound to make matching the entire system highly unlikely $(.9 \times .9 = .81; .9 \times .9 \times .9 \times .9 = .66$, and so on$)$. Existing companies that try to reposition or straddle will be forced to reconfigure many activities. And even new entrants, though they do not confront the trade-offs facing established rivals, still face formidable barriers to imitation.

The more a company's positioning rests on activity systems with second- and third-order fit, the more sustainable its advantage will be. Such systems, by their very nature, are usually difficult to untangle from outside the company and therefore hard to imitate. And even if rivals can identify the relevant interconnections, they will have difficulty replicating them. Achieving fit is difficult because it requires the integration of decisions and actions across many independent subunits.

A competitor seeking to match an activity system gains little by imitating only some activities and not matching the whole. Performance does not improve; it can decline. Recall Continental Lite's disastrous attempt to imitate Southwest.

Finally, fit among a company's activities creates pressures and incentives to improve operational effectiveness, which makes imitation even harder. Fit means that poor performance in one activity will degrade the performance in others, so that weaknesses are exposed and more prone to get attention. Conversely, improvements in one activity will pay dividends in others. Companies with strong fit among their activities are rarely inviting targets. Their superiority in strategy and in execution only compounds their advantages and raises the hurdle for imitators.

When activities complement one another, rivals will get little benefit from imitation unless they successfully match the whole system. Such situations tend to promote winner-take-all competition. The company that builds the best activity system—Toys R Us, for instance—wins, while rivals with similar strategies—Child World and Lionel Leisure— fall behind. Thus finding a new strategic position is often preferable to being the second or third imitator of an occupied position.

The most viable positions are those whose activity systems are incompatible because of trade-offs. Strategic positioning sets the trade-off rules that define how individual activities will be configured and integrated. Seeing strategy in terms of activity systems only makes it clearer why organizational structure, systems, and processes need to be strategy-specific. Tailoring organization to strategy, in turn, makes complementarities more achievable and contributes to sustainability.

One implication is that strategic positions should have a horizon of a decade or more, not of a single planning cycle. Continuity fosters improvements in individual activities and the fit across activities, allowing an organization to build unique capabilities and skills tailored to its strategy. Continuity also reinforces a company's identity.

Conversely, frequent shifts in positioning are costly. Not only must a company reconfigure individual activities, but it must also realign entire systems. Some activities may never catch up to the vacillating strategy. The inevitable result of frequent shifts in strategy, or of failure to choose a distinct position in the first place, is "me-too" or hedged activity configurations, inconsistencies across functions, and organizational dissonance.

What is strategy? We can now complete the answer to this question. Strategy is creating fit among a company's activities. The success of a strategy depends on doing many things well—not just a few—and integrating among them. If there is no fit among activities, there is no distinctive strategy and little sustainability. Management reverts to the simpler task of overseeing independent functions, and operational effectiveness determines an organization's relative performance.

Rediscovering Strategy

Why do so many companies fail to have a strategy? Why do managers avoid making strategic choices? Or, having made them in the past, why do managers so often let strategies decay and blur? (See the insert "Reconnecting with Strategy.")

Commonly, the threats to strategy are seen to emanate from outside a company because of changes in technology or the behavior of competitors. Although external changes can be the problem, the greater threat to strategy often comes from within. A sound strategy is undermined by a misguided view of competition, by organizational failures, and, especially, by the desire to grow.

THE FAILURE TO CHOOSE

Managers have become confused about the necessity of making choices. When many companies operate far from the productivity frontier, trade-offs appear unnecessary. It can seem that a well-run company should be able to beat its ineffective rivals on all dimensions simultaneously. Taught by popular management thinkers that they do not have to make trade-offs, managers have acquired a macho sense that to do so is a sign of weakness.

Unnerved by forecasts of hypercompetition, managers increase its likelihood by imitating everything about their competitors. Exhorted to think in terms of revolution, managers chase every new technology for its own sake.

The pursuit of operational effectiveness is seductive because it is concrete and actionable. Over the past decade, managers have been under increasing pressure to deliver tangible, measurable performance improvements. Programs in operational effectiveness produce reassuring progress, although superior profitability may remain elusive. Business

Reconnecting with Strategy

Most companies owe their initial success to a unique strategic position involving clear trade-offs. Activities once were aligned with that position. The passage of time and the pressures of growth, however, led to compromises that were, at first, almost imperceptible. Through a succession of incremental changes that each seemed sensible at the time, many established companies have compromised their way to homogeneity with their rivals.

The issue here is not with the companies whose historical position is no longer viable; their challenge is to start over, just as a new entrant would. At issue is a far more common phenomenon: the established company achieving mediocre returns and lacking a clear strategy. Through incremental additions of product varieties, incremental efforts to serve new customer groups, and emulation of rivals' activities, the existing company loses its clear competitive position. Typically, the company has matched many of its competitors' offerings and practices and attempts to sell to most customer groups.

A number of approaches can help a company reconnect with strategy. The first is a careful look at what it already does. Within most well-established companies is a core of uniqueness. It is identified by an-

swering questions such as the following:

- Which of our product or service varieties are the most distinctive?
- Which of our product or service varieties are the most profitable?
- Which of our customers are the most satisfied?
- Which customers, channels, or purchase occasions are the most profitable?
- Which of the activities in our value chain are the most different and effective?

Around this core of uniqueness are encrustations added incrementally over time. Like barnacles, they must be removed to reveal the underlying strategic positioning. A small percentage of varieties or customers may well account for most of a company's sales and especially its profits. The challenge, then, is to refocus on the unique core and realign the company's activities with it. Customers and product varieties at the periphery can be sold or allowed through inattention or price increases to fade away.

A company's history can also be instructive. What was the vision of the founder? What were the products and customers that made the company? Looking backward, one can re-examine the original strategy to see if it is still valid. Can the historical positioning be implemented in a modern way, one consistent with today's technologies and practices? This sort of thinking may lead to a commitment to renew the strategy and may challenge the organization to recover its distinctiveness. Such a challenge can be galvanizing and can instill the confidence to make the needed trade-offs.

Table 2.1   Alternative Views of Strategy

The Implicit Strategy Model of the Past Decade	Sustainable Competitive Advantage
One ideal competitive position in the industry	Unique competitive position for the company
Benchmarking of all activities and achieving best practice	Activities tailored to stratgy
Aggressive outsourcing and partnering to gain efficiencies	Clear trade-offs and choices vis-à-vis competitors
Advantages rest on a few key success factors, critical resources, core competencies	Competitive advantage arises from fit across activities
Flexibility and rapid responses to all competitive and market changes	Sustainability comes from the activity system, not the parts
	Operational effectiveness a given

---

publications and consultants flood the market with information about what other companies are doing, reinforcing the best-practice mentality. Caught up in the race for operational effectiveness, many managers simply do not understand the need to have a strategy.

Companies avoid or blur strategic choices for other reasons as well. Conventional wisdom within an industry is often strong, homogenizing competition. Some managers mistake "customer focus" to mean they must serve all customer needs or respond to every request from distribution channels. Others cite the desire to preserve flexibility.

Organizational realities also work against strategy. Trade-offs are frightening, and making no choice is sometimes preferred to risking blame for a bad choice. Companies imitate one another in a type of herd behavior, each assuming rivals know something they do not. Newly empowered employees, who are urged to seek every possible source of improvement, often lack a vision of the whole and the perspective to recognize trade-offs. The failure to choose sometimes comes down to the reluctance to disappoint valued managers or employees.

THE GROWTH TRAP

Among all other influences, the desire to grow has perhaps the most perverse effect on strategy. Trade-offs and limits appear to constrain growth. Serving one group of customers and excluding others, for instance, places a real or imagined limit on revenue growth. Broadly targeted strategies emphasizing low price result in lost sales with customers sensitive to features or service. Differentiators lose sales to price-sensitive customers.

Managers are constantly tempted to take incremental steps that surpass those limits but blur a company's strategic position. Eventually, pressures to grow or apparent saturation of the target market lead managers to broaden the position by extending product lines, adding new features, imitating competitors' popular services, matching processes, and even making acquisitions. For years, Maytag Corporation's success was based on its focus on reliable, durable washers and dryers, later extended to include dishwashers. However, conventional wisdom emerging within the industry supported the notion of selling a full line of products. Concerned with slow industry growth and competition from broad-line appliance makers, Maytag was pressured by dealers and encouraged by customers to extend its line. Maytag expanded into refrigerators and cooking products under the Maytag brand and acquired other brands—Jenn-Air, Hardwick Stove, Hoover, Admiral, and Magic Chef—with disparate positions. Maytag has grown substantially from $684 million in 1985 to a peak of $3.4 billion in 1994, but return on sales has declined from 8 percent to 12 percent in the 1970s and 1980s to an average of less than 1 percent between 1989 and 1995. Cost cutting will improve this performance, but laundry and dishwasher products still anchor Maytag's profitability.

Neutrogena may have fallen into the same trap. In the early 1990s, its U.S. distribution broadened to include mass merchandisers such as Wal-Mart Stores. Under the Neutrogena name, the company expanded into a wide variety of products—eye-makeup remover and shampoo, for example—in which it was not unique and which diluted its image, and it began turning to price promotions.

Compromises and inconsistencies in the pursuit of growth will erode the competitive advantage a company had with its original varieties or target customers. Attempts to compete in several ways at once create confusion and undermine organizational motivation and focus. Profits fall, but more revenue is seen as the answer. Managers are unable to make choices, so the company embarks on a new round of broadening and compromises. Often, rivals continue to match each other until desperation breaks the cycle, resulting in a merger or downsizing to the original positioning.

PROFITABLE GROWTH

Many companies, after a decade of restructuring and cost-cutting, are turning their attention to growth. Too often, efforts to grow blur uniqueness, create compromises, reduce fit, and ultimately undermine competitive advantage. In fact, the growth imperative is hazardous to strategy.

What approaches to growth preserve and reinforce strategy? Broadly, the prescription is to concentrate on deepening a strategic position rather than broadening and compromising it. One approach is to look for extensions of the strategy that leverage the existing activity system by offering features or services that rivals would find impossible or costly to match on a stand-alone basis. In other words, managers can ask themselves which activities, features, or forms of competition are feasible or less costly to them because of complementary activities that their company performs.

Deepening a position involves making the company's activities more distinctive, strengthening fit, and communicating the strategy better to those customers who should value it. But many companies succumb to the temptation to chase "easy" growth by adding hot features, products, or services without screening them or adapting them to their strategy. Or they target new customers or markets in which the company has little special to offer. A company can often grow faster—and far more profitably—by better penetrating needs and varieties where it is distinctive than by slugging it out in potentially higher growth arenas in which the company lacks uniqueness. Carmike, now the largest theater chain in the United States, owes its rapid growth to its disciplined concentration on small markets. The company quickly sells any big-city theaters that come to it as part of an acquisition.

Globalization often allows growth that is consistent with strategy, opening up larger markets for a focused strategy. Unlike broadening domestically, expanding globally is likely to leverage and reinforce a company's unique position and identity.

Companies seeking growth through broadening within their industry can best contain the risks to strategy by creating stand-alone units, each with its own brand name and tailored activities. Maytag has clearly struggled with this issue. On the one hand, it has organized its premium and value brands into separate units with different strategic positions. On the other, it has created an umbrella appliance company for all its brands to gain critical mass. With shared design, manufacturing, distribution, and customer service, it will be hard to avoid homogenization. If a given business unit attempts to compete with different positions for different products or customers, avoiding compromise is nearly impossible.

THE ROLE OF LEADERSHIP

The challenge of developing or reestablishing a clear strategy is often primarily an organizational one and depends on leadership. With so many forces at work against making choices and trade-offs in organizations, a clear intellectual framework to guide strategy is a necessary counterweight. Moreover, strong leaders willing to make choices are essential.

In many companies, leadership has degenerated into orchestrating operational improvements and making deals. But the leader's role is broader and far more important. General management is more than the stewardship of individual functions. Its core is strategy: defining and communicating the company's unique position, making trade-offs, and forging fit among activities. The leader must provide the discipline to decide which industry changes and customer needs the company will respond to, while avoiding organizational distractions and maintaining the company's distinctiveness. Managers at lower levels lack the perspective and the confidence to maintain a strategy. There will be constant pressures to compromise, relax trade-offs, and emulate rivals. One of the leader's jobs is to teach others in the organization about strategy— and to say no.

Strategy renders choices about what not to do as important as choices about what to do. Indeed, setting limits is another function of leadership. Deciding which target group of customers, varieties, and needs the company should serve is fundamental to developing a strategy. But so is deciding not to serve other customers or needs and not to offer certain features or services. Thus strategy requires constant discipline and clear communication. Indeed, one of the most important functions of an explicit, communicated strategy is to guide employees in making choices that arise because of trade-offs in their individual activities and in day-to-day decisions.

Improving operational effectiveness is a necessary part of management, but it is *not* strategy. In confusing the two, managers have unintentionally backed into a way of thinking about competition that is driving many industries toward competitive convergence, which is in no one's best interest and is not inevitable.

Managers must clearly distinguish operational effectiveness from strategy. Both are essential, but the two agendas are different.

The operational agenda involves continual improvement everywhere there are no trade-offs. Failure to do this creates vulnerability even for companies with a good strategy. The operational agenda is the proper place for constant change, flexibility, and relentless efforts to achieve best practice. In contrast, the strategic agenda is the right place for defining a unique position, making clear trade-offs, and tightening fit. It involves the continual search for ways to reinforce and extend the company's position. The strategic agenda demands discipline and continuity; its enemies are distraction and compromise.

Strategic continuity does not imply a static view of competition. A company must continually improve its operational effectiveness and actively try to shift the productivity frontier; at the same time, there needs to be ongoing effort to extend its uniqueness while strengthening the fit among its activities. Strategic continuity, in fact, should make an organization's continual improvement more effective.

A company may have to change its strategy if there are major structural changes in its industry. In fact, new strategic positions often arise because of industry changes, and new entrants unencumbered by history often can exploit them more easily. However, a company's choice of a

---

Emerging Industries and Technologies

Developing a strategy in a newly emerging industry or in a business undergoing revolutionary technological changes is a daunting proposition. In such cases, managers face a high level of uncertainty about the needs of customers, the products and services that will prove to be the most desired, and the best configuration of activities and technologies to deliver them. Because of all this uncertainty, imitation and hedging are rampant: unable to risk being wrong or left behind, companies match all features, offer all new services, and explore all technologies.

During such periods in an industry's development, its basic productivity frontier is being established or reestablished. Explosive growth can make such times profitable for many companies, but profits will be temporary because imitation and strategic convergence will ultimately destroy industry profitability. The companies that are enduringly successful will be those that begin as early as possible to define and embody in their activities a unique competitive position. A period of imitation may be inevitable in emerging industries, but that period reflects the level of uncertainty rather than a desired state of affairs.

In high-tech industries, this imitation phase often continues much longer than it should. Enraptured by technological change itself, companies pack more features—most of which are never used—into their products while slashing prices across the board. Rarely are trade-offs even considered. The drive for growth to satisfy market pressures leads companies into every product area. Although a few companies with fundamental advantages prosper, the majority are doomed to a rat race no one can win.

Ironically, the popular business press, focused on hot, emerging industries, is prone to presenting these special cases as proof that we have entered a new era of competition in which none of the old rules are valid. In fact, the opposite is true.

new position must be driven by the ability to find new trade-offs and leverage a new system of complementary activities into a sustainable advantage. (See the insert "Emerging Industries and Technologies.")

NOTES

1. I first described the concept of activities and its use in understanding competitive advantage in *Competitive Advantage* (New York: The Free Press, 1985). The ideas in this article build on and extend that thinking.

2. Paul Milgrom and John Roberts have begun to explore the economics of systems of complementary functions, activities, and functions. Their focus is on the emergence of "modern manufacturing" as a new set of complementary activities, on the tendency of companies to react to external changes with coherent bundles of internal responses, and on the need for central coordination—a strategy—to align functional managers. In the latter case, they model what has long been a bedrock principle of strategy. See Paul Milgrom and John Roberts, "The Economics of Modern Manufacturing: Technology, Strategy, and Organization," *American Economic Review* 80 (1990): 511–528; Paul Milgrom, Yingyi Qian, and John Roberts, "Complementarities, Momentum, and Evolution of Modern Manufacturing," *American Economic Review* 81 (1991) 84–88; and Paul Milgrom and John Roberts, "Complementarities and Fit: Strategy, Structure, and Organizational Changes in Manufacturing," *Journal of Accounting and Economics*, vol. 19 (March–May 1995): 179–208.

3. Material on retail strategies is drawn in part from Jan Rivkin, "The Rise of Retail Category Killers," unpublished working paper, January 1995. Nicolaj Siggelkow prepared the case study on the Gap.

CHAPTER 3

How Information
Gives You
Competitive Advantage

Michael E. Porter

Victor E. Millar

———————————

THE INFORMATION REVOLUTION IS sweeping through our economy. No company can escape its effects. Dramatic reductions in the cost of obtaining, processing, and transmitting information are changing the way we do business.

Most general managers know that the revolution is under way, and few dispute its importance. As more and more of their time and investment capital is absorbed in information technology and its effects, executives have a growing awareness that the technology can no longer be the exclusive territory of EDP or IS departments. As they see their rivals use information for competitive advantage, these executives recognize the need to become directly involved in the management of the new technology. In the face of rapid change, however, they don't know how.

This chapter aims to help general managers respond to the challenges of the information revolution. How will advances in information technology affect competition and the sources of competitive advantage? What strategies should a company pursue to exploit the technology?

Author's note: We wish to thank Monitor Company and Arthur Andersen for their assistance in preparing this article. F. Warren McFarlan also provided valuable comments.

———————————

July–August 1985

What are the implications of actions that competitors may already have taken? Of the many opportunities for investment in information technology, which are the most urgent?

To answer these questions, managers must first understand that information technology is more than just computers. Today, information technology must be conceived of broadly to encompass the information that businesses create and use as well as a wide spectrum of increasingly convergent and linked technologies that process the information. In addition to computers, then, data recognition equipment, communications technologies, factory automation, and other hardware and services are involved.

The information revolution is affecting competition in three vital ways:

- It changes industry structure and, in so doing, alters the rules of competition.

- It creates competitive advantage by giving companies new ways to outperform their rivals.

- It spawns whole new businesses, often from within a company's existing operations.

We discuss the reasons why information technology has acquired strategic significance and how it is affecting all businesses. We then describe how the new technology changes the nature of competition and how astute companies have exploited this. Finally, we outline a procedure managers can use to assess the role of information technology in their business and to help define investment priorities to turn the technology to their competitive advantage.

Strategic Significance

Information technology is changing the way companies operate. It is affecting the entire process by which companies create their products. Furthermore, it is reshaping the product itself: the entire package of physical goods, services, and information companies provide to create value for their buyers.

An important concept that highlights the role of information technology in competition is the "value chain."[1] This concept divides a company's activities into the technologically and economically distinct activities it performs to do business. We call these "value activities." The value a company creates is measured by the amount that buyers are willing to pay for a product or service. A business is profitable if the value it creates exceeds the cost of performing the value activities. To gain competitive advantage over its rivals, a company must either perform these activities at a lower cost or perform them in a way that leads to differentiation and a premium price (more value).[2]

A company's value activities fall into nine generic categories (see Figure 3.1). Primary activities are those involved in the physical creation of the product, its marketing and delivery to buyers, and its support and servicing after sale. Support activities provide the inputs and infrastructure that allow the primary activities to take place. Every activity employs purchased inputs, human resources, and a combination of technologies. Firm infrastructure, including such functions as general management, legal work, and accounting, supports the entire chain. Within each of these generic categories, a company will perform a number of discrete activities, depending on the particular business. Service, for example, frequently includes activities such as installation, repair, adjustment, upgrading, and parts inventory management.

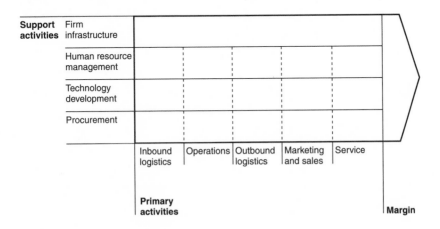

Figure 3.1   The Value Chain

A company's value chain is a system of interdependent activities, which are connected by linkages. Linkages exist when the way in which one activity is performed affects the cost or effectiveness of other activities. Linkages often create trade-offs in performing different activities that should be optimized. This optimization may require trade-offs. For example, a more costly product design and more expensive raw materials can reduce after-sale service costs. A company must resolve such trade-offs, in accordance with its strategy, to achieve competitive advantage.

Linkages also require activities to be coordinated. On-time delivery requires that operations, outbound logistics, and service activities (installation, for example) should function smoothly together. Good coordination allows on-time delivery without the need for costly inventory. Careful management of linkages is often a powerful source of competitive advantage because of the difficulty rivals have in perceiving them and in resolving trade-offs across organizational lines.

The value chain for a company in a particular industry is embedded in a larger stream of activities that we term the "value system" (see Figure 3.2). The value system includes the value chains of suppliers, who provide inputs (such as raw materials, components, and purchased services) to the company's value chain. The company's product often passes through its channels' value chains on its way to the ultimate buyer. Finally, the product becomes a purchased input to the value chains of its buyers, who use it to perform one or more buyer activities.

Linkages not only connect value activities inside a company but also create interdependencies between its value chain and those of its suppliers and channels. A company can create competitive advantage by optimizing or coordinating these links to the outside. For example, a candy manufacturer may save processing steps by persuading its suppliers to deliver chocolate in liquid form rather than in molded bars. Just-in-time

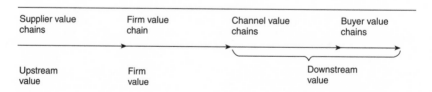

Figure 3.2   The Value System

deliveries by the supplier may have the same effect. But the opportunities for savings through coordinating with suppliers and channels go far beyond logistics and order processing. The company, suppliers, and channels can all benefit through better recognition and exploitation of such linkages.

Competitive advantage in either cost or differentiation is a function of a company's value chain. A company's cost position reflects the collective cost of performing all its value activities relative to rivals. Each value activity has cost drivers that determine the potential sources of a cost advantage. Similarly, a company's ability to differentiate itself reflects the contribution of each value activity toward fulfillment of buyer needs. Many of a company's activities—not just its physical product or service—contribute to differentiation. Buyer needs, in turn, depend not only on the impact of the company's product on the buyer but also on the company's other activities (for example, logistics or after-sale services).

In the search for competitive advantage, companies often differ in competitive scope—or the breadth of their activities. Competitive scope has four key dimensions: segment scope, vertical scope (degree of vertical integration), geographic scope, and industry scope (or the range of related industries in which the company competes).

Competitive scope is a powerful tool for creating competitive advantage. Broad scope can allow the company to exploit interrelationships between the value chains serving different industry segments, geographic areas, or related industries. For example, two business units may share one sales force to sell their products, or the units may coordinate the procurement of common components. Competing nationally or globally with a coordinated strategy can yield a competitive advantage over local or domestic rivals. By employing a broad vertical scope, a company can exploit the potential benefits of performing more activities internally rather than use outside suppliers.

By selecting a narrow scope, on the other hand, a company may be able to tailor the value chain to a particular target segment to achieve lower cost or differentiation. The competitive advantage of a narrow scope comes from customizing the value chain to best serve particular product varieties, buyers, or geographic regions. If the target segment has unusual needs, broad-scope competitors will not serve it well.

TRANSFORMING THE VALUE CHAIN

Information technology is permeating the value chain at every point, transforming the way value activities are performed and the nature of the linkages among them. It also is affecting competitive scope and reshaping the way products meet buyer needs. These basic effects explain why information technology has acquired strategic significance and is different from the many other technologies businesses use.

Every value activity has both a physical and an information-processing component. The physical component includes all the physical tasks required to perform the activity. The information-processing component encompasses the steps required to capture, manipulate, and channel the data necessary to perform the activity.

Every value activity creates and uses information of some kind. A logistics activity, for example, uses information like scheduling promises, transportation rates, and production plans to ensure timely and cost-effective delivery. A service activity uses information about service requests to schedule calls and order parts, and generates information on product failures that a company can use to revise product designs and manufacturing methods.

An activity's physical and information-processing components may be simple or quite complex. Different activities require a different mix of the two components. For instance, metal stamping uses more physical processing than information processing; processing of insurance claims requires just the opposite balance.

For most of industrial history, technological progress principally affected the physical component of what businesses do. During the Industrial Revolution, companies achieved competitive advantage by substituting machines for human labor. Information processing at that time was mostly the result of human effort.

Now the pace of technological change is reversed. Information technology is advancing faster than technologies for physical processing. The costs of information storage, manipulation, and transmittal are falling rapidly and the boundaries of what is feasible in information processing are at the same time expanding. During the Industrial Revolution, the railroad cut the travel time from Boston, Massachusetts, to Concord, New Hampshire, from five days to four hours, a factor of thirty.[3] But the advances in information technology are even greater. The cost of computer power relative to the cost of manual information processing is at least 8,000 times less expensive than the cost thirty years ago. Between 1958 and 1980 the time for one electronic operation fell by a factor of 80 million. Department of Defense studies show that the error rate in recording data through bar coding is 1 in 3,000,000, compared to 1 error in 300 manual data entries.[4]

This technological transformation is expanding the limits of what companies can do faster than managers can explore the opportunities. The information revolution affects all nine categories of value activity, from allowing computer-aided design in technology development to incorporating automation in warehouses (see Figure 3.3). The new technology substitutes machines for human effort in information processing. Paper ledgers and rules of thumb have given way to computers.

Initially, companies used information technology mainly for accounting and record-keeping functions. In these applications, the computers automated repetitive clerical functions such as order processing. Today information technology is spreading throughout the value chain and is performing optimization and control functions as well as more judgmental executive functions. General Electric, for instance, uses a data base that includes the accumulated experience and (often intuitive) knowledge of its appliance service engineers to provide support to customers by phone.

Information technology is generating more data as a company performs its activities and is permitting it to collect or capture information that was not available before. Such technology also makes room for a more comprehensive analysis and use of the expanded data. The number of variables that a company can analyze or control has grown dramatically. Hunt-Wesson, for example, developed a computer model to aid it in studying distribution-center expansion and relocation issues. The model enabled the company to evaluate many more different variables, scenarios, and alternative strategies than had been possible before. Similarly, information technology helped Sulzer Brothers' engineers improve the design of diesel engines in ways that manual calculations could not.

Information technology is also transforming the physical processing component of activities. Computer-controlled machine tools are faster, more accurate, and more flexible in manufacturing than the older, manu-

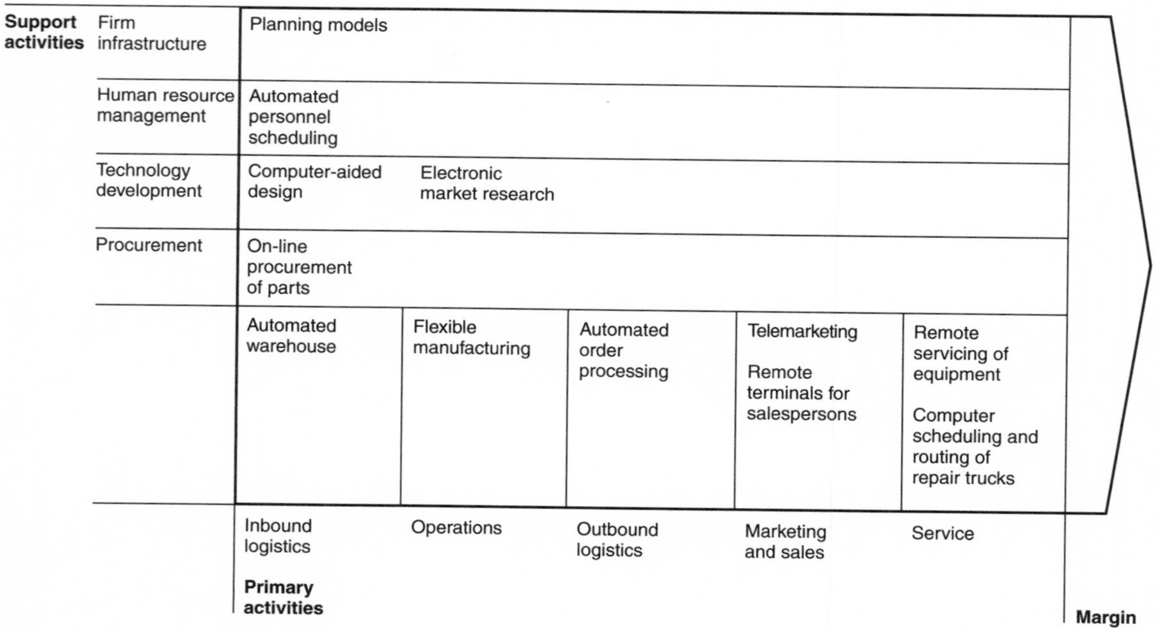

Figure 3.3 Information Technology Permeates the Value Chain

Support activities	Firm infrastructure	Planning models				
	Human resource management	Automated personnel scheduling				
	Technology development	Computer-aided design	Electronic market research			
	Procurement	On-line procurement of parts				
		Automated warehouse	Flexible manufacturing	Automated order processing	Telemarketing Remote terminals for salespersons	Remote servicing of equipment Computer scheduling and routing of repair trucks
		Inbound logistics	Operations	Outbound logistics	Marketing and sales	Service
		Primary activities				

Margin

ally operated machines. Schlumberger has developed an electronic device permitting engineers to measure the angle of a drill bit, the temperature of a rock, and other variables while drilling oil wells. The result: drilling time is reduced and some well-logging steps are eliminated. On the West Coast, some fishermen now use weather satellite data on ocean temperatures to identify promising fishing grounds. This practice greatly reduces the fishermen's steaming time and fuel costs.

Information technology not only affects how individual activities are performed but, through new information flows, it is also greatly enhancing a company's ability to exploit linkages between activities, both within and outside the company. The technology is creating new linkages between activities, and companies can now coordinate their actions more closely with those of their buyers and suppliers. For example, McKesson, the nation's largest drug distributor, provides its drugstore customers with terminals. The company makes it so easy for clients to order, receive, and prepare invoices that the customers, in return, are willing to place larger orders. At the same time, McKesson has streamlined its order processing.

Finally, the new technology has a powerful effect on competitive scope. Information systems allow companies to coordinate value activities in far-flung geographic locations. (For example, Boeing engineers work on designs on-line with foreign suppliers.) Information technology is also creating many new interrelationships among businesses, expanding the scope of industries in which a company must compete to achieve competitive advantage.

So pervasive is the impact of information technology that it confronts executives with a tough problem: too much information. This problem creates new uses of information technology to store and analyze the flood of information available to executives.

TRANSFORMING THE PRODUCT

Most products have always had both a physical and an information component. The latter, broadly defined, is everything that the buyer needs to know to obtain the product and use it to achieve the desired result. That is, a product includes information about its characteristics and how it should be used and supported. For example, convenient, accessible information on maintenance and service procedures is an important buyer criterion in consumer appliances.

Historically, a product's physical component has been more important than its information component. The new technology, however, makes it feasible to supply far more information along with the physical product. For example, General Electric's appliance service data base supports a consumer hotline that helps differentiate GE's service support from its rivals'. Similarly, some railroad and trucking companies offer up-to-the-minute information on the whereabouts of shippers' freight, which improves coordination between shippers and the railroad. The new technology is also making it increasingly possible to offer products with no physical component at all. Compustat's customers have access to corporate financial data filed with the Securities and Exchange Commission, and many companies have sprung up to perform energy use analyses of buildings.

Many products also process information in their normal functioning. A dishwasher, for example, requires a control system that directs the various components of the unit through the washing cycle and displays the process to the user. The new information technology is enhancing product performance and is making it easier to boost a product's information content. Electronic control of the automobile, for example, is becoming more visible in dashboard displays, talking dashboards, diagnostic messages, and the like.

There is an unmistakable trend toward expanding the information content in products. This component, combined with changes in companies' value chains, underscores the increasingly strategic role of information technology. There are no longer mature industries; rather, there are mature ways of doing business.

DIRECTION & PACE OF CHANGE

Although a trend toward information intensity in companies and products is evident, the role and importance of the technology differs in each industry. Banking and insurance, for example, have always been information intensive. Such industries were naturally among the first and most enthusiastic users of data processing. On the other hand, physical processing will continue to dominate in industries that produce,

say, cement, despite increased information processing in such businesses.

Figure 3.4, which relates information intensity in the value chain to
information content in the product, illuminates the differences in the
role and intensity of information among various industries. The banking
and newspaper industries have a high information-technology content
in both product and process. The oil-refining industry has a high use of
information in the refining process but a relatively low information
content in the product dimension.

Because of the falling cost and growing capacity of the new technology,
many industries seem to be moving toward a higher information content
in both product and process. It should be emphasized that technology

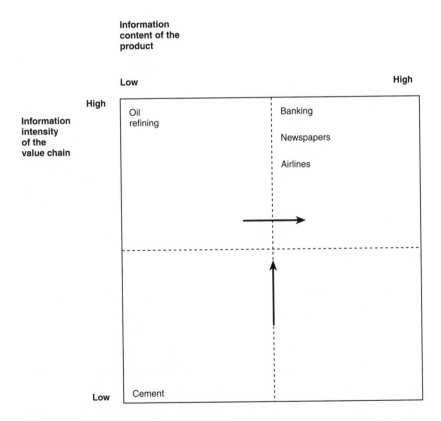

Figure 3.4   Information Intensity Matrix

will continue to improve rapidly. The cost of hardware will continue to drop, and managers will continue to distribute the technology among even the lower levels of the company. The cost of developing software, now a key constraint, will fall as more packages become available that are easily tailored to customers' circumstances. The applications of information technology that companies are using today are only a beginning.

Information technology is not only transforming products and processes but also the nature of competition itself. Despite the growing use of information technology, industries will always differ in their position in Figure 3.4 and their pace of change.

Changing the Nature of Competition

After surveying a wide range of industries, we find that information technology is changing the rules of competition in three ways. First, advances in information technology are changing the industry structure. Second, information technology is an increasingly important lever that companies can use to create competitive advantage. A company's search for competitive advantage through information technology often also spreads to affect industry structure as competitors imitate the leader's strategic innovations. Finally, the information revolution is spawning completely new businesses. These three effects are critical for understanding the impact of information technology on a particular industry and for formulating effective strategic responses.

CHANGING INDUSTRY STRUCTURE

The structure of an industry is embodied in five competitive forces that collectively determine industry profitability: the power of buyers, the power of suppliers, the threat of new entrants, the threat of substitute products, and the rivalry among existing competitors (see Figure 3.5). The collective strength of the five forces varies from industry to industry, as does average profitability. The strength of each of the five forces can also change, either improving or eroding the attractiveness of an industry.[5]

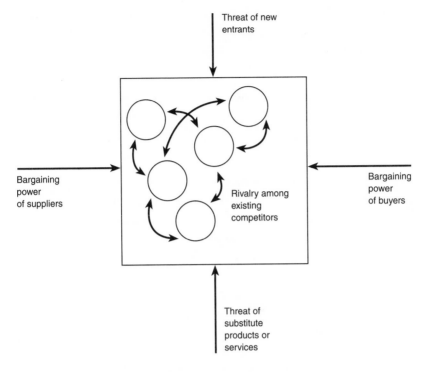

Figure 3.5   Determinants of Industry Attractiveness

Information technology can alter each of the five competitive forces and, hence, industry attractiveness as well. The technology is unfreezing the structure of many industries, creating the need and opportunity for change. For example:

- Information technology increases the power of buyers in industries assembling purchased components. Automated bills for materials and vendor quotation files make it easier for buyers to evaluate sources of materials and make-or-buy decisions.

- Information technologies requiring large investments in complex software have raised the barriers to entry. For example, banks competing in cash management services for corporate clients now need advanced software to give customers on-line account information. These banks may also need to invest in improved computer hardware and other facilities.

• Flexible computer-aided design and manufacturing systems have influenced the threat of substitution in many industries by making it quicker, easier, and cheaper to incorporate enhanced features into products.

• The automation of order processing and customer billing has increased rivalry in many distribution industries. The new technology raises fixed costs at the same time as it displaces people. As a result, distributors must often fight harder for incremental volume.

Industries such as airlines, financial services, distribution, and information suppliers (see the upper right-hand corner of Figure 3.4) have felt these effects so far.[6] (See the insert "Information Technology and Industry Structure" for more examples.)

Information technology has had a particularly strong impact on bargaining relationships between suppliers and buyers since it affects the linkages between companies and their suppliers, channels, and buyers. Information systems that cross company lines are becoming common. In some cases, the boundaries of industries themselves have changed.[7]

Systems that connect buyers and suppliers are spreading. Xerox gives manufacturing data to suppliers electronically to help them deliver materials. To speed up order entry, Westinghouse Electric Supply Company and American Hospital Supply have furnished their customers with terminals. Among other things, many systems raise the costs of switching to a new partner because of the disruption and retraining required. These systems tend to tie companies more closely to their buyers and suppliers.

Information technology is altering the relationship among scale, automation, and flexibility with potentially profound consequences. Large-scale production is no longer essential to achieve automation. As a result, entry barriers in a number of industries are falling.

At the same time, automation no longer necessarily leads to inflexibility. For example, General Electric rebuilt its Erie locomotive facility as a large-scale yet flexible factory using computers to store all design and manufacturing data. Ten types of motor frames can be accommodated without manual adjustments to the machines. After installation of a "smart" manufacturing system, BMW can build customized cars (each with its own tailored gearbox, transmission system, interior, and other

Information Technology and Industry Structure

Buyer Power

Videotex home shopping services, such as Comp-U-Card, increase buyers' information. Buyers use their personal computers to browse through electronic catalogs and compare prices and product specifications. Customers can make purchases at any hour at prices typically 25 percent to 30 percent below suggested retail levels. Comp-U-Card is growing quickly: revenues have quintupled in two years to $9.5 million and membership is now 15,000. According to some projections, by the mid-1990s, 75 percent of U.S. households will have access to such services.

Buyer Power

Shelternet, an electronic information exchange offered by First Boston Corporation, allows real estate brokers to determine quickly and easily what mortgage packages are available and whether the buyer will qualify for financing. This improves the position of both brokers and homebuyers in shopping for mortgages. The parties can make preliminary commitments within thirty minutes.

Substitution

Electronic data bases, such as NEXIS, are substituting for library research and consulting firms. NEXIS subscribers can quickly search the full text of any article in 225 periodicals. Users drastically reduce the time spent in literature searches. In addition, the buyer avoids the cost of journal subscriptions and pays only for the information required.

features) on the normal assembly line. Automation and flexibility are achieved simultaneously, a pairing that changes the pattern of rivalry among competitors.

The increasing flexibility in performing many value activities combined with the falling costs of designing products has triggered an avalanche of opportunities to customize and to serve small market niches. Computer-aided design capability not only reduces the cost of designing new products but also dramatically reduces the cost of modifying or adding features to existing products. The cost of tailoring products to market segments is falling, again affecting the pattern of industry rivalry.

While managers can use information technology to improve their industry structure, the technology also has the potential to destroy that structure. For example, information systems now permit the airline industry to alter fares frequently and to charge many different fares between any two points. At the same time, however, the technology makes the flight and fare schedules more readily available and allows travel agents and individuals to shop around quickly for the lowest fare. The result is a lower fare structure than might otherwise exist. Information technology has made a number of professional service industries less attractive by reducing personal interaction and making service more of a commodity. Managers must look carefully at the structural implications of the new technology to realize its advantages or to be prepared for its consequences.

CREATING COMPETITIVE ADVANTAGE

In any company, information technology has a powerful effect on competitive advantage in either cost or differentiation. The technology affects value activities themselves or allows companies to gain competitive advantage by exploiting changes in competitive scope.

Lowering Cost. As we have seen, information technology can alter a company's costs in any part of the value chain.[8] The technology's historical impact on cost was confined to activities in which repetitive information processing played a large part. These limits no longer exist, however. Even activities like assembly that mainly involve physical processing now have a large information-processing component.

Canon, for example, built a low-cost copier assembly process around an automated parts-selection and materials-handling system. Assembly workers have bins containing all the parts needed for the particular copier. Canon's success with this system derives from the software that controls parts inventory and selection. In insurance brokerage, a number of insurance companies usually participate in underwriting a contract. The costs of documenting each company's participation are high. Now a computer model can optimize (and often reduce) the number of insurers per contract, lowering the broker's total cost. In garment production, equipment such as automated pattern drawers, fabric cutters, and systems for delivering cloth to the final sewing station have reduced the labor time for manufacturing by up to 50 percent. (See the insert "Aim: A Competitive Edge" for further examples.)

In addition to playing a direct role in cost, information technology often alters the cost drivers of activities in ways that can improve (or erode) a company's relative cost position. For example, Louisiana Oil & Tire has taken all ten of its salespeople off the road and made them into telemarketers. As a result, sales expenses have fallen by 10 percent and sales volume has doubled. However, the move has made the national scale of operations the key determinant of the cost of selling, rather than regional scale.

Enhancing Differentiation. The impact of information technology on differentiation strategies is equally dramatic. As noted earlier, the role of a company and its product in the buyer's value chain is the key determinant of differentiation. The new information technology makes it possible to customize products. Using automation, for instance, Sulzer Brothers has increased from five to eight the number of cylinder bore sizes of new low-speed marine diesel engines. Shipowners now choose an engine that is more precisely suited to their needs and thereby recoup

---

Aim: A Competitive Edge

Lowering Cost

Casinos spend up to 20% of revenues on complimentary services for high rollers. One assignment for pit bosses has always been to keep an eye out for the big spenders. Now, however, many casinos have developed computer systems to analyze data on customers. Caesar's Palace lowered its complimentary budget more than 20% by developing a player-rating system for more accurate identification of big spenders.

Enhancing Differentiation

American Express has developed differentiated travel services for corporate customers through the use of information technology. The services include arranging travel and close monitoring of individual expenses. Computers search for the lowest airplane fares, track travel expenses for each cardholder, and issue monthly statements.

significant fuel savings. Similarly, Digital Equipment's artificial intelligence system, XCON, uses decision rules to develop custom computer configurations. This dramatically reduces the time required to fill orders and increases accuracy—which enhances Digital's image as a quality provider.

By bundling more information with the physical product package sold to the buyer, the new technology affects a company's ability to differentiate itself. For example, a magazine distributor offers retailers processing credits for unsold items more efficiently than its competitors. Similarly, the embedding of information systems in the physical product itself is an increasingly powerful way to distinguish it from competing goods.

Changing Competitive Scope. Information technology can alter the relationship between competitive scope and competitive advantage. The technology increases a company's ability to coordinate its activities regionally, nationally, and globally. It can unlock the power of broader geographic scope to create competitive advantage. Consider the newspaper industry. Dow Jones, publisher of the *Wall Street Journal,* pioneered the page transmission technology that links its seventeen U.S. printing plants to produce a truly national newspaper. Such advances in communication plants have also made it possible to move toward a global strategy. Dow Jones has started the *Asian Wall Street Journal* and the *Wall Street Journal-European Edition* and shares much of the editorial content while printing the papers in plants all over the world.

The information revolution is creating interrelationships among industries that were previously separate. The merging of computer and telecommunications technologies is an important example. This convergence has profound effects on the structure of both industries. For example, AT&T is using its position in telecommunications as a staging point for entry into the computer industry. IBM, which recently acquired Rolm, the telecommunications equipment manufacturer, is now joining the competition from the other direction. Information technology is also at the core of growing interrelationships in financial services, where the banking, insurance, and brokerage industries are merging, and in office equipment, where once distinct functions such as typing, photocopying, and data and voice communications can now be combined.

Broad-line companies are increasingly able to segment their offerings in ways that were previously feasible only for focused companies. In the trucking industry, Intermodal Transportation Services, Inc. of Cincinnati has completely changed its system for quoting prices. In the past, each local office set prices using manual procedures. Intermodal now uses microcomputers to link its offices to a center that calculates all prices. The new system gives the company the capacity to introduce a new pricing policy to offer discounts to national accounts, which place their orders from all over the country. Intermodal is tailoring its value chain to large national customers in a way that was previously impossible.

As information technology becomes more widespread, the opportunities to take advantage of a new competitive scope will only increase. The benefits of scope (and the achievement of linkages), however, can accrue only when the information technology spread throughout the organization can communicate. Completely decentralized organizational design and application of information technology will thwart these possibilities, because the information technology introduced in various parts of a company will not be compatible.

SPAWNING NEW BUSINESSES

The information revolution is giving birth to completely new industries in three distinct ways. First, it makes new businesses technologically feasible. For example, modern imaging and telecommunications technology blend to support new facsimile services such as Federal Express's Zapmail. Similarly, advances in microelectronics made personal computing possible. Services such as Merrill Lynch's Cash Management Account required new information technology to combine several financial products into one.

Second, information technology can also spawn new businesses by creating derived demand for new products. One example is Western Union's EasyLink service, a sophisticated, high-speed, data-communications network that allows personal computers, word processors, and other electronic devices to send messages to each other and to telex machines throughout the world. This service was not needed before the spread of information technology caused a demand for it.

Third, information technology creates new businesses within old ones. A company with information processing embedded in its value chain may have excess capacity or skills that can be sold outside. Sears took advantage of its skills in processing credit card accounts and of its massive scale to provide similar services to others. It sells credit-authorization and transaction-processing services to Phillips Petroleum and retail remittance-processing services to Mellon Bank. Similarly, a manufacturer of automotive parts, A.O. Smith, developed data-communications expertise to meet the needs of its traditional businesses. When a bank consortium went looking for a contractor to run a network of automated teller machines, A.O. Smith got the job. Eastman Kodak recently began offering long-distance telephone and data-transmission services through its internal telecommunications system. Where the information technology used in a company's value chain is sensitive to scale, a company may improve its overall competitive advantage by increasing the scale of information processing and lowering costs. By selling extra capacity outside, it is at the same time generating new revenue.

Companies also are increasingly able to create and sell to others information that is a by-product of their operations. National Benefit Life reportedly merged with American Can in part to gain access to data on the nine million customers of American Can's direct-mail retailing subsidiary. The use of bar-code scanners in supermarket retailing has turned grocery stores into market research labs. Retailers can run an ad in the morning newspaper and find out its effect by early afternoon. They can also sell this data to market research companies and to food processors.

Competing in the Age of Information

Senior executives can follow five steps to take advantage of opportunities that the information revolution has created.

1. **Assess information intensity.** A company's first task is to evaluate the existing and potential information intensity of the products and processes of its business units. To help managers accomplish this, we

have developed some measures of the potential importance of information technology.

It is very likely that information technology will play a strategic role in an industry that is characterized by one or more of the following features:

- Potentially high information intensity in the value chain—a large number of suppliers or customers with whom the company deals directly, a product requiring a large quantity of information in selling, a product line with many distinct product varieties, a product composed of many parts, a large number of steps in a company's manufacturing process, a long cycle time from the initial order to the delivered product.

- Potentially high information intensity in the product—a product that mainly provides information, a product whose operation involves substantial information processing, a product whose use requires the buyer to process a lot of information, a product requiring especially high costs for buyer training, a product that has many alternative uses or is sold to a buyer with high information intensity in his or her own business.

These may help identify priority business units for investment in information technology. When selecting priority areas, remember the breadth of information technology—it involves more than simple computing.

2. Determine the role of information technology in industry structure. Managers should predict the likely impact of information technology on their industry's structure. They must examine how information technology might affect each of the five competitive forces. Not only is each force likely to change but industry boundaries may change as well. Chances are that a new definition of the industry may be necessary.

Many companies are partly in control of the nature and pace of change in the industry structure. Companies have permanently altered the bases of competition in their favor in many industries through aggressive investments in information technology and have forced other companies to follow. Citibank, with its automated teller machines and transaction processing; American Airlines, with its computerized reservations system; and *USA Today*, with its newspaper page transmission to decentralized printing plants, are pioneers that have used information technology to alter industry structure. A company should understand how structural change is forcing it to respond and look for ways to lead change in the industry.

3. **Identify and rank the ways in which information technology might create competitive advantage.** The starting assumption must be that the technology is likely to affect every activity in the value chain. Equally important is the possibility that new linkages among activities are being made possible. By taking a careful look, managers can identify the value activities that are likely to be most affected in terms of cost and differentiation. Obviously, activities that represent a large proportion of cost or that are critical to differentiation bear closest scrutiny, particularly if they have a significant information-processing component. Activities with important links to other activities inside and outside the company are also critical. Executives must examine such activities for ways in which information technology can create sustainable competitive advantage.

In addition to taking a hard look at its value chain, a company should consider how information technology might allow a change in competitive scope. Can information technology help the company serve new segments? Will the flexibility of information technology allow broad-line competitors to invade areas that were once the province of niche competitors? Will information technology provide the leverage to expand the business globally? Can managers harness information technology to exploit interrelationships with other industries? Or, can the technology help a company create competitive advantage by narrowing its scope?

A fresh look at the company's product may also be in order:

Can the company bundle more information with the product?

Can the company embed information technology in it?

4. **Investigate how information technology might spawn new businesses.** Managers should consider opportunities to create new businesses from existing ones. Information technology is an increasingly important avenue for corporate diversification. Lockheed, for example,

entered the data base business by perceiving an opportunity to use its spare computer capacity.

Identifying opportunities to spawn new businesses requires answering questions such as:

What information generated (or potentially generated) in the business could the company sell?

What information-processing capacity exists internally to start a new business?

Does information technology make it feasible to produce new items related to the company's product?

5. **Develop a plan for taking advantage of information technology.** The first four steps should lead to an action plan to capitalize on the information revolution. This action plan should rank the strategic investments necessary in hardware and software, and in new product development activities that reflect the increasing information content in products. Organizational changes that reflect the role that the technology plays in linking activities inside and outside the company are likely to be necessary.

The management of information technology can no longer be the sole province of the EDP department. Increasingly, companies must employ information technology with a sophisticated understanding of the requirements for competitive advantage. Organizations need to distribute the responsibility for systems development more widely in the organization. At the same time, general managers must be involved to ensure that cross-functional linkages, more possible to achieve with information technology, are exploited.

These changes do not mean that a central information-technology function should play an insignificant role. Rather than control information technology, however, an information services manager should coordinate the architecture and standards of the many applications throughout the organization, as well as provide assistance and coaching in systems development. Unless the numerous applications of information technology inside a company are compatible with each other, many benefits may be lost.

Information technology can help in the strategy implementation process. Reporting systems can track progress toward milestones and success factors. By using information systems, companies can measure their activities more precisely and help motivate managers to implement strategies successfully.[9]

The importance of the information revolution is not in dispute. The question is not whether information technology will have a significant impact on a company's competitive position; rather the question is when and how this impact will strike. Companies that anticipate the power of information technology will be in control of events. Companies that do not respond will be forced to accept changes that others initiate and will find themselves at a competitive disadvantage.

NOTES

1. For more information on the value chain concept, see Michael E. Porter, *Competitive Advantage* (New York: Free Press, 1985).

2. For a discussion of the two basic types of competitive advantage, see Michael E. Porter, *Competitive Strategy* (New York: Free Press, 1980), Chapter 2.

3. Alfred D. Chandler, Jr., *The Visible Hand* (Cambridge: Belknap Press of Harvard University Press, 1977), p. 86.

4. James L. McKenney and F. Warren McFarlan, "The Information Archipelago—Maps and Bridges," *Harvard Business Review* 60, no. 5 (1982): 109.

5. See Michael E. Porter, "How Competitive Forces Shape Strategy," *Harvard Business Review* 57, no. 2 (1979): 137.

6. See F. Warren McFarlan, "Information Technology Changes the Way You Compete," *Harvard Business Review* 62, no. 3 (1984): 98.

7. James I. Cash, Jr. and Benn R. Konsynski, "IS Redraws Competitive Boundaries," *Harvard Business Review* 63, no. 2 (1985): 134.

8. See Gregory L. Parsons, "Information Technology: A New Competitive Weapon," *Sloan Management Review*, Fall 1983, p. 3.

9. Victor E. Millar, "Decision-Oriented Information," *Datamation*, January 1984, p. 159.

CHAPTER 4

Strategy and the Internet

Michael E. Porter

THE INTERNET IS AN EXTREMELY IMPOR-
tant new technology, and it is no surprise that it has received so much
attention from entrepreneurs, executives, investors, and business observers. Caught up in the general fervor, many have assumed that the
Internet changes everything, rendering all the old rules about companies
and competition obsolete. That may be a natural reaction, but it is a
dangerous one. It has led many companies, dot-coms and incumbents
alike, to make bad decisions—decisions that have eroded the attractiveness of their industries and undermined their own competitive advantages. Some companies, for example, have used Internet technology
to shift the basis of competition away from quality, features, and service
and toward price, making it harder for anyone in their industries to
turn a profit. Others have forfeited important proprietary advantages
by rushing into misguided partnerships and outsourcing relationships.
Until recently, the negative effects of these actions have been obscured
by distorted signals from the marketplace. Now, however, the consequences are becoming evident.

The time has come to take a clearer view of the Internet. We need
to move away from the rhetoric about "Internet industries," "e-business
strategies," and a "new economy" and see the Internet for what it is:
an enabling technology—a powerful set of tools that can be used, wisely
or unwisely, in almost any industry and as part of almost any strategy.
We need to ask fundamental questions: Who will capture the economic
benefits that the Internet creates? Will all the value end up going to
customers, or will companies be able to reap a share of it? What will
be the Internet's impact on industry structure? Will it expand or shrink

---

March 2001

97

the pool of profits? And what will be its impact on strategy? Will the Internet bolster or erode the ability of companies to gain sustainable advantages over their competitors?

In addressing these questions, much of what we find is unsettling. I believe that the experiences companies have had with the Internet thus far must be largely discounted and that many of the lessons learned must be forgotten. When seen with fresh eyes, it becomes clear that the Internet is not necessarily a blessing. It tends to alter industry structures in ways that dampen overall profitability, and it has a leveling effect on business practices, reducing the ability of any company to establish an operational advantage that can be sustained.

The key question is not whether to deploy Internet technology—companies have no choice if they want to stay competitive—but how to deploy it. Here, there is reason for optimism. Internet technology provides better opportunities for companies to establish distinctive strategic positionings than did previous generations of information technology. Gaining such a competitive advantage does not require a radically new approach to business. It requires building on the proven principles of effective strategy. The Internet per se will rarely be a competitive advantage. Many of the companies that succeed will be ones that use the Internet as a complement to traditional ways of competing, not those that set their Internet initiatives apart from their established operations. That is particularly good news for established companies, which are often in the best position to meld Internet and traditional approaches in ways that buttress existing advantages. But dot-coms can also be winners—if they understand the trade-offs between Internet and traditional approaches and can fashion truly distinctive strategies. Far from making strategy less important, as some have argued, the Internet actually makes strategy more essential than ever.

Distorted Market Signals

Companies that have deployed Internet technology have been confused by distorted market signals, often of their own creation. It is understandable, when confronted with a new business phenomenon, to look to marketplace outcomes for guidance. But in the early stages of the rollout of any important new technology, market signals can be unreliable. New technologies trigger rampant experimentation, by both companies and customers, and the experimentation is often economically unsustainable. As a result, market behavior is distorted and must be interpreted with caution.

That is certainly the case with the Internet. Consider the revenue side of the profit equation in industries in which Internet technology is widely used. Sales figures have been unreliable for three reasons. First, many companies have subsidized the purchase of their products and services in hopes of staking out a position on the Internet and attracting a base of customers. (Governments have also subsidized on-line shopping by exempting it from sales taxes.) Buyers have been able to purchase goods at heavy discounts, or even obtain them for free, rather than pay prices that reflect true costs. When prices are artificially low, unit demand becomes artificially high. Second, many buyers have been drawn to the Internet out of curiosity; they have been willing to conduct transactions on-line even when the benefits have been uncertain or limited. If Amazon.com offers an equal or lower price than a conventional bookstore and free or subsidized shipping, why not try it as an experiment? Sooner or later, though, some customers can be expected to return to more traditional modes of commerce, especially if subsidies end, making any assessment of customer loyalty based on conditions so far suspect. Finally, some "revenues" from on-line commerce have been received in the form of stock rather than cash. Much of the estimated $450 million in revenues that Amazon has recognized from its corporate partners, for example, has come as stock. The sustainability of such revenue is questionable, and its true value hinges on fluctuations in stock prices.

If revenue is an elusive concept on the Internet, cost is equally fuzzy. Many companies doing business on-line have enjoyed subsidized inputs. Their suppliers, eager to affiliate themselves with and learn from dot-com leaders, have provided products, services, and content at heavily discounted prices. Many content providers, for example, rushed to provide their information to Yahoo! for next to nothing in hopes of establishing a beachhead on one of the Internet's most visited sites. Some providers have even paid popular portals to distribute their content. Further masking true costs, many suppliers—not to mention employees

—have agreed to accept equity, warrants, or stock options from Internet-related companies and ventures in payment for their services or products. Payment in equity does not appear on the income statement, but it is a real cost to shareholders. Such supplier practices have artificially depressed the costs of doing business on the Internet, making it appear more attractive than it really is. Finally, costs have been distorted by the systematic understatement of the need for capital. Company after company touted the low asset intensity of doing business on-line, only to find that inventory, warehouses, and other investments were necessary to provide value to customers.

Signals from the stock market have been even more unreliable. Responding to investor enthusiasm over the Internet's explosive growth, stock valuations became decoupled from business fundamentals. They no longer provided an accurate guide as to whether real economic value was being created. Any company that has made competitive decisions based on influencing near-term share price or responding to investor sentiments has put itself at risk.

Distorted revenues, costs, and share prices have been matched by the unreliability of the financial metrics that companies have adopted. The executives of companies conducting business over the Internet have, conveniently, downplayed traditional measures of profitability and economic value. Instead, they have emphasized expansive definitions of revenue, numbers of customers, or, even more suspect, measures that might someday correlate with revenue, such as numbers of unique users ("reach"), numbers of site visitors, or click-through rates. Creative accounting approaches have also multiplied. Indeed, the Internet has given rise to an array of new performance metrics that have only a loose relationship to economic value, such as pro forma measures of income that remove "nonrecurring" costs like acquisitions. The dubious connection between reported metrics and actual profitability has served only to amplify the confusing signals about what has been working in the marketplace. The fact that those metrics have been taken seriously by the stock market has muddied the waters even further. For all these reasons, the true financial performance of many Internet-related businesses is even worse than has been stated.

One might argue that the simple proliferation of dot-coms is a sign of the economic value of the Internet. Such a conclusion is premature at best. Dot-coms multiplied so rapidly for one major reason: they were able to raise capital without having to demonstrate viability. Rather than signaling a healthy business environment, the sheer number of dot-coms in many industries often revealed nothing more than the existence of low barriers to entry, always a danger sign.

A Return to Fundamentals

It is hard to come to any firm understanding of the impact of the Internet on business by looking at the results to date. But two broad conclusions can be drawn. First, many businesses active on the Internet are artificial businesses competing by artificial means and propped up by capital that until recently had been readily available. Second, in periods of transition such as the one we have been going through, it often appears as if there are new rules of competition. But as market forces play out, as they are now, the old rules regain their currency. The creation of true economic value once again becomes the final arbiter of business success.

Economic value for a company is nothing more than the gap between price and cost, and it is reliably measured only by sustained profitability. To generate revenues, reduce expenses, or simply do something useful by deploying Internet technology is not sufficient evidence that value has been created. Nor is a company's current stock price necessarily an indicator of economic value. Shareholder value is a reliable measure of economic value only over the long run.

In thinking about economic value, it is useful to draw a distinction between the uses of the Internet (such as operating digital marketplaces, selling toys, or trading securities) and Internet technologies (such as site-customization tools or real-time communications services), which can be deployed across many uses. Many have pointed to the success of technology providers as evidence of the Internet's economic value. But this thinking is faulty. It is the uses of the Internet that ultimately create economic value. Technology providers can prosper for a time irrespective of whether the uses of the Internet are profitable. In periods of heavy experimentation, even sellers of flawed technologies can thrive. But unless the uses generate sustainable revenues or savings in excess of their cost of deployment, the opportunity for technology providers will shrivel as companies realize that further investment is economically unsound.

So how can the Internet be used to create economic value? To find the answer, we need to look beyond the immediate market signals to the two fundamental factors that determine profitability:

- *industry structure,* which determines the profitability of the average competitor; and

- *sustainable competitive advantage,* which allows a company to outperform the average competitor.

These two underlying drivers of profitability are universal; they transcend any technology or type of business. At the same time, they vary widely by industry and company. The broad, supra-industry classifications so common in Internet parlance, such as business-to-consumer (or "B2C") and business-to-business (or "B2B") prove meaningless with respect to profitability. Potential profitability can be understood only by looking at individual industries and individual companies.

The Internet and Industry Structure

The Internet has created some new industries, such as on-line auctions and digital marketplaces. However, its greatest impact has been to enable the reconfiguration of existing industries that had been constrained by high costs for communicating, gathering information, or accomplishing transactions. Distance learning, for example, has existed for decades, with about one million students enrolling in correspondence courses every year. The Internet has the potential to greatly expand distance learning, but it did not create the industry. Similarly, the Internet provides an efficient means to order products, but catalog retailers with toll-free numbers and automated fulfillment centers have been around for decades. The Internet only changes the front end of the process.

Whether an industry is new or old, its structural attractiveness is determined by five underlying forces of competition: the intensity of rivalry among existing competitors, the barriers to entry for new competitors, the threat of substitute products or services, the bargaining power of suppliers, and the bargaining power of buyers. In combination, these forces determine how the economic value created by any product, service, technology, or way of competing is divided between, on the one hand, companies in an industry and, on the other, customers, suppliers, distributors, substitutes, and potential new entrants. Although some have argued that today's rapid pace of technological change makes industry analysis less valuable, the opposite is true. Analyzing the forces illuminates an industry's fundamental attractiveness, exposes the underlying drivers of average industry profitability, and provides insight into how profitability will evolve in the future. The five competitive forces still determine profitability even if suppliers, channels, substitutes, or competitors change.

Because the strength of each of the five forces varies considerably from industry to industry, it would be a mistake to draw general conclusions about the impact of the Internet on long-term industry profitability; each industry is affected in different ways. Nevertheless, an examination of a wide range of industries in which the Internet is playing a role reveals some clear trends, as summarized in figure 4.1. Some of the trends are positive. For example, the Internet tends to dampen the bargaining power of channels by providing companies with new, more direct avenues to customers. The Internet can also boost an industry's efficiency in various ways, expanding the overall size of the market by improving its position relative to traditional substitutes.

But most of the trends are negative. Internet technology provides buyers with easier access to information about products and suppliers, thus bolstering buyer bargaining power. The Internet mitigates the need for such things as an established sales force or access to existing channels, reducing barriers to entry. By enabling new approaches to meeting needs and performing functions, it creates new substitutes. Because it is an open system, companies have more difficulty maintaining proprietary offerings, thus intensifying the rivalry among competitors. The use of the Internet also tends to expand the geographic market, bringing many more companies into competition with one another. And Internet technologies tend to reduce variable costs and tilt cost structures toward fixed cost, creating significantly greater pressure for companies to engage in destructive price competition.

While deploying the Internet can expand the market, then, doing so often comes at the expense of average profitability. The great paradox of the Internet is that its very benefits—making information widely

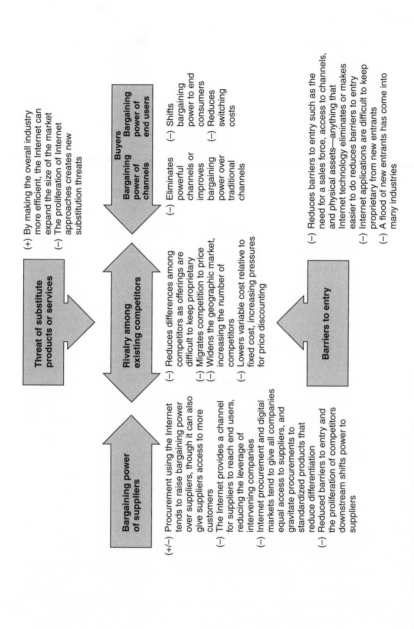

Figure 4.1 How the Internet Influences Industry Structure

This discussion is drawn from the author's research with David Sutton. For a fuller discussion, see M. E. Porter, *Competitive Strategy*, Free Press, 1980.

Threat of substitute products or services

(+) By making the overall industry more efficient, the Internet can expand the size of the market

(−) The proliferation of Internet approaches creates new substitution threats

Buyers

Bargaining power of channels

(−) Eliminates powerful channels or improves bargaining power over traditional channels

Bargaining power of end users

(−) Shifts bargaining power to end consumers

(−) Reduces switching costs

Rivalry among existing competitors

(−) Reduces differences among competitors as offerings are difficult to keep proprietary

(−) Migrates competition to price

(−) Widens the geographic market, increasing the number of competitors

(−) Lowers variable cost relative to fixed cost, increasing pressures for price discounting

Bargaining power of suppliers

(+/−) Procurement using the Internet tends to raise bargaining power over suppliers, though it can also give suppliers access to more customers

(−) The Internet provides a channel for suppliers to reach end users, reducing the leverage of intervening companies

(−) Internet procurement and digital markets tend to give all companies equal access to suppliers, and gravitate procurements to standardized products that reduce differentiation

(−) Reduced barriers to entry and the proliferation of competitors downstream shifts power to suppliers

Barriers to entry

(−) Reduces barriers to entry such as the need for a sales force, access to channels, and physical assets—anything that Internet technology eliminates or makes easier to do reduces barriers to entry

(−) Internet applications are difficult to keep proprietary from new entrants

(−) A flood of new entrants has come into many industries

available; reducing the difficulty of purchasing, marketing, and distribution; allowing buyers and sellers to find and transact business with one another more easily—also make it more difficult for companies to capture those benefits as profits.

We can see this dynamic at work in automobile retailing. The Internet allows customers to gather extensive information about products easily, from detailed specifications and repair records to wholesale prices for new cars and average values for used cars. Customers can also choose among many more options from which to buy, not just local dealers but also various types of Internet referral networks (such as Autoweb and AutoVantage) and on-line direct dealers (such as Autobytel.com, AutoNation, and CarsDirect.com). Because the Internet reduces the importance of location, at least for the initial sale, it widens the geographic market from local to regional or national. Virtually every dealer or dealer group becomes a potential competitor in the market. It is more difficult, moreover, for on-line dealers to differentiate themselves, as they lack potential points of distinction such as showrooms, personal selling, and service departments. With more competitors selling largely undifferentiated products, the basis for competition shifts ever more toward price. Clearly, the net effect on the industry's structure is negative.

That does not mean that every industry in which Internet technology is being applied will be unattractive. For a contrasting example, look at Internet auctions. Here, customers and suppliers are fragmented and thus have little power. Substitutes, such as classified ads and flea markets, have less reach and are less convenient to use. And though the barriers to entry are relatively modest, companies can build economies of scale, both in infrastructure and, even more important, in the aggregation of many buyers and sellers, that deter new competitors or place them at a disadvantage. Finally, rivalry in this industry has been defined, largely by eBay, the dominant competitor, in terms of providing an easy-to-use marketplace in which revenue comes from listing and sales fees, while customers pay the cost of shipping. When Amazon and other rivals entered the business, offering free auctions, eBay maintained its prices and pursued other ways to attract and retain customers. As a result, the destructive price competition characteristic of other on-line businesses has been avoided.

EBay's role in the auction business provides an important lesson: industry structure is not fixed but rather is shaped to a considerable degree by the choices made by competitors. EBay has acted in ways that strengthen the profitability of its industry. In stark contrast, Buy.com, a prominent Internet retailer, acted in ways that undermined its industry, not to mention its own potential for competitive advantage. Buy.com achieved $100 million in sales faster than any company in history, but it did so by defining competition solely on price. It sold products not only below full cost but at or below cost of goods sold, with the vain hope that it would make money in other ways. The company had no plan for being the low-cost provider; instead, it invested heavily in brand advertising and eschewed potential sources of differentiation by outsourcing all fulfillment and offering the bare minimum of customer service. It also gave up the opportunity to set itself apart from competitors by choosing not to focus on selling particular goods; it moved quickly beyond electronics, its initial category, into numerous other product categories in which it had no unique offering. Although the company has been trying desperately to reposition itself, its early moves have proven extremely difficult to reverse.

The Myth of the First Mover

Given the negative implications of the Internet for profitability, why was there such optimism, even euphoria, surrounding its adoption? One reason is that everyone tended to focus on what the Internet could do and how quickly its use was expanding rather than on how it was affecting industry structure. But the optimism can also be traced to a widespread belief that the Internet would unleash forces that would enhance industry profitability. Most notable was the general assumption that the deployment of the Internet would increase switching costs and create strong network effects, which would provide first movers with competitive advantages and robust profitability. First movers would reinforce these advantages by quickly establishing strong new-economy brands. The result would be an attractive industry for the victors. This thinking does not, however, hold up to close examination.

Consider switching costs. Switching costs encompass all the costs incurred by a customer in changing to a new supplier—everything from hashing out a new contract to reentering data to learning how to use a different product or service. As switching costs go up, customers' bargaining power falls and the barriers to entry into an industry rise. While switching costs are nothing new, some observers argued that the Internet would raise them substantially. A buyer would grow familiar with one company's user interface and would not want to bear the cost of finding, registering with, and learning to use a competitor's site, or, in the case of industrial customers, integrating a competitor's systems with its own. Moreover, since Internet commerce allows a company to accumulate knowledge of customers' buying behavior, the company would be able to provide more tailored offerings, better service, and greater purchasing convenience—all of which buyers would be loath to forfeit. When people talk about the "stickiness" of Web sites, what they are often talking about is high switching costs.

In reality, though, switching costs are likely to be lower, not higher, on the Internet than they are for traditional ways of doing business, including approaches using earlier generations of information systems such as EDI. On the Internet, buyers can often switch suppliers with just a few mouse clicks, and new Web technologies are systematically reducing switching costs even further. For example, companies like PayPal provide settlement services or Internet currency—so-called e-wallets—that enable customers to shop at different sites without having to enter personal information and credit card numbers. Content-consolidation tools such as OnePage allow users to avoid having to go back to sites over and over to retrieve information by enabling them to build customized Web pages that draw needed information dynamically from many sites. And the widespread adoption of XML standards will free companies from the need to reconfigure proprietary ordering systems and to create new procurement and logistical protocols when changing suppliers.

What about network effects, through which products or services become more valuable as more customers use them? A number of important Internet applications display network effects, including e-mail, instant messaging, auctions, and on-line message boards or chat rooms.

Where such effects are significant, they can create demand-side econo-mies of scale and raise barriers to entry. This, it has been widely argued, sets off a winner-take-all competition, leading to the eventual domi-nance of one or two companies.

But it is not enough for network effects to be present; to provide barriers to entry they also have to be proprietary to one company. The openness of the Internet, with its common standards and protocols and its ease of navigation, makes it difficult for a single company to capture the benefits of a network effect. (America Online, which has managed to maintain borders around its on-line community, is an exception, not the rule.) And even if a company is lucky enough to control a network effect, the effect often reaches a point of diminishing returns once there is a critical mass of customers. Moreover, network effects are subject to a self-limiting mechanism. A particular product or service first at-tracts the customers whose needs it best meets. As penetration grows, however, it will tend to become less effective in meeting the needs of the remaining customers in the market, providing an opening for competitors with different offerings. Finally, creating a network effect requires a large investment that may offset future benefits. The network effect is, in many respects, akin to the experience curve, which was also supposed to lead to market-share dominance—through cost advan-tages, in that case. The experience curve was an oversimplification, and the single-minded pursuit of experience curve advantages proved disastrous in many industries.

Internet brands have also proven difficult to build, perhaps because the lack of physical presence and direct human contact makes virtual businesses less tangible to customers than traditional businesses. De-spite huge outlays on advertising, product discounts, and purchasing incentives, most dot-com brands have not approached the power of established brands, achieving only a modest impact on loyalty and barri-ers to entry.

Another myth that has generated unfounded enthusiasm for the In-ternet is that partnering is a win-win means to improve industry eco-nomics. While partnering is a well-established strategy, the use of Internet technology has made it much more widespread. Partnering takes two forms. The first involves complements: products that are used in tandem with another industry's product. Computer software, for example, is a complement to computer hardware. In Internet commerce, complements have proliferated as companies have sought to offer broader arrays of products, services, and information. Partnering to assemble complements, often with companies who are also competitors, has been seen as a way to speed industry growth and move away from narrow-minded, destructive competition.

But this approach reveals an incomplete understanding of the role of complements in competition. Complements are frequently important to an industry's growth—spreadsheet applications, for example, accelerated the expansion of the personal computer industry—but they have no direct relationship to industry profitability. While a close substitute reduces potential profitability, for example, a close complement can exert either a positive or a negative influence. Complements affect industry profitability indirectly through their influence on the five competitive forces. If a complement raises switching costs for the combined product offering, it can raise profitability. But if a complement works to standardize the industry's product offering, as Microsoft's operating system has done in personal computers, it will increase rivalry and depress profitability.

With the Internet, widespread partnering with producers of complements is just as likely to exacerbate an industry's structural problems as mitigate them. As partnerships proliferate, companies tend to become more alike, which heats up rivalry. Instead of focusing on their own strategic goals, moreover, companies are forced to balance the many potentially conflicting objectives of their partners while also educating them about the business. Rivalry often becomes more unstable, and since producers of complements can be potential competitors, the threat of entry increases.

Another common form of partnering is outsourcing. Internet technologies have made it easier for companies to coordinate with their suppliers, giving widespread currency to the notion of the "virtual enterprise"—a business created largely out of purchased products, components, and services. While extensive outsourcing can reduce near-term costs and improve flexibility, it has a dark side when it comes to industry structure. As competitors turn to the same vendors, purchased inputs become more homogeneous, eroding company distinctiveness and increasing price competition. Outsourcing also usually lowers barriers to entry because a new entrant need only assemble purchased inputs rather than build its own capabilities. In addition, companies lose control over important elements of their business, and crucial experience in components, assembly, or services shifts to suppliers, enhancing their power in the long run.

The Future of Internet Competition

While each industry will evolve in unique ways, an examination of the forces influencing industry structure indicates that the deployment of Internet technology will likely continue to put pressure on the profitability of many industries. Consider the intensity of competition, for example. Many dot-coms are going out of business, which would seem to indicate that consolidation will take place and rivalry will be reduced. But while some consolidation among new players is inevitable, many established companies are now more familiar with Internet technology and are rapidly deploying on-line applications. With a combination of new and old companies and generally lower entry barriers, most industries will likely end up with a net increase in the number of competitors and fiercer rivalry than before the advent of the Internet.

The power of customers will also tend to rise. As buyers' initial curiosity with the Web wanes and subsidies end, companies offering products or services on-line will be forced to demonstrate that they provide real benefits. Already, customers appear to be losing interest in services like Priceline.com's reverse auctions because the savings they provide are often outweighed by the hassles involved. As customers become more familiar with the technology, their loyalty to their initial suppliers will also decline; they will realize that the cost of switching is low.

A similar shift will affect advertising-based strategies. Even now, advertisers are becoming more discriminating, and the rate of growth of Web advertising is slowing. Advertisers can be expected to continue to exercise their bargaining power to push down rates significantly, aided and abetted by new brokers of Internet advertising.

Not all the news is bad. Some technological advances will provide opportunities to enhance profitability. Improvements in streaming video and greater availability of low-cost bandwidth, for example, will make it easier for customer service representatives, or other company personnel, to speak directly to customers through their computers. Internet sellers will be able to better differentiate themselves and shift buyers' focus away from price. And services such as automatic bill paying by banks may modestly boost switching costs. In general, however, new Internet technologies will continue to erode profitability by shifting power to customers.

To understand the importance of thinking through the longer-term structural consequences of the Internet, consider the business of digital marketplaces. Such marketplaces automate corporate procurement by linking many buyers and suppliers electronically. The benefits to buyers include low transaction costs, easier access to price and product information, convenient purchase of associated services, and, sometimes, the ability to pool volume. The benefits to suppliers include lower selling costs, lower transaction costs, access to wider markets, and the avoidance of powerful channels.

From an industry structure standpoint, the attractiveness of digital marketplaces varies depending on the products involved. The most important determinant of a marketplace's profit potential is the intrinsic power of the buyers and sellers in the particular product area. If either side is concentrated or possesses differentiated products, it will gain bargaining power over the marketplace and capture most of the value generated. If buyers and sellers are fragmented, however, their bargaining power will be weak, and the marketplace will have a much better chance of being profitable. Another important determinant of industry structure is the threat of substitution. If it is relatively easy for buyers and sellers to transact business directly with one another, or to set up their own dedicated markets, independent marketplaces will be unlikely to sustain high levels of profit. Finally, the ability to create barriers to entry is critical. Today, with dozens of marketplaces competing in some industries and with buyers and sellers dividing their purchases or operating their own markets to prevent any one marketplace from gaining power, it is clear that modest entry barriers are a real challenge to profitability.

Competition among digital marketplaces is in transition, and industry structure is evolving. Much of the economic value created by marketplaces derives from the standards they establish, both in the underlying technology platform and in the protocols for connecting and exchanging information. But once these standards are put in place, the added value of the marketplace may be limited. Anything buyers or suppliers provide to a marketplace, such as information on order specifications or inventory availability, can be readily provided on their own proprietary sites. Suppliers and customers can begin to deal directly on-line without the need for an intermediary. And new technologies will undoubtedly make it easier for parties to search for and exchange goods and information with one another.

In some product areas, marketplaces should enjoy ongoing advantages and attractive profitability. In fragmented industries such as real estate and furniture, for example, they could prosper. And new kinds of value-added services may arise that only an independent marketplace could provide. But in many product areas, marketplaces may be superceded by direct dealing or by the unbundling of purchasing, information, financing, and logistical services; in other areas, they may be taken over by participants or industry associations as cost centers. In such cases, marketplaces will provide a valuable "public good" to participants but will not themselves be likely to reap any enduring benefits. Over the long haul, moreover, we may well see many buyers back away from open marketplaces. They may once again focus on building close, proprietary relationships with fewer suppliers, using Internet technologies to gain efficiency improvements in various aspects of those relationships.

The Internet and Competitive Advantage

If average profitability is under pressure in many industries influenced by the Internet, it becomes all the more important for individual companies to set themselves apart from the pack—to be more profitable than the average performer. The only way to do so is by achieving a sustainable competitive advantage—by operating at a lower cost, by commanding a premium price, or by doing both. Cost and price advantages can be achieved in two ways. One is operational effectiveness—doing the same things your competitors do but doing them better. Operational effectiveness advantages can take myriad forms, including better technologies, superior inputs, better-trained people, or a more effective management structure. The other way to achieve advantage is strategic positioning—doing things differently from competitors, in a way that delivers a unique type of value to customers. This can mean offering a different set of features, a different array of services, or different logistical arrangements. The Internet affects operational effectiveness and strategic positioning in very different ways. It makes it harder for companies to sustain operational advantages, but it opens new opportunities for achieving or strengthening a distinctive strategic positioning.

OPERATIONAL EFFECTIVENESS

The Internet is arguably the most powerful tool available today for enhancing operational effectiveness. By easing and speeding the exchange of real-time information, it enables improvements throughout the entire value chain, across almost every company and industry. And because it is an open platform with common standards, companies can often tap into its benefits with much less investment than was required to capitalize on past generations of information technology.

But simply improving operational effectiveness does not provide a competitive advantage. Companies only gain advantages if they are able to achieve and sustain higher levels of operational effectiveness than competitors. That is an exceedingly difficult proposition even in the best of circumstances. Once a company establishes a new best practice, its rivals tend to copy it quickly. Best practice competition eventually leads to competitive convergence, with many companies doing the same things in the same ways. Customers end up making decisions based on price, undermining industry profitability.

The nature of Internet applications makes it more difficult to sustain operational advantages than ever. In previous generations of information technology, application development was often complex, arduous, time consuming, and hugely expensive. These traits made it harder to gain an IT advantage, but they also made it difficult for competitors to imitate information systems. The openness of the Internet, combined with advances in software architecture, development tools, and modularity, makes it much easier for companies to design and implement applications. The drugstore chain CVS, for example, was able to roll out a complex Internet-based procurement application in just 60 days. As the fixed costs of developing systems decline, the barriers to imitation fall as well.

Today, nearly every company is developing similar types of Internet applications, often drawing on generic packages offered by third-party developers. The resulting improvements in operational effectiveness will be broadly shared, as companies converge on the same applications with the same benefits. Very rarely will individual companies be able to gain durable advantages from the deployment of "best-of-breed" applications.

STRATEGIC POSITIONING

As it becomes harder to sustain operational advantages, strategic positioning becomes all the more important. If a company cannot be more operationally effective than its rivals, the only way to generate higher levels of economic value is to gain a cost advantage or price premium by competing in a distinctive way. Ironically, companies today define competition involving the Internet almost entirely in terms of operational effectiveness. Believing that no sustainable advantages exist, they seek speed and agility, hoping to stay one step ahead of the competition. Of course, such an approach to competition becomes a self-fulfilling prophecy. Without a distinctive strategic direction, speed and flexibility lead nowhere. Either no unique competitive advantages are created, or improvements are generic and cannot be sustained.

Having a strategy is a matter of discipline. It requires a strong focus on profitability rather than just growth, an ability to define a unique value proposition, and a willingness to make tough trade-offs in choosing what not to do. A company must stay the course, even during times of upheaval, while constantly improving and extending its distinctive positioning. Strategy goes far beyond the pursuit of best practices. It involves the configuration of a tailored value chain—the series of activities required to produce and deliver a product or service—that enables a company to offer unique value. To be defensible, moreover, the value chain must be highly integrated. When a company's activities fit together as a self-reinforcing system, any competitor wishing to imitate a strategy must replicate the whole system rather than copy just one or two discrete product features or ways of performing particular activities. (See the insert "The Six Principles of Strategic Positioning.")

The Six Principles of Strategic Positioning

To establish and maintain a distinctive strategic positioning, a company needs to follow six fundamental principles.

First, it must start with the *right goal:* superior long-term return on investment. Only by grounding strategy in sustained profitability will real economic value be generated. Economic value is created when customers are willing to pay a price for a product or service that exceeds the cost of producing it. When goals are defined in terms of volume or market share leadership, with profits assumed to follow, poor strategies often result. The same is true when strategies are set to respond to the perceived desires of investors.

Second, a company's strategy must enable it to deliver a *value proposition,* or set of benefits, different from those that competitors offer. Strategy, then, is neither a quest for the universally best way of competing nor an effort to be all things to every customer. It defines a way of competing that delivers unique value in a particular set of uses or for a particular set of customers.

Third, strategy needs to be reflected in a *distinctive value chain.* To establish a sustainable competitive advantage, a company must perform different activities than rivals or perform similar activities in different ways. A company must configure the way it conducts manufacturing, logistics, service delivery, marketing, human resource management, and so on differently from rivals and tailored to its unique value proposition. If a company focuses on adopting best practices, it will end up performing most activities similarly to competitors, making it hard to gain an advantage.

Fourth, robust strategies involve *trade-offs.* A company must abandon or forgo some product features, services, or activities in order to be unique at others. Such trade-offs, in the product and in the value chain, are what make a company truly distinctive. When improvements in the product or in the value chain do not require trade-offs, they often become new best practices that are imitated because competitors can do so with no sacrifice to their existing ways of competing. Trying to be all things to all customers almost guarantees that a company will lack any advantage.

Fifth, strategy defines how all the elements of what a company does *fit* together. A strategy involves making choices throughout the value chain that are interdependent; all a company's activities must be mutually reinforcing. A company's product design, for example, should reinforce its approach to the manufacturing process, and both should leverage the way it conducts after-sales service. Fit not only increases competitive advantage but also makes a strategy harder to imitate. Rivals can copy one activity or product feature fairly easily, but will have much more difficulty duplicating a whole system of competing. Without fit, discrete improvements in manufacturing, marketing, or distribution are quickly matched.

Finally, strategy involves *continuity* of direction. A company must define a distinctive value proposition that it will stand for, even if that means forgoing certain opportunities. Without continuity of direction, it is difficult for companies to develop unique skills and assets or build strong reputations with customers. Frequent corporate "reinvention," then, is usually a sign of poor strategic thinking and a route to mediocrity. Continuous improvement is a necessity, but it must always be guided by a strategic direction.

The Absence of Strategy

Many of the pioneers of Internet business, both dot-coms and established companies, have competed in ways that violate nearly every precept of good strategy. Rather than focus on profits, they have sought to maximize revenue and market share at all costs, pursuing customers indiscriminately through discounting, giveaways, promotions, channel incentives, and heavy advertising. Rather than concentrate on delivering real value that earns an attractive price from customers, they have pursued indirect revenues from sources such as advertising and click-through fees from Internet commerce partners. Rather than make trade-offs, they have rushed to offer every conceivable product, service, or type of information. Rather than tailor the value chain in a unique way, they have aped the activities of rivals. Rather than build and maintain control over proprietary assets and marketing channels, they have entered into a rash of partnerships and outsourcing relationships, further eroding their own distinctiveness. While it is true that some companies have avoided these mistakes, they are exceptions to the rule.

By ignoring strategy, many companies have undermined the structure of their industries, hastened competitive convergence, and reduced the likelihood that they or anyone else will gain a competitive advantage. A destructive, zero-sum form of competition has been set in motion that confuses the acquisition of customers with the building of profitability. Worse yet, price has been defined as the primary if not the sole competitive variable. Instead of emphasizing the Internet's ability to support convenience, service, specialization, customization, and other forms of value that justify attractive prices, companies have turned competition into a race to the bottom. Once competition is defined this way, it is very difficult to turn back. (See the insert "Words for the Unwise: The Internet's Destructive Lexicon.")

Even well-established, well-run companies have been thrown off track by the Internet. Forgetting what they stand for or what makes them unique, they have rushed to implement hot Internet applications and copy the offerings of dot-coms. Industry leaders have compromised their existing competitive advantages by entering market segments to which

---

Words for the Unwise: The Internet's Destructive Lexicon

The misguided approach to competition that characterizes business on the Internet has even been embedded in the language used to discuss it. Instead of talking in terms of strategy and competitive advantage, dot-coms and other Internet players talk about "business models." This seemingly innocuous shift in terminology speaks volumes. The definition of a business model is murky at best. Most often, it seems to refer to a loose conception of how a company does business and generates revenue. Yet simply having a business model is an exceedingly low bar to set for building a company. Generating revenue is a far cry from creating economic value, and no business model can be evaluated independently of industry structure. The business model approach to management becomes an invitation for faulty thinking and self-delusion.

Other words in the Internet lexicon also have unfortunate consequences. The terms "e-business" and "e-strategy" have been particularly problematic. By encouraging managers to view their Internet operations in isolation from the rest of the business, they can lead to simplistic approaches to competing using the Internet and increase the pressure for competitive imitation. Established companies fail to integrate the Internet into their proven strategies and thus never harness their most important advantages.

they bring little that is distinctive. Merrill Lynch's move to imitate the low-cost on-line offerings of its trading rivals, for example, risks undermining its most precious advantage—its skilled brokers. And many established companies, reacting to misguided investor enthusiasm, have hastily cobbled together Internet units in a mostly futile effort to boost their value in the stock market.

It did not have to be this way—and it does not have to be in the future. When it comes to reinforcing a distinctive strategy, tailoring activities, and enhancing fit, the Internet actually provides a better technological platform than previous generations of IT. Indeed, IT worked against strategy in the past. Packaged software applications were hard to customize, and companies were often forced to change the way they conducted activities in order to conform to the "best practices" embedded in the software. It was also extremely difficult to connect discrete applications to one another. Enterprise resource planning (ERP) systems linked activities, but again companies were forced to adapt their ways of doing things to the software. As a result, IT has been a force for standardizing activities and speeding competitive convergence.

Internet architecture, together with other improvements in software architecture and development tools, has turned IT into a far more powerful tool for strategy. It is much easier to customize packaged Internet applications to a company's unique strategic positioning. By providing a common IT delivery platform across the value chain, Internet architecture and standards also make it possible to build truly integrated and customized systems that reinforce the fit among activities. (See the insert "The Internet and the Value Chain.")

To gain these advantages, however, companies need to stop their rush to adopt generic, "out of the box" packaged applications and instead tailor their deployment of Internet technology to their particular strategies. Although it remains more difficult to customize packaged applications, the very difficulty of the task contributes to the sustainability of the resulting competitive advantage.

The Internet as Complement

To capitalize on the Internet's strategic potential, executives and entrepreneurs alike will need to change their points of view. It has been

The Internet and the Value Chain

The basic tool for understanding the influence of information technology on companies is the value chain— the set of activities through which a product or service is created and delivered to customers. When a company competes in any industry, it performs a number of discrete but interconnected value-creating activities, such as operating a sales force, fabricating a component, or delivering products, and these activities have points of connection with the activities of suppliers, channels, and customers. The value chain is a framework for identifying all these activities and analyzing how they affect both a company's costs and the value delivered to buyers.

Because every activity involves the creation, processing, and communication of information, information technology has a pervasive influence on the value chain. The special advantage of the Internet is the ability to link one activity with others and make real-time data created in one activity widely available, both within the company and with outside suppliers, channels, and customers. By incorporating a common, open set of communication protocols, Internet technology provides a standardized infrastructure, an intuitive browser interface for information access and delivery, bidirectional communication, and ease of connectivity—all at much lower cost than private networks and electronic data interchange, or EDI.

Many of the most prominent applications of the Internet in the value chain are shown in the figure on the next page. Some involve moving physical activities on-line, while others involve making physical activities more cost effective.

But for all its power, the Internet does not represent a break from the past; rather, it is the latest stage in the ongoing evolution of information technology.[1] Indeed, the technological possibilities available today derive not just from the Internet architecture but also from complementary technological advances such as scanning, object-oriented programming, relational databases, and wireless communications.

To see how these technological improvements will ultimately affect the value chain, some historical perspective is illuminating.[2] The evolution of information technology in business can be thought of in terms of five overlapping stages, each of which evolved out of constraints presented by the previous generation. The earliest IT systems automated discrete transactions such as order entry and accounting. The next stage involved the fuller automation and functional enhancement of individual activities such as human

Firm Infrastructure
- Web-based, distributed financial and ERP systems
- On-line investor relations (e.g., information dissemination, broadcast conference calls)

Human Resource Management
- Self-service personnel and benefits administration
- Web-based training
- Internet-based sharing and dissemination of company information
- Electronic time and expense reporting

Technology Development
- Collaborative product design across locations and among multiple value-system participants
- Knowledge directories accessible from all parts of the organization
- Real-time access by R&D to online sales and service information

Procurement
- Internet-enabled demand planning; real-time available-to-promise/capable-to-promise and fulfillment
- Other linkage of purchase, inventory, and forecasting systems with suppliers
- Automated "requisition to pay"
- Direct and indirect procurement via marketplaces, changes, auctions, and buyer-seller matching

Inbound Logistics	Operations	Outbound Logistics	Marketing and Sales	After-Sales Service
• Real-time integrated scheduling, shipping, warehouse management, demand management and planning, and advanced planning and scheduling across the company and its suppliers • Dissemination throughout the company of real-time inbound and in-progress inventory data	• Integrated information exchange, scheduling, and decision making in in-house plants, contract assemblers, and components suppliers • Real-time available-to-promise and capable-to-promise information available to the sales force and channels	• Real-time transaction of orders whether initiated by an end consumer, a sales person, or a channel partner • Automated customer-specific agreements and contract terms • Customer and channel access to product development and delivery status • Collaborative integration with customer forecasting systems • Integrated channel management including information exchange, warranty claims, and contract management (versioning, process control)	• On-line sales channels including Web sites and marketplaces • Real-time inside and outside access to customer information, product catalogs, dynamic pricing, inventory availability, on-line submission of quotes, and order entry • On-line product configurations • Customer-tailored marketing via customer profiling • Push advertising • Tailored on-line access • Real-time customer feedback through Web surveys, opt-in/opt-out marketing, and promotion response tracking	• On-line support of customer service representatives through e-mail response management, billing integration, co-browse, chat, "call me now," voice-over-IP, and other uses of video streaming • Customer self-service via Web sites, and intelligent service request processing including updates to billing and shipping profiles • Real-time field service access to customer account review, schematic review, parts availability and ordering, work-order update, and service parts management

← • Web-distributed supply chain management →

Prominent Applications of the Internet in the Value Chain

resource management, sales force operations, and product design. The third stage, which is being accelerated by the Internet, involves cross-activity integration, such as linking sales activities with order processing. Multiple activities are being linked together through such tools as customer relationship management (CRM), supply chain management (SCM), and enterprise resource planning (ERP) systems. The fourth stage, which is just beginning, enables the integration of the value chain and entire value system, that is, the set of value chains in an entire industry, encompassing those of tiers of suppliers, channels, and customers. SCM and CRM are starting to merge, as end-to-end applications involving customers, channels, and suppliers link orders to, for example, manufacturing, procurement, and service delivery. Soon to be integrated is product development, which has been largely separate. Complex product models will be exchanged among parties, and Internet procurement will move from standard commodities to engineered items.

In the upcoming fifth stage, information technology will be used not only to connect the various activities and players in the value system but to optimize its workings in real time. Choices will be made based on information from multiple activities and

corporate entities. Production decisions, for example, will automatically factor in the capacity available at multiple facilities and the inventory available at multiple suppliers. While early fifth-stage applications will involve relatively simple optimization of sourcing, production, logistical, and servicing transactions, the deeper levels of optimization will involve the product design itself. For example, product design will be optimized and customized based on input not only from factories and suppliers but also from customers.

The power of the Internet in the value chain, however, must be kept in perspective. While Internet applications have an important influence on the cost and quality of activities, they are neither the only nor the dominant influence. Conventional factors such as scale, the skills of personnel, product and process technology, and investments in physical assets also play prominent roles. The Internet is transformational in some respects, but many traditional sources of competitive advantage remain intact.

1. See M. E. Porter and V. E. Millar, "How Information Gives You Competitive Advantage," (HBR July–August 1985) for a framework that helps put the Internet's current influence in context.

2. This discussion is drawn from the author's research with Philip Bligh.

widely assumed that the Internet is cannibalistic, that it will replace all conventional ways of doing business and overturn all traditional advantages. That is a vast exaggeration. There is no doubt that real trade-offs can exist between Internet and traditional activities. In the record industry, for example, on-line music distribution may reduce the need for CD-manufacturing assets. Overall, however, the trade-offs are modest in most industries. While the Internet will replace certain elements of industry value chains, the complete cannibalization of the value chain will be exceedingly rare. Even in the music business, many traditional activities—such as finding and promoting talented new artists, producing and recording music, and securing airplay—will continue to be highly important.

The risk of channel conflict also appears to have been overstated. As on-line sales have become more common, traditional channels that were initially skeptical of the Internet have embraced it. Far from always cannibalizing those channels, Internet technology can expand opportunities for many of them. The threat of disintermediation of channels appears considerably lower than initially predicted.

Frequently, in fact, Internet applications address activities that, while necessary, are not decisive in competition, such as informing customers, processing transactions, and procuring inputs. Critical corporate assets—skilled personnel, proprietary product technology, efficient logistical systems—remain intact, and they are often strong enough to preserve existing competitive advantages.

In many cases, the Internet complements, rather than cannibalizes, companies' traditional activities and ways of competing. Consider Walgreens, the most successful pharmacy chain in the United States. Walgreens introduced a Web site that provides customers with extensive information and allows them to order prescriptions on-line. Far from cannibalizing the company's stores, the Web site has underscored their value. Fully 90 percent of customers who place orders over the Web prefer to pick up their prescriptions at a nearby store rather than have them shipped to their homes. Walgreens has found that its extensive network of stores remains a potent advantage, even as some ordering shifts to the Internet.

Another good example is W.W. Grainger, a distributor of maintenance products and spare parts to companies. A middleman with stocking locations all over the United States, Grainger would seem to be a text-book case of an old-economy company set to be made obsolete by the Internet. But Grainger rejected the assumption that the Internet would undermine its strategy. Instead, it tightly coordinated its aggressive on-line efforts with its traditional business. The results so far are revealing. Customers who purchase on-line also continue to purchase through other means—Grainger estimates a 9 percent incremental growth in sales for customers who use the on-line channel above the normalized sales of customers who use only traditional means. Grainger, like Wal-greens, has also found that Web ordering increases the value of its physical locations. Like the buyers of prescription drugs, the buyers of industrial supplies often need their orders immediately. It is faster and cheaper for them to pick up supplies at a local Grainger outlet than to wait for delivery. Tightly integrating the site and stocking locations not only increases the overall value to customers, it reduces Grainger's costs as well. It is inherently more efficient to take and process orders over the Web than to use traditional methods, but more efficient to make bulk deliveries to a local stocking location than to ship individual orders from a central warehouse.

Grainger has also found that its printed catalog bolsters its on-line operation. Many companies' first instinct is to eliminate printed catalogs once their content is replicated on-line. But Grainger continues to pub-lish its catalog, and it has found that each time a new one is distributed, on-line orders surge. The catalog has proven to be a good tool for promot-ing the Web site while continuing to be a convenient way of packaging information for buyers.

In some industries, the use of the Internet represents only a modest shift from well-established practices. For catalog retailers like Lands' End, providers of electronic data interchange services like General Elec-tric, direct marketers like Geico and Vanguard, and many other kinds of companies, Internet business looks much the same as traditional business. In these industries, established companies enjoy particularly important synergies between their on-line and traditional operations, which make it especially difficult for dot-coms to compete. Examining segments of industries with characteristics similar to those supporting on-line businesses—in which customers are willing to forgo personal service and immediate delivery in order to gain convenience or lower prices, for instance—can also provide an important reality check in estimating the size of the Internet opportunity. In the prescription drug business, for example, mail orders represented only about 13% of all purchases in the late 1990s. Even though on-line drugstores may draw more customers than the mail-order channel, it is unlikely that they will supplant their physical counterparts.

Virtual activities do not eliminate the need for physical activities, but often amplify their importance. The complementarity between Internet activities and traditional activities arises for a number of reasons. First, introducing Internet applications in one activity often places greater demands on physical activities elsewhere in the value chain. Direct ordering, for example, makes warehousing and shipping more important. Second, using the Internet in one activity can have systemic consequences, requiring new or enhanced physical activities that are often unanticipated. Internet-based job-posting services, for example, have greatly reduced the cost of reaching potential job applicants, but they have also flooded employers with electronic résumés. By making it easier for job seekers to distribute résumés, the Internet forces employers to sort through many more unsuitable candidates. The added back-end costs, often for physical activities, can end up outweighing the up-front savings. A similar dynamic often plays out in digital marketplaces. Suppliers are able to reduce the transactional cost of taking orders when they move on-line, but they often have to respond to many additional requests for information and quotes, which, again, places new strains on traditional activities. Such systemic effects underscore the fact that Internet applications are not stand-alone technologies; they must be integrated into the overall value chain.

Third, most Internet applications have some shortcomings in comparison with conventional methods. While Internet technology can do many useful things today and will surely improve in the future, it cannot do everything. Its limits include the following:

• Customers cannot physically examine, touch, and test products or get hands-on help in using or repairing them.

• Knowledge transfer is restricted to codified knowledge, sacrificing the spontaneity and judgment that can result from interaction with skilled personnel.

- The ability to learn about suppliers and customers (beyond their mere purchasing habits) is limited by the lack of face-to-face contact.

- The lack of human contact with the customer eliminates a powerful tool for encouraging purchases, trading off terms and conditions, providing advice and reassurance, and closing deals.

- Delays are involved in navigating sites and finding information and are introduced by the requirement for direct shipment.

- Extra logistical costs are required to assemble, pack, and move small shipments.

- Companies are unable to take advantage of low-cost, nontransactional functions performed by sales forces, distribution channels, and purchasing departments (such as performing limited service and maintenance functions at a customer site).

- The absence of physical facilities circumscribes some functions and reduces a means to reinforce image and establish performance.

- Attracting new customers is difficult given the sheer magnitude of the available information and buying options.

Traditional activities, often modified in some way, can compensate for these limits, just as the shortcomings of traditional methods—such as lack of real-time information, high cost of face-to-face interaction, and high cost of producing physical versions of information—can be offset by Internet methods. Frequently, in fact, an Internet application and a traditional method benefit each other. For example, many companies have found that Web sites that supply product information and support direct ordering make traditional sales forces more, not less, productive and valuable. The sales force can compensate for the limits of the site by providing personalized advice and after-sales service, for instance. And the site can make the sales force more productive by automating the exchange of routine information and serving as an efficient new conduit for leads. The fit between company activities, a cornerstone of strategic positioning, is in this way strengthened by the deployment of Internet technology.

Once managers begin to see the potential of the Internet as a comple-ment rather than a cannibal, they will take a very different approach to organizing their on-line efforts. Many established companies, believing that the new economy operated under new rules, set up their Internet operations in stand-alone units. Fear of cannibalization, it was argued, would deter the mainstream organization from deploying the Internet aggressively. A separate unit was also helpful for investor relations, and it facilitated IPOs, tracking stocks, and spin-offs, enabling companies to tap into the market's appetite for Internet ventures and provide special incentives to attract Internet talent.

But organizational separation, while understandable, has often under-mined companies' ability to gain competitive advantages. By creating separate Internet strategies instead of integrating the Internet into an overall strategy, companies failed to capitalize on their traditional assets, reinforced me-too competition, and accelerated competitive conver-gence. Barnes & Noble's decision to establish Barnesandnoble.com as a separate organization is a vivid example. It deterred the on-line store from capitalizing on the many advantages provided by the network of physical stores, thus playing into the hands of Amazon.

Rather than being isolated, Internet technology should be the responsi-bility of mainstream units in all parts of a company. With support from IT staff and outside consultants, companies should use the technology strategically to enhance service, increase efficiency, and leverage ex-isting strengths. While separate units may be appropriate in some cir-cumstances, everyone in the organization must have an incentive to share in the success of Internet deployment.

The End of the New Economy

The Internet, then, is often not disruptive to existing industries or established companies. It rarely nullifies the most important sources of competitive advantage in an industry; in many cases it actually makes those sources even more important. As all companies come to embrace Internet technology, moreover, the Internet itself will be neutralized as a source of advantage. Basic Internet applications will become table stakes—companies will not be able to survive without them, but they will not gain any advantage from them. The more robust competitive advantages will arise instead from traditional strengths such as unique products, proprietary content, distinctive physical activities, superior product knowledge, and strong personal service and relationships. Internet technology may be able to fortify those advantages, by tying a company's activities together in a more distinctive system, but it is unlikely to supplant them.

Ultimately, strategies that integrate the Internet and traditional competitive advantages and ways of competing should win in many industries. On the demand side, most buyers will value a combination of online services, personal services, and physical locations over stand-alone Web distribution. They will want a choice of channels, delivery options, and ways of dealing with companies. On the supply side, production and procurement will be more effective if they involve a combination of Internet and traditional methods, tailored to strategy. For example, customized, engineered inputs will be bought directly, facilitated by Internet tools. Commodity items may be purchased via digital markets, but purchasing experts, supplier sales forces, and stocking locations will often also provide useful, value-added services.

The value of integrating traditional and Internet methods creates potential advantages for established companies. It will be easier for them to adopt and integrate Internet methods than for dot-coms to adopt and integrate traditional ones. It is not enough, however, just to graft the Internet onto historical ways of competing in simplistic "clicks-and-mortar" configurations. Established companies will be most successful when they deploy Internet technology to reconfigure traditional activities or when they find new combinations of Internet and traditional approaches.

Dot-coms, first and foremost, must pursue their own distinctive strategies, rather than emulate one another or the positioning of established companies. They will have to break away from competing solely on price and instead focus on product selection, product design, service, image, and other areas in which they can differentiate themselves. Dot-coms can also drive the combination of Internet and traditional methods. Some will succeed by creating their own distinctive ways of doing so. Others will succeed by concentrating on market segments that exhibit real trade-offs between Internet and traditional methods—either those in which a pure Internet approach best meets the needs of a particular set of customers or those in which a particular product or service can be best delivered without the need for physical assets. (See the insert "Strategic Imperatives for Dot-Coms and Established Companies.")

These principles are already manifesting themselves in many industries, as traditional leaders reassert their strengths and dot-coms adopt

---

Strategic Imperatives for Dot-Coms and Established Companies

At this critical juncture in the evolution of Internet technology, dot-coms and established companies face different strategic imperatives. Dot-coms must develop real strategies that create economic value. They must recognize that current ways of competing are destructive and futile and benefit neither themselves nor, in the end, customers. Established companies, in turn, must stop deploying the Internet on a stand-alone basis and instead use it to enhance the distinctiveness of their strategies.

The most successful dot-coms will focus on creating benefits that customers will pay for, rather than pursuing advertising and click-through revenues from third parties. To be competitive, they will often need to widen their value chains to encompass other activities besides those conducted over the Internet and to develop other assets, including physical ones. Many are already doing so. Some on-line retailers, for example, distributed paper catalogs for the 2000 holiday season as an added convenience to their shoppers. Others are introducing proprietary products under their own brand names, which not only boosts margins but provides real differentiation. It is such new activities in the value chain, not minor differences in Web sites, that hold the key to whether dot-coms gain competitive advantages. AOL, the Internet pioneer, recognized these principles. It charged for its services even in the face of free competitors. And not resting on initial advantages gained from its Web site and Internet technologies (such as instant messaging), it moved early to develop or acquire proprietary content.

Yet dot-coms must not fall into the trap of imitating established companies. Simply adding conventional activities is a me-too strategy that will not provide a competitive advantage. Instead, dot-coms need to create strategies that involve new, hybrid value chains, bringing together virtual and physical activities in unique configurations. For example, E*Trade is planning to install stand-alone kiosks, which will not require full-time staffs, on the sites of some corporate customers. VirtualBank, an on-line bank, is cobranding with corporations to create in-house credit unions. Juniper, another on-line bank, allows customers to deposit checks at Mail Box Etc. locations. While none of these approaches is certain to be successful, the strategic thinking behind them is sound.

Another strategy for dot-coms is to seek out trade-offs, concentrating exclusively on segments where an Internet-only model offers real advantages. Instead of attempting to force the Internet model on the entire market, dot-coms can pursue customers that do not have a strong need for functions delivered outside the Internet—even if such customers represent only a modest portion of the overall industry. In such segments, the challenge will be to find a value proposition for the company that will distinguish it from other Internet rivals and address low entry barriers.

Successful dot-coms will share the following characteristics:

• Strong capabilities in Internet technology

• A distinctive strategy vis-à-vis established companies and other dot-coms, resting on a clear focus and meaningful advantages

• Emphasis on creating customer value and charging for it directly, rather than relying on ancillary forms of revenue

• Distinctive ways of performing physical functions and assembling non-Internet assets that complement their strategic positions

• Deep industry knowledge to allow proprietary skills, information, and relationships to be established

Established companies, for the most part, need not be afraid of the Internet—the predictions of their demise at the hands of dot-coms were greatly exaggerated. Established companies possess traditional competitive advantages that will often continue to prevail; they also have inherent strengths in deploying Internet technology.

The greatest threat to an established company lies in either failing to deploy the Internet or failing to deploy it strategically. Every company needs an aggressive program to deploy the Internet throughout its value chain, using the technology to reinforce traditional competitive advantages and complement existing ways of competing. The key is not to imitate rivals but to tailor Internet applications to a company's overall strategy in ways that extend its competitive advantages and make them more sustainable. Schwab's expansion of its brick-and-mortar branches by one-third since it started on-line trading, for example, is extending its advantages over Internet-only competitors. The Internet, when used properly, can support greater strategic focus and a more tightly integrated activity system.

Edward Jones, a leading brokerage firm, is a good example of tailoring the Internet to strategy. Its strategy is to provide conservative, personalized advice to investors who value asset preservation and seek trusted, individualized guidance in investing. Target customers include retirees and small-business owners. Edward Jones does not offer commodities, futures, options, or other risky forms of investment. Instead, the company stresses a buy-and-hold approach to investing involving mutual funds, bonds, and blue-chip equities. Edward Jones operates a network of about 7,000 small offices, which are located conveniently to customers and are designed to encourage personal relationships with brokers.

Edward Jones has embraced the Internet for internal management functions, recruiting (25% of all job inquiries come via the Internet), and for providing account statements and other information to customers. However, it has no plan to offer on-line trading, as its competitors do. Self-directed, on-line trading does not fit Jones's strategy nor the value it aims to deliver to its customers. Jones, then, has tailored the use of the Internet to its strategy rather than imitated rivals. The company is thriving, outperforming rivals whose me-too Internet deployments have reduced their distinctiveness.

The established companies that will be most successful will be those that use Internet technology to make traditional activities better and those that find and implement new combinations of virtual and physical activities that were not previously possible.

more focused strategies. In the brokerage industry, Charles Schwab has gained a larger share (18 percent at the end of 1999) of on-line trading than E*Trade (15 percent). In commercial banking, established institutions like Wells Fargo, Citibank, and Fleet have many more on-line accounts than Internet banks do. Established companies are also gaining dominance over Internet activities in such areas as retailing, financial information, and digital marketplaces. The most promising dot-coms are leveraging their distinctive skills to provide real value to their customers. ECollege, for example, is a full-service provider that works with universities to put their courses on the Internet and operate the required delivery network for a fee. It is vastly more successful than competitors offering free sites to universities under their own brand names, hoping to collect advertising fees and other ancillary revenue.

When seen in this light, the "new economy" appears less like a new economy than like an old economy that has access to a new technology. Even the phrases "new economy" and "old economy" are rapidly losing their relevance, if they ever had any. The old economy of established companies and the new economy of dot-coms are merging, and it will soon be difficult to distinguish them. Retiring these phrases can only be healthy because it will reduce the confusion and muddy thinking that have been so destructive of economic value during the Internet's adolescent years.

In our quest to see how the Internet is different, we have failed to see how the Internet is the same. While a new means of conducting business has become available, the fundamentals of competition remain unchanged. The next stage of the Internet's evolution will involve a shift in thinking from e-business to business, from e-strategy to strategy. Only by integrating the Internet into overall strategy will this powerful new technology become an equally powerful force for competitive advantage.

CHAPTER 5

From Competitive Advantage to Corporate Strategy

Michael E. Porter

CORPORATE STRATEGY, THE OVERALL PLAN for a diversified company, is both the darling and the stepchild of contemporary management practice—the darling because CEOs have been obsessed with diversification since the early 1960s, the stepchild because almost no consensus exists about what corporate strategy is, much less about how a company should formulate it.

A diversified company has two levels of strategy: business unit (or competitive) strategy and corporate (or companywide) strategy. Competitive strategy concerns how to create competitive advantage in each of the businesses in which a company competes. Corporate strategy concerns two different questions: what businesses the corporation should be in and how the corporate office should manage the array of business units.

Corporate strategy is what makes the corporate whole add up to more than the sum of its business unit parts. The track record of corporate strategies has been dismal. I studied the diversification records of thirty-three large, prestigious U.S. companies over the 1950-1986 period and found that most of them had divested many more acquisitions than they had kept. The corporate strategies of most companies have dissipated instead of created shareholder value.

The need to rethink corporate strategy could hardly be more urgent. By taking over companies and breaking them up, corporate raiders thrive

May–June 1987

on failed corporate strategy. Fueled by junk bond financing and growing acceptability, raiders can expose any company to takeover, no matter how large or blue chip.

Recognizing past diversification mistakes, some companies have initiated large-scale restructuring programs. Others have done nothing at all. Whatever the response, the strategic questions persist. Those who have restructured must decide what to do next to avoid repeating the past; those who have done nothing must awake to their vulnerability. To survive, companies must understand what good corporate strategy is.

A Sober Picture

While there is disquiet about the success of corporate strategies, none of the available evidence satisfactorily indicates the success or failure of corporate strategy. Most studies have approached the question by measuring the stock market valuation of mergers, captured in the movement of the stock prices of acquiring companies immediately before and after mergers are announced.

These studies show that the market values mergers as neutral or slightly negative, hardly cause for serious concern.[1] Yet the short-term market reaction is a highly imperfect measure of the long-term success of diversification, and no self-respecting executive would judge a corporate strategy this way.

Studying the diversification programs of a company over a long period of time is a much more telling way to determine whether a corporate strategy has succeeded or failed. My study of thirty-three companies, many of which have reputations for good management, is a unique look at the track record of major corporations. (For an explanation of the

---

Where the Data Come From

We studied the 1950–1986 diversification histories of thirty-three large diversified U.S. companies. They were chosen at random from many broad sectors of the economy.

To eliminate distortions caused by World War II, we chose 1950 as the base year and then identified each business the company was in. We tracked every acquisition, joint venture, and start-up made over this period—3,788 in all. We classified each as an entry into an entirely new sector or field (financial services, for example), a new industry within a field the company was already in (insurance, for example), or a geographic extension of an existing product or service. We also classified each new field as related or unrelated to existing units. Then we tracked whether and when each entry was divested or shut down and the number of years each remained part of the corporation.

Our sources included annual reports, 10K forms, the F&S Index, and Moody's, supplemented by our judgment and general knowledge of the industries involved. In a few cases, we asked the companies specific questions.

It is difficult to determine the success of an entry without knowing the full purchase or start-up price, the profit history, the amount and timing of ongoing investments made in the unit, whether any write-offs or write-downs were taken, and the selling price and terms of sale. Instead, we employed a relatively simple way to gauge success: *whether the entry was divested or shut down.* The underlying assumption is that a company will generally not divest or close down a successful business except in a comparatively few special cases. Companies divested many of the entries in our sample within five years, a reflection of disappointment with performance. Of the compara-

tively few divestments where the company disclosed a loss or gain, the divestment resulted in a reported loss in more than half the cases.

The data in Table 5.1 cover the entire 1950–1986 period. However, the divestment ratios in Table 5.2 and Table 5.3 do not compare entries and divestments over the entire period because doing so would over-state the success of diversification. Companies usually do not shut down or divest new entries immediately but hold them for some time to give them an opportunity to succeed. Our data show that the average holding period is five to slightly more than ten years, though many divestments occur within five years. To accurately gauge the success of diversification, we calculated the percentage of entries made by 1975 and by 1980 that were divested or closed down as of January 1987. If we had included more recent entries, we would have biased upward our assessment of how successful these entries had been.

As compiled, these data probably understate the rate of failure. Companies tend to announce acquisitions and other forms of new entry with a flourish but divestments and shutdowns with a whimper, if at all. We have done our best to root out every such transaction, but we have undoubtedly missed some. There may also be new entries that we did not uncover, but our best impression is that the number is not large.

research, see the insert "Where the Data Come From.") Each company entered an average of eighty new industries and twenty-seven new fields. Just over 70 percent of the new entries were acquisitions, 22 percent were start-ups, and 8 percent were joint ventures. IBM, Exxon, Du Pont, and 3M, for example, focused on start-ups, while ALCO Standard, Beatrice, and Sara Lee diversified almost solely through acquisitions (Table 5.1 has a complete rundown).

My data paint a sobering picture of the success ratio of these moves (see Table 5.2). I found that on average corporations divested more than half their acquisitions in new industries and more than 60 percent of their acquisitions in entirely new fields. Fourteen companies left more than 70 percent of all the acquisitions they had made in new fields. The track record in unrelated acquisitions is even worse—the average divestment rate is a startling 74 percent (see Table 5.3). Even a highly respected company like General Electric divested a very high percentage of its acquisitions, particularly those in new fields. Companies near the top of the list in Table 5.2 achieved a remarkably low rate of divestment. Some bear witness to the success of well-thought-out corporate strategies. Others, however, enjoy a lower rate simply because they have not faced up to their problem units and divested them.

I calculated total shareholder returns (stock price appreciation plus dividends) over the period of the study for each company so that I could compare them with its divestment rate. While companies near the top of the list have above-average shareholder returns, returns are not a reliable measure of diversification success. Shareholder return often depends heavily on the inherent attractiveness of companies' base industries. Companies like CBS and General Mills had extremely profitable base businesses that subsidized poor diversification track records.

I would like to make one comment on the use of shareholder value to judge performance. Linking shareholder value quantitatively to diversification performance only works if you compare the share-holder value that is with the shareholder value that might have been without diversification. Because such a comparison is virtually impossible to make, measuring diversification success—the number of units retained by the company—seems to be as good an indicator as any of the contribution of diversification to corporate performance.

My data give a stark indication of the failure of corporate strategies.[2] Of the thirty-three companies, six had been taken over as my study was being completed (see the note on Table 5.2). Only the lawyers, investment bankers, and original sellers have prospered in most of these acquisitions, not the shareholders.

Premises of Corporate Strategy

Any successful corporate strategy builds on a number of premises. These are facts of life about diversification. They cannot be altered, and when ignored, they explain in part why so many corporate strategies fail.

Competition Occurs at the Business Unit Level. Diversified companies do not compete; only their business units do. Unless a corporate strategy places primary attention on nurturing the success of each unit, the strategy will fail, no matter how elegantly constructed. Successful corporate strategy must grow out of and reinforce competitive strategy.

Diversification Inevitably Adds Costs and Constraints to Business Units. Obvious costs such as the corporate overhead allocated to a unit may not be as important or subtle as the hidden costs and constraints. A business unit must explain its decisions to top management, spend time complying with planning and other corporate systems, live with parent company guidelines and personnel policies, and forgo the opportunity to motivate employees with direct equity ownership. These costs and constraints can be reduced but not entirely eliminated.

Shareholders Can Readily Diversify Themselves. Shareholders can diversify their own portfolios of stocks by selecting those that best match their preferences and risk profiles.[3] Shareholders can often diversify more cheaply than a corporation because they can buy shares at the market price and avoid hefty acquisition premiums. These premises mean that corporate strategy cannot succeed unless it truly adds value—to business units by providing tangible benefits that offset the inherent costs of lost independence and to shareholders by diversifying in a way they could not replicate.

Table 5.1 Diversification Profiles of 33 Leading U.S. Companies, 1950–1986

Company	Number Total Entries	All Entries into New Industries	Percent Acquisitions	Percent Joint Ventures
ALCO Standard	221	165	99%	0%
Allied Corp.	77	49	67	10
Beatrice	382	204	97	1
Borden	170	96	77	4
CBS	148	81	67	16
Continental Group	75	47	77	6
Cummins Engine	30	24	54	17
Du Pont	80	39	33	16
Exxon	79	56	34	5
General Electric	160	108	47	20
General Foods	92	53	91	4
General Mills	110	102	84	7
W.R. Grace	275	202	83	7
Gulf & Western	178	140	91	4
IBM	46	38	18	18
IC Industries	67	41	85	3
ITT	246	178	89	2
Johnson & Johnson	88	77	77	0
Mobil	41	32	53	16
Procter & Gamble	28	23	61	0
Raytheon	70	58	86	9
RCA	53	46	35	15
Rockwell	101	75	73	24
Sara Lee	197	141	96	1
Scovill	52	36	97	0
Signal	53	45	67	4
Tenneco	85	62	81	6
3M	144	125	54	2
TRW	119	82	77	10
United Technologies	62	49	57	18
Westinghouse	129	73	63	11
Wickes	71	47	83	0
Xerox	59	50	66	6
Total	**3,788**	**2,644**		
Average	**114.8**	**80.1**	**70.3**	**7.9**

Notes: Beatrice, Continental Group, General Foods, RCA, Scovill, and Signal were taken over as the study was being completed. Their data cover the period up through takeover but not subsequent divestments. The percentage averages may not add up to 100% because of rounding off.

Percent Start-ups	Entries into New Industries That Represented Entirely New Fields	Percent Acquisitions	Percent Joint Ventures	Percent Start-ups
1%	56	100%	0%	0%
22	17	65	6	29
2	61	97	0	3
19	32	75	3	22
17	28	65	21	14
17	19	79	11	11
29	13	46	23	31
51	19	37	0	63
61	17	29	6	65
33	29	48	14	38
6	22	86	5	9
9	27	74	7	19
10	66	74	5	21
6	48	88	2	10
63	16	19	0	81
12	17	88	6	6
9	50	92	0	8
23	18	56	0	44
31	15	60	7	33
39	14	79	0	21
5	16	81	19	6
50	19	37	21	42
3	27	74	22	4
4	41	95	2	2
3	12	92	0	8
29	20	75	0	25
13	26	73	8	19
45	34	71	3	56
13	28	64	11	25
24	17	23	17	39
26	36	61	3	36
17	22	68	0	32
28	18	50	11	39
	906			
21.8	27.4	67.9	7.0	25.9

Table 5.2 Acquisition Track Records of Leading U.S. Diversifiers Ranked by Percent Divested, 1950–1986

Company	All Acquisitions in New Industries	Percent Made by 1980 and Then Divested	Percent Made by 1975 and Then Divested
Johnson & Johnson	59	17%	12%
Procter & Gamble	14	17	17
Raytheon	50	17	26
United Technologies	28	25	13
3M	67	26	27
TRW	63	27	31
IBM	7	33	0*
Du Pont	13	38	43
Mobil	17	38	57
Borden	74	39	40
IC Industries	35	42	50
Tenneco	50	43	47
Beatrice	198	46	45
ITT	159	52	52
Rockwell	55	56	57
Allied Corp.	33	57	45
Exxon	19	62	20*
Sara Lee	135	62	65
General Foods	48	63	62
Scovill	35	64	77
Signal	30	65	63
ALCO Standard	164	65	70
W.R. Grace	167	65	70
General Electric	51	65	78
Wickes	38	67	72
Westinghouse	46	68	69
Xerox	33	71	79
Continental Group	36	71	72
General Mills	86	75	73
Gulf & Western	127	79	78
Cummins Engine	13	80	80
RCA	16	80	92
CBS	54	87	89
Total	**2,021**		
Average per company†	**61.2**	**53.4%**	**56.5%**

*Companies with three or fewer acquisitions by the cutoff year.

†Companies with three or fewer acquisitions by the cutoff year are excluded from the average to minimize statistical distortions.

Note: Beatrice, Continental Group, General Foods, RCA, Scovill, and Signal were taken over as the study was being completed. Their data cover the period up through takeover but not subsequent divestments.

Acquisitions in New Industries That Represented Entirely New Fields	Percent Made by 1980 and Then Divested	Percent Made by 1975 and Then Divested
10	33%	14%
11	17	17
13	25	33
10	17	0
24	42	45
18	40	38
3	33	0*
7	60	75
9	50	50
24	45	50
15	46	44
19	27	33
59	52	51
46	61	61
20	71	71
11	80	67
5	80	50*
39	80	76
19	93	93
11	64	70
15	70	67
56	72	76
49	71	70
14	100	100
15	73	70
22	61	59
9	100	100
15	60	60
20	65	60
42	75	72
6	83	83
7	86	100
18	88	88
661		
20.0	**61.2%**	**61.1%**

Table 5.3 Diversification Performance in Joint Ventures, Start-ups, and Unrelated Acquisitions, 1950–1986 (Companies in same order as in Exhibit 2)

Company	Joint Ventures as a Percent of New Entries	Percent Made by 1980 and Then Divested	Percent Made by 1975 and Then Divested	Start-Ups as a Percent of New Entries
Johnson & Johnson	0%	†	†	23%
Procter & Gamble	0	†	†	39
Raytheon	9	60%	60%	5
United Technologies	18	50	50	24
3M	2	100*	100*	45
TRW	10	20	25	13
IBM	18	100*	†	63
Du Pont	16	100*	†	51
Mobil	16	33	33	31
Borden	4	33	33	19
IC Industries	3	100*	100*	13
Tenneco	6	67	67	13
Beatrice	1	†	†	2
ITT	2	0*	†	8
Rockwell	24	38	42	3
Allied Corp.	10	100	75	22
Exxon	5	0	0	61
Sara Lee	1	†	†	4
General Foods	4	†	†	6
Scovill	0	†	†	3
Signal	4	†	†	29
ALCO Standard	0	†	†	1
W.R. Grace	7	33	38	10
General Electric	20	20	33	33
Wickes	0	†	†	17
Westinghouse	11	0*	0*	26
Xerox	6	100*	100*	28
Continental Group	6	67	67	17
General Mills	7	71	71	9
Gulf & Western	4	75	50	6
Cummins Engine	17	50	50	29
RCA	15	67	67	50
CBS	16	71	71	17
Average per company‡‡	**7.9%**	**50.3%**	**48.9%**	**21.8%**

*Companies with two or fewer entries.

†No entries in this category.

‡‡Average excludes companies with two or fewer entries to minimize statistical distortions.

Note: Beatrice, Continental Group, General Foods, RCA, Scovill, and Signal were taken over as the study was being completed. Their data cover the period up through takeover, but not subsequent divestments.

Percent Made by 1980 and Then Divested	Percent Made by 1975 and Then Divested	Acquisitions in Unrelated New Fields as a Percent of Total Acquisitions in New Fields	Percent Made by 1980 and Then Divested	Percent Made by 1975 and Then Divested
14%	20%	0%	†	†
0	0	9	†	†
50	50	46	40%	40%
11	20	40	0*	0*
2	3	33	75	86
63	71	39	71	71
20	22	33	100*	100*
61	61	43	0*	0*
50	56	67	60	100
17	13	21	80	80
80	30	33	50	50
67	80	42	33	40
0	0	63	59	53
38	57	61	67	64
0	0	35	100	100
38	29	45	50	0
27	19	100	80	50*
75	100*	41	73	73
67	50	42	86	83
100	100*	45	80	100
20	11	67	50	50
†	†	63	79	81
71	71	39	65	65
33	44	36	100	100
63	57	60	80	75
44	44	36	57	67
50	56	22	100	100
14	0	40	83	100
89	80	65	77	67
100	100	74	77	74
0	0	67	100	100
99	55	36	100	100
86	80	39	100	100
44.0%	**40.9%**	**46.1%**	**74.0%**	**74.4%**

Passing the Essential Tests

To understand how to formulate corporate strategy, it is necessary to specify the conditions under which diversification will truly create shareholder value. These conditions can be summarized in three essential tests:

1. *The attractiveness test.* The industries chosen for diversification must be structurally attractive or capable of being made attractive.
2. *The cost-of-entry test.* The cost of entry must not capitalize all the future profits.
3. *The better-off test.* Either the new unit must gain competitive advantage from its link with the corporation or vice versa.

Of course, most companies will make certain that their proposed strategies pass some of these tests. But my study clearly shows that when companies ignored one or two of them, the strategic results were disastrous.

HOW ATTRACTIVE IS THE INDUSTRY?

In the long run, the rate of return available from competing in an industry is a function of its underlying structure, which I have described in another *Harvard Business Review* article.[4] An attractive industry with a high average return on investment will be difficult to enter because entry barriers are high, suppliers and buyers have only modest bargaining power, substitute products or services are few, and the rivalry among competitors is stable. An unattractive industry like steel will have structural flaws, including a plethora of substitute materials, powerful and price-sensitive buyers, and excessive rivalry caused by high fixed costs and a large group of competitors, many of whom are state supported.

Diversification cannot create shareholder value unless new industries have favorable structures that support returns exceeding the cost of capital. If the industry doesn't have such returns, the company must be able to restructure the industry or gain a sustainable competitive advantage that leads to returns well above the industry average. An industry need not be attractive before diversification. In fact, a company might benefit from entering before the industry shows its full potential. The diversification can then transform the industry's structure.

In my research, I often found companies had suspended the attractiveness test because they had a vague belief that the industry "fit" very closely with their own businesses. In the hope that the corporate "comfort" they felt would lead to a happy outcome, the companies ignored fundamentally poor industry structures. Unless the close fit allows substantial competitive advantage, however, such comfort will turn into pain when diversification results in poor returns. Royal Dutch Shell and other leading oil companies have had this unhappy experience in a number of chemicals businesses, where poor industry structures overcame the benefits of vertical integration and skills in process technology.

Another common reason for ignoring the attractiveness test is a low entry cost. Sometimes the buyer has an inside track or the owner is anxious to sell. Even if the price is actually low, however, a one-shot gain will not offset a perpetually poor business. Almost always, the company finds it must reinvest in the newly acquired unit, if only to replace fixed assets and fund working capital.

Diversifying companies are also prone to use rapid growth or other simple indicators as a proxy for a target industry's attractiveness. Many that rushed into fast-growing industries (personal computers, video games, and robotics, for example) were burned because they mistook early growth for long-term profit potential. Industries are profitable not because they are sexy or high tech; they are profitable only if their structures are attractive.

WHAT IS THE COST OF ENTRY?

Diversification cannot build shareholder value if the cost of entry into a new business eats up its expected returns. Strong market forces, however, are working to do just that. A company can enter new industries by acquisition or start-up. Acquisitions expose it to an increasingly efficient merger market. An acquirer beats the market if it pays a price not fully reflecting the prospects of the new unit. Yet multiple bidders are commonplace, information flows rapidly, and investment bankers and other intermediaries work aggressively to make the market as efficient as possible. In recent years, new financial instruments such as junk bonds have brought new buyers into the market and made even large companies vulnerable to takeover. Acquisition premiums are high and reflect the acquired company's future prospects—sometimes too well. Philip Morris paid more than four times book value for Seven-Up Company, for example. Simple arithmetic meant that profits had to more than quadruple to sustain the preacquisition ROI. Since there proved to be little Philip Morris could add in marketing prowess to the sophisticated marketing wars in the soft-drink industry, the result was the unsatisfactory financial performance of Seven-Up and ultimately the decision to divest.

In a start-up, the company must overcome entry barriers. It's a real catch-22 situation, however, since attractive industries are attractive because their entry barriers are high. Bearing the full cost of the entry barriers might well dissipate any potential profits. Otherwise, other entrants to the industry would have already eroded its profitability.

In the excitement of finding an appealing new business, companies sometimes forget to apply the cost-of-entry test. The more attractive a new industry, the more expensive it is to get into.

WILL THE BUSINESS BE BETTER OFF?

A corporation must bring some significant competitive advantage to the new unit, or the new unit must offer potential for significant advantage to the corporation. Sometimes, the benefits to the new unit accrue only once, near the time of entry, when the parent instigates a major overhaul of its strategy or installs a first-rate management team. Other diversification yields ongoing competitive advantage if the new unit can market its product through the well-developed distribution system of its sister units, for instance. This is one of the important underpinnings of the merger of Baxter Travenol and American Hospital Supply.

When the benefit to the new unit comes only once, the parent company has no rationale for holding the new unit in its portfolio over the long term. Once the results of the one-time improvement are clear, the diversified company no longer adds value to offset the inevitable costs imposed on the unit. It is best to sell the unit and free up corporate resources.

The better-off test does not imply that diversifying corporate risk creates shareholder value in and of itself. Doing something for shareholders that they can do themselves is not a basis for corporate strategy. (Only in the case of a privately held company, in which the company's and the shareholder's risk are the same, is diversification to reduce risk valuable for its own sake.) Diversification of risk should only be a by-product of corporate strategy, not a prime motivator.

Executives ignore the better-off test most of all or deal with it through arm waving or trumped-up logic rather than hard strategic analysis. One reason is that they confuse company size with shareholder value. In the drive to run a bigger company, they lose sight of their real job. They may justify the suspension of the better-off test by pointing to the way they manage diversity. By cutting corporate staff to the bone and giving business units nearly complete autonomy, they believe they avoid the pitfalls. Such thinking misses the whole point of diversification, which is to create shareholder value rather than to avoid destroying it.

Concepts of Corporate Strategy

The three tests for successful diversification set the standards that any corporate strategy must meet; meeting them is so difficult that most diversification fails. Many companies lack a clear concept of corporate strategy to guide their diversification or pursue a concept that does not address the tests. Others fail because they implement a strategy poorly.

My study has helped me identify four concepts of corporate strategy that have been put into practice—portfolio management, restructuring, transferring skills, and sharing activities. While the concepts are not always mutually exclusive, each rests on a different mechanism by which the corporation creates shareholder value and each requires the diversified company to manage and organize itself in a different way. The first two require no connections among business units; the second two depend on them. (See Table 5.4.) While all four concepts of strategy have succeeded under the right circumstances, today some make more sense than others. Ignoring any of the concepts is perhaps the quickest road to failure.

PORTFOLIO MANAGEMENT

The concept of corporate strategy most in use is portfolio management, which is based primarily on diversification through acquisition. The corporation acquires sound, attractive companies with competent man-

Table 5.4 Concepts of Corporate Strategy

	Portfolio Management	Restructuring	Transferring Skills	Sharing Activities
Strategic Prerequisites	Superior insight into identifying and acquiring undervalued companies	Superior insight into identifying restructuring opportunities	Proprietary skills in activities important to competitive advantage in target industries	Activities in existing units that can be shared with new business units to gain competitive advantage
	Willingness to sell off losers quickly or to opportunistically divest good performers when buyers are willing to pay large premiums	Willingness and capability to intervene to transform acquired units	Ability to accomplish the transfer of skills among units on an ongoing basis	Benefits of sharing that outweigh the costs
	Broad guidelines for and constraints on the types of units in the portfolio so that senior management can play the review role effectively	Broad similarities among the units in the portfolio. Willingness to cut losses by selling off units where restructuring proves unfeasible	Acquisitions of beachhead positions in new industries as a base	Both start-ups and acquisitions as entry vehicles
	A private company or undeveloped capital markets	Willingness to sell units when restructuring is complete, the results are clear, and market conditions are favorable		Ability to overcome organizational resistance to business unit collaboration
	Ability to shift away from portfolio management as the capital markets get more efficient or the company gets unwieldy			

	Autonomous business units	Autonomous business units	Largely autonomous but collaborative business units	Strategic business units that are encouraged to share activities
Organizational Prerequisites	A very small, low-cost, corporate staff Incentives based largely on business unit results	A corporate organization with the talent and resources to oversee the turnarounds and strategic repositionings of acquired units Incentives based largely on acquired units' results	High-level corporate staff members who see their role primarily as integrators Cross-business-unit committees, task forces, and other forms to serve as focal points for capturing and transferring skills Objectives of line managers that include skills transfer Incentives based in part on corporate resutls	An active strategic planning role at group, sector, and corporate levels High-level corporate staff members who see their roles primarily as integrators Incentives based heavily on group and corporate results
Common Pitfalls	Pursuing portfolio management in countries with efficient capital marketing and a developed pool of professional management talent Ignoring the fact that industry structure is not attractive	Mistaking rapid growth or a "hot" indsutry as sufficient evidence of a restructuring opportunity Lacking the resolve or resources to take on troubled situations and to intervene in management Ignoring the fact that industry structure is not attractive Paying lip service to restructuring but actually practicing passive portfolio managment	Mistaking similarity or comfort with new businesses as sufficient basis for diversification Providing no practical way for skills transfer to occur Ignoring the fact that industry structure is not attractive	Sharing for its own sake rather than because it leads to competitive advantage Assuming sharing will occur naturally without senior management playing an active role Ignoring the fact that industry structure is not attractive

agers who agree to stay on. While acquired units do not have to be in the same industries as existing units, the best portfolio managers generally limit their range of businesses in some way, in part to limit the specific expertise needed by top management.

The acquired units are autonomous, and the teams that run them are compensated according to the unit results. The corporation supplies capital and works with each to infuse it with professional management techniques. At the same time, top management provides objective and dispassionate review of business unit results. Portfolio managers categorize units by potential and regularly transfer resources from units that generate cash to those with high potential and cash needs.

In a portfolio strategy, the corporation seeks to create shareholder value in a number of ways. It uses its expertise and analytical resources to spot attractive acquisition candidates that the individual share-holder could not. The company provides capital on favorable terms that reflect corporatewide fundraising ability. It introduces professional management skills and discipline. Finally, it provides high-quality review and coaching, unencumbered by conventional wisdom or emotional attachments to the business.

The logic of the portfolio management concept rests on a number of vital assumptions. If a company's diversification plan is to meet the attractiveness and cost-of-entry test, it must find good but undervalued companies. Acquired companies must be truly undervalued because the parent does little for the new unit once it is acquired. To meet the better-off test, the benefits the corporation provides must yield a significant competitive advantage to acquired units. The style of operating through highly autonomous business units must both develop sound business strategies and motivate managers.

In most countries, the days when portfolio management was a valid concept of corporate strategy are past. In the face of increasingly well-developed capital markets, attractive companies with good managements show up on everyone's computer screen and attract top dollar in terms of acquisition premium. Simply contributing capital isn't contributing much. A sound strategy can easily be funded; small to medium-size companies don't need a munificent parent.

Other benefits have also eroded. Large companies no longer corner the market for professional management skills; in fact, more and more observers believe managers cannot necessarily run anything in the absence of industry-specific knowledge and experience. Another supposed advantage of the portfolio management concept—dispassionate review—rests on similarly shaky ground since the added value of review alone is questionable in a portfolio of sound companies.

The benefit of giving business units complete autonomy is also questionable. Increasingly, a company's business units are interrelated, drawn together by new technology, broadening distribution channels, and changing regulations. Setting strategies of units independently may well undermine unit performance. The companies in my sample that have succeeded in diversification have recognized the value of interrelationships and understood that a strong sense of corporate identity is as important as slavish adherence to parochial business unit financial results.

But it is the sheer complexity of the management task that has ultimately defeated even the best portfolio managers. As the size of the company grows, portfolio managers need to find more and more deals just to maintain growth. Supervising dozens or even hundreds of disparate units and under chain-letter pressures to add more, management begins to make mistakes. At the same time, the inevitable costs of being part of a diversified company take their toll and unit performance slides while the whole company's ROI turns downward. Eventually, a new management team is installed that initiates wholesale divestments and pares down the company to its core businesses. The experiences of Gulf & Western, Consolidated Foods (now Sara Lee), and ITT are just a few comparatively recent examples. Reflecting these realities, the U.S. capital markets today reward companies that follow the portfolio management model with a "conglomerate discount"; they value the whole less than the sum of the parts.

In developing countries, where large companies are few, capital markets are undeveloped, and professional management is scarce, portfolio management still works. But it is no longer a valid model for corporate strategy in advanced economies. Nevertheless, the technique is in the limelight today in the United Kingdom, where it is supported so far by a newly energized stock market eager for excitement. But this enthusiasm will wane—as well it should. Portfolio management is no way to conduct corporate strategy.

RESTRUCTURING

Unlike its passive role as a portfolio manager, when it serves as banker and reviewer, a company that bases its strategy on restructuring becomes an active restructurer of business units. The new businesses are not necessarily related to existing units. All that is necessary is unrealized potential.

The restructuring strategy seeks out undeveloped, sick, or threatened organizations or industries on the threshold of significant change. The parent intervenes, frequently changing the unit management team, shifting strategy, or infusing the company with new technology. Then it may make follow-up acquisitions to build a critical mass and sell off unneeded or unconnected parts and thereby reduce the effective acquisition cost. The result is a strengthened company or a transformed industry. As a coda, the parent sells off the stronger unit once results are clear because the parent is no longer adding value and top management decides that its attention should be directed elsewhere. (See the insert "An Uncanny British Restructurer" for an example of restructuring.)

When well implemented, the restructuring concept is sound, for it passes the three tests of successful diversification. The restructurer meets the cost-of-entry test through the types of company it acquires. It limits acquisition premiums by buying companies with problems and lackluster images or by buying into industries with as yet unforeseen potential. Intervention by the corporation clearly meets the better-off test. Provided that the target industries are structurally attractive, the restructuring model can create enormous shareholder value. Some restructuring companies are Loew's, BTR, and General Cinema. Ironically, many of today's restructurers are profiting from yesterday's portfolio management strategies.

To work, the restructuring strategy requires a corporate management team with the insight to spot undervalued companies or positions in industries ripe for transformation. The same insight is necessary to actually turn the units around even though they are in new and unfamiliar businesses.

These requirements expose the restructurer to considerable risk and usually limit the time in which the company can succeed at the strategy. The most skillful proponents understand this problem, recognize their mistakes, and move decisively to dispose of them. The best companies

An Uncanny British Restructurer

Hanson Trust, on its way to becoming Britain's largest company, is one of several skillful followers of the restructuring concept. A conglomerate with units in many industries, Hanson might seem on the surface a portfolio manager. In fact, Hanson and one or two other conglomerates have a much more effective corporate strategy. Hanson has acquired companies such as London Brick, Ever Ready Batteries, and SCM, which the city of London rather disdainfully calls "low tech."

Although a mature company suffering from low growth, the typical Hanson target is not just in any industry; it has an attractive structure. Its customer and supplier power is low and rivalry with competitors moderate. The target is a market leader, rich in assets but formerly poor in management. Hanson pays little of the present value of future cash flow out in an acquisition premium and reduces purchase price even further by aggressively selling off businesses that it cannot improve. In this way, it recoups just over a third of the cost of a typical acquisition during the first six months of ownership. Imperial Group's plush properties in London lasted barely two months under Hanson ownership, while Hanson's recent sale of Courage Breweries to Elders recouped £1.4 billion of the original £2.1 billion acquisition price of Imperial Group.

Like the best restructurers, Hanson approaches each unit with a modus operandi that it has perfected through repetition.

Hanson emphasizes low costs and tight financial controls. It has cut an average of 25 percent of labor costs out of acquired companies, slashed fixed overheads, and tightened capital expenditures. To reinforce its strategy of keeping costs low, Hanson carves out detailed one-year financial budgets with divisional managers and (through generous use of performance-related bonuses and share option schemes) gives them incentive to deliver the goods.

It's too early to tell whether Hanson will adhere to the last tenet of restructuring-selling turned-around units once the results are clear. If it succumbs to the allure of bigness, Hanson may take the course of the failed U.S. conglomerates.

realize they are not just acquiring companies but restructuring an industry. Unless they can integrate the acquisitions to create a whole new strategic position, they are just portfolio managers in disguise. Another important difficulty surfaces if so many other companies join the action that they deplete the pool of suitable candidates and bid their prices up.

Perhaps the greatest pitfall, however, is that companies find it very hard to dispose of business units once they are restructured and performing well. Human nature fights economic rationale. Size supplants shareholder value as the corporate goal. The company does not sell a unit even though the company no longer adds value to the unit. While the transformed units would be better off in another company that had related businesses, the restructuring company instead retains them. Gradually, it becomes a portfolio manager. The parent company's ROI declines as the need for reinvestment in the units and normal business risks eventually offset restructuring's one-shot gain. The perceived need to keep growing intensifies the pace of acquisition; errors result and standards fall. The restructuring company turns into a conglomerate with returns that only equal the average of all industries at best.

TRANSFERRING SKILLS

The purpose of the first two concepts of corporate strategy is to create value through a company's relationship with each autonomous unit. The corporation's role is to be a selector, a banker, and an intervenor.

The last two concepts exploit the interrelationships between businesses. In articulating them, however, one comes face-to-face with the often ill-defined concept of synergy. If you believe the text of the countless corporate annual reports, just about anything is related to just about anything else! But imagined synergy is much more common than real synergy. GM's purchase of Hughes Aircraft simply because cars were going electronic and Hughes was an electronics concern demonstrates the folly of paper synergy. Such corporate relatedness is an ex post facto rationalization of a diversification undertaken for other reasons.

Even synergy that is clearly defined often fails to materialize. Instead of cooperating, business units often compete. A company that can define the synergies it is pursuing still faces significant organizational impediments in achieving them.

But the need to capture the benefits of relationships between businesses has never been more important. Technological and competitive developments already link many businesses and are creating new possibilities for competitive advantage. In such sectors as financial services, computing, office equipment, entertainment, and health care, interrelationships among previously distinct businesses are perhaps the central concern of strategy.

To understand the role of relatedness in corporate strategy, we must give new meaning to this ill-defined idea. I have identified a good way to start—the value chain.[5] Every business unit is a collection of discrete activities ranging from sales to accounting that allow it to compete. I call them value activities. It is at this level, not in the company as a whole, that the unit achieves competitive advantage. I group these activities in nine categories. *Primary* activities create the product or service, deliver and market it, and provide after-sale support. The categories of primary activities include inbound logistics, operations, outbound logistics, marketing and sales, and service. *Support* activities provide the inputs and infrastructure that allow the primary activities to take place. The categories are company infrastructure, human resource management, technology development, and procurement.

The value chain defines the two types of interrelationships that may create synergy. The first is a company's ability to transfer skills or expertise among similar value chains. The second is the ability to share activities. Two business units, for example, can share the same sales force or logistics network.

The value chain helps expose the last two (and most important) concepts of corporate strategy. The transfer of skills among business units in the diversified company is the basis for one concept. While each business unit has a separate value chain, knowledge about how to perform activities is transferred among the units. For example, a toiletries business unit, expert in the marketing of convenience products, transmits ideas on new positioning concepts, promotional techniques, and packaging possibilities to a newly acquired unit that sells cough syrup. Newly entered industries can benefit from the expertise of existing units and vice versa.

These opportunities arise when business units have similar buyers or channels, similar value activities like government relations or procurement, similarities in the broad configuration of the value chain (for example, managing a multisite service organization), or the same strategic concept (for example, low cost). Even though the units operate separately, such similarities allow the sharing of knowledge.

Of course, some similarities are common; one can imagine them at some level between almost any pair of businesses. Countless companies have fallen into the trap of diversifying too readily because of similarities; mere similarity is not enough.

Transferring skills leads to competitive advantage only if the similarities among businesses meet three conditions:

1. The activities involved in the businesses are similar enough that sharing expertise is meaningful. Broad similarities (marketing intensiveness, for example, or a common core process technology such as bending metal) are not a sufficient basis for diversification. The resulting ability to transfer skills is likely to have little impact on competitive advantage.

2. The transfer of skills involves activities important to competitive advantage. Transferring skills in peripheral activities such as government relations or real estate in consumer goods units may be beneficial but is not a basis for diversification.

3. The skills transferred represent a significant source of competitive advantage for the receiving unit. The expertise or skills to be transferred are both advanced and proprietary enough to be beyond the capabilities of competitors.

The transfer of skills is an active process that significantly changes the strategy or operations of the receiving unit. The prospect for change must be specific and identifiable. Almost guaranteeing that no shareholder value will be created, too many companies are satisfied with vague prospects or faint hopes that skills will transfer. The transfer of skills does not happen by accident or by osmosis. The company will have to reassign critical personnel, even on a permanent basis, and the participation and support of high-level management in skills transfer is essential. Many companies have been defeated at skills transfer because they have not provided their business units with any incentives to participate.

Transferring skills meets the tests of diversification if the company truly mobilizes proprietary expertise across units. This makes certain the company can offset the acquisition premium or lower the cost of overcoming entry barriers.

The industries the company chooses for diversification must pass the attractiveness test. Even a close fit that reflects opportunities to transfer skills may not overcome poor industry structure. Opportunities to transfer skills, however, may help the company transform the structures of newly entered industries and send them in favorable directions.

The transfer of skills can be one-time or ongoing. If the company exhausts opportunities to infuse new expertise into a unit after the initial postacquisition period, the unit should ultimately be sold. The corporation is no longer creating shareholder value. Few companies have grasped this point, however, and many gradually suffer mediocre returns. Yet a company diversified into well-chosen businesses can transfer skills eventually in many directions. If corporate management conceives of its role in this way and creates appropriate organizational mechanisms to facilitate cross-unit interchange, the opportunities to share expertise will be meaningful.

By using both acquisitions and internal development, companies can build a transfer-of-skills strategy. The presence of a strong base of skills sometimes creates the possibility for internal entry instead of the acquisition of a going concern. Successful diversifiers that employ the concept of skills transfer may, however, often acquire a company in the target industry as a beachhead and then build on it with their internal expertise. By doing so, they can reduce some of the risks of internal entry and speed up the process. Two companies that have diversified using the transfer-of-skills concept are 3M and Pepsico.

SHARING ACTIVITIES

The fourth concept of corporate strategy is based on sharing activities in the value chains among business units. Procter & Gamble (P&G), for example, employs a common physical distribution system and sales force in both paper towels and disposable diapers. McKesson, a leading distribution company, will handle such diverse lines as pharmaceuticals and liquor through superwarehouses.

The ability to share activities is a potent basis for corporate strategy because sharing often enhances competitive advantage by lowering cost or raising differentiation. But not all sharing leads to competitive advantage, and companies can encounter deep organizational resistance to even beneficial sharing possibilities. These hard truths have led many companies to reject synergy prematurely and retreat to the false simplicity of portfolio management.

A cost-benefit analysis of prospective sharing opportunities can determine whether synergy is possible. Sharing can lower costs if it achieves economies of scale, boosts the efficiency of utilization, or helps a company move more rapidly down the learning curve. The costs of General Electric's advertising, sales, and after-sales service activities in major appliances are low because they are spread over a wide range of appliance products. Sharing can also enhance the potential for differentiation. A shared order-processing system, for instance, may allow new features and services that a buyer will value. Sharing can also reduce the cost of differentiation. A shared service network, for example, may make more advanced, remote servicing technology economically feasible. Often, sharing will allow an activity to be wholly reconfigured in ways that can dramatically raise competitive advantage.

Sharing must involve activities that are significant to competitive advantage, not just any activity. P&G's distribution system is such an instance in the diaper and paper towel business, where products are bulky and costly to ship. Conversely, diversification based on the opportunities to share only corporate overhead is rarely, if ever, appropriate.

Sharing activities inevitably involves costs that the benefits must outweigh. One cost is the greater coordination required to manage a shared activity. More important is the need to compromise the design or performance of an activity so that it can be shared. A salesperson handling the products of two business units, for example, must operate in a way that is usually not what either unit would choose were it independent. And if compromise greatly erodes the unit's effectiveness, then sharing may reduce rather than enhance competitive advantage.

Many companies have only superficially identified their potential for sharing. Companies also merge activities without consideration of whether they are sensitive to economies of scale. When they are not, the coordination costs kill the benefits. Companies compound such errors by not identifying costs of sharing in advance, when steps can be taken to minimize them. Costs of compromise can frequently be mitigated by redesigning the activity for sharing. The shared salesperson, for example, can be provided with a remote computer terminal to boost productivity and provide more customer information. Jamming business units together without such thinking exacerbates the costs of sharing.

Despite such pitfalls, opportunities to gain advantage from sharing activities have proliferated because of momentous developments in technology, deregulation, and competition. The infusion of electronics and information systems into many industries creates new opportunities to link businesses. The corporate strategy of sharing can involve both acquisition and internal development. Internal development is often possible because the corporation can bring to bear clear resources in launching a new unit. Start-ups are less difficult to integrate than acquisitions. Companies using the shared-activities concept can also make acquisitions as beachhead landings into a new industry and then integrate the units through sharing with other units. Prime examples of companies that have diversified via using shared activities include P&G, Du Pont, and IBM. The fields into which each has diversified are a cluster of tightly related units. Marriott illustrates both successes and failures in sharing activities over time. (See the insert "Adding Value with Hospitality.")

Adding Value with Hospitality

Marriott began in the restaurant business in Washington, D.C. Because its customers often ordered takeouts on the way to the national airport, Marriott eventually entered airline catering. From there, it jumped into food service management for institutions. Marriott then began broadening its base of family restaurants and entered the hotel industry. More recently, it has moved into restaurants, snack bars, and merchandise shops in airport terminals and into gourmet restaurants. In addition, Marriott has branched out from its hotel business into cruise ships, theme parks, wholesale travel agencies, budget motels, and retirement centers.

Marriott's diversification has exploited well-developed skills in food service and hospitality. Marriott's kitchens prepare food according to more than 6,000 standardized recipe cards; hotel procedures are also standardized and painstakingly documented in elaborate manuals. Marriott shares a number of important activities across units. A shared procurement and distribution system for food serves all Marriott units through nine regional procurement centers. As a result, Marriott earns 50 percent higher margins on food service than any other hotel company. Marriott also has a fully integrated real estate unit that brings corporatewide power to bear on site acquisitions as well as on the designing and building of all Marriott locations.

Marriott's diversification strategy balances acquisitions and start-ups. Start-ups or small acquisitions are used for initial entry, depending on how close the opportunities for shar-

ing are. To expand its geographic base, Marriott acquires companies and then disposes of the parts that do not fit.

Apart from this success, it is important to note that Marriott has divested 36 percent of both its acquisitions and its start-ups. While this is an above-average record, Marriott's mistakes are quite illuminating. Marriott has largely failed in diversifying into gourmet restaurants, theme parks, cruise ships, and wholesale travel agencies. In the first three businesses, Marriott discovered it could not transfer skills despite apparent similarities. Standardized menus did not work well in gourmet restaurants. Running cruise ships and theme parks was based more on entertainment and pizzazz than the carefully disciplined management of hotels and mid-price restaurants. The wholesale travel agencies were ill fated from the start because Marriott had to compete with an important customer for its hotels and had no proprietary skills or opportunities to share with which to add value.

Following the shared-activities model requires an organizational context in which business unit collaboration is encouraged and reinforced. Highly autonomous business units are inimical to such collaboration. The company must put into place a variety of what I call horizontal mechanisms—a strong sense of corporate identity, a clear corporate mission statement that emphasizes the importance of integrating business unit strategies, an incentive system that rewards more than just business unit results, cross-business-unit task forces, and other methods of integrating.

A corporate strategy based on shared activities clearly meets the better-off test because business units gain ongoing tangible advantages from others within the corporation. It also meets the cost-of-entry test by reducing the expense of surmounting the barriers to internal entry. Other bids for acquisitions that do not share opportunities will have lower reservation prices. Even widespread opportunities for sharing activities do not allow a company to suspend the attractiveness test, however. Many diversifiers have made the critical mistake of equating the close fit of a target industry with attractive diversification. Target industries must pass the strict requirement test of having an attractive structure as well as a close fit in opportunities if diversification is to ultimately succeed.

Choosing a Corporate Strategy

Each concept of corporate strategy allows the diversified company to create shareholder value in a different way. Companies can succeed with any of the concepts if they clearly define the corporation's role and objectives, have the skills necessary for meeting the concept's prerequisites, organize themselves to manage diversity in a way that fits the strategy, and find themselves in an appropriate capital market environment. The caveat is that portfolio management is only sensible in limited circumstances.

A company's choice of corporate strategy is partly a legacy of its past. If its business units are in unattractive industries, the company must start from scratch. If the company has few truly proprietary skills or activities it can share in related diversification, then its initial diversification must rely on other concepts. Yet corporate strategy should not be a once-and-for-all choice but a vision that can evolve. A company should choose its long-term preferred concept and then proceed pragmatically toward it from its initial starting point.

Both the strategic logic and the experience of the companies studied over the last decade suggest that a company will create shareholder value through diversification to a greater and greater extent as its strategy moves from portfolio management toward sharing activities. Because they do not rely on superior insight or other questionable assumptions about the company's capabilities, sharing activities and transferring skills offer the best avenues for value creation.

Each concept of corporate strategy is not mutually exclusive of those that come before, a potent advantage of the third and fourth concepts. A company can employ a restructuring strategy at the same time it transfers skills or shares activities. A strategy based on shared activities becomes more powerful if business units can also exchange skills. As the Marriott case illustrates, a company can often pursue the two strategies together and even incorporate some of the principles of restructuring with them. When it chooses industries in which to transfer skills or share activities, the company can also investigate the possibility of transforming the industry structure. When a company bases its strategy on interrelationships, it has a broader basis on which to create shareholder value than if it rests its entire strategy on transforming companies in unfamiliar industries.

My study supports the soundness of basing a corporate strategy on the transfer of skills or shared activities. The data on the sample companies' diversification programs illustrate some important characteristics of successful diversifiers. They have made a disproportionately low percentage of unrelated acquisitions, *unrelated* being defined as having no clear opportunity to transfer skills or share important activities (see Table 5.3). Even successful diversifiers such as 3M, IBM, and TRW have terrible records when they have strayed into unrelated acquisitions. Successful acquirers diversify into fields, each of which is related to many others. P&G and IBM, for example, operate in eighteen and nineteen interrelated fields respectively and so enjoy numerous opportunities to transfer skills and share activities.

Companies with the best acquisition records tend to make heavier-than-average use of start-ups and joint ventures. Most companies shy away from modes of entry besides acquisition. My results cast doubt on the conventional wisdom regarding start-ups. Table 5.3 demonstrates that while joint ventures are about as risky as acquisitions, start-ups are not. Moreover, successful companies often have very good records with start-up units, as 3M, P&G, Johnson & Johnson, IBM, and United Technologies illustrate. When a company has the internal strength to start up a unit, it can be safer and less costly to launch a company than to rely solely on an acquisition and then have to deal with the problem of integration. Japanese diversification histories support the soundness of start-up as an entry alternative.

My data also illustrate that none of the concepts of corporate strategy works when industry structure is poor or implementation is bad, no matter how related the industries are. Xerox acquired companies in related industries, but the businesses had poor structures and its skills were insufficient to provide enough competitive advantage to offset implementation problems.

AN ACTION PROGRAM

To translate the principles of corporate strategy into successful diversification, a company must first take an objective look at its existing businesses and the value added by the corporation. Only through such an assessment can an understanding of good corporate strategy grow. That understanding should guide future diversification as well as the development of skills and activities with which to select further new businesses. The following action program provides a concrete approach to conducting such a review. A company can choose a corporate strategy by:

1. *Identifying the interrelationships among already existing business units*. A company should begin to develop a corporate strategy by identifying all the opportunities it has to share activities or transfer skills in its existing portfolio of business units. The company will not only find ways to enhance the competitive advantage of existing units but also come upon several possible diversification avenues. The lack of meaningful interrelationships in the portfolio is an equally important finding, suggesting the need to justify the value added by the corporation or, alternately, a fundamental restructuring.

2. *Selecting the core businesses that will be the foundation of the corporate strategy.* Successful diversification starts with an understanding of the core businesses that will serve as the basis for corporate strategy. Core businesses are those that are in an attractive industry, have the potential to achieve sustainable competi-

tive advantage, have important interrelationships with other business units, and provide skills or activities that represent a base from which to diversify.

The company must first make certain its core businesses are on sound footing by upgrading management, internationalizing strategy, or improving technology. The study shows that geographic extensions of existing units, whether by acquisition, joint venture, or start-up, had a substantially lower divestment rate than diversification.

The company must then patiently dispose of the units that are not core businesses. Selling them will free resources that could be better deployed elsewhere. In some cases disposal implies immediate liquidation, while in others the company should dress up the units and wait for a propitious market or a particularly eager buyer.

3. *Creating horizontal organizational mechanisms to facilitate interrelationships among the core businesses and lay the groundwork for future related diversification.* Top management can facilitate interrelationships by emphasizing cross-unit collaboration, grouping units organizationally and modifying incentives, and taking steps to build a strong sense of corporate identity.

4. *Pursuing diversification opportunities that allow shared activities.* This concept of corporate strategy is the most compelling, provided a company's strategy passes all three tests. A company should inventory activities in existing business units that represent the strongest foundation for sharing, such as strong distribution channels or world-class technical facilities. These will in turn lead to potential new business areas. A company can use acquisitions as a beachhead or employ start-ups to exploit internal capabilities and minimize integrating problems.

5. *Pursuing diversification through the transfer of skills if opportunities for sharing activities are limited or exhausted.* Companies can pursue this strategy through acquisition, although they may be able to use start-ups if their existing units have important skills they can readily transfer.

Such diversification is often riskier because of the tough conditions necessary for it to work. Given the uncertainties, a company should avoid diversifying on the basis of skills transfer alone. Rather it should also be viewed as a stepping-stone to subsequent diversification using shared activities. New industries should be chosen that will lead naturally to other businesses. The goal is to build a cluster of related and mutually reinforcing business units. The strategy's logic implies that the company should not set the rate of return standards for the initial foray into a new sector too high.

6. ***Pursuing a strategy of restructuring if this fits the skills of management or no good opportunities exist for forging corporate interrelationships.*** When a company uncovers undermanaged companies and can deploy adequate management talent and resources to the acquired units, then it can use a restructuring strategy. The more developed the capital markets and the more active the market for companies, the more restructuring will require a patient search for that special opportunity rather than a headlong race to acquire as many bad apples as possible. Restructuring can be a permanent strategy, as it is with Loew's, or a way to build a group of businesses that supports a shift to another corporate strategy.

7. ***Paying dividends so that the shareholders can be the portfolio managers.*** Paying dividends is better than destroying shareholder value through diversification based on shaky underpinnings. Tax considerations, which some companies cite to avoid dividends, are hardly legitimate reasons to diversify if a company cannot demonstrate the capacity to do it profitably.

Creating a Corporate Theme

Defining a corporate theme is a good way to ensure that the corporation will create shareholder value. Having the right theme helps unite the efforts of business units and reinforces the ways they interrelate as well as guides the choice of new businesses to enter. NEC Corporation, with its "C&C" theme, provides a good example. NEC integrates its computer, semiconductor, telecommunications, and consumer elec-tronics businesses by merging computers and communication.

It is all too easy to create a shallow corporate theme. CBS wanted to be an "entertainment company," for example, and built a group of businesses related to leisure time. It entered such industries as toys, crafts, musical instruments, sports teams, and hi-fi retailing. While this corporate theme sounded good, close listening revealed its hollow ring. None of these businesses had any significant opportunity to share activi-ties or transfer skills among themselves or with CBS's traditional broad-casting and record businesses. They were all sold, often at significant losses, except for a few of CBS's publishing-related units. Saddled with the worst acquisition record in my study, CBS has eroded the shareholder value created through its strong performance in broadcasting and records.

Moving from competitive strategy to corporate strategy is the business equivalent of passing through the Bermuda Triangle. The failure of corporate strategy reflects the fact that most diversified companies have failed to think in terms of how they really add value. A corporate strategy that truly enhances the competitive advantage of each business unit is the best defense against the corporate raider. With a sharper focus on the tests of diversification and the explicit choice of a clear concept of corporate strategy, companies' diversification track records from now on can look a lot different.

NOTES

1. The studies also show that sellers of companies capture a large fraction of the gains from merger. See Michael C. Jensen and Richard S. Ruback, "The Market for Corporate Control: The Scientific Evidence," *Journal of Financial Economics* (April 1983): 5, and Michael C. Jensen, "Takeovers: Folklore and Science," *Harvard Business Review* 62, no. 5 (1984): 109.

2. Some recent evidence also supports the conclusion that acquired companies often suffer eroding performance after acquisition. See Frederick M. Scherer, "Mergers, Sell-Offs and Managerial Behavior," in *The Economics of Strategic Planning*, ed. Lacy Glenn Thomas (Lexington, Mass.: Lexington Books, 1986), p. 143; and David A. Ravenscraft and Frederick M. Scherer, "Mergers and Managerial Performance," paper presented at the Conference on Takeovers and Contests for Corporate Control, Colum-bia Law School, 1985.

3. This observation has been made by a number of authors. See, for example, Malcolm S. Salter and Wolf A. Weinhold, *Diversification Through Acquisition* (New York: Free Press, 1979).

4. See Michael E. Porter, "How Competitive Forces Shape Strategy," *Harvard Business Review* 57, no. 2 (1979): 86.

5. See Michael E. Porter, *Competitive Advantage* (New York: Free Press, 1985).

Part II The Competitiveness of Locations

CHAPTER 6

The Competitive Advantage of Nations

Michael E. Porter

NATIONAL PROSPERITY IS CREATED, not inherited. It does not grow out of a country's natural endowments, its labor pool, its interest rates, or its currency's value, as classical economics insists.

A nation's competitiveness depends on the capacity of its industry to innovate and upgrade. Companies gain advantage against the world's best competitors because of pressure and challenge. They benefit from having strong domestic rivals, aggressive home-based suppliers, and demanding local customers.

In a world of increasingly global competition, nations have become more, not less, important. As the basis of competition has shifted more and more to the creation and assimilation of knowledge, the role of the nation has grown. Competitive advantage is created and sustained through a highly localized process. Differences in national values, culture, economic structures, institutions, and histories all contribute to competitive success. There are striking differences in the patterns of competitiveness in every country; no nation can or will be competitive in every or even most industries. Ultimately, nations succeed in particular industries because their home environment is the most forward-looking, dynamic, and challenging.

Author's note: Michael J. Enright, who served as project coordinator for this study, has contributed valuable suggestions.

March–April 1990

These conclusions, the product of a four-year study of the patterns of competitive success in ten leading trading nations, contradict the conventional wisdom that guides the thinking of many companies and national governments—and that is pervasive today in the United States. (For more about the study, see the insert "Patterns of National Competitive Success.") According to prevailing thinking, labor costs, interest rates, exchange rates, and economies of scale are the most potent determinants of competitiveness. In companies, the words of the day are merger, alliance, strategic partnerships, collaboration, and supranational

---

Patterns of National Competitive Success

To investigate why nations gain competitive advantage in particular industries and the implications for company strategy and national economies, I conducted a four-year study of ten important trading nations: Denmark, Germany, Italy, Japan, Korea, Singapore, Sweden, Switzerland, the United Kingdom, and the United States. I was assisted by a team of more than 30 researchers, most of whom were natives of and based in the nation they studied. The researchers all used the same methodology.

Three nations—the United States, Japan, and Germany—are the world's leading industrial powers. The other nations represent a variety of population sizes, government policies toward industry, social philosophies, geographical sizes, and locations. Together, the ten nations accounted for fully 50 percent of total world exports in 1985, the base year for statistical analysis.

Most previous analyses of national competitiveness have focused on single nation or bilateral comparisons. By studying nations with widely varying characteristics and circumstances, this study sought to separate the fundamental forces underlying national competitive advantage from the idiosyncratic ones.

In each nation, the study consisted of two parts. The first identified all industries in which the nation's companies were internationally successful, using available statistical data, supplementary published sources, and field interviews. We defined a nation's industry as internationally successful if it *possessed competitive advantage relative to the best worldwide competitors.* Many measures of competitive advantage, such as reported profitability, can be misleading. We chose as the best indicators the presence of substantial and sustained exports to a wide array of other nations and/or significant outbound foreign investment based on skills and assets created in the home country. A nation was considered the home base for a company if it was either a locally owned, indigenous enterprise or managed autonomously although owned by a foreign company or investors. We then created a profile of all the industries in which each nation was internationally successful at three points in time: 1971, 1978, and 1985. The pattern of competitive industries in each economy was far from random: the task was to explain it and how it had changed over time. Of particular interest were the connections or relationships among the nation's competitive industries.

In the second part of the study, we examined the history of competition in particular industries to understand how competitive advantage was created. On the basis of national profiles, we selected over 100 industries or industry groups for detailed study; we examined many more in less detail. We went back as far as necessary to understand how and why the industry began in the nation, how it grew, when and why companies from the nation developed international competitive advantage, and the process by which competitive advantage had been either sustained or lost. The resulting case histories fall short of the work of a good historian in their level of detail, but they do provide insight into the development of both the industry and the nation's economy.

We chose a sample of industries for each nation that represented the most important groups of competitive industries in the economy. The industries studied accounted for a large share of total exports in each nation: more than 20 percent of total exports in Japan, Germany, and Switzerland, for example, and more than 40 percent in South Korea. We studied some of the most famous and important international success stories —German high-performance autos and chemicals, Japanese semi-conductors and VCRs, Swiss banking and pharmaceuticals, Italian footwear and textiles, U.S. commercial aircraft and motion pictures—and some relatively obscure but highly competitive industries—South Korean pianos, Italian ski boots, and British biscuits. We also added a few industries because they appeared to be paradoxes: Japanese home demand for Western-character typewriters is nearly nonexistent, for example, but Japan holds a strong export and foreign investment position in the industry. We avoided industries that were highly dependent on natural resources: such industries do not form the backbone of advanced economies, and the capacity to compete in them is more explicable using classical theory. We did, however, include a number of more technologically intensive, natural-resource-related industries such as newsprint and agricultural chemicals.

The sample of nations and industries offers a rich empirical foundation for developing and testing the new theory of how countries gain competitive advantage. The accompanying article concentrates on the determinants of competitive advantage in individual industries and also sketches out some of the study's overall implications for government policy and company strategy. A fuller treat-

ment in my book, *The Competitive Advantage of Nations,* develops the theory and its implications in greater depth and provides many additional examples. It also contains detailed descriptions of the nations we studied and the future prospects for their economies.

globalization. Managers are pressing for more government support for particular industries. Among governments, there is a growing tendency to experiment with various policies intended to promote national competitiveness—from efforts to manage exchange rates to new measures to manage trade to policies to relax antitrust—which usually end up only undermining it. (See the insert "What Is National Competitiveness?")

These approaches, now much in favor in both companies and governments, are flawed. They fundamentally misperceive the true sources of competitive advantage. Pursuing them, with all their short term appeal, will virtually guarantee that the United States—or any other advanced nation—never achieves real and sustainable competitive advantage.

We need a new perspective and new tools—an approach to competitiveness that grows directly out of an analysis of internationally successful industries, without regard for traditional ideology or current intellectual fashion. We need to know, very simply, what works and why. Then we need to apply it.

What Is National Competitiveness?

National competitiveness has become one of the central preoccupations of government and industry in every nation. Yet for all the discussion, debate, and writing on the topic, there is still no persuasive theory to explain national competitiveness. What is more, there is not even an accepted definition of the term

"competitiveness" as applied to a nation. While the notion of a competitive company is clear, the notion of a competitive nation is not.

Some see national competitiveness as a macroeconomic phenomenon, driven by variables such as exchange rates, interest rates, and government deficits. But Japan, Italy, and South Korea have all enjoyed rapidly rising living standards despite budget deficits; Germany and Switzerland despite appreciating currencies; and Italy and Korea despite high interest rates.

Others argue that competitiveness is a function of cheap and abundant labor. But Germany, Switzerland, and Sweden have all prospered even with high wages and labor shortages. Besides, shouldn't a nation seek higher wages for its workers as a goal of competitiveness?

Another view connects competitiveness with bountiful natural resources. But how, then, can one explain the success of Germany, Japan, Switzerland, Italy, and South Korea—countries with limited natural resources?

More recently, the argument has gained favor that competitiveness is driven by government policy: targeting, protection, import promotion, and subsidies have propelled Japanese and South Korean auto, steel, shipbuilding, and semiconductor industries into global preeminence. But a closer look reveals a spotty record. In Italy, government intervention has been ineffectual— but Italy has experienced a boom in world export share second only to Japan. In Germany, direct government intervention in exporting industries is rare. And even in Japan and South Korea, government's role in such important industries as facsimile machines, copiers, robotics,

and advanced materials has been modest; some of the most frequently cited examples, such as sewing machines, steel, and shipbuilding, are now quite dated.

A final popular explanation for national competitiveness is differences in management practices, including management-labor relations. The problem here, however, is that different industries require different approaches to management. The successful management practices governing small, private, and loosely organized Italian family companies in footwear, textiles, and jewelry, for example, would produce a management disaster if applied to German chemical or auto companies, Swiss pharmaceutical makers, or American aircraft producers. Nor is it possible to generalize about management-labor relations. Despite the commonly held view that powerful unions undermine competitive advantage, unions are strong in Germany and Sweden—and both countries boast internationally preeminent companies.

Clearly, none of these explanations is fully satisfactory; none is sufficient by itself to rationalize the competitive position of industries within a national border. Each contains some truth; but a broader, more complex set of forces seems to be at work.

The lack of a clear explanation signals an even more fundamental question. What is a "competitive" nation in the first place? Is a "competitive" nation one where every company or industry is competitive? No nation meets this test. Even Japan has large sectors of its economy that fall far behind the world's best competitors.

Is a "competitive" nation one whose exchange rate makes its goods price competitive in international markets? Both Germany and Japan have enjoyed remarkable gains in their standards of living—and experienced sustained periods of strong currency and rising prices. Is a "competitive" nation one with a large positive balance of trade? Switzerland has roughly balanced trade; Italy has a chronic trade deficit—both nations enjoy strongly rising national income. Is a "competitive" nation one with low labor costs? India and Mexico both have low wages and low labor costs—but neither seems an attractive industrial model.

The only meaningful concept of competitiveness at the national level is *productivity*. The principal goal of a nation is to produce a high and rising standard of living for its citizens. The ability to do so depends on the productivity with which a nation's labor and capital are employed. Productivity is the value of the output produced by a unit of labor or capital. Productivity depends on both the quality and features of products (which determine the prices that they can command) and the ef-

ficiency with which they are produced. Productivity is the prime determinant of a nation's long-run standard of living; it is the root cause of national per capita income. The productivity of human resources determines employee wages; the productivity with which capital is employed determines the return it earns for its holders.

A nation's standard of living depends on the capacity of its companies to achieve high levels of productivity—and to increase productivity over time. Sustained productivity growth requires that an economy continually *upgrade itself*. A nation's companies must relentlessly improve productivity in existing industries by raising product quality, adding desirable features, improving product technology, or boosting production efficiency. They must develop the necessary capabilities to compete in more and more sophisticated industry segments, where productivity is generally high. They must finally develop the capability to compete in entirely new, sophisticated industries.

International trade and foreign investment can both improve a nation's productivity as well as threaten it. They support rising national productivity by allowing a nation to specialize in those industries and segments of industries where its companies are more productive and to import where its companies are less productive. No nation can be competitive in everything. The ideal is to deploy the nation's limited pool of human and other resources into the most productive uses. Even those nations with the highest standards of living have many industries in which local companies are uncompetitive.

Yet international trade and foreign investment also can threaten productivity growth. They expose a nation's industries to the test of international standards of productivity. An industry will lose out if its productivity is not sufficiently higher than foreign rivals' to offset any advantages in local wage rates. If a nation loses the ability to compete in a range of high-productivity/high-wage industries, its standard of living is threatened.

Defining national competitiveness as achieving a trade surplus or balanced trade per se is inappropriate. The expansion of exports because of low wages and a weak currency, at the same time that the nation imports sophisticated goods that its companies cannot produce competitively, may bring trade into balance or surplus but lowers the nation's standard of living. Competitiveness also does not mean jobs. It's the *type* of jobs, not just the ability to employ citizens at low wages, that is decisive for economic prosperity.

Seeking to explain "competitiveness" at the national level, then, is to answer the wrong question. What we must understand instead is the determinants of productivity and the

rate of productivity growth. To find answers, we must focus not on the economy as a whole but on *specific industries and industry segments.* We must understand how and why commercially viable skills and technology are created, which can only be fully understood at the level of particular industries. It is the outcome of the thousands of struggles for competitive advantage against foreign rivals in particular segments and industries, in which products and processes are created and improved, that underpins the process of upgrading national productivity.

When one looks closely at any national economy, there are striking differences among a nation's industries in competitive success. International advantage is often concentrated in particular industry segments. German exports of cars are heavily skewed toward high performance cars, while Korean exports are all compacts and subcompacts. In many industries and segments of industries, the competitors with true international competitive advantage are *based in only a few nations.*

Our search, then, is for the decisive characteristic of a nation that allows its companies to create and sustain competitive advantage in particular fields—the search is for the competitive advantage of nations. We are particularly concerned with the determinants of international success in technology and skill-intensive segments and industries, which underpin high and rising productivity.

Classical theory explains the success of nations in particular industries based on so-called factors of production such as land, labor, and natural resources. Nations gain factor-based comparative advantage in industries that make intensive use of the factors they possess in abundance. Classical theory, however, has been overshadowed in advanced industries and economies by the globalization of competition and the power of technology.

A new theory must recognize that in modern international competition, companies compete with global strategies involving not only trade but also foreign investment. What a new theory must explain is why a nation provides a favorable home base for companies that compete internationally. The home base is the nation in which the essential competitive advantages of the enterprise are created and sustained. It is where a company's strategy is set, where the core product and process technology is created and maintained, and where the most productive jobs and most advanced skills are located. The presence of the home base in a nation has the greatest positive influence on other linked domestic industries and leads to other benefits in the nation's economy. While the ownership of the company is often concentrated at the home base, the nationality of shareholders is secondary.

A new theory must move beyond comparative advantage to the competitive advantage of a nation. It must reflect a rich conception of competition that includes segmented markets, differentiated products, technology differences, and economies of scale. A new theory must go beyond cost and explain why companies from some nations are better than others at creating advantages based on quality, features, and new product innovation. A new theory must begin from the premise that competition is dynamic and evolving; it must answer the questions: Why do some companies based in some nations innovate more than others? Why do some nations provide an environment that enables companies to improve and innovate faster than foreign rivals?

How Companies Succeed in International Markets

Around the world, companies that have achieved international leadership employ strategies that differ from each other in every respect. But while every successful company will employ its own particular strategy, the underlying mode of operation—the character and trajectory of all successful companies—is fundamentally the same.

Companies achieve competitive advantage through acts of innovation. They approach innovation in its broadest sense, including both new technologies and new ways of doing things. They perceive a new basis for competing or find better means for competing in old ways. Innovation can be manifested in a new product design, a new production process, a new marketing approach, or a new way of conducting training. Much innovation is mundane and incremental, depending more on a cumulation of small insights and advances than on a single, major technological breakthrough. It often involves ideas that are not even "new"—ideas that have been around, but never vigorously pursued. It always involves investments in skill and knowledge, as well as in physical assets and brand reputations.

Some innovations create competitive advantage by perceiving an entirely new market opportunity or by serving a market segment that others have ignored. When competitors are slow to respond, such innovation yields competitive advantage. For instance, in industries such as autos and home electronics, Japanese companies gained their initial advantage by emphasizing smaller, more compact, lower capacity models that foreign competitors disdained as less profitable, less important, and less attractive.

In international markets, innovations that yield competitive advantage anticipate both domestic and foreign needs. For example, as international concern for product safety has grown, Swedish companies like Volvo, Atlas Copco, and AGA have succeeded by anticipating the market opportunity in this area. On the other hand, innovations that respond to concerns or circumstances that are peculiar to the home market can actually retard international competitive success. The lure of the huge U.S. defense market, for instance, has diverted the attention of U.S. materials and machine-tool companies from attractive, global commercial markets.

Information plays a large role in the process of innovation and improvement—information that either is not available to competitors or that they do not seek. Sometimes it comes from simple investment in research and development or market research; more often, it comes from effort and from openness and from looking in the right place unencumbered by blinding assumptions or conventional wisdom.

This is why innovators are often outsiders from a different industry or a different country. Innovation may come from a new company, whose founder has a nontraditional background or was simply not appreciated in an older, established company. Or the capacity for innovation may come into an existing company through senior managers who are new to the particular industry and thus more able to perceive opportunities and more likely to pursue them. Or innovation may occur as a company diversifies, bringing new resources, skills, or perspectives to another industry. Or innovations may come from another nation with different circumstances or different ways of competing.

With few exceptions, innovation is the result of unusual effort. The company that successfully implements a new or better way of competing pursues its approach with dogged determination, often in the face of harsh criticism and tough obstacles. In fact, to succeed, innovation usually requires pressure, necessity, and even adversity: the fear of loss often proves more powerful than the hope of gain.

Once a company achieves competitive advantage through an innovation, it can sustain it only through relentless improvement. Almost any advantage can be imitated. Korean companies have already matched the ability of their Japanese rivals to mass-produce standard color televisions and VCRs; Brazilian companies have assembled technology and designs comparable to Italian competitors in casual leather footwear.

Competitors will eventually and inevitably overtake any company that stops improving and innovating. Sometimes early-mover advantages such as customer relationships, scale economies in existing technologies, or the loyalty of distribution channels are enough to permit a stagnant company to retain its entrenched position for years or even decades. But sooner or later, more dynamic rivals will find a way to innovate around these advantages or create a better or cheaper way of doing things. Italian appliance producers, which competed successfully on the basis of cost in selling midsize and compact appliances through large retail chains, rested too long on this initial advantage. By developing more differentiated products and creating strong brand franchises, German competitors have begun to gain ground.

Ultimately, the only way to sustain a competitive advantage is to *upgrade it*—to move to more sophisticated types. This is precisely what Japanese automakers have done. They initially penetrated foreign markets with small, inexpensive compact cars of adequate quality and competed on the basis of lower labor costs. Even while their labor-cost advantage persisted, however, the Japanese companies were upgrading. They invested aggressively to build large modern plants to reap economies of scale. Then they became innovators in process technology, pioneering just-in-time production and a host of other quality and productivity practices. These process improvements led to better product quality, better repair records, and better customer-satisfaction ratings than foreign competitors had. Most recently, Japanese auto makers have advanced to the vanguard of product technology and are introducing new, premium brand names to compete with the world's most prestigious passenger cars.

The example of the Japanese automakers also illustrates two additional prerequisites for sustaining competitive advantage. First, a company must adopt a global approach to strategy. It must sell its product worldwide, under its own brand name, through international marketing channels that it controls. A truly global approach may even require the company to locate production or R&D facilities in other nations to take advantage of lower wage rates, to gain or improve market access, or to take advantage of foreign technology. Second, creating more sustainable advantages often means that a company must make its existing advantage obsolete—even while it is still an advantage. Japanese auto companies recognized this; either they would make their advantage obsolete, or a competitor would do it for them.

As this example suggests, innovation and change are inextricably tied together. But change is an unnatural act, particularly in successful companies; powerful forces are at work to avoid and defeat it. Past approaches become institutionalized in standard operating procedures and management controls. Training emphasizes the one correct way to do anything; the construction of specialized, dedicated facilities solidifies past practice into expensive brick and mortar; the existing strategy takes on an aura of invincibility and becomes rooted in the company culture.

Successful companies tend to develop a bias for predictability and stability; they work on defending what they have. Change is tempered by the fear that there is much to lose. The organization at all levels filters out information that would suggest new approaches, modifications, or departures from the norm. The internal environment operates like an immune system to isolate or expel "hostile" individuals who challenge current directions or established thinking. Innovation ceases; the company becomes stagnant; it is only a matter of time before aggressive competitors overtake it.

The Diamond of National Advantage

Why are certain companies based in certain nations capable of consistent innovation? Why do they ruthlessly pursue improvements, seeking an ever more sophisticated source of competitive advantage? Why are they able to overcome the substantial barriers to change and innovation that so often accompany success?

The answer lies in four broad attributes of a nation, attributes that individually and as a system constitute the diamond of national advantage, the playing field that each nation establishes and operates for its industries. These attributes are:

1. *Factor Conditions.* The nation's position in factors of production, such as skilled labor or infrastructure, necessary to compete in a given industry.
2. *Demand Conditions.* The nature of home-market demand for the industry's product or service.
3. *Related and Supporting Industries.* The presence or absence in the nation of supplier industries and other related industries that are internationally competitive.
4. *Firm Strategy, Structure, and Rivalry.* The conditions in the nation governing how companies are created, organized, and managed, as well as the nature of domestic rivalry.

These determinants create the national environment in which companies are born and learn how to compete. (See Figure 6.1.) Each point on the diamond—and the diamond as a system—affects essential ingredients for achieving international competitive success: the availability of resources and skills necessary for competitive advantage in an industry; the information that shapes the opportunities that companies perceive and the directions in which they deploy their resources and skills; the

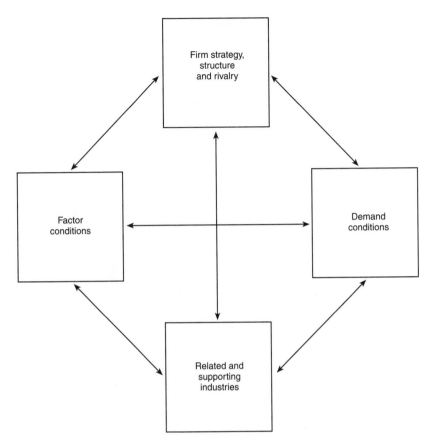

Figure 6.1 Determinants of National Competitive Advantage

goals of the owners, managers, and individuals in companies; and most important, the pressures on companies to invest and innovate. (See the insert "How the Diamond Works: The Italian Ceramic Tile Industry.")

When a national environment permits and supports the most rapid accumulation of specialized assets and skills—sometimes simply because of greater effort and commitment—companies gain a competitive advantage. When a national environment affords better ongoing information and insight into product and process needs, companies gain a competitive advantage. Finally, when the national environment pressures companies to innovate and invest, companies both gain a competitive advantage and upgrade those advantages over time.

How the Diamond Works: The Italian Ceramic Tile Industry

Michael J. Enright and Paolo Tenti

In 1987, Italian companies were world leaders in the production and export of ceramic tiles, a $10 billion industry. Italian producers, concentrated in and around the small town of Sassuolo in the Emilia-Romagna region, accounted for about 30 percent of world production and almost 60 percent of world exports. The Italian trade surplus that year in ceramic tiles was about $1.4 billion.

The development of the Italian ceramic tile industry's competitive advantage illustrates how the diamond of national advantage works. Sassuolo's sustainable competitive advantage in ceramic tiles grew not from any static or historical advantage but from dynamism and change. Sophisticated and demanding local buyers, strong and unique distribution channels, and intense rivalry among local companies created constant pressure for innovation. Knowledge grew quickly from continuous experimentation and cumulative production experience. Private ownership of the companies and loyalty to the community spawned intense commitment to invest in the industry.

Tile producers benefited as well from a highly developed set of local machinery suppliers and other supporting industries, producing materials, services, and infrastructure. The presence of world-class, Italian-related industries also reinforced Italian strength in tiles. Finally, the geographic concentration of the entire cluster supercharged the whole process. Today foreign companies compete against an entire subculture. The organic nature of this system represents the most sustainable advantage of Sassuolo's ceramic tile companies.

The Origins of the Italian Industry

Tile production in Sassuolo grew out of the earthenware and crockery industry, whose history traces back to the thirteenth century. Immediately after World War II, there were only a handful of ceramic tile manufacturers in and around Sassuolo, all serving the local market exclusively.

Demand for ceramic tiles within Italy began to grow dramatically in the immediate postwar years, as the reconstruction of Italy triggered a boom in building materials of all kinds. Italian demand for ceramic tiles was particularly great due to the climate, local tastes, and building techniques.

Because Sassuolo was in a relatively prosperous part of Italy, there were many who could combine the modest amount of capital and necessary organizational skills to start a tile company. In 1955, there were 14 Sassuolo area tile companies; by 1962, there were 102.

The new tile companies benefited from a local pool of mechanically trained workers. The region around Sassuolo was home to Ferrari, Maserati, Lamborghini, and other technically sophisticated companies. As the tile industry began to grow and prosper, many engineers and skilled workers gravitated to the successful companies.

The Emerging Italian Tile Cluster

Initially, Italian tile producers were dependent on foreign sources of raw materials and production technology. In the 1950s, the principal raw materials used to make tiles were kaolin (white) clays. Since there were red but no white-clay deposits near Sassuolo, Italian producers had to import the clays from the United Kingdom. Tile making equipment was also imported in the 1950s and 1960s: kilns from Germany, America, and France; presses for forming tiles from Germany. Sassuolo tile makers had to import even simple glazing machines.

Over time, the Italian tile producers learned how to modify imported equipment to fit local circumstances: red versus white clays, natural gas versus heavy oil. As process technicians from tile companies left

to start their own equipment companies, a local machinery industry arose in Sassuolo. By 1970, Italian companies had emerged as world-class producers of kilns and presses; the earlier situation had exactly reversed: were exporting their red-clay equipment for foreigners to use with white clays.

The relationship between Italian tile and equipment manufacturers was a mutually supporting one, made even more so by close proximity. In the mid-1980s, there were some 200 Italian equipment manufacturers; more than 60 percent were located in the Sassuolo area. The equipment manufacturers competed fiercely for local business, and tile manufacturers benefited from better prices and more advanced equipment than their foreign rivals.

As the emerging tile cluster grew and concentrated in the Sassuolo region, a pool of skilled workers and technicians developed, including engineers, production specialists, maintenance workers, service technicians, and design personnel. The industry's geographic concentration encouraged other supporting companies to form, offering molds, packaging materials, glazes, and transportation services. An array of small, specialized consulting companies emerged to give advice to tile producers on plant design, logistics, and commercial, advertising, and fiscal matters.

With its membership concentrated in the Sassuolo area, Assopiastrelle, the ceramic tile industry association, began offering services in areas of common interest: bulk purchasing, foreign-market research, and consulting on fiscal and legal matters. The growing tile cluster stimulated the formation of a new, specialized factor-creating institution: in 1976, a consortium of the University of Bologna, regional agencies, and the ceramic industry association founded the Centro Ceramico di Bologna, which conducted process research and product analysis.

Sophisticated Home Demand

By the mid-1960s, per-capita tile consumption in Italy was considerably higher than in the rest of the world. The Italian market was also the world's most sophisticated. Italian customers, who were generally the first to adopt new designs and features, and Italian producers, who constantly innovated to improve manufacturing methods and create new designs, progressed in a mutually reinforcing process.

The uniquely sophisticated character of domestic demand also extended to retail outlets. In the 1960s, specialized tile showrooms began opening in Italy. By 1985, there were roughly 7,600 specialized showrooms handling approximately 80 percent of domestic sales, far more than in other nations. In 1976, the Italian company Piemme introduced tiles by famous designers to gain distribution outlets and to build brand name awareness among consumers. This innovation drew on another related industry, design services, in which Italy was world leader, with over $10 billion in exports.

Sassuolo Rivalry

The sheer number of tile companies in the Sassuolo area created intense rivalry. News of product and process innovations spread rapidly, and companies seeking technological, design, and distribution leadership had to improve constantly.

Proximity added a personal note to the intense rivalry. All of the producers were privately held, most were family run. The owners all lived in the same area, knew each other, and were the leading citizens of the same towns.

Pressures to Upgrade

In the early 1970s, faced with intense domestic rivalry, pressure from retail customers, and the shock of the 1973 energy crisis, Italian tile companies struggled to reduce gas and labor costs. These efforts led to a technological breakthrough, the rapid single-firing process, in which the hardening process, material transformation, and glaze-fixing all occurred in one pass through the kiln. A process that took 225 employees using the double-firing method needed only ninety employees using single-firing roller kilns. Cycle time dropped from sixteen to twenty hours to only fifty to fifty-five minutes.

The new, smaller, and lighter equipment was also easier to export. By the early 1980s, exports from Italian equipment manufacturers exceeded domestic sales; in 1988, exports represented almost 80 percent of total sales.

Working together, tile manufacturers and equipment manufacturers made the next important breakthrough during the mid and late 1970s: the development of materials-handling equipment that transformed tile manufacture from a batch process to a continuous process. The innovation reduced high labor costs—which had been a substantial selective factor disadvantage facing Italian tile manufacturers.

The common perception is that Italian labor costs were lower during this period than those in the United States and Germany. In those two countries, however, different jobs had widely different wages. In Italy, wages for different skill categories were compressed, and work rules constrained manufacturers from using overtime or multiple shifts. The restriction proved costly: once cool, kilns are expensive to reheat and are best run continuously. Because of this factor disadvantage, the Italian companies were the first to develop continuous, automated production.

Internationalization

By 1970, Italian domestic demand had matured. The stagnant Italian market led companies to step up their efforts to pursue foreign markets. The presence of related and supporting Italian industries helped in the export drive. Individual tile manufacturers began advertising in Italian and foreign home-design and architectural magazines, publications with wide global circulation among architects, designers, and consumers. This heightened awareness reinforced the quality image of Italian tiles. Tile makers were also able to capitalize on Italy's leading world export positions in related industries like marble, building stone, sinks, washbasins, furniture, lamps, and home appliances.

Assopiastrelle, the industry association, established trade-promotion offices in the United States in 1980, in Germany in 1984, and in France in 1987. It organized elaborate trade shows in cities ranging from Bologna to Miami and ran sophisticated advertising. Between 1980 and 1987, the association spent roughly $8 million to promote Italian tiles in the United States.

Michael J. Enright and
Paolo Tenti

Michael J. Enright, a doctoral student in business economics at the Harvard Business School, performed numerous research and supervisory tasks for The Competitive Advantage of Nations. *Paolo Tenti was responsible for the Italian part of research undertaken for the book. He is a consultant in strategy and finance for Monitor Company and Analysis F.A.—Milan.*

FACTOR CONDITIONS

According to standard economic theory, factors of production—labor, land, natural resources, capital, infrastructure—will determine the flow of trade. A nation will export those goods that make most use of the factors with which it is relatively well endowed. This doctrine, whose origins date back to Adam Smith and David Ricardo and that is embedded in classical economics, is at best incomplete and at worst incorrect.

In the sophisticated industries that form the backbone of any advanced economy, a nation does not inherit but instead creates the most important factors of production—such as skilled human resources or a scientific base. Moreover, the stock of factors that a nation enjoys at a particular time is less important than the rate and efficiency with which it creates, upgrades, and deploys them in particular industries.

The most important factors of production are those that involve sustained and heavy investment and are specialized. Basic factors, such as a pool of labor or a local raw-material source, do not constitute an advantage in knowledge-intensive industries. Companies can access them easily through a global strategy or circumvent them through technology. Contrary to conventional wisdom, simply having a general work force that is high school or even college educated represents no competitive advantage in modern international competition. To support competitive advantage, a factor must be highly specialized to an industry's particular needs—a scientific institute specialized in optics, a pool of venture capital to fund software companies. These factors are more scarce, more difficult for foreign competitors to imitate—and they require sustained investment to create.

Nations succeed in industries where they are particularly good at factor creation. Competitive advantage results from the presence of world-class institutions that first create specialized factors and then continually work to upgrade them. Denmark has two hospitals that concentrate in studying and treating diabetes—and a world-leading export position in insulin. Holland has premier research institutes in the cultivation, packaging, and shipping of flowers, where it is the world's export leader.

What is not so obvious, however, is that selective disadvantages in the more basic factors can prod a company to innovate and upgrade—a disadvantage in a static model of competition can become an advantage in a dynamic one. When there is an ample supply of cheap raw materials or abundant labor, companies can simply rest on these advantages and often deploy them inefficiently. But when companies face a selective disadvantage, like high land costs, labor shortages, or the lack of local raw materials, they must innovate and upgrade to compete.

Implicit in the oft-repeated Japanese statement, "We are an island nation with no natural resources,' is the understanding that these deficiencies have only served to spur Japan's competitive innovation. Just-in-time production, for example, economized on prohibitively expensive space. Italian steel producers in the Brescia area faced a similar set of disadvantages: high capital costs, high energy costs, and no local raw materials. Located in Northern Lombardy, these privately owned companies faced staggering logistics costs due to their distance from southern ports and the inefficiencies of the state-owned Italian transportation system. The result: they pioneered technologically advanced minimills that require only modest capital investment, use less energy, employ scrap metal as the feedstock, are efficient at small scale, and permit producers to locate close to sources of scrap and end-use customers. In other words, they converted factor disadvantages into competitive advantage.

Disadvantages can become advantages only under certain conditions. First, they must send companies proper signals about circumstances that will spread to other nations, thereby equipping them to innovate in advance of foreign rivals. Switzerland, the nation that experienced the first labor shortages after World War II, is a case in point. Swiss companies responded to the disadvantage by upgrading labor productivity and seeking higher value, more sustainable market segments. Companies in most other parts of the world, where there were still ample workers, focused their attention on other issues, which resulted in slower upgrading.

The second condition for transforming disadvantages into advantages is favorable circumstances elsewhere in the diamond—a consideration that applies to almost all determinants. To innovate, companies must have access to people with appropriate skills and have home-demand conditions that send the right signals. They must also have active domestic rivals who create pressure to innovate. Another precondition is company goals that lead to sustained commitment to the industry. Without such a commitment and the presence of active rivalry, a company may take an easy way around a disadvantage rather than using it as a spur to innovation.

For example, U.S. consumer-electronics companies, faced with high relative labor costs, chose to leave the product and production process largely unchanged and move labor-intensive activities to Taiwan and other Asian countries. Instead of upgrading their sources of advantage, they settled for labor-cost parity. On the other hand, Japanese rivals, confronted with intense domestic competition and a mature home market, chose to eliminate labor through automation. This led to lower assembly costs, to products with fewer components and to improved quality and reliability. Soon Japanese companies were building assembly plants in the United States—the place U.S. companies had fled.

DEMAND CONDITIONS

It might seem that the globalization of competition would diminish the importance of home demand. In practice, however, this is simply not the case. In fact, the composition and character of the home market usually has a disproportionate effect on how companies perceive, interpret, and respond to buyer needs. Nations gain competitive advantage in industries where the home demand gives their companies a clearer or earlier picture of emerging buyer needs, and where demanding buyers pressure companies to innovate faster and achieve more sophisticated competitive advantages than their foreign rivals. The size of home demand proves far less significant than the character of home demand.

Home-demand conditions help build competitive advantage when a particular industry segment is larger or more visible in the domestic market than in foreign markets. The larger market segments in a nation receive the most attention from the nation's companies; companies accord smaller or less desirable segments a lower priority. A good example is hydraulic excavators, which represent the most widely used type of construction equipment in the Japanese domestic market—but which comprise a far smaller proportion of the market in other advanced nations. This segment is one of the few where there are vigorous Japanese international competitors and where Caterpillar does not hold a substantial share of the world market.

More important than the mix of segments per se is the nature of domestic buyers. A nation's companies gain competitive advantage if domestic buyers are the world's most sophisticated and demanding buyers for the product or service. Sophisticated, demanding buyers provide a window into advanced customer needs; they pressure companies to meet high standards; they prod them to improve, to innovate, and to upgrade into more advanced segments. As with factor conditions, demand conditions provide advantages by forcing companies to respond to tough challenges.

Especially stringent needs arise because of local values and circumstances. For example, Japanese consumers, who live in small, tightly packed homes, must contend with hot, humid summers and high-cost electrical energy—a daunting combination of circumstances. In response, Japanese companies have pioneered compact, quiet air-conditioning units powered by energy-saving rotary compressors. In industry after industry, the tightly constrained requirements of the Japanese market have forced companies to innovate, yielding products that are *kei-haku-tan-sho*—light, thin, short, small—and that are internationally accepted.

Local buyers can help a nation's companies gain advantage if their needs anticipate or even shape those of other nations—if their needs provide ongoing "early-warning indicators" of global market trends. Sometimes anticipatory needs emerge because a nation's political values foreshadow needs that will grow elsewhere. Sweden's long-standing concern for handicapped people has spawned an increasingly competitive industry focused on special needs. Denmark's environmentalism has led to success for companies in water-pollution control equipment and windmills.

More generally, a nation's companies can anticipate global trends if the nation's values are spreading—that is, if the country is exporting its values and tastes as well as its products. The international success of U.S. companies in fast food and credit cards, for example, reflects not only the American desire for convenience but also the spread of these tastes to the rest of the world. Nations export their values and tastes through media, through training foreigners, through political influence, and through the foreign activities of their citizens and companies.

RELATED AND SUPPORTING INDUSTRIES

The third broad determinant of national advantage is the presence in the nation of related and supporting industries that are internationally competitive. Internationally competitive home-based suppliers create advantages in downstream industries in several ways. First, they deliver the most cost-effective inputs in an efficient, early, rapid, and sometimes preferential way. Italian gold and silver jewelry companies lead the world in that industry in part because other Italian companies supply two-thirds of the world's jewelry-making and precious-metal recycling machinery.

Far more significant than mere access to components and machinery, however, is the advantage that home-based related and supporting industries provide in innovation and upgrading—an advantage based on close working relationships. Suppliers and end-users located near each other can take advantage of short lines of communication, quick and constant flow of information, and an ongoing exchange of ideas and innovations. Companies have the opportunity to influence their suppliers' technical efforts and can serve as test sites for R&D work, accelerating the pace of innovation.

Figure 6.2, "The Italian Footwear Cluster," offers a graphic example of how a group of close-by, supporting industries creates competitive advantage in a range of interconnected industries that are all internationally competitive. Shoe producers, for instance, interact regularly with leather manufacturers on new styles and manufacturing techniques and learn about new textures and colors of leather when they are still on the drawing boards. Leather manufacturers gain early insights into fashion trends, helping them to plan new products. The interaction is mutually advantageous and self-reinforcing, but it does not happen automatically: it is helped by proximity, but occurs only because companies and suppliers work at it.

The nation's companies benefit most when the suppliers are, themselves, global competitors. It is ultimately self-defeating for a company or country to create "captive" suppliers who are totally dependent on

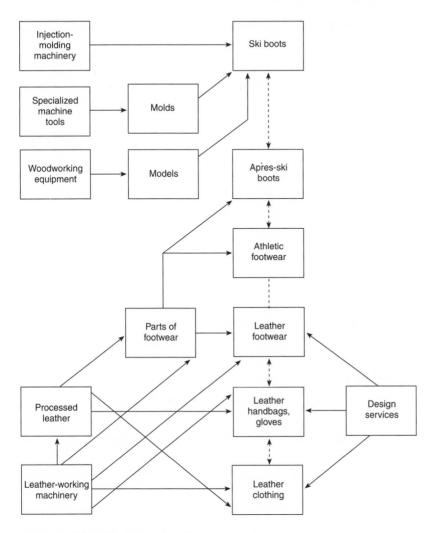

Figure 6.2   The Italian Footwear Cluster

the domestic industry and prevented from serving foreign competitors. By the same token, a nation need not be competitive in all supplier industries for its companies to gain competitive advantage. Companies can readily source from abroad materials, components, or technologies without a major effect on innovation or performance of the industry's products. The same is true of other generalized technologies—like electronics or software—where the industry represents a narrow application area.

Home-based competitiveness in related industries provides similar benefits: information flow and technical interchange speed the rate of innovation and upgrading. A home-based related industry also increases the likelihood that companies will embrace new skills, and it also provides a source of entrants who will bring a novel approach to competing. The Swiss success in pharmaceuticals emerged out of previous international success in the dye industry, for example; Japanese dominance in electronic musical keyboards grows out of success in acoustic instruments combined with a strong position in consumer electronics.

FIRM STRATEGY, STRUCTURE, AND RIVALRY

National circumstances and context create strong tendencies in how companies are created, organized, and managed, as well as what the nature of domestic rivalry will be. In Italy, for example, successful international competitors are often small or medium-sized companies that are privately owned and operated like extended families; in Germany, in contrast, companies tend to be strictly hierarchical in organization and management practices, and top managers usually have technical backgrounds.

No one managerial system is universally appropriate—notwithstanding the current fascination with Japanese management. Competitiveness in a specific industry results from convergence of the management practices and organizational modes favored in the country and the sources of competitive advantage in the industry. In industries where Italian companies are world leaders—such as lighting, furniture, footwear, woolen fabrics, and packaging machines—a company strategy that emphasizes focus, customized products, niche marketing, rapid change, and breathtaking flexibility fits both the dynamics of the industry and the character of the Italian management system. The German management system, in contrast, works well in technical or engineering-oriented industries—optics, chemicals, complicated machinery—where complex products demand precision manufacturing, a careful development process, after-sale service, and thus a highly disciplined management structure. German success is much rarer in consumer goods and services where image marketing and rapid new-feature and model turn-over are important to competition.

Countries also differ markedly in the goals that companies and individuals seek to achieve. Company goals reflect the characteristics of national capital markets and the compensation practices for managers. For example, in Germany and Switzerland, where banks comprise a substantial part of the nation's shareholders, most shares are held for long-term appreciation and are rarely traded. Companies do well in mature industries, where ongoing investment in R&D and new facilities is essential but returns may be only moderate. The United States is at the opposite extreme, with a large pool of risk capital but widespread trading of public companies and a strong emphasis by investors on quarterly and annual share-price appreciation. Management compensation is heavily based on annual bonuses tied to individual results. America does well in relatively new industries, like software and bio-technology, or ones where equity funding of new companies feeds active domestic rivalry, like specialty electronics and services. Strong pressures leading to underinvestment, however, plague more mature industries.

Individual motivation to work and expand skills is also important to competitive advantage. Outstanding talent is a scarce resource in any nation. A nation's success largely depends on the types of education its talented people choose, where they choose to work, and their commitment and effort. The goals a nation's institutions and values set for individuals and companies, and the prestige it attaches to certain industries, guide the flow of capital and human resources—which, in turn, directly affects the competitive performance of certain industries. Nations tend to be competitive in activities that people admire or depend on—the activities from which the nation's heroes emerge. In Switzerland, it is banking and pharmaceuticals. In Israel, the highest callings have been agriculture and defense-related fields. Sometimes it is hard to distinguish between cause and effect. Attaining international success can make an industry prestigious, reinforcing its advantage.

The presence of strong local rivals is a final, and powerful, stimulus to the creation and persistence of competitive advantage. This is true of small countries, like Switzerland, where the rivalry among its pharmaceutical companies, Hoffmann-La Roche, Ciba-Geigy, and Sandoz, contributes to a leading worldwide position. It is true in the United States in the computer and software industries. Nowhere is the role of fierce rivalry more apparent than in Japan, where there are 112 companies competing in machine tools, thirty-four in semiconductors, twenty-five in audio equipment, fifteen in cameras—in fact, there are usually double figures in the industries in which Japan boasts global dominance. (See Table 6.1.) Among all the points on the diamond, domestic rivalry is

Table 6.1   Estimated Number of Japanese Rivals in Selected Industries

Air conditioners	13
Audio Equipment	25
Automobiles	9
Cameras	15
Car Audio	12
Carbon Fibers	7
Construction Equipment*	15
Copiers	14
Facsimile Machines	10
Large-scale Computers	6
Lift Trucks	8
Machine Tools	112
Microwave Equipment	5
Motorcycles	4
Musical Instruments	4
Personal Computers	16
Semiconductors	34
Sewing Machines	20
Shipbuilding†	33
Steel‡	5
Synthetic Fibers	8
Television Sets	15
Truck and Bus Tires	5
Trucks	11
Typewriters	14
Videocassette Recorders	10

Sources: Field interviews; *Nippon Kogyo Shinbun, Nippon Kogyo Nenkan,* 1987; Yano Research, *Market Share Jitan,* 1987; researchers' estimates.
*The number of companies varied by product area. The smallest number, ten, produced bulldozers. Fifteen companies produced shovel trucks, truck cranes, and asphalt-paving equipment. There were twenty companies in hydraulic excavators, a product area where Japan was particularly strong.
†Six companies had annual production exports in excess of 10,000 tons.
‡Integrated companies.

arguably the most important because of the powerfully stimulating effect it has on all the others.

Conventional wisdom argues that domestic competition is wasteful: it leads to duplication of effort and prevents companies from achieving economies of scale. The "right solution" is to embrace one or two national champions, companies with the scale and strength to tackle foreign competitors, and to guarantee them the necessary resources, with the government's blessing. In fact, however, most national champions are uncompetitive, although heavily subsidized and protected by their government. In many of the prominent industries in which there is only one national rival, such as aerospace and telecommunications, government has played a large role in distorting competition.

Static efficiency is much less important than dynamic improvement, which domestic rivalry uniquely spurs. Domestic rivalry, like any rivalry, creates pressure on companies to innovate and im-prove. Local rivals push each other to lower costs, improve quality and service, and create new products and processes. But unlike rivalries with foreign competitors, which tend to be analytical and distant, local rivalries often go beyond pure economic or business competition and become intensely personal Domestic rivals engage in active feuds; they compete not only for market share but also for people, for technical excellence, and perhaps most important, for "bragging rights." One domestic rival's success proves to others that advancement is possible and often attracts new rivals to the industry. Companies often attribute the success of foreign rivals to "unfair" advantages. With domestic rivals, there are no excuses.

Geographic concentration magnifies the power of domestic rivalry. This pattern is strikingly common around the world: Italian jewelry companies are located around two towns, Arezzo and Valenza Po; cutlery companies in Solingen, West Germany and Seki, Japan; pharmaceutical companies in Basel, Switzerland; motorcycles and musical instruments in Hamamatsu, Japan. The more localized the rivalry, the more intense. And the more intense, the better.

Another benefit of domestic rivalry is the pressure it creates for constant upgrading of the sources of competitive advantage. The presence of domestic competitors automatically cancels the types of advantage that come from simply being in a particular nation—factor costs, access to or preference in the home market, or costs to foreign competitors who import into the market. Companies are forced to move beyond them, and as a result, gain more sustainable advantages. Moreover, competing domestic tons. rivals will keep each other honest in obtaining government support. Companies are less likely to get hooked on the narcotic of government contracts or creeping industry protectionism. Instead, the industry will seek—and benefit from—more constructive forms of government support, such as assistance in opening foreign markets, as well as investments in focused educational institutions or other specialized factors.

Ironically, it is also vigorous domestic competition that ultimately pressures domestic companies to look at global markets and toughens them to succeed in them. Particularly when there are economies of scale, local competitors force each other to look out-ward to foreign markets to capture greater efficiency and higher profitability. And having been tested by fierce domestic competition, the stronger companies are well equipped to win abroad. If Digital Equipment can hold its own against IBM, Data General, Prime, and Hewlett-Packard, going up against Siemens or Machines Bull does not seem so daunting a prospect.

The Diamond as a System

Each of these four attributes defines a point on the diamond of national advantage; the effect of one point often depends on the state of others. Sophisticated buyers will not translate into advanced products, for example, unless the quality of human resources permits companies to meet buyer needs. Selective disadvantages in factors of production will not motivate innovation unless rivalry is vigorous and company goals support sustained investment. At the broadest level, weaknesses in any one determinant will constrain an industry's potential for advancement and upgrading.

But the points of the diamond are also self-reinforcing: they constitute a system. Two elements, domestic rivalry and geographic concentration, have especially great power to transform the diamond into a system— domestic rivalry because it promotes improvement in all the other determinants and geographic concentration because it elevates and magnifies the interaction of the four separate influences.

The role of domestic rivalry illustrates how the diamond operates as a self-reinforcing system. Vigorous domestic rivalry stimulates the development of unique pools of specialized factors, particularly if the rivals are all located in one city or region: the University of California at Davis has become the world's leading center of wine-making research, working closely with the California wine industry. Active local rivals also upgrade domestic demand in an industry. In furniture and shoes, for example, Italian consumers have learned to expect more and better products because of the rapid pace of new product development that is driven by intense domestic rivalry among hundreds of Italian companies. Domestic rivalry also promotes the formation of related and supporting industries. Japan's world-leading group of semiconductor producers, for instance, has spawned world-leading Japanese semiconductor-equipment manufacturers.

The effects can work in all directions: sometimes world-class suppliers become new entrants in the industry they have been supplying. Or highly sophisticated buyers may themselves enter a supplier industry, particularly when they have relevant skills and view the new industry as strategic. In the case of the Japanese robotics industry, for example, Matsushita and Kawasaki originally designed robots for internal use before beginning to sell robots to others. Today they are strong competitors in the robotics industry. In Sweden, Sandvik moved from specialty steel into rock drills, and SKF moved from specialty steel into ball bearings.

Another effect of the diamond's systemic nature is that nations are rarely home to just one competitive industry; rather, the diamond creates an environment that promotes clusters of competitive industries. Competitive industries are not scattered helter-skelter throughout the economy but are usually linked together through vertical (buyer-seller) or horizontal (common customers, technology, channels) relationships. Nor are clusters usually scattered physically; they tend to be concentrated geographically. One competitive industry helps to create another in a mutually reinforcing process. Japan's strength in consumer electronics, for example, drove its success in semiconductors toward the memory chips and integrated circuits these products use. Japanese strength in laptop computers, which contrasts to limited success in other segments, reflects the base of strength in other compact, portable products and leading expertise in liquid-crystal display gained in the calculator and watch industries.

Once a cluster forms, the whole group of industries becomes mutually supporting. Benefits flow forward, backward, and horizontally. Aggressive rivalry in one industry spreads to others in the cluster, through spin-offs, through the exercise of bargaining power, and through diversification by established companies. Entry from other industries within the cluster spurs upgrading by stimulating diversity in R&D approaches and facilitating the introduction of new strategies and skills. Through the conduits of suppliers or customers who have contact with multiple competitors, information flows freely and innovations diffuse rapidly. Interconnections within the cluster, often unanticipated, lead to perceptions of new ways of competing and new opportunities. The cluster becomes a vehicle for maintaining diversity and overcoming the inward focus, inertia, inflexibility, and accommodation among rivals that slows or blocks competitive upgrading and new entry.

The Role of Government

In the continuing debate over the competitiveness of nations, no topic engenders more argument or creates less understanding than the role of the government. Many see government as an essential helper or supporter of industry, employing a host of policies to contribute directly to the competitive performance of strategic or target industries. Others accept the "free market" view that the operation of the economy should be left to the workings of the invisible hand.

Both views are incorrect. Either, followed to its logical outcome, would lead to the permanent erosion of a country's competitive capabilities. On one hand, advocates of government help for industry frequently propose policies that would actually hurt companies in the long run and only create the demand for more helping. On the other hand, advocates of a diminished government presence ignore the legitimate role that government plays in shaping the context and institutional structure surrounding companies and in creating an environment that stimulates companies to gain competitive advantage.

Government's proper role is as a catalyst and challenger; it is to encourage—or even push—companies to raise their aspirations and move to higher levels of competitive performance, even though this process may be inherently unpleasant and difficult. Government cannot create competitive industries; only companies can do that. Government plays a role that is inherently partial, that succeeds only when working in tandem with favorable underlying conditions in the diamond. Still, government's role of transmitting and amplifying the forces of the diamond is a powerful one. Government policies that succeed are those that create an environment in which companies can gain competitive advantage rather than those that involve government directly in the process, except in nations early in the development process. It is an indirect, rather than a direct, role.

Japan's government, at its best, understands this role better than anyone—including the point that nations pass through stages of competitive development and that government's appropriate role shifts as the economy progresses. By stimulating early demand for advanced products, confronting industries with the need to pioneer frontier technology through symbolic cooperative projects, establishing prizes that reward quality, and pursuing other policies that magnify the forces of the diamond, the Japanese government accelerates the pace of innovation. But like government officials anywhere, at their worst Japanese bureaucrats can make the same mistakes: attempting to manage industry structure, protecting the market too long, and yielding to political pressure to insulate inefficient retailers, farmers, distributors, and industrial companies from competition.

It is not hard to understand why so many governments make the same mistakes so often in pursuit of national competitiveness: competitive time for companies and political time for governments are fundamentally at odds. It often takes more than a decade for an industry to create competitive advantage; the process entails the long upgrading of human skills, investing in products and processes, building clusters, and penetrating foreign markets. In the case of the Japanese auto industry, for instance, companies made their first faltering steps toward exporting in the 1950s—yet did not achieve strong international positions until the 1970s.

But in politics, a decade is an eternity. Consequently, most governments favor policies that offer easily perceived short-term benefits, such as subsidies, protection, and arranged mergers—the very policies that retard innovation. Most of the policies that would make a real difference either are too slow and require too much patience for politicians or, even worse, carry with them the sting of short-term pain. Deregulating a protected industry, for example, will lead to bankruptcies sooner and to stronger, more competitive companies only later.

Policies that convey static, short-term cost advantages but that unconsciously undermine innovation and dynamism represent the most common and most profound error in government industrial policy. In a desire to help, it is all too easy for governments to adopt policies such as joint projects to avoid "wasteful" R&D that undermine dynamism and competition. Yet even a 10 percent cost saving through economies of scale is easily nullified through rapid product and process improvement and the pursuit of volume in global markets—something that such policies undermine.

There are some simple, basic principles that governments should embrace to play the proper supportive role for national competitiveness: encourage change, promote domestic rivalry, stimulate innovation. Some of the specific policy approaches to guide nations seeking to gain competitive advantage include the following.

FOCUS ON SPECIALIZED FACTOR CREATION

Government has critical responsibilities for fundamentals like the primary and secondary education systems, basic national infrastructure, and research in areas of broad national concern such as health care. Yet these kinds of generalized efforts at factor creation rarely produce competitive advantage. Rather, the factors that translate into competitive advantage are advanced, specialized, and tied to specific industries or industry groups. Mechanisms such as specialized apprenticeship programs, research efforts in universities connected with an industry, trade association activities, and, most important, the private investments of companies ultimately create the factors that will yield competitive advantage.

AVOID INTERVENING IN FACTOR AND CURRENCY MARKETS

By intervening in factor and currency markets, governments hope to create lower factor costs or a favorable exchange rate that will help companies compete more effectively in international markets. Evidence from around the world indicates that these policies—such as the Reagan administration's dollar devaluation—are often counterproductive. They work against the upgrading of industry and the search for more sustainable competitive advantage.

The contrasting case of Japan is particularly instructive, although both Germany and Switzerland have had similar experiences. Over the past twenty years, the Japanese have been rocked by the sudden Nixon currency devaluation shock, two oil shocks, and, most recently, the yen shock—all of which forced Japanese companies to upgrade their competitive advantages. The point is not that government should pursue policies that intentionally drive up factor costs or the exchange rate. Rather, when market forces create rising factor costs or a higher exchange rate, government should resist the temptation to push them back down.

ENFORCE STRICT PRODUCT, SAFETY, AND ENVIRONMENTAL STANDARDS

Strict government regulations can promote competitive advantage by stimulating and upgrading domestic demand. Stringent standards for product performance, product safety, and environmental impact pressure companies to improve quality, upgrade technology, and provide features that respond to consumer and social demands. Easing standards, however tempting, is counterproductive.

When tough regulations anticipate standards that will spread internationally, they give a nation's companies a head start in developing products and services that will be valuable elsewhere. Sweden's strict standards for environmental protection have promoted competitive advantage in many industries. Atlas Copco, for example, produces quiet compressors that can be used in dense urban areas with minimal disruption to residents. Strict standards, however, must be combined with a rapid and streamlined regulatory process that does not absorb resources and cause delays.

SHARPLY LIMIT DIRECT COOPERATION AMONG INDUSTRY RIVALS

The most pervasive global policy fad in the competitiveness arena today is the call for more cooperative research and industry consortia. Operating on the belief that independent research by rivals is wasteful and duplicative, that collaborative efforts achieve economies of scale, and that individual companies are likely to underinvest in R&D because they cannot reap all the benefits, governments have embraced the idea of more direct cooperation. In the United States, antitrust laws have been modified to allow more cooperative R&D; in Europe, megaprojects such as ESPRIT, an information-technology project, bring together companies from several countries. Lurking behind much of this thinking is the fascination of Western governments with—and fundamental misunderstanding of—the countless cooperative research projects sponsored by the Ministry of International Trade and Industry (MITI), projects that appear to have contributed to Japan's competitive rise.

But a closer look at Japanese cooperative projects suggests a different story. Japanese companies participate in MITI projects to maintain good relations with MITI, to preserve their corporate images, and to hedge the risk that competitors will gain from the project—largely defensive reasons. Companies rarely contribute their best scientists and engineers to cooperative projects and usually spend much more on their own private research in the same field. Typically, the government makes only a modest financial contribution to the project.

The real value of Japanese cooperative research is to signal the importance of emerging technical areas and to stimulate proprietary company research. Cooperative projects prompt companies to explore new fields and boost internal R&D spending because companies know that their domestic rivals are investigating them.

Under certain limited conditions, cooperative research can prove beneficial. Projects should be in areas of basic product and process research, not in subjects closely connected to a company's proprietary sources of advantage. They should constitute only a modest portion of a company's overall research program in any given field. Cooperative research should be only indirect, channeled through independent organizations to which most industry participants have access. Organizational structures, like university labs and centers of excellence, reduce management problems and minimize the risk to rivalry. Finally, the most useful cooperative projects often involve fields that touch a number of industries and that require substantial R&D investments.

PROMOTE GOALS THAT LEAD TO SUSTAINED INVESTMENT

Government has a vital role in shaping the goals of investors, managers, and employees through policies in various areas. The manner in which capital markets are regulated, for example, shapes the incentives of investors and, in turn, the behavior of companies. Government should aim to encourage sustained investment in human skills, in innovation, and in physical assets. Perhaps the single most powerful tool for raising the rate of sustained investment in industry is a tax incentive for long-term(five years or more) capital gains restricted to new investment in corporate equity. Long-term capital gains incentives should also be applied to pension funds and other currently untaxed investors, who now have few reasons not to engage in rapid trading.

DEREGULATE COMPETITION

Regulation of competition through such policies as maintaining a state monopoly, controlling entry into an industry, or fixing prices has two strong negative consequences: it stifles rivalry and innovation as companies become preoccupied with dealing with regulators and protecting what they already have; and it makes the industry a less dynamic and less desirable buyer or supplier. Deregulation and privatization on their own, however, will not succeed without vigorous domestic rivalry—and that requires, as a corollary, a strong and consistent antitrust policy.

ENFORCE STRONG DOMESTIC ANTITRUST POLICIES

A strong antitrust policy—especially for horizontal mergers, alliances, and collusive behavior—is fundamental to innovation. While it is fashionable today to call for mergers and alliances in the name of globalization and the creation of national champions, these often undermine the creation of competitive advantage. Real national competitiveness requires governments to disallow mergers, acquisitions, and alliances that involve industry leaders. Furthermore, the same standards for mergers and alliances should apply to both domestic and foreign companies. Finally, government policy should favor internal entry, both domestic and international, over acquisition. Companies should, however, be allowed to acquire small companies in related industries when the move promotes the transfer of skills that could ultimately create competitive advantage.

REJECT MANAGED TRADE

Managed trade represents a growing and dangerous tendency for dealing with the fallout of national competitiveness. Orderly marketing agreements, voluntary restraint agreements, or other devices that set quantitative targets to divide up markets are dangerous, ineffective, and often enormously costly to consumers. Rather than promoting innovation in a nation's industries, managed trade guarantees a market for inefficient companies.

Government trade policy should pursue open market access in every foreign nation. To be effective, trade policy should not be a passive instrument; it cannot respond only to complaints or work only for those industries that can muster enough political clout; it should not require a long history of injury or serve only distressed industries. Trade policy should seek to open markets wherever a nation has competitive advantage and should actively address emerging industries and incipient problems.

Where government finds a trade barrier in another nation, it should concentrate its remedies on dismantling barriers, not on regulating imports or exports. In the case of Japan, for example, pressure to accelerate the already rapid growth of manufactured imports is a more effective approach than a shift to managed trade. Compensatory tariffs that punish companies for unfair trade practices are better than market quotas. Other increasingly important tools to open markets are restrictions that prevent companies in offending nations from investing in acquisitions or production facilities in the host country—thereby blocking the unfair country's companies from using their advantage to establish a new beachhead that is immune from sanctions.

Any of these remedies, however, can backfire. It is virtually impossible to craft remedies to unfair trade practices that avoid both reducing incentives for domestic companies to innovate and export and harming domestic buyers. The aim of remedies should be adjustments that allow the remedy to disappear.

The Company Agenda

Ultimately, only companies themselves can achieve and sustain competitive advantage. To do so, they must act on the fundamentals described above. In particular, they must recognize the central role of innovation— and the uncomfortable truth that innovation grows out of pressure and challenge. It takes leadership to create a dynamic, challenging environment. And it takes leadership to recognize the all-too-easy escape routes that appear to offer a path to competitive advantage, but are actually short-cuts to failure. For example, it is tempting to rely on cooperative research and development projects to lower the cost and risk of research. But they can divert company attention and resources from proprietary research efforts and will all but eliminate the prospects for real innovation.

Competitive advantage arises from leadership that harnesses and amplifies the forces in the diamond to promote innovation and upgrading. Here are just a few of the kinds of company policies that will support that effort:

CREATE PRESSURES FOR INNOVATION

A company should seek out pressure and challenge, not avoid them. Part of strategy is to take advantage of the home nation to create the impetus for innovation. To do that, companies can sell to the most sophisticated and demanding buyers and channels; seek out those buyers with the most difficult needs; establish norms that exceed the toughest regulatory hurdles or product standards; source from the most advanced suppliers; treat employees as permanent in order to stimulate upgrading of skills and productivity.

SEEK OUT THE MOST CAPABLE COMPETITORS AS MOTIVATORS

To motivate organizational change, capable competitors and respected rivals can be a common enemy. The best managers always run a little scared; they respect and study competitors. To stay dynamic, companies must make meeting challenge a part of the organization's norms. For example, lobbying against strict product standards signals the organization that company leadership has diminished aspirations. Companies that value stability, obedient customers, dependent suppliers, and sleepy competi tors are inviting inertia and, ultimately, failure.

ESTABLISH EARLY-WARNING SYSTEMS

Early-warning signals translate into early-mover advantages. Companies can take actions that help them see the signals of change and act on them, thereby getting a jump on the competition. For example, they can find and serve those buyers with the most anticipatory needs; investigate all emerging new buyers or channels; find places whose regulations foreshadow emerging regulations elsewhere; bring some outsiders into the management team; maintain ongoing relationships with research centers and sources of talented people.

IMPROVE THE NATIONAL DIAMOND

Companies have a vital stake in making their home environment a better platform for international success. Part of a company's responsibility is to play an active role in forming clusters and to work with its home-nation buyers, suppliers, and channels to help them upgrade and extend their own competitive advantages. To upgrade home demand, for example, Japanese musical instrument manufacturers, led by Yamaha, Kawai, and Suzuki, have established music schools. Similarly, companies can stimulate and support local suppliers of important specialized inputs—including encouraging them to compete globally. The health and strength of the national cluster will only enhance the company's own rate of innovation and upgrading.

In nearly every successful competitive industry, leading companies also take explicit steps to create specialized factors like human resources, scientific knowledge, or infrastructure. In industries like wool cloth, ceramic tiles, and lighting equipment, Italian industry associations invest in market information, process technology, and common infrastructure. Companies can also speed innovation by putting their headquarters and other key operations where there are concentrations of sophisticated buyers, important suppliers, or specialized factor-creating mechanisms, such as universities or laboratories.

WELCOME DOMESTIC RIVALRY

To compete globally, a company needs capable domestic rivals and vigorous domestic rivalry. Especially in the United States and Europe today, managers are wont to complain about excessive competition and to argue for mergers and acquisitions that will produce hoped-for economies of scale and critical mass. The complaint is only natural—but the argument is plain wrong. Vigorous domestic rivalry creates sustainable competitive advantage. Moreover, it is better to grow internationally than to dominate the domestic market. If a company wants an acquisition, a foreign one that can speed globalization and supplement home-based advantages or offset home-based disadvantages is usually far better than merging with leading domestic competitors.

GLOBALIZE TO TAP SELECTIVE ADVANTAGES IN OTHER NATIONS

In search of "global" strategies, many companies today abandon their home diamond. To be sure, adopting a global perspective is important to creating competitive advantage. But relying on foreign activities that supplant domestic capabilities is always a second-best solution. Innovating to offset local factor disadvantages is better than outsourcing; developing domestic suppliers and buyers is better than relying solely on foreign ones. Unless the critical underpinnings of competitiveness are present at home, companies will not sustain competitive advantage in the long run. The aim should be to upgrade home-base capabilities so that foreign activities are selective and supplemental only to over-all competitive advantage.

The correct approach to globalization is to tap selectively into sources of advantage in other nations' diamonds. For example, identifying sophisticated buyers in other countries helps companies understand different needs and creates pressures that will stimulate a faster rate of innovation. No matter how favorable the home diamond, moreover, important research is going on in other nations. To take advantage of foreign research, companies must station high-quality people in overseas bases and mount a credible level of scientific effort. To get anything back from foreign research ventures, companies must also allow access to their own ideas—recognizing that competitive advantage comes from continuous improvement, not from protecting today's secrets.

USE ALLIANCES ONLY SELECTIVELY

Alliances with foreign companies have become another managerial fad and cure-all: they represent a tempting solution to the problem of a company wanting the advantages of foreign enterprises or hedging against risk, without giving up independence. In reality, however, while alliances can achieve selective benefits, they always exact significant costs: they involve coordinating two separate operations, reconciling goals with an independent entity, creating a competitor, and giving up profits. These costs ultimately make most alliances short-term transitional devices, rather than stable, long-term relationships.

Most important, alliances as a broad-based strategy will only ensure a company's mediocrity, not its international leadership. No company can rely on another outside, independent company for skills and assets that are central to its competitive advantage. Alliances are best used as a selective tool, employed on a temporary basis or involving noncore activities.

LOCATE THE HOME BASE TO SUPPORT COMPETITIVE ADVANTAGE

Among the most important decisions for multinational companies is the nation in which to locate the home base for each distinct business. A company can have different home bases for distinct businesses or segments. Ultimately, competitive advantage is created at home: it is where strategy is set, the core product and process technology is created, and a critical mass of production takes place. The circumstances in the home nation must support innovation; otherwise the company has no choice but to move its home base to a country that stimulates innovation and that provides the best environment for global competitiveness. There are no half measures: the management team must move as well.

The Role of Leadership

Too many companies and top managers misperceive the nature of competition and the task before them by focusing on improving financial performance, soliciting government assistance, seeking stability, and reducing risk through alliances and mergers.

Today's competitive realities demand leadership. Leaders believe in change; they energize their organizations to innovate continuously; they recognize the importance of their home country as integral to their competitive success and work to upgrade it. Most important, leaders recognize the need for pressure and challenge. Because they are willing to encourage appropriate—and painful—government policies and regulations, they often earn the title "statesmen," although few see themselves that way. They are prepared to sacrifice the easy life for difficulty and, ultimately, sustained competitive advantage. That must be the goal, for both nations and companies: not just surviving, but achieving international competitiveness.

And not just once, but continuously.

CHAPTER 7

Clusters and Competition

New Agendas for
Companies, Governments,
and Institutions

Michael E. Porter

THINKING ABOUT COMPETITION and strategy at the company level has been dominated by what goes on inside companies. Thinking about the competitiveness of nations and states has focused on the economy as a whole, with national economic policy seen as the dominant influence. In both competition and competitiveness the role of location is all but absent. If anything, the tendency has been to see location as diminishing in importance.[1] Globalization allows companies to source capital, goods, and technology from anywhere and to locate operations wherever it is most cost effective. Governments are widely seen as losing their influence over competition to global forces.

This perspective, although widespread, does not accord with competitive reality. In *The Competitive Advantage of Nations* (1990), I put forward a theory of national, state, and local competitiveness within the context of a global economy. This theory gives clusters a prominent role. Clusters are geographic concentrations of interconnected companies, specialized suppliers, service providers, firms in related industries, and associated institutions (for example, universities, standards agencies, and trade associations) in particular fields that compete but also

This article has benefited from extensive research by Veronica H. Ingham and from research assistance by John Kelleher and Raymond Fisman. I am also grateful for comments by Joseph Babiec, Gregory Bond, Michael Fairbanks, Ifor Ffowcs-Williams, Anne Habiby, Bennett Harrison, David L. Kang, Lucia Marshall, Ian Smith, Claas van der Linde, and Marjorie Williams.

cooperate. Critical masses of unusual competitive success in particular business areas, clusters are a striking feature of virtually every national, regional, state, and even metropolitan economy, especially those of more economically advanced nations.

While the phenomenon of clusters in one form or another has been recognized and explored in a range of literatures, clusters cannot be understood independently of a broader theory of competition and the influence of location in the global economy. (See the insert "Historical and Intellectual Antecedents of Cluster Theory.") The prevalence of clusters in economies, rather than isolated firms and industries, reveals important insights into the nature of competition and the role of location in competitive advantage. Even though old reasons for clustering have diminished in importance with globalization, new roles of clusters in competition have taken on growing importance in an increasingly complex, knowledge-based, and dynamic economy.

The cluster concept represents a new way of thinking about national, state, and city economies, and points to new roles for companies, governments, and other institutions striving to enhance competitiveness. The presence of clusters suggests that much of competitive advantage lies outside a given company or even outside its industry, residing instead in the *locations* of its business units. The odds of building a world-class mutual fund company are much higher in Boston than in most any other location; a similar statement applies to textile-related companies in North and South Carolina, high performance auto companies in southern Germany, or fashion shoe companies in Italy.

The importance of clusters creates new management agendas that are rarely recognized. Companies have a tangible stake in the business environments where they are located in ways that go far beyond taxes, electricity costs, and wage rates. The health of the cluster is important to the health of the company. A company may actually benefit from the presence of local competitors. Trade associations can be competitive assets, as well as lobbying and social organizations.

Clusters also create new roles for government. The proper macroeconomic policies for fostering competitiveness are increasingly well understood but they are necessary and not sufficient. Government's more decisive influences are often at the microeconomic level. Removing obstacles to the growth and upgrading of existing and emerging clusters should be a priority. Clusters are a driving force in increasing exports and magnets for attracting foreign investment. They constitute a forum in which new types of dialogue can, and must, take place among firms, government agencies, and institutions (such as schools, universities, and public utilities).

Knowledge about cluster theory has advanced and continues to spread since publication of *The Competitive Advantage of Nations*, which triggered an ever growing number of formal cluster initiatives at the city, state, country, and even regional level (as in Central America, for example). In this essay, I will assess the current state of knowledge about clusters, their role in competition, and their implications. I will describe the theory of clusters, the process by which they grow and decline, the appropriate roles of the private sector, government, and other institutions in cluster upgrading, and some of the implications clusters hold for company strategy. Finally, I will draw on my participation in many cluster studies and initiatives and on other literature to explore the best ways to organize such initiatives to catalyze positive economic improvement. (An extensive bibliography on clusters and cluster initiatives appears at the end of this chapter.)

What Is a Cluster?

A cluster is a geographically proximate group of interconnected companies and associated institutions in a particular field, linked by commonalities and complementarities. The geographic scope of a cluster can range from a single city or state to a country or even a network of neighboring countries.[2] Clusters take varying forms depending on their depth and sophistication, but most include end-product or service companies; suppliers of specialized inputs, components, machinery, and services; financial institutions; and firms in related industries. Clusters also often include firms in downstream industries (that is, channels or customers); producers of complementary products; specialized infrastructure providers; government and other institutions providing specialized training, education, information, research, and technical support (such as universities, think tanks, vocational training providers); and standards-setting agencies. Government agencies that significantly influence a cluster can be considered part of it. Finally, many clusters include trade associations and other collective private sector bodies that support cluster members. (See the insert "Historical and Intellectual Antecedents of Cluster Theory.")

Identifying the constituent parts of a cluster involves starting with a large firm or concentration of like firms and then looking upstream and downstream in the vertical chain of firms and institutions. The next step is to look horizontally to identify industries that pass through common channels or that produce complementary products and services. Additional horizontal chains of industries are identified based on the use of similar specialized inputs or technologies or with other supply-side linkages. The next step after identification of a cluster's industries and firms involves isolating the institutions that provide it with specialized skills, technology, information, capital, or infrastructure and any collective bodies covering cluster participants. The final step is to seek out government or other regulatory bodies that significantly influence participants in the cluster.

Figures 7.1 and 7.2 present schematic diagrams of the Italian leather footwear and fashion cluster and the California wine cluster. While

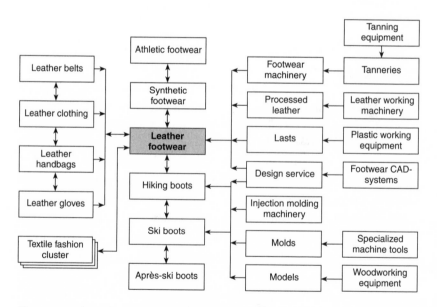

Figure 7.1   The Italian Footwear and Fashion Cluster
Source: Research by Claas van der Linde, 1993.

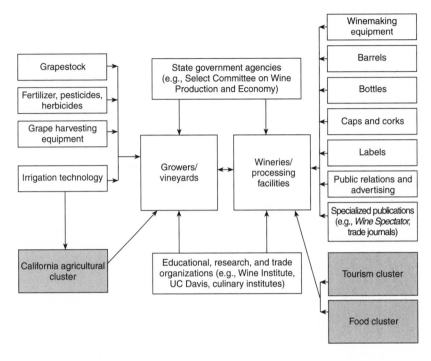

Figure 7.2   The California Wine Cluster
Sources: Based on research by Harvard MBA students R. Alexander, R. Arney,
N. Black, E. Frost, and A. Shivananda.

neither diagram can include all the entities comprising the respective clusters, each illustrates important cluster attributes. Figure 7.1, for example, demonstrates the several chains of related industries involved in the Italian leather footwear and fashion cluster, including those relating to different types of leather goods (complementary products, common, common inputs, similar technologies), different types of footwear (overlapping channels, similar inputs, and technologies), and different types of fashion goods (complementary products). These industries also employ common marketing media and compete with similar images in similar customer segments. The extraordinary strength of the Italian cluster can be attributed, at least in part, to the multiple cross-firm linkages and synergies that Italian firms enjoy.

The California wine cluster includes an extensive complement of supporting industries to both winemaking and grape growing. On the

growing side, there are strong connections to the larger California agricultural cluster. On the winemaking side, the cluster enjoys strong
links to both the California restaurant and food preparation industries
(complementary products) and the tourism cluster in Napa and other
wine-producing regions of the state. Figure 7.2 also illustrates the host of
local institutions involved with wine, for example, the world-renowned
viticulture and enology program at the University of California at Davis
and special committees of the California senate and assembly.

Drawing cluster boundaries is often a matter of degree, and involves a
creative process informed by understanding the most important linkages
and complementarities across industries and institutions to competition. The strength of these "spillovers" and their importance to productivity and innovation determine the ultimate boundaries. The institutional furnishings cluster located in the Grand Rapids, Michigan, area
illustrates the kinds of choices made when drawing cluster boundaries
(see Figure 7.3). Office furniture and partitions clearly belong in the
cluster, as does seating for stadia, classrooms, and transportation vehicles. These products have important commonalities in product attributes, features, components, and technology. Nearby metal parts and
equipment manufacturers, plastics manufacturers, and printing companies are cluster suppliers. These supplier industries may also be part of
other clusters, because they serve other customer industries such as
automobile manufacturers. Particularly in metal parts, the prior existence of automotive suppliers serving the nearby Detroit automotive
cluster contributed importantly to development of the furnishing
cluster. Cluster boundaries should encompass all firms, industries, and
institutions with strong linkages, whether vertical, horizontal, or institutional; those with weak or non-existent linkages can safely be left
out.[3]

Clusters encompassing broad groupings, such as manufacturing, consumer goods, or high tech, have been too broadly conceived. Such aggre-
gates exhibit, at best, weak connections among the industries included.
Discussions about cluster constraints and bottlenecks in such groupings
fall into generalities. Conversely, labeling a single industry as a cluster
overlooks crucial cross-industry and institutional interconnections that
strongly affect competitiveness.[4]

Clusters occur in many types of industries, in both larger and smaller
fields, and even in some local businesses, such as restaurants, car dealers,

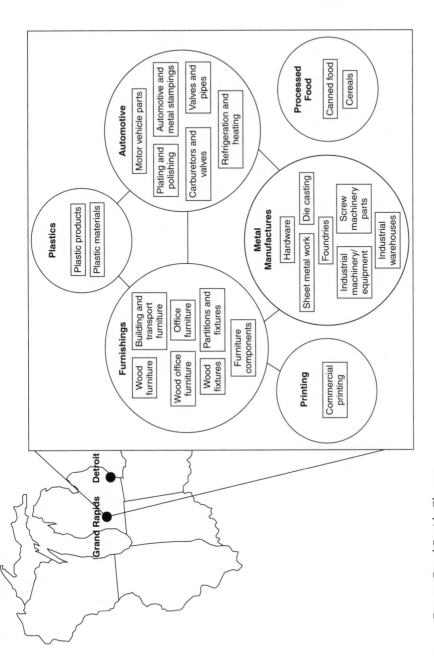

Figure 7.3 Greater Grand Rapids Clusters

and antique shops. They are present in large and small economies, in rural and urban areas, and at several geographic levels (for example, nations, states, metropolitan regions, and cities). Clusters occur in both advanced and developing economies, although clusters in advanced economies tend to be far better developed.

Cluster boundaries rarely conform to standard industrial classification systems, which fail to capture many important actors in competition as well as linkages across industries. Clusters normally consist of a combination of end-product, machinery, materials, and service industries, usually classified in separate categories. They often involve (or potentially involve) both traditional and high-tech industries. Clusters, then, represent a distinct way of organizing economic data and viewing the economy.

Because parts of a cluster often fall within different traditional industrial or service categories, significant clusters may be obscured or even go unrecognized. In Massachusetts, for example, more than four hundred companies, representing at least 39,000 high-paying jobs, were involved in some way in medical devices. The cluster long remained all but invisible, however, buried within several larger and overlapping industry categories, such as electronic equipment and plastic products. Executives in the cluster had never come together before despite the fact that firms shared many common constraints, problems, and opportunities. The discovery of this cluster, the subsequent organization of an association, MassMedic, and the initiation of a productive dialogue with government will be explored below.

Clusters vary in size, breadth, and state of development. Some clusters consist primarily of small- and medium-sized firms (for example, the Italian footwear and the North Carolina home furniture clusters).[5] Other clusters involve both large and small firms (for example, Hollywood or the German chemical clusters). Some clusters center on research universities, while others have no important university connection.[6] These differences in the nature of clusters reflect differences in the structures of their constituent industries. More developed clusters have deeper and more specialized supplier bases, a wider array of related industries, and more extensive supporting institutions.

The boundaries of clusters continually evolve as new firms and industries emerge, established industries shrink or decline, and local institutions develop and change. Technological and market developments spawn new industries, create new linkages, or alter served markets. Regulatory changes also contribute to shifting boundaries, as they have, for example, in telecommunications and transport.

Clusters can be examined at various levels of aggregation, thus exposing different issues. In California, for example, there is a large agribusiness cluster. Mapping and analyzing this broad cluster reveals important competitive insights. The wine cluster already discussed is embedded within the broad cluster. Analysis at this level reveals some more specific and distinct issues (for example, the linkage with the tourism clusters).

The appropriate definition of a cluster can differ in different locations, depending on the segments in which the member companies compete and the strategies they employ. The lower Manhattan multimedia cluster, for example, consists primarily of content providers and firms in related industries, such as publishing, broadcast media, and graphics and visual arts. The San Francisco Bay area multimedia cluster, in contrast, contains many hardware and software industries that provide enabling technology.

Why view economies through the lens of clusters rather than of more traditional groupings such as companies, industries, or sectors, such as manufacturing or services? Foremost because clusters align better with the nature of competition and the sources of competitive advantage. Clusters, broader than industries, capture important linkages, complementarities, and spillovers of technology, skills, information, marketing, and customer needs that cut across firms and industries. As will be discussed below, such connections are fundamental to competition, to productivity, and, especially, to the direction and pace of new business formation and innovation. Most cluster participants do not compete directly, but serve different industry segments. Yet they do share many common needs and opportunities and encounter many common constraints and obstacles to productivity. Viewing a group of companies and institutions as a cluster highlights opportunities for coordination and mutual improvement in areas of common concern without threatening or distorting competition or limiting the intensity of rivalry. The cluster provides a constructive and efficient forum for dialogue among related companies and their suppliers, government, and other salient institutions. Public and private investments to improve conditions for clusters benefit many firms.

Viewing the world in terms of industries or narrow sectors such as automotive products, in contrast, often degenerates into lobbying over subsidies and tax breaks by the participating companies. Resulting public investments create fewer spillover benefits for other industries and may, therefore, distort markets. Because a large proportion of participants directly compete, there is a very real threat that the intensity of rivalry will be diminished. Companies are also often hesitant about participating for fear of aiding direct competitors. An industry or narrow sectoral perspective tends to result in distorting competition, then, while a cluster perspective focuses on enhancing competition. I will return to these issues when I explore the implications of clusters for companies and governments.

Historical and Intellectual Antecedents of Cluster Theory

Clusters have long been part of the economic landscape, with geographic concentrations of trades and companies in particular industries dating back for centuries. However, the role of clusters was arguably more limited. The depth and breadth of clusters, however, have increased as competition has evolved and as modern economies have grown in complexity. Globalization, together with rising knowledge intensity, have greatly altered the role of clusters in competition.

Intellectual antecedents of cluster theory date back at least to Alfred Marshall, who included a fascinating chapter on the externalities of specialized industrial locations in his *Principles of Economics* (originally published in 1890). During the first fifty years of this century, economic geography was a recognized field with an extensive literature. With the mid-century advent of neoclassical economics, however, location moved out of the economics mainstream. More recently, increasing returns have started to play a central role in new theories of growth and international trade, and interest in the field of economic geography has been growing.[a]

In the management literature, as well, attention to geography or location has been minimal. If treated at all, consideration of geography has often been reduced to assessments of cultural and other differences when doing business in various countries. Corporate location has been treated as a narrow subspecialty of operations management. The recent preoccupation with globalization has, if anything, created a tendency to regard location as of diminished and diminishing importance.

A variety of bodies of literature have in some respects recognized and shed light on the phenomenon of clusters, including those on growth poles and backward and forward linkages,[b] agglomeration economies,[c] economic geography,[d] urban and regional economics,[e] national innovation systems,[f] regional science,[g] industrial districts,[h] and social networks.[i]

The literature on urban economics and on regional science focuses on generalized urban agglomeration economies, reflected in the infrastructure, communications technology, input access, diverse industrial base, and markets available in concentrated urban areas. These types of economies, which are independent of the types of firms and clusters present, appear to be most important in developing countries. Overall, however, generalized urban agglomeration economies seem to be diminishing in importance as the opening of trade and the fall in communication and transportation costs allow easier access to inputs and markets and as more locations and countries develop comparable infrastructures.[j]

Other studies focus on geographic concentrations of companies operating in particular fields, which can be seen as special cases of clusters. Italian-style industrial districts of small- and medium-sized firms dominating a local economy prevail in some types of industries. In other fields, a mixture of large domestic firms, large foreign-owned firms, and an array of smaller companies is the rule.

Some clusters center on research universities, while others draw little on the resources of formal technological institutions. Clusters occur both in high tech and traditional industries, in manufacturing as well as in service industries. Indeed, clusters often mix high tech, low tech, manufacturing, and services. Some regions contain a single dominant cluster, while others contain several. Clusters appear in both developing and advanced economies, though the lack of depth of clusters in developing nations is a characteristic constraint to development.

Earlier studies have, nonetheless, contributed to our understanding of the influence of clusters on competition. The literature on agglomeration economies stresses input cost minimization, input specialization made possible because of the extent of the local market, and the advantages of locating near markets. The economic development literature focuses on induced demand and supply, certainly an element of cluster formation. The normative implication of the concept of backward and forward linkages, however, emphasizes the need to build industries with linkages to many others. Cluster theory, in contrast, advocates building on emerging concentrations of companies and encouraging the development of those fields with the strongest linkages to or spillovers within each cluster.

Overall, most past theories address particular aspects of clusters or clusters of a particular type. Many traditional agglomeration arguments for the existence of clusters have been undercut by the globalization of supply sources and markets. Yet the modern, knowledge-based economy creates a far more textured role for clusters.

The broader role of clusters in competition is only now becoming widely recognized. To understand this role requires embedding clusters in a broader and dynamic theory of competition that encompasses both cost and differentiation and both static efficiency and continuous improvement and innovation, and that recognizes a world of global factor and product markets. Some of the most important agglomeration economies represent dynamic rather than static efficiencies and revolve around innovation and the rate of learning. Clusters occupy a more complex and integral role in the modern economy than has been previously recognized.

Clusters, then, constitute an important multi-organizational form, a central influence on competition, and a prominent characteristic of market economies. The state of an economy's clusters reveals important insights into its productive potential and the constraints on its future development. The role of clusters in competition raises important implications for companies, government, and other institutions.

c. There is an extensive literature on agglomeration including Weber (1929); Lösch (1954); Harris (1954); Isard (1956); Lloyd and Dicken (1977); Goldstein and Gronberg (1984); Rivera-Batiz (1988); McCann (1995B); Ciccone and Hall (1996); and Fujita and Thisse (1996).

d. See Storper and Salais (1997A, 1997B); Storper (1997); Amin and Thrift (1992); and papers by Storper, Gertler, Mair, Swyngedouw, and Cox in Cox (1993).

e. Scott (1991); Glaeser, Kallal, Sheinkman, and Shleifer (1992); Glaeser (1994); Henderson (1994); Glaeser, Scheinkman and Shleifer (1995); Henderson, Kuncoro, and Turner (1995); and Henderson (1996) are some interesting examples.

f. See Bengt-Åke (1992); Dosi, Gianetti, and Toninelli (1992); Nelson (1993); and Cimoli and Dosi (1995).

g. See, for example, Giarratani (1994) and Markusen (1995A).

h. This literature includes the work of Piore and Sabel (1984); Becattini (1987); Pyke, Becattini, and Sengenberger (1990);Pyke and Sengenberger (1992); and Harrison (1992).

i. See, for example, Burt (1997); Granovetter (1985); Henton, Melville, and Walesh (1997); Nohria (1992); Perrow (1992); Putnam, Leonardi, and Nanetti (1993); Fukuyama (1995); and Harrison and Weiss (1998).

j. Harrison, Kelley, and Grant (1996) construct an imaginative test of the relative importance of industry and urbanization economies in the diffusion of innovation in machining and find that urbanization effects are more significant. They acknowledge, however, that the test is far from definitive. This is because, among other reasons, they picked a widely applicable (versus specialized) innovation in a not very geographically concentrated field. Metalworking, indeed, is not normally a cluster itself but part of other clusters.

---

a. See Krugman (1991A, 1991B).
b. Hirschman (1958).

Location and Competition

In recent decades, thinking about the influence of location on competition has taken a relatively simple view of how companies compete. Competition has been seen as largely static and as resting on cost minimization in relatively closed economies. Here comparative advantage in factors of production (labor and capital) is decisive, or, in the most recent analyses, economies of scale.

Yet this picture fails to represent real competition. Competition is dynamic and rests on innovation and the search for strategic differences. Three conditions contribute to rendering factor inputs per se less valuable: the expanded input supply as more countries open to the global economy; the greater efficiency of national and international factor markets; and the diminishing factor intensity of competition. Instead, close linkages with buyers, suppliers, and other institutions contribute importantly not only to efficiency but to the rate of improvement and innovation. While extensive vertical integration (for example, in-house production of parts, services, or training) may have once been the norm, a more dynamic environment can render vertical integration inefficient, ineffective, and inflexible.

In this broader and more dynamic view of competition, location affects competitive advantage through its influence on *productivity* and especially on *productivity growth*. Productivity is the value created per day of work and unit of capital or physical resources employed. Generic factor inputs themselves are usually abundant and readily accessed. Prosperity depends on the productivity with which factors are used and upgraded in a particular location.

The productivity and prosperity of a location rest not on the industries in which its firms compete, but on *how* they compete. Firms can be more productive in any industry—shoes, agriculture, or semiconductors—if they employ sophisticated methods, use advanced technology, and offer unique products and services. All industries can employ high technology, all industries can be knowledge intensive. The term *high tech*, normally used to refer to fields such as information technology and biotechnology, thus has questionable relevance. A more descriptive term might be *enabling technology*, signifying fields providing tools that enhance technology in many industries.

Conversely, the mere presence of high tech in an industry does not by itself guarantee prosperity if the firms are unproductive. Traditional distinctions between industries, such as high or low tech, manufacturing or services, resource-based or knowledge-based have in themselves little relevance. The proper goal is to improve the productivity of *all* industries, enhancing prosperity both directly and indirectly, as the improved productivity of one industry increases the productivity of others.

The prosperity of a location depends, then, on the productivity of what firms located there choose to do. This sets the wages that can be sustained and the profits that can be earned. Both domestic and foreign firms contribute to the prosperity of a location, based on the productivity of their activities there. The presence of sophisticated foreign firms often enhances the productivity of domestic firms and vice versa.

The sophistication and productivity with which companies compete in a location is strongly influenced by the *quality of the business environment*. Firms cannot employ advanced logistical techniques, for example, unless a high-quality transportation infrastructure is available. Firms cannot compete using high-service strategies unless they can access well-educated people. Firms cannot operate efficiently under onerous amounts of regulatory red tape, requiring endless dialogue with government, or under a court system that fails to resolve disputes quickly and fairly. All of these situations consume resources and management time without contributing to customer value. The effects of some aspects of the business environment, such as the road system, corporate tax rates, and the legal system, cut across all industries. These economywide (or horizontal) areas can represent the binding constraints to competitiveness in developing economies. For both more advanced economies and, increasingly, everywhere, however, the more decisive aspects of the business environment are often *cluster specific* (for example, the presence of particular types of suppliers or university departments). Cluster thinking thus assumes an important role in both company strategy and economic policy.

Capturing the nature of the business environment in a location is challenging given the myriad of locational influences on productivity and productivity growth. In *The Competitive Advantage of Nations*, I modeled the effect of location on competition using four interrelated influences, graphically depicted in a diamond, a metaphor that has become a shorthand reference to the theory (see Figure 7.4).[7] A few elements of this framework deserve highlighting here because they are important to understanding the role of clusters in competition.

As Figure 7.4 shows, factor inputs include tangible assets (such as physical infrastructure), information, the legal system, and university research institutes that firms draw upon in competition. To increase productivity, factor inputs must improve in efficiency, quality, and, ultimately specialization to particular cluster areas. Specialized factors, especially those integral to innovation and upgrading (for example, a specialized university research institute), not only foster high levels of productivity but tend to be less tradable or available from elsewhere.

The context for firm strategy and rivalry refers to the rules, incentives, and norms governing the type and intensity of local rivalry. Economies with low productivity demonstrate little local rivalry: Most competition, if it is present at all, comes from imports; local rivalry, if it occurs at all, involves imitation. Price is the sole competitive variable, and firms

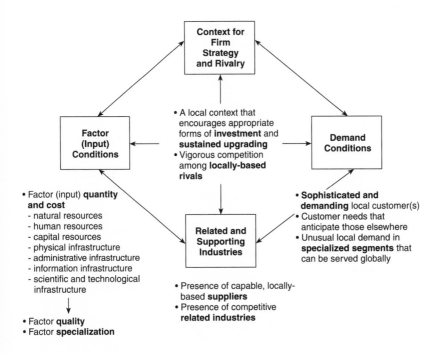

Figure 7.4 Sources of Locational Competitive Advantage

hold down wages to lower cost. Such competition involves minimal investment.

The move to an advanced economy requires developing vigorous local rivalry. Rivalry must shift from low wages to low total cost, which requires upgrading the efficiency of manufacturing and service delivery. Ultimately, rivalry must also evolve beyond cost to include differentiation. Competition must shift from imitation to innovation and from low investment to high investment, not only in physical assets but in intangibles such as skills and technology. Clusters, as will be evident, play an integral role in these transitions.

The context for strategy and rivalry can be divided into two primary dimensions. One is the climate for investment in its various forms. A rising investment intensity of competition is necessary for support of more sophisticated forms of competition and higher levels of productivity. Macroeconomic and political stability sets the context for investment, but microeconomic policies are also important: the structure of the tax system, the corporate governance system, labor market policies affecting workforce development incentives, and intellectual property rules and their enforcement, among others.

The other dimension of the context for competition is local policies affecting rivalry itself. Openness to trade and foreign investment, government ownership, licensing rules, antitrust policy, and the influence of corruption, among other things, have a vital role in setting the intensity of local rivalry. The character of rivalry is also strongly influenced by many other aspects of the business environment (such as the available factors and local demand conditions).

Demand conditions at home have much to do with whether firms can and will move from imitative, low-quality products and services to competing on differentiation. Firms in low productivity economies learn about demand primarily from foreign markets. Advancement requires the development of increasingly demanding local markets. The presence or emergence of sophisticated and demanding home customers presses firms to improve and provides insights into existing and future needs difficult to gain through foreign markets alone. Local demand can also reveal market segments in which firms can differentiate. In a global economy, the *quality* of local demand matters far more than its size.

Clusters of linked industries play a central role in setting demand conditions.

Clusters and Competitive Advantage

Clusters constitute one facet of the diamond (related and supporting industries), but they are best seen as a manifestation of the interactions among all four facets. Clusters affect competition in three broad ways: first, by increasing the productivity of constituent firms or industries; second, by increasing their capacity for innovation and thus for productivity growth; and third, by stimulating new business formation that supports innovation and expands the cluster. Many cluster advantages rest on external economies or spillovers across firms and industries of various sorts. (Many cluster advantages also apply to sub-units *within* firms, such as R&D and production.) A cluster may thus be defined as a system of interconnected firms and institutions whose value as a whole is greater than the sum of its parts.

As noted above, scholars have sought to explain concentrations of firms in terms of economies of agglomeration.[8] These have normally been seen as arising either at the industry level or in a diversified urban economy. Many treatments of agglomeration economies stress cost minimization due to proximity to inputs or proximity to markets. These explanations, though, have been undercut by the globalization of markets, technology, and supply sources, increased mobility, and lower transportation and communication costs. Today, economies of agglomeration have shifted in nature, becoming increasingly important at the cluster level and not just within narrowly-defined industries.

The competitive advantages of clusters will not be equally great in all fields, although clusters appear to occur quite broadly in economies. Generally, the stronger the advantages of clusters and the more tradable the products and services involved, the fewer the number of viable cluster locations. The importance of clusters rises with the sophistication of competition, meaning clusters tend to increase in number as economies develop.

Each of the three broad influences of clusters on competition depends to some extent on personal relationships, face-to-face communication, and interaction among networks of individuals and institutions. While the existence of a cluster makes such relationships more likely to develop and more effective once in place, the process is far from automatic. Formal and informal organizing mechanisms and cultural norms often play a role in the development and functioning of clusters, as will become more evident below.

CLUSTERS AND PRODUCTIVITY

Access to Specialized Inputs and Employees. Locating within a cluster can provide superior or lower-cost access to specialized inputs such as components, machinery, business services, and personnel, as compared to the alternatives—vertical integration, formal alliances with outside entities, or "importing" inputs from distant locations. The cluster, then, represents a spatial organizational form that can be an inherently more efficient or effective means of assembling inputs—if competitive local suppliers are available. Sourcing outside the cluster may be necessary where competent local suppliers are unavailable, but that is not the ideal arrangement.

Sourcing inputs from cluster participants ("local" outsourcing) can result in lower transactions costs than those incurred when using distant sources ("distant" outsourcing). Local outsourcing minimizes the need for inventory and eliminates importing costs and delays. It curbs opportunistic behavior by suppliers to overprice or renege on commitments because of the transparency and ongoing nature of local relationships and the adverse effect poor performance will have on their reputations with other cluster participants. Sourcing within the cluster eases communication, reduces the cost of tailoring, and facilitates the joint provision of ancillary or support services, such as installation, debugging, user training, troubleshooting, and timely repair. Other things being equal, then, local outsourcing often dominates distant outsourcing, especially for advanced and specialized inputs involving embedded technology, information, or service content. (Note that "local" refers to a firm with substantial investment within the cluster, including technical resources, even though the parent company is headquartered elsewhere.)

Formal alliances with distant suppliers can mitigate some of the disadvantages of distant outsourcing. However, forming formal alliances with either distant or nearby firms introduces complex bargaining and governance problems and can inhibit a firm's flexibility. The close, informal relationships possible between firms in a local cluster can offer a superior solution.

Access to inputs within a cluster can also be more efficient or effective than vertical integration. Outside specialists are often more cost effective and responsive than in-house units, not only in component production but also in areas such as training. Vertical integration consumes management attention that may be better spent elsewhere. In contrast, obtaining inputs from nearby vendors with whom a firm has close and special relationships offers cost and quality advantages. Proximity of vendors allows efficient quasi-vertical integration while preserving strong incentives.

Expanding the range of inputs available from specialized suppliers at a single location has long been observed to be one of the benefits of agglomeration.[9] This remains true, although the globalization of markets undercuts the traditional rationale. The division of labor is no longer limited by the extent of the market, because the market is international. Suppliers rarely need to rely on the local market for most of their volume.

In the modern economy, the greater depth and specialization of suppliers within clusters arises from the easier recognition of market opportunities and from risk reduction due to the presence of multiple local customers. Moreover, developed clusters consist not only of one industry but of a number of related industries. These industries frequently draw on common or very similar inputs, thus expanding opportunities for suppliers. For this reason, and because of the importance of externalities and spillovers within clusters, the breadth and depth of a cluster rather than the size of individual firms or industries within the cluster is often more significant for competitive advantage.

Clusters also offer advantages in obtaining inputs best sourced from a distance. The presence of a cluster can lower the costs of importing distant inputs because suppliers will price more aggressively and firms can use more efficient means of delivery. (Lower supplier prices will reflect not only the attractiveness of penetrating a large, concentrated potential market but also the efficiencies in serving it.) Suppliers may also be willing to make greater investments to make their products or services more available. Because of the depth of Boston's financial services cluster, for example, senior executives on road shows invariably visit Boston, substantially lowering the cost to Boston institutions of direct contact with the managements of the companies in which they invest.

Clusters offer similar, although not identical, sourcing advantages in the area of specialized and experienced employees. A cluster represents a pool of such employees. This lowers search and transactions costs for recruiting and makes possible more efficient matching of jobs to people. In addition, because a cluster signals opportunity and reduces the risk to employees of relocation, clusters may reduce the cost of sourcing specialized employees from other locations.[10]

Working against a cluster's advantages in assembling inputs and labor is the possibility that such concentration will render these resources scarce and bid up their cost. (Another potential cost of clustering, costs of congestion, apply more to large, diversified urban concentrations rather than to clusters per se.) Yet the ability to outsource many inputs limits any cost penalty relative to other locations. More importantly, the presence of a cluster not only increases the demand for specialized inputs but also increases their supply. Where a cluster exists, the availability of specialized personnel, services, and components and the number of entities creating them usually far exceeds the levels at other locations, a distinct benefit, despite the greater competition.

The absence of capable, locally based suppliers also works against cluster input advantages. If competitive suppliers or other institutions are entrenched elsewhere, distant outsourcing or formal alliances may be necessary. Given the inherent benefits of clusters, however, forces encouraging local suppliers to upgrade will be strong, and cluster constituent firms will have an incentive to encourage the entry of new suppliers or local investments by distant suppliers.

Access to Information. Extensive market, technical, and other specialized information accumulates within a cluster in firms and local institutions. This can be accessed better or at lower cost from within the cluster, thus allowing firms to enhance productivity and get closer to the productivity frontier. This effect also applies to the flow of information between units of the same company.[11] Proximity, supply and technological linkages, and the existence of repeated, personal relationships and community ties fostering trust facilitate the information flow within clusters. (These conditions all make sticky or impacted information more transferable.) An important special case of the informational benefits of clusters is the availability of information about current buyer needs. Sophisticated buyers are often part of clusters, and other cluster participants often gain and share information about buyer needs.[12]

Complementarities. A cluster enhances productivity not only via the acquisition and assembly of inputs but by facilitating complementarities between the activities of cluster participants. The most obvious form of complementarities are among products. In tourism, for example, the quality of the visitor's experience depends not only on the appeal of the primary attraction (for example, beaches or historical sites) but also on the comfort and service of area hotels, restaurants, souvenir outlets, airport and other transportation facilities, and so on. As this example illustrates, the parts of the cluster are often truly mutually dependent. Bad performance by one part of the cluster can undermine the success of the others.

Such complementarities across products to create buyer value are pervasive, not only in service delivery but in product design, logistics, and after-sales service. Coordination and internal pressures for improvement among parts of a cluster, made possible by co-location, can substantially improve its overall quality or efficiency. Co-location makes it easier to achieve technological linkages and accomplish ongoing coordination. As with access to inputs, achieving these and other complementarities internally within a cluster offers advantages over having to resort to formal alliances.

Marketing provides another form of complementarity within clusters. The presence of a group of related firms and industries in a location offers efficiencies in joint marketing (for example, firm referrals, trade fairs, trade magazines, and marketing delegations). It can also enhance the reputation of a location in a particular field, making it more likely that buyers will consider a vendor or manufacturer based there. Italy, for example, has established a strong reputation for fashion and design that benefits firms in footwear, leather goods, apparel, and accessories. This reputation constitutes a type of public good for all Italian-based companies in fashion-related industries.

The presence of a cluster also can enhance buying efficiency. Visiting buyers can see numerous firms in a single trip. The presence in a location of multiple sources for a product or service can also reduce perceived buying risk by offering buyers the potential to multisource or switch vendors if the need arises. Hong Kong thrives as a source of fashion apparel in part for this reason.[13]

Other complementarities arising within clusters involve the better alignment of activities among cluster participants. In the wood products cluster, for example, the efficiency of sawmills depends on a reliable supply of good-quality timber and the ability to maximize the utilization of timber in either furniture (highest quality), pallets and boxes (lower quality), or wood chips (lowest quality). Portuguese sawmills suffered from poor timber quality because landowners would not invest in timber management.[14] Hence most timber was processed for use in pallets and boxes, a lower value use that limited the price paid to landowners. Substantial improvement in productivity was possible, but only if several parts of the cluster changed simultaneously. Logging operations, for example, had to modify cutting and sorting procedures while sawmills had to develop the capacity to process in more sophisticated ways. Coordination to develop standard wood classifications and measures was an important enabling step. Such linkages can be recognized and captured more easily within clusters than among dispersed participants.

Access to Institutions and Public Goods. Clusters make many inputs that would otherwise be costly into public or quasi-public goods. The ability to recruit employees trained in local programs, for example, eliminates or lowers the cost of internal training. Firms can often access benefits, such as specialized infrastructure or advice from experts in local institutions at very low cost. Indeed, the information built up in a cluster can in itself be seen as a quasi-public good.

The public goods held in clusters may better be termed quasi-public goods, because accessing them involves some cost, although well below full cost. The analysis of public goods in economics has been limited to the pure cases of a fairly narrow range of largely governmental functions. Clusters create a far broader array of circumstances in which something approaching a public-good asset arises and include many instances in which *private* institutions and investments help create them.

Some of the public or quasi-public goods available in clusters are similar to conventional public goods in that they are closely linked to government and to public institutions. Public investment in specialized infrastructure, educational programs, information, trade fairs, and other forms that benefit a cluster is encouraged by the number and visibility of cluster participants and by the number of firms likely to experience spillover benefits from such investment. Other quasi-public goods available to cluster participants arise as natural by-products of competition. These include information and technology pools, the reputation accrued by the cluster location, and some of the marketing and sourcing advantages described above.

In addition, public or quasi-public goods at cluster locations often result from *private* investments in training programs, infrastructure, quality centers, and so on. While public goods are associated with public institutions, they may also arise in private or partially private institutions created at cluster locations (for example, testing laboratories or trade journals). Such private investments are common because cluster participants perceive the potential for collective benefits. Often such investments take place via trade associations or other collective mechanisms.

Incentives and Performance Measurement. Clusters help to solve or mitigate some agency problems that arise in more isolated locations and in more vertically integrated firms. Clusters improve the incentives within companies for achieving high productivity for several reasons. Foremost is competitive pressure. Rivalry with locally based competitors has particularly strong incentive effects because of the ease of constant comparison and because local rivals have similar general circumstances (for example, labor costs and local market access), so that competition must take place on other things. In addition, peer pressure amplifies competitive pressure within a cluster, even among indirectly competing or non-competing firms. Pride and the desire to look good in the local community motivate firms in their attempts to outdo each other.

Clusters also facilitate measurement of the performance of in-house activities because, often, other local firms perform similar functions. Managers gain wider opportunities to compare internal costs with arms-length transactions, and lower employee monitoring costs by comparing employee performance with others locally. The accumulation of cluster knowledge in financial institutions, for example, should make loan decisions and other financing choices better informed and improve customer monitoring. As mentioned above, clusters also offer the advantage of limiting opportunistic behavior as when one participant takes advantage of another or provides shoddy products or services.[15] Because of repeated interactions, the easy spread of information, the spread of reputation, and the desire to maintain a standing in the local community, cluster participants usually strive for constructive interactions that will positively affect their long-term interests.

*　*　*

As has been noted, many of these productivity advantages of clusters involve location-specific public goods or benefits that depend on physical proximity, face-to-face contact, close and ongoing relationships, and "insider" access to information. The benefits of cluster membership can thus be difficult if not impossible to access unless firms participate actively, with a significant local presence. Clusters can and do include foreign firms, but only when such firms make a permanent investment in achieving a significant local presence.

Many of the advantages of clustering also apply to sub-units *within a single company*. Co-locating R&D, component fabrication, assembly, marketing, customer support, and other activities can facilitate internal efficiencies in sourcing and information flow, as well as complementarities and other benefits. Companies sometimes disperse units in order to lower costs of labor, utilities, or taxes, thus unwittingly sacrificing the powerful system cost benefits of clusters and their advantages in fostering dynamism and innovation.

CLUSTERS AND INNOVATION

The benefits of clusters in innovation and productivity growth, compared to an isolated location, can be more important than those in current productivity, though there are some risks as well. Some of the same cluster characteristics that enhance current productivity are even more important to innovation.

Firms within a cluster are often able to more clearly and rapidly perceive new buyer needs. Just as with current buyer needs, firms in a cluster benefit from the concentration of firms with buyer knowledge and relationships, the juxtaposition of firms in related industries, the concentration of specialized information-generating entities, and buyer sophistication. Cluster firms can often discern buyer trends faster than can isolated competitors. Silicon Valley and Austin-based computer companies, for example, plug into customer needs and trends quickly and effectively, with an ease impossible to match elsewhere.

Cluster participation also offers advantages in perceiving new technological, operating, or delivery possibilities. Participants learn early and consistently about evolving technology, component and machinery availability, service and marketing concepts, and so on, facilitated by ongoing relationships with other cluster entities, the ease of site visits, and frequent face-to-face contacts. Cluster membership makes possible direct observation of other firms. The isolated firm, in contrast, faces higher costs and steeper impediments to acquiring information and a corresponding increase in the need to devote resources to generating such knowledge internally.[16]

The potential advantages of clusters in perceiving both the need and the opportunity for innovation are significant, but equally important can be the flexibility and capacity they provide to act rapidly on these insights. A firm within a cluster often can more rapidly source the new components, services, machinery, and other elements needed to implement innovations, whether a new product line, a new process, or a new logistical model. Local suppliers and partners can and do get closely involved in the innovation process, thus ensuring that the inputs they supply better meet the firm's requirements. New, specialized personnel can often be recruited locally to fill gaps required to pursue new approaches. The complementarities involved in innovating are more easily achieved among nearby participants.

Firms within a cluster can experiment at lower cost and can delay large commitments until they are more assured that a new product, process, or service will pan out. In contrast, a firm relying on distant outsourcing faces greater challenges in contracting, securing delivery, obtaining associated technical and service support, and coordinating across complementary entities, and a firm relying on vertical integration faces inertia, difficult tradeoffs if the innovation erodes the value of in-house assets, and constraints if current products or processes must be maintained while new ones are developed.

Reinforcing these other advantages for innovation is the sheer pressure —competitive pressure, peer pressure, and constant comparison— occurring in geographically concentrated clusters. The similarity of basic circumstances (for example, labor and utility costs) combined with the presence of multiple rivals forces firms to distinguish themselves creatively. The pressure to innovate is elevated. Individual firms in the cluster have difficulty staying ahead for long, but many firms progress faster than do those based at other locations.

Under certain circumstances, however, cluster participation can re-tard innovation. When a cluster shares a uniform approach to competing, a sort of groupthink often reinforces old behaviors, suppresses new ideas, and creates rigidities that prevent adoption of improvements.[17] Clusters also may not support truly radical innovation, which tends to invalidate the existing pools of talent, information, suppliers, and infrastructure. In these circumstances, a cluster participant may be no worse off, in principle, than an isolated firm (because both can outsource), but the firm in an established cluster may suffer from greater barriers to perceiv-ing the need to change and from inertia against severing past relation-ships that no longer contribute to competitive advantage. I will explore these issues further in the context of the processes by which clusters emerge and decline.

*   *   *

The geographic concentration of clusters occurs because proximity serves to amplify many of the productivity and innovation benefits of clustering already described.[18] Transactions costs are reduced, the creation and flow of information improves, local institutions respond more readily to a cluster's specialized needs, and peer pressure and competitive pressure are more keenly felt.

Clusters clearly represent a combination of competition and coopera-tion. Vigorous competition occurs in winning customers and retaining them. The presence of multiple rivals and strong incentives often accen-tuates the intensity of competition among clusters. Yet cooperation must occur in a variety of areas I identified above. Much of it is vertical, involves related industries and is with local institutions. Competition and cooperation can coexist because they occur on different dimensions and between different players; cooperation in some dimensions aids successful competition in others.

A number of the mechanisms through which clusters affect productivity and innovation echo findings in other literatures. Management literature shows growing awareness of the importance of close linkages with suppliers and buyers and of the value of outsourcing or partnering. The literature on innovation highlights the role of customers, suppliers, and universities in the innovation process, while the literature on the diffusion of innovation stresses such notions as demonstration effects, contagion, experimentation, and ease of observability—all clearly influenced by the presence of clusters.[19] Many studies in economics highlight the importance of transactions costs, and others explore the organizational incentive problems that stand in the way of efficiency.

Little of this thinking, however, has been connected to location. It is as if linkages, transactions, and information flow took place outside time and space. Yet proximity clearly affects linkages and transactions costs. Incentive misalignments difficult to resolve with feasible contracts may right themselves under the strong influence of repeated interaction and other aspects of location and clusters. The resort to formal partnerships and alliances, undertaken despite complex incentive and governance problems, overlooks the relative ease of achieving many of the same benefits more simply and informally within clusters. Bringing these various theoretical approaches together with an understanding of location and clusters can extend their usefulness and deepen our understanding of the effect of clusters on competition.

More broadly, the geographically proximate cluster of independent and informally linked firms and institutions represents a robust organizational form in the continuum between markets and hierarchies—but one still little explored in theory. Location can powerfully shape the tradeoffs between markets and hierarchies. Clusters offer obvious advantages in transactions cost over other forms and seem to ameliorate many incentive problems. Repeated interactions and informal contracts within a cluster structure result from living and working in a circumscribed geographic area and foster trust, open communication, and lower the costs of severing and recombining market relationships.

CLUSTERS AND NEW BUSINESS FORMATION

Many if not most new businesses (that is, headquarters, not branch offices or ancillary facilities) form within existing clusters rather than at isolated locations. This occurs for a variety of reasons. First, clusters provide inducement to entry through better information about opportunities. The existence of a cluster in itself signals an opportunity. Individuals working somewhere in or near the cluster more easily perceive gaps in products, services, or suppliers to fill. Having had this insight, these individuals more readily leave established firms to start new ones aimed at filling the perceived gaps.

Opportunities perceived at cluster locations are pursued there because *barriers to entry are lower than elsewhere.* Needed assets, skills, inputs, and staff, often readily available at the cluster location, can be assembled more easily for a new enterprise. Local financial institutions and investors, already possessing familiarity with the cluster, may require a lower risk premium on capital. In addition, the cluster often presents a significant local market. The entrepreneur seeking to benefit from established relationships often prefers to stay in the same community. All of these factors—lower entry barriers, multiple potential local customers, established relationships, and the presence of other local firms that have "made it"— reduce the perceived risks of entry. The barriers to exit at a cluster can also be lower due to reduced need for specialized investment, deeper markets for specialized assets, and other factors.[20]

While local entrepreneurs are likely entrants to a cluster, entrepreneurs based outside a cluster frequently relocate, sooner or later, to a cluster location. The same lower entry barriers attract them, as does the potential to create more economic value from their ideas and skills at the cluster location or the ability to operate more productively.

Established companies based in non-cluster locations (foreign and domestic) often establish subsidiaries at clusters, seeking the productivity benefits and innovation advantages discussed above. The presence of an established cluster not only lowers the barriers to entry for outside firms, but it also reduces, as noted above, the perceived risk. (This is particularly the case where other "foreign" firms have already moved into the cluster.) Many firms have relocated entire business units to a cluster location or have designated their cluster-based subsidiary as their regional or world headquarters for that particular line of business.

The advantages of a cluster in new business formation can play a major role in speeding up the process of cluster innovation. Large companies often face constraints or impediments of various sorts to innovating. Spin-off companies often pick up the slack, sometimes with the blessing of the original company. (A large company, for example, may support a smaller firm serving a niche it cannot address economically.) Larger companies in a cluster develop close relationships with innovative smaller ones, helping in their establishment, and acquiring them if they become successful.

Because of new business formation, clusters often grow in depth and breadth over time, further enhancing cluster advantages. The intense competition within a cluster, together with lower entry and exit barriers, sometimes leads to high rates of both entry and exit at these locations. The net result is that many of the surviving firms in the cluster can gain position vis-à-vis rivals at other locations. Location and the state of clusters not only affect barriers to entry and exit but most other aspects of industry structure. Analysts are just beginning to explore the connections between location and industrial organization.

The Socioeconomy of Clusters

The mere presence of firms, suppliers, and institutions in a location creates the *potential* for economic value, but it does not necessarily ensure the realization of this potential. Social glue binds clusters together, contributing to the value creation process. Many of the competitive advantages of clusters depend on the free flow of information, the discovery of value-adding exchanges or transactions, the willingness to align agendas and to work across organizations, and strong motivation for improvement. Relationships, networks, and a sense of common interest undergird these circumstances. The social structure of clusters thus takes on central importance.

A growing economic and organizational literature examines the importance of network relationships found in effective companies and communities.[21] Economic activities are seen as "embedded" in ongoing social relationships. Much research undertakes to map these networks, to understand the number of nodes feasible, and to verify the importance of repeated interaction and of time in making networks effective. Examinations of the structure of networks has revealed that the social relationships among individuals, or their "social capital," greatly facilitates access to important resources and information.

Cluster theory focuses on how juxtaposition of economically linked firms and institutions in a specific geographic location affects competitiveness. While some cluster advantages are largely independent of social relationships (for example, available pools of capital or employees), most if not all have at least a relationship component. A firm's identification with and sense of community, derived from membership in a cluster, and its "civic engagement" beyond its own narrow confines as a single entity translate directly, according to cluster theory, into economic value. Cluster theory further extends notions of social capital by exploring the mechanisms through which a structure of network relationships within a geographic location produce benefits for particular firms. The benefits of trust and organizational permeability, fostered through repeated interactions and a sense of mutual dependence within a region or city, clearly grease the interactions within clusters that enhance productivity, spur innovation, and result in the creation of new businesses.

Cluster theory bridges network theory and competition. A cluster is a form of a network that occurs within a geographic location, in which the proximity of firms and institutions ensures certain forms of commonality and increases the frequency and impact of interactions. Well-functioning clusters move beyond hierarchical networks to become lattices of numerous overlapping and fluid connections among individuals, firms, and institutions. These connections are repeated, constantly shift, and often expand to related industries. Both "strong ties" and "weak ties" occur together. Modest changes in the pattern of relationships within a cluster may have significant consequences for productivity and the direction of innovation.

Network theory can greatly inform understanding of the way clusters work and of how clusters can become more productive. As will be discussed further, successful cluster upgrading depends on paying explicit attention to relationship building, an important characteristic of cluster development initiatives. Trade associations play important roles in facilitating the formation of networks.

For its part, cluster theory also provides a way to connect theories of networks, social capital, and civic engagements more tightly to business competition and economic prosperity—and to extend them. Cluster theory identifies who needs to be in the network for what relationships and why. Clusters offer a new way of exploring the mechanisms by which networks, social capital, and civic engagement affect competition and market outcomes. Cluster theory helps isolate the most beneficial forms of networks. Relationships and trust resulting in cartels, for example, undermine economic value, while those facilitating open information exchange between customers and suppliers enhance it. The workings of clusters also suggest the efficiency and flexibility possible in network structures built on proximity and informal local links compared to those defined by formal or hierarchical relationships between companies or between institutions and companies. Cluster theory may also reveal how network relationships form and how social capital is acquired, helping to unscramble questions of cause and effect; for example, do strong relationships and trust arise because a cluster exists or are clusters more likely to develop from existing networks? Cluster theory, then, helps illuminate the causes of network structure, the substance of network activity, and the link between network characteristics and outcomes.

Clusters and Economic Geography

Specialization characterizes the economic geography of cities, states, and nations, especially of prosperous ones, and appears to increase as an economy becomes more advanced.[22] A relatively small number of clusters usually account for a major share of the economy within a geographic area as well as an overwhelming share of the outward-oriented economic activity (for example, exports to other locations and investment in other locations by locally based firms).[23] Outward-oriented clusters are juxtaposed with two other types of business: localized industries and clusters that do not compete with other locations (for example, restaurants, entertainment, logistical services, real estate, and construction); and local subsidiaries of competitive firms based elsewhere that primarily serve the local market (for example, sales offices, customer support centers, branch offices, and assembly plants).

The outward-oriented clusters based in a geographic area constitute the area's primary *long-run* source of economic growth and prosperity. Such clusters can grow far beyond the size of the local market, absorbing workers from less productive firms and industries. The demand for local industries, in contrast, is inherently limited and derives primarily, either directly or indirectly, from the success of outward-oriented clusters.

The partial cluster map in Figure 7.5 illustrates the geographic distribution of clusters in the United States, a highly advanced economy. The map shows just a few of the many geographically concentrated clusters present in the United States, ranging from familiar ones, such as entertainment in Hollywood, finance in New York City, and household furniture in High Point, North Carolina, to less familiar clusters, such as golf equipment in Carlsbad, California, and optics in Arizona. Figure 7.6 shows regional clusters in a less advanced economy, Portugal. Figure 7.7 maps the dominant clusters in a single U.S. state, Massachusetts, and Figure 7.8 shows the clusters in a single U.S. metropolitan region, greater Pittsburgh. Not evident from these maps are the striking differences in cluster specialization even between nearby economic areas: The Massachusetts economy, for example, looks quite different from that of neighboring Connecticut.

In identifying clusters, outward-oriented industries must be distinguished from those that primarily serve the local market. Every economy will include local clusters, such as real estate and construction, as well as the local operations of exporting clusters based elsewhere. It is also important to recognize that the co-location of parts of a cluster does not ensure that linkages and interactions within the cluster function effectively. In Pittsburgh, for example, the potential for innovation within and across clusters has not been fully realized.

While cluster boundaries often fit within political boundaries, they may also cross state and even national borders, especially in smaller states and nations and in cities located near borders. A thriving photonics (or electro-optics) cluster in Massachusetts, centered around Sturbridge, for example, extends into Connecticut, where another 135 companies are based, about 50 of them in counties abutting the Massachusetts border. In another example, a European chemicals cluster encompasses

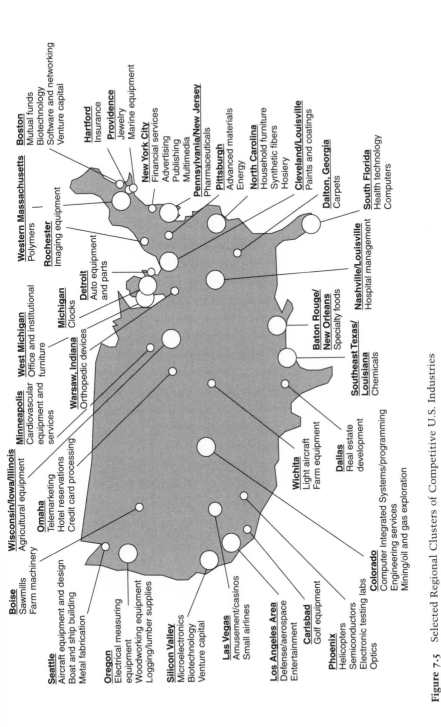

Boise
Sawmills
Farm machinery

Seattle
Aircraft equipment and design
Boat and ship building
Metal fabrication

Oregon
Electrical measuring
equipment
Woodworking equipment
Logging/lumber supplies

Silicon Valley
Microelectronics
Biotechnology
Venture capital

Las Vegas
Amusement/casinos
Small airlines

Los Angeles Area
Defense/aerospace
Entertainment

Carlsbad
Golf equipment

Phoenix
Helicopters
Semiconductors
Electronic testing labs
Optics

Colorado
Computer Integrated Systems/programming
Engineering services
Mining/oil and gas exploration

Wisconsin/Iowa/Illinois
Agricultural equipment

Omaha
Telemarketing
Hotel reservations
Credit card processing

Minneapolis
Cardiovascular
equipment and
services

West Michigan
Office and institutional
furniture

Warsaw, Indiana
Orthopedic devices

Michigan
Clocks

Detroit
Auto equipment
and parts

Rochester
Imaging equipment

Western Massachusetts
Polymers

Boston
Mutual funds
Biotechnology
Software and networking
Venture capital

Hartford
Insurance

Providence
Jewelry
Marine equipment

New York City
Financial services
Advertising
Publishing
Multimedia

Pennsylvania/New Jersey
Pharmaceuticals

Pittsburgh
Advanced materials
Energy

North Carolina
Household furniture
Synthetic fibers
Hosiery

Cleveland/Louisville
Paints and coatings

Dalton, Georgia
Carpets

South Florida
Health technology
Computers

Nashville/Louisville
Hospital management

**Baton Rouge/
New Orleans**
Specialty foods

**Southeast Texas/
Louisiana**
Chemicals

Dallas
Real estate
development

Wichita
Light aircraft
Farm equipment

Figure 7.5 Selected Regional Clusters of Competitive U.S. Industries

Figure 7.6   Selected Regional Clusters in Portugal
Source: Monitor Company, Cambridge, Massachusetts.

firms in both Germany and the German-speaking part of Switzerland. Clusters are more likely to span political borders where there is a common language, short physical distances (e.g., 200 miles or less between business locations), similar legal systems and other institutions, and minimal trade or investment barriers.

CLUSTERS AND DEVELOPING ECONOMIES

Clusters are normally most pronounced in advanced economies, where the depth and breadth of clusters is usually greater. In developing economies, a greater proportion of industries are locally based or are foreign

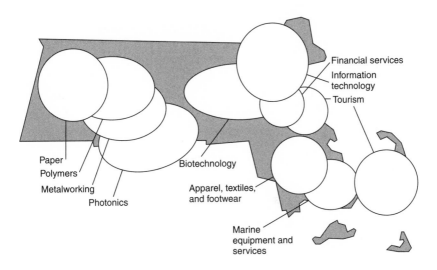

Financial services

Information technology

Tourism

Paper

Polymers

Metalworking

Photonics

Biotechnology

Apparel, textiles, and footwear

Marine equipment and services

Figure 7.7   Massachusetts Clusters

subsidiaries serving the local market. Exporting industries tend to be resource- or labor-intensive. Clusters in developing economies tend to be shallow and to rely primarily on foreign components, services, and technology. Firms in such locations must often vertically integrate, producing not only their own components but even back-up electricity as well; they must sometimes also build and operate not only physical infrastructure but their own schools and other services. The relatively competitive companies in developing economies tend to operate more like islands rather than as cluster participants.[24] Figure 7.9 contrasts the forest products cluster in Sweden, an advanced economy, with that of Portugal, a middle income economy, illustrating some of these differences.

As compared to those in advanced economies, clusters in developing economies not only involve fewer participants but often differ as well in their sociometrics. Many take the form of hierarchical, hub-and-spoke networks surrounding a few large companies, government entities, or distributors. Communication is limited, and linkages between existing firms and institutions are not well developed. In contrast, successful clusters in advanced economies involve a dense mesh of continually evolving relationships and linkages.

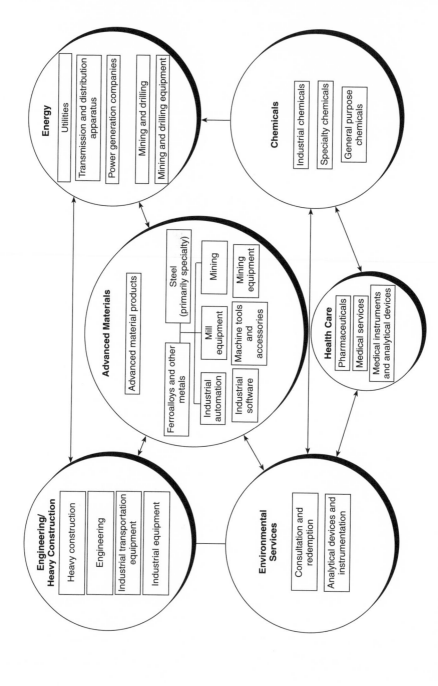

Figure 7.8 Greater Pittsburgh Clusters

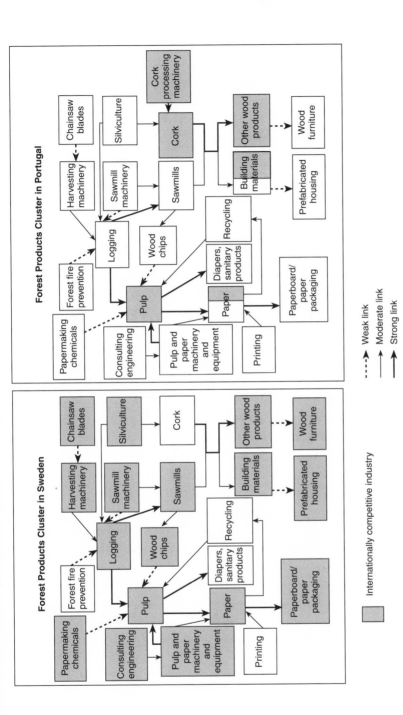

Figure 7.9 Forest Products Clusters in Sweden and Portugal
Sources: Monitor Company (1994) and Porter, Sölvell, and Zander (1991).

The development of well-functioning clusters is one of the essential steps in moving to an advanced economy. In developing economies, cluster formation is impeded by low local education and skill levels, weaknesses in technology, lack of access to capital, and poorly developed institutions. Government policy may also work against cluster formation. Restrictions on industrial location and subsidies artificially spread out companies. University and technical school curricula, centrally dictated, fail to adapt to cluster needs. Finally, protected from competition, companies engage in monopolistic behavior that further retards cluster development.

The paucity of clusters in developing countries does not mean that such countries cannot compete, but it impedes upgrading and productivity improvement. While exports can grow for a time based on low-cost local labor or natural resources exploited with imported technology, such an approach is ultimately limiting. To improve profits, wages, and the standard of living, the challenge over time is to raise productivity and increase product value. To allow a location to become more productive, develop local capacity to improve products and processes, and, ultimately, to innovate, a cluster must build up over time. Otherwise, the natural tendency for local costs to rise over time cannot be counteracted, and other locations with lower factor costs or offering greater subsidies will take over production.

The successful deepening and broadening of clusters, then, is integral to successful economic development.[25] Cluster development seems to be a controlling factor in moving from a lower middle income (per capita income of $8,000 to 15,000) to an advanced economy. Even in advanced, high-wage economies, however, the need for cluster upgrading is never-ending. It remains essential to allow the continuing rise of productivity and incomes. The wealthier the economy, the more necessary becomes true innovation in products, services, and methods of production to support rising wages and to replace jobs freed up by improvements in efficiency.

INTERNAL TRADE AND INVESTMENT

While international trade and investment are widely recognized as powerful forces for productivity growth, the role of internal trade and investment has been largely ignored. The geographic dispersion of clusters and the specialization of geographic regions by cluster is normally greatest in advanced economies. In nations such as the United States, Italy, Switzerland, and Germany, internal specialization, trade, and investment contribute significantly to productivity and productivity growth. Internal competition motivates improvements by state and local governments and by local institutions, because these entities face far more competitive pressure than do federal government or institutional monopolies. Trading within a nation, made easier by proximity, national similarities, and, often, fewer trade barriers outside of a nation's control, provides a stepping-stone from which firms can build the skills needed to internationalize.

In developing economies, a large proportion of economic activity tends to concentrate around large capital cities, such as in Bangkok and Bogota. This concentration reflects the absence of infrastructure and institutions in outlying areas and the almost total lack of available suppliers. It may also reflect an intrusive role by the central government in controlling competition, a force that leads firms to locate near the seat of power and the agencies whose approval they require to do business. In many developing economies, industries crowd together, and little or no activity takes place in outlying areas, other than agriculture and resource production.

This pattern of economic geography inflicts high costs in terms of productivity as compared to geographic dispersion and specialization. Congestion, bottlenecks, and inflexibility lead to high administrative costs and major inefficiencies, not to mention a diminished quality of life. Companies cannot easily move out from the center, however, because neither infrastructure nor rudimentary clusters exist in the smaller cities and towns. The transition from a concentrated to a dispersed economy, with specialized industries and clusters, represents another essential challenge of economic development. (The building of a tourism cluster in developing economies can be a positive force in improving outlying infrastructure and dispersing economic activity.)

Even in advanced economies, however, economic activity may be concentrated in a few geographic areas. Japan offers a particularly striking case, with nearly 50 percent of total manufacturing shipments located around Tokyo and Osaka. This is due less to inadequacies in infrastructure in outlying areas and more to the powerful and intrusive central government, with its centralizing bias in policies and institutions. The Japanese case illustrates vividly the major inefficiencies and productivity costs resulting from such an economic geography even for advanced nations. Addressing its pattern of economic geography is a major policy issue facing Japan.

Traditional treatments of economic geography often stress the benefits of highly diversified metropolitan economies, citing advantages in terms of available inputs, infrastructure, communication, and access to a large local market. The forces of globalization have greatly diminished such generalized urbanization advantages, while cluster-specific advantages have increased. In advanced economies, even large metropolitan areas are often quite specialized in terms of exporting clusters. An economic geography characterized by a number of metropolitan areas, each specializing in an array of clusters, appears to be a far more productive industrial organization than one based on one or two huge, diversified cities. Most developing countries also suffer from the lack of multiple metropolitan areas that compete with one another.

THE LOCATION PARADOX

Economic geography in an era of global competition, then, involves a paradox. In an economy with rapid transportation and communication and accessible global markets, location remains fundamental to competition. It has been widely recognized that changes in technology and competition have diminished many of the traditional roles of location. Resources, capital, and other inputs can be efficiently sourced in global markets. Firms can access immobile inputs via corporate networks. They need no longer locate near large markets.

Naturally, perhaps, the first response to globalization has been to pursue these benefits by moving assembly plants and other factor cost-sensitive activities to low-cost locations. Anything that can be efficiently sourced from a distance, however, has been essentially *nullified* as a competitive advantage in advanced economies. Information and relationships that can be accessed and maintained via fax or e-mail are available to anyone. While global sourcing and communication mitigates disadvantages, it does not create advantages. Moreover, distant sourcing is normally a second-best solution compared to accessing a competitive local cluster, in terms of both total productivity and innovation.

Paradoxically, then, the enduring competitive advantages in a global economy are often heavily local, arising from concentrations of highly specialized skills and knowledge, institutions, rivals, related businesses, and sophisticated customers in a particular nation or region. Proximity in geographic, cultural, and institutional terms allows special access, special relationships, better information, powerful incentives, and other advantages in productivity and productivity growth that are difficult to tap from a distance. Standard inputs, information, and technologies are readily available via globalization, then, while more advanced dimensions of competition remain geographically bounded. Location matters, albeit in different ways at the turn of the twenty-first century than in earlier decades.[26]

Economic geography in many parts of the world, however, remains in a state of major transition. The relaxation of barriers to trade and investment, still comparatively recent in many countries, is incomplete. The fall of transportation and communication costs has been rapid, while investments in plant and equipment often last for many decades. As a result, many overly broad national and subnational economies persist, as do many clusters in countries and regions that lack a real competitive advantage.

The Birth, Evolution, and Decline of Clusters

A cluster's roots can often be traced to parts of the diamond that are present in a location due to historical circumstances.[27] One prominent motivation for the formation of early companies is the availability of pools of factors, such as specialized skills, university research expertise, an efficient physical location, or particularly good or appropriate infrastructure. Many Massachusetts clusters, for example, had their beginnings in research done at MIT or Harvard while a number of prominent Finnish clusters emerged from the presence of natural resources. The Dutch transportation cluster owes much to a central location within Europe, a network of waterways, the efficiency of the port of Rotterdam, and the skills accumulated by the Dutch through Holland's long maritime history.

Clusters may also arise from unusual, sophisticated, or stringent local demand. Israel's cluster in irrigation equipment and other advanced agricultural technologies reflects that nation's strong desire for a self-sufficient food supply, coupled with its scarcity of water and its hot, arid growing conditions. Finland's environmental cluster emerged from pollution problems created by local process industries (for example, metals, forestry, chemicals, energy), as did the environment cluster in greater Pittsburgh (see Figure 7.8).

Prior existence of supplier industries, related industries, or entire related clusters provides yet another seed for new clusters. The golf equipment cluster near San Diego, California, for example, has its roots in the southern California aerospace cluster. This cluster created a pool of available suppliers for castings and advanced materials and of engineers with the requisite experience in working with these technologies.

New clusters may also arise from one or two innovative companies that stimulate the growth of many others. Medtronic played this role in helping to create the Minneapolis medical devices cluster. Similarly, MCI and America OnLine have been spin-off hubs for the telecommunications cluster in the Washington, D.C., metropolitan area.

Chance events are often important to the birth of a cluster. The early formation of companies in a location often reflects acts of entrepreneurship not completely explainable by reference to favorable local circumstances. These companies, in other words, could have sprouted at any one of a number of comparable locations. The establishment of cluster pioneer Callaway Golf in Carlsbad rather than another southern California town had much to do with chance.

Chance, however, often has locational antecedents, making its role less than it at first appears. The location of pacemaker pioneer Medtronic in the Minneapolis area provides an interesting example. Medtronic, which now employs over twelve thousand people, provided the seed for the entire Minnesota medical devices cluster, now encompassing more than one hundred Minnesota companies—all with roots traceable to Medtronic employees or technologies.[28] In 1949, Earl Bakken, an electrical engineering graduate student working part time at a Minneapolis hospital, founded Medtronic, with Palmer Hermundslie, as a medical equipment repair company. By the early 1950s, Medtronic was building custom equipment for medical researchers. In the mid 1950s, the company developed a relationship with Dr. C. W. Lillehei, a pioneer in open heart surgery at the University of Minnesota Medical School. The university had a national reputation in both electrical engineering and surgery. Medtronic engineers worked with Dr. Lillehei to improve the bulky and dangerous devices then being used to stimulate heart activity. By 1957, the breakthrough Bakken battery-powered pacemaker was in use. The next breakthrough, in electrodes, was developed in 1958, the result of a collaboration with Dr. Samuel Hunter of St. Joseph Hospital in St. Paul. By 1960, Medtronic had evolved into a world-recognized pacemaker competitor. While the developments leading to the company's initial success arose partly by chance, the founding and success of the company were inextricably entwined with the area's local university and medical institutions.

Chance events can also be important in the chain of causality leading to company formation by creating advantageous factor or demand conditions. The telemarketing cluster in Omaha, Nebraska, for example, owes much to the decision by the U.S. Air Force to locate the Strategic Air Command (SAC) there. Charged with a key role in America's nuclear deterrence strategy, SAC was the site of the first installation of fiber-optic telecommunications cables in the United States. In addition, the local Bell operating company (now U.S. West) developed unusual capability through dealing with such a demanding customer. The extraordinary telecommunication infrastructure that consequently developed in Omaha, coupled with less unique attributes, such as its central time zone location and easy-to-understand local accent, provided the underpinnings of the area's telemarketing cluster.

Some recent treatments of industry evolution have emphasized chance, but chance must be considered in its locational context. What looks like chance may be as much the result of preexisting local circumstances, as the above examples, and others, suggest. Moreover, even when chance provides a central explanation for a development, it is almost never the sole explanation. The influences of location not only raise the odds that chance events will occur, they also raise the odds that chance events will lead to competitive firms and industries. Chance alone rarely explains why a cluster takes root or its subsequent growth and development.

The limited explanatory role of chance raises serious doubts about whether clusters can be seeded in locations where no important advantages already exist. The appropriate policy towards cluster development, then, should be to *build on existing or emerging fields* that have passed a market test, a subject to which I will return below.

CLUSTER DEVELOPMENT

While the birth of clusters has many causes, the development or lack of development of clusters is more predictable. Though there is no guarantee that a cluster will develop, once the process gets started it is like a chain reaction in which the lines of causality quickly become blurred. The process depends heavily on the efficacy of the diamond's arrows or feedback loops, on how well, for example, local educational, regulatory, and other institutions respond to the cluster's needs, or how rapidly capable suppliers respond to the cluster opportunity. Three particular areas deserve special attention: intensity of local competition, the location's overall environment for new business formation, and the efficacy of formal and informal mechanisms for bringing cluster participants together. Healthy rivalry is an essential driver of rapid improvement and entrepreneurship. The entrepreneurial climate is important because the creation of new firms and institutions is so integral to cluster development. Finally, organizational and relationship-building mechanisms are necessary because a cluster's advantages rely heavily on linkages and connections among individuals and groups.

In a healthy cluster, the initial critical mass of firms triggers a self-reinforcing process in which specialized suppliers emerge; information accumulates; local institutions develop specialized training, research, infrastructure and appropriate regulations; and cluster visibility and prestige grows. Perceiving a market opportunity and facing falling entry barriers, entrepreneurs create new companies. Spinoffs from existing companies develop, and new suppliers emerge. Recognition of the cluster's existence constitutes a milestone. As more institutions and firms recognize the cluster's importance, a growing number of specialized products and services become available and specialized expertise responsive to the cluster arises among local financial services providers, construction firms, and the like. Informal and formal organizations and modes of communication involving cluster participants develop.[29] As the cluster grows, it develops greater influence not only over what other firms do but also over public and private institutions and government policies. Policies that have deterred cluster upgrading are often modified.

From numerous case studies, it appears that clusters require a decade or more to develop depth and to gain real competitive advantage—one reason why government attempts to create clusters normally fail. Clusters at different locations often develop unique subspecializations, notably in product segment coverage, the array of suppliers and complementary industries, and the prevailing modes of competing.

Cluster development often becomes particularly vibrant at the intersection of clusters. Here, insights, skills, and technologies from different fields merge, sparking new businesses. The presence of multiple intersecting clusters further lowers barriers to entry, because potential entrants and spinoffs come from several directions. Diversity of learning stimulates innovation. Germany, for example, has both a home appliance cluster and a household furniture cluster. At the intersection of these clusters is built-in kitchens and built-in appliances, products in which Germany has a higher share of world exports than in either appliances or furniture overall. Figure 7.10 illustrates some cluster intersections in Massachusetts that have proven to be fertile breeding grounds for new companies.

In a national or global economy, cluster development can be greatly accelerated by attracting cluster participants from other states or nations. A growing cluster begins to attract in-bound foreign direct investment (FDI) in the form of manufacturing or service operations and supplier facilities. Companies relocate from less productive locations or invest in subsidiaries to access cluster expertise in particular segments. This occurred in golf equipment, for example, when east coast manufacturers established R&D centers and operations in Carlsbad, California. Suppliers move to the emerging location to gain better access and closer relationships with a growing customer base.

Developing clusters also attract—and cluster participants seek out—people and ideas that reinforce the cluster. Growing clusters attract

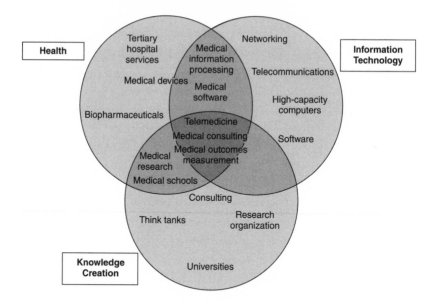

Figure 7.10   Cluster Intersections in Massachusetts

skilled people through offering greater opportunities. Entrepreneurs or individuals with ideas migrate to the cluster from other locations, as well, because a growing cluster signals opportunity. A cluster's success stories help attract the best talent.

As noted, cluster participants often play a role in this process, seeking out people, technologies, and even suppliers from elsewhere. The later history of Medtronic provides a good example. In 1960, two Buffalo, New York, physicians and an electrical engineer published a paper on a self-contained, transistorized, implantable pacemaker. Medtronic, working on the same problem, immediately recognized the significance of the work, and within months had contracted for exclusive rights to the new pacemaker. Lacking a local cluster, the Buffalo inventors quickly realized that the economic value of their idea would be much greater if an established company in a growing cluster commercialized it.

As a cluster evolves, cluster participants tend to develop increasingly global strategies. They market products in more and more countries, and sometimes source the more generic or basic inputs from other locations. Over time, less productive activities are internationalized to lower cost and improve access to foreign markets. As long as such internationalization results not from internal rigidities but from active pursuit of opportunities, this process makes the cluster more competitive. A cluster in which many participants compete globally is healthier because this not only opens up more growth opportunities but enriches knowledge and stimulates new ideas. Any effort to keep cluster participants local to protect advantages is misguided and ultimately counterproductive.

Nascent clusters can never develop if the market forces and feedback loops of the kind described here prove weak or nonfunctioning. Local institutions may have other agendas. Inbound foreign investments may be blocked by government policy. Dominant firms or cartels may keep out new competition. Dominant suppliers may be entrenched elsewhere. Artificial barriers to new business formation may stunt competition and retard innovation and specialization. Government policy can also impede clustering and cluster upgrading in a myriad of ways.

In a world economy in which many national and local markets are still protected to some extent or are only slowly opening, there are still numerous clusters lacking any competitive advantage. As more and more of the world economy opens to competition, however, these clusters will shrink and wither away.

CLUSTER DECLINE

Clusters can maintain vibrancy as competitive locations for centuries, and most successful clusters prosper at least for decades. Just as the development of a cluster is not assured, however, neither is its continued ability to compete.

The causes of cluster atrophy and decline can also be found in the elements of the diamond. They can be grouped into two broad categories: endogenous, or deriving from the location itself, and exogenous, or due to developments or discontinuities in the external environment.

Internal sources of decline stem from internal rigidities that diminish productivity and innovation. The onset of restrictive union rules or regulatory inflexibility can slow down productivity improvement. Over-consolidation, mutual understandings, cartels, or other barriers to competition can undermine local rivalry. Institutions such as schools and universities can suffer from their own rigidities and fail to upgrade and change. Groupthink among cluster participants, another form of rigidity, was discussed above.

Such rigidities in clusters tend to arise in locations in which government is prone to suspend or intervene in competition. When internal rigidities arise, the rate of improvement and innovation in a cluster falters. Increases in the cost of doing business begin to outrun the ability to upgrade. Such internal rigidities currently work against a variety of clusters in Switzerland and Germany.

As long as rivalry remains sufficiently vigorous, companies can partially compensate for local problems through globalization. Outsourcing can compensate for supplier problems, and foreign production can offset local wages that rise ahead of productivity. German firms in the 1990s, for example, have been rapidly outsourcing and outlocating to mitigate the effect of local cost problems. Unless internal rigidities ease, however, a cluster will eventually lose its productivity and dynamism. Competitive advantage will migrate to other locations.

External threats to cluster success arise in several areas. Technological discontinuities are perhaps the most significant, because they can neutralize many cluster advantages simultaneously. Market information, employee skills, scientific and technical expertise, and supplier bases may be rendered inappropriate. Unless the requisite new technologies and skills are available from other local institutions or can be rapidly developed, competitive advantage will shift to another location. The shift of golf equipment manufacturing from New England to California provides a good example. The New England cluster was based on steel shafts, steel irons, and wooden-headed woods. When the notion of making golf clubs with advanced materials was pioneered, east coast producers had difficulty competing. Some east coast firms joined the California cluster; others died or declined.

A shift in buyer needs, creating a divergence between local needs and needs elsewhere, constitutes another external threat to cluster productivity and innovation. American firms in a variety of clusters, for example, suffered when energy efficiency grew in importance in most parts of the world while the United States maintained low energy prices, retarding innovation. As this example illustrates, however, the threat posed by external developments often relates to local choices and policies.

As with internal threats to cluster competitiveness, aggressive firms in a location can, for a time, use globalization to compensate for external discontinuities. Technology can be licensed or sourced from other locations, product development can be moved elsewhere, and components and equipment can be outsourced. Over time, however, a location that fails to build up a critical mass in a major new technology or in meeting a major new need will wane as a home base for innovative companies.

The competitive decline of a cluster should not be confused with reductions in employment or total revenue that may result from upgrading. Rising local wages and profits reflect economic success. This means that less skilled and less productive activities *should* move to other locations. The ultimate test of the health or decline of a cluster is its rate of innovation. A cluster that is investing and innovating at home is of far less concern than one that improves productivity only through shrinking and outsourcing.

The Role of Government

Government inevitably plays a variety of roles in an economy. Identifying the broad types of these roles helps put government's proper policies toward clusters in context.

Goverment's most basic role in an economy is to achieve macroeconomic and political stability. It does this by establishing stable government institutions, a consistent basic economic framework, and sound macroeconomic policies, including prudent government finances and low inflation. Government's second role is to improve general microeconomic capacity of the economy by improving the efficiency and quality of the general purpose inputs to business identified in the diamond (an educated workforce, appropriate physical infrastructure, and accurate and timely economic information) and the institutions that provide them. Such inputs are required across the entire economy and are a foundation upon which everything else is built. Government's third role is to establish the overall microeconomic rules and incentives governing competition that will encourage productivity growth. Such rules and incentives, present throughout the diamond, include a competition policy enhancing rivalry, a tax system and intellectual property laws encouraging investment, a fair and efficient legal system, laws providing consumer recourse, corporate governance rules holding managers accountable for performance, and an efficient regulatory process promoting innovation rather than freezing the status quo.

While these roles of government are necessary for economic progress, however, they may not be sufficient. Especially as government begins to make headway in its more basic roles, a fourth role—that of facilitating cluster development and upgrading—takes on prominence. Government should aim to reinforce the development and upgrading of *all* clusters, not choose among them. While the general business environment is central to competitiveness, cluster circumstances are increasingly important in allowing an economy to move beyond factor-cost competition. Government policies inevitably affect the opportunities for upgrading clusters. At the same time, many of the productivity and innovation advantages of clusters rest on spillovers and externalities that involve government entities. In addition to modifying its own policies and practices, government can also motivate, facilitate, and provide incentives for collective action by the private sector. (Government's role in cluster development and upgrading is not the same as so-called industrial policy. See the insert "Clusters versus Industrial Policy.")

Government's final role in an economy is in developing and implementing a positive, distinctive, long-term economic action program or change process which mobilizes government, business, institutions, and citizens to upgrade both the general business environment and the array of local clusters. Economic progress is thwarted as much by inaction as by a lack of knowing what steps are necessary. Strong forces oppose economic upgrading, ranging from obsolete views about competitiveness to entrenched interests that prosper from the status quo. Only a long-term process, with accompanying institutions, can counteract these forces. The process must involve all key constituencies and rise above the politics of any particular administration or government. The process must encompass the general conditions affecting all industries as well as the upgrading of clusters. Ideally, such a process will occur not only at the national level but at the state and city level as well.

GOVERNMENT POLICY AT THE CLUSTER LEVEL

All clusters offer opportunities to improve productivity and support rising wages, even those that do not compete with other locations. Every cluster not only contributes directly to national productivity but can affect the productivity of *other* clusters as well. This means that traditional clusters, such as agriculture, should not be abandoned but upgraded. Efforts to upgrade clusters may have to be sequenced for practical reasons, but the goal should be to encompass all of them eventually. Not all clusters will succeed, of course, and upgrading in some clusters will reduce employment as firms move to more productive activities. These outcomes should be determined by market forces, however, not by government decisions.

Government should reinforce and build on established and emerging clusters, rather than attempt to create entirely new ones. New industries and new clusters emerge best from established ones. Businesses involving advanced technology do not succeed in a vacuum, but where there is already a base of less sophisticated activities in the field. Most clusters form independently of government action—and sometimes in spite of it. Clusters form where a foundation of locational advantages exists to build on. To justify cluster development efforts, some seeds of a cluster should have already passed a market test.

Cluster development efforts must embrace the pursuit of competitive advantage and specialization, rather than attempt to imitate exactly what is present in other locations. This requires building on local differences and sources of uniqueness where possible, turning them into strengths. Finding areas of specialization normally proves more effective than head-on competition with well-established rival locations. Specialization also offers the potential to meet new needs and expand the market.

Cluster development can be seeded and reinforced by inbound FDI. The most effective efforts at attracting FDI concentrate on attracting multiple companies in the same field, supported by parallel investments in specialized training, infrastructure, and other aspects of the business environment.

Cluster upgrading involves recognizing the presence of a cluster, and then removing obstacles, relaxing constraints, and eliminating inefficiencies that impede cluster productivity and innovation. Constraints include those of human resources, infrastructure, and regulation. Some can be addressed to varying degrees by private initiatives, but others result from government policies and institutions and must be addressed by government. Government regulations, for example, may create unnecessary inefficiencies; important infrastructure may be lacking; education and training policies may overlook cluster needs. Ideally, all government policies that inflict costs on firms without conferring any compensating, long-term competitive value should be minimized or eliminated. Upgrading clusters, then, requires going beyond improvements in the general business environment to evaluating and, if necessary, changing policies and institutions that affect particular concentrations of related firms and industries.

Governments are often drawn into developing policies, such as subsidiaries or technology grants, that attempt to enhance the competitiveness of individual firms. Much policy attention has also addressed the industry level, also narrower than clusters. Conversely, other policy thinking is concerned with broad sectors, such as machinery, manufacturing, or services. None of these approaches is well aligned with modern competition. Setting policies to benefit individual firms distorts markets and

---

Clusters versus Industrial Policy

A cluster-based approach to economic development is sometimes confused with industrial policy. In reality, cluster theory and industrial policy differ fundamentally in both their intellectual foundations and their implications for government policy.

Industrial policy rests on a view of international (or more generally, locational) competition in which some industries offer greater wealth-creating prospects than others. Desirable industries—that is, those that are growing or industries that employ high tech—should be "targeted" for support. Industrial policy sees competitive advantage as heavily determined by increasing returns to scale.

Given the importance of scale, governments should nurture priority emerging, "infant" industries until they reach a critical mass, through subsidies, eliminating "destructive" or "wasteful" internal competition, selective protection from imports, and restricting foreign investment. Subsidies and suspension of internal competition should concentrate on scale-sensitive areas, such as R&D and facilities investment. Through such intervention, government attempts to tilt competitive outcomes (and international market share) in a nation's favor. Sometimes the notion of industrial policy seems to reflect a zero-sum view of international competition, where there is a fixed pool of demand to be served and the goal is to gain a larger share for a particular nation.[a]

Cluster theory could hardly be more different. The concept of clusters rests on a broader, more dynamic view of competition among firms and locations based on the growth of productivity. Interconnections and spillovers within a cluster often influence productivity growth more than does the scale of individual firms.

All clusters can be desirable, and all offer the potential to contribute to prosperity. What matters is not what a nation (location) competes in, but how. Instead of targeting, therefore, all existing and emerging clusters deserve attention. All clusters can improve their productivity. Rather than recommending the exclusion of foreign firms, cluster theory calls for welcoming them. Foreign firms enhance cluster externalities and productivity, and their activities in a nation contribute directly to local employment and investment. Rather than advocate blocking imports, cluster theory stresses the need for timely and steady opening of the local market to imports that boost local efficiency, provide needed inputs, upgrade local demand conditions, and stimulate rivalry.

While industrial policy aims to distort competition in favor of a particular location, cluster theory focuses on removing constraints to productivity and productivity growth. Cluster theory emphasizes not market share but dynamic improvement. This results in a positive sum underlying view of competition, in which productivity improvements and trade expand the market and many locations prosper if they can become more productive and innovative.

---

a. The intellectual foundations of industrial policy go back for centuries and can be traced to works on mercantilism and arguments for protecting of infant industries, among others. Industrial policy received major impetus in work that viewed it as an important explanation for Japan's economic success. The intellectual rigor of industrial policy was also greatly enhanced by "strategic trade theory." See, for example, Krugman (1986) and Tyson (1992).

uses government resources inefficiently. Focusing policy at the industry level presumes that some industries are better than others and runs grave risks of distorting or limiting competition. Often, firms are wary of participating along with their competitors. Sectors, in contrast, are too broad to be competitively significant, and distinctions such as manufacturing versus services or high tech versus low tech no longer hold meaning.

A cluster focus highlights the externalities, linkages, spillovers, and supporting institutions so important to competition. By grouping together firms, suppliers, related industries, service providers, and institutions, government initiatives and investments address problems common to many firms and industries without threatening competition. A government role in cluster upgrading, then, will encourage competition rather than distort it. A cluster focus will also encourage the buildup of public or quasi-public goods that significantly impact many linked businesses. Government investments focused on improving the business environment in clusters, then, other things being equal, may well earn a higher return than those aimed at individual firms or industries or at the broad economy.

Emphasizing clusters might seem to encourage unhealthy economic specialization, but upgrading all clusters rather than choosing among them avoids this. Moreover, clusters function as powerful sources of new business formation, and new clusters often emerge out of existing ones. Also, the presence of clusters can facilitate the adjustment of local firms to changing economic conditions, reducing risk to the local economy rather than increasing it.[30]

More broadly, clusters represent a new and complementary way of dividing and understanding an economy, organizing economic development thinking and practice, and setting public policy. Clusters, together with the diamond model, reveal the process by which wealth is actually created in an economy and make competitiveness more concrete and operational. (Nonbusiness constituencies, especially, benefit from the demystification of competition.) Policy analyses and recommendations can address systematically the needs of business. In the Netherlands, for example, cluster development represents an important priority of government policy. Clusters provide a vehicle for bringing companies, government, and local institutions together in a constructive dialogue about upgrading and offer a new mechanism for business-government collaboration. Dialogue with more broadly defined business groupings inevitably gravitates toward discussion of the general business environment, and issues such as taxes, currency value, and overall complaints about the inefficiencies of government. Businesses get to vent their grievances against the government, but quickly lose patience. Government gains little useful information from such critiques and representatives quickly tire of listening to repetitive lobbying over the same old issues. A business-government dialogue convened around narrowly defined industries inhibits productive interchange as participants grow wary of revealing their needs and problems in front of competitors. Such discussions often gravitate toward subsidies, import protections, and limits to competition. Dialogues that engage cluster participants, in contrast, avoid these difficulties by bringing together all the affected players and focusing on common constraints and linkages among related firms. The presence of suppliers, channels, and often customers checks any incipient effort to suppress competition.

GOVERNMENT INFLUENCES ON CLUSTER UPGRADING

Figure 7.11 illustrates some specific government roles in cluster upgrading. Government influences on a cluster appear throughout the diamond. At one end of the spectrum, governments might convene forums of

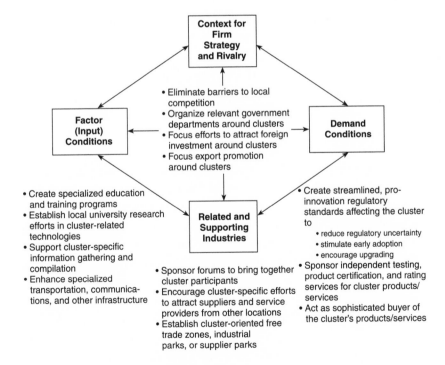

Figure 7.11   Government Influences on Cluster Upgrading

firms, institutions, and appropriate government agencies. At the other end, government has more direct roles such as collecting and compiling cluster-specific information; setting educational policies encouraging public universities and schools to respond to local cluster needs; clarifying and simplifying regulations significantly affecting the cluster; and improving the sophistication of local demand for cluster products and services. At times, cluster upgrading can be as simple as colocating public with private investments. In New Zealand forestry, for example, the cluster centers on the North Island, while the main university institution supporting the cluster, at the University of Canterbury, is on the South Island. (See the insert "Microclusters in Catalonia" for another specific case example.)

Clusters offer a new way for governments to collect and organize information. The Standard Industrial Classification System, for example, aligns poorly with clusters and with the actual nature of competition; dated groupings, such as machinery, products, and services, fail to capture the most important linkages among industries. Some regions, such as Massachusetts, have begun to retabulate economic data focusing on clusters, although much remains to be done.[31]

As clusters mature and develop and as the sources of their competitive advantage shift, the appropriate government priorities change. Early priorities involve improving infrastructure and eliminating diamond disadvantages. Later roles revolve more around removing constraints and impediments to innovation.

An important tool for encouraging cluster growth in developing countries is attracting foreign investment. Attracting one or two multinationals in a field can attract others, which in turn triggers local developments. In Costa Rica, for example, an Intel plant announced in November 1996 and a Microsoft investment announced in September 1997 have led to serious expressions of interest in the nation from other information technology producers. Foreign investment alone, however, is insufficient to build clusters. Also necessary are systematic efforts to improve local conditions throughout the diamond. Costa Rica's plan to create the conditions for growing an information technology cluster includes initiatives in areas such as improving training, enhancing the data communications infrastructure, and encouraging use of computers in schools.

Even when attempting to seed clusters with FDI, however, success requires the presence of prior locational advantages. Costa Rica spends 6 percent of GDP on education, one of the highest expenditures in the region. It also has an established network of research centers and enjoys the highest index of computers per capita in Latin America. These conditions, together with a long history of political stability, were what attracted Intel and Microsoft in the first place.

In developing economies, foreign investment promotion, free trade zones, and industrial parks also act as prominent policy levers favoring cluster growth. Free trade zones and industrial parks can better foster economic upgrading if they have a cluster rather than a general focus, supported by tailored regulations and supporting infrastructure. Free trade zones and industrial parks may have to begin as enclaves in an otherwise inefficient business environment, with virtually all inputs imported, all outputs exported, and little or no contact with the rest of the economy. Over time, however, such zones should build links with the rest of the economy. Programs and regulations must encourage the use and development of local suppliers, for example, and the forging of links with local educational and training institutions. In addition, government must move aggressively to improve infrastructure and reduce inefficiencies *throughout* the economy. The use of enclaves cannot be allowed to reduce the sense of urgency about needed improvements in the general business environment, still the only way to achieve sustained improvements in prosperity.

CLUSTERS AND OVERALL ECONOMIC POLICY

The cluster concept provides a way of organizing thinking about many policy areas that goes beyond the common needs of the entire economy, as shown in Figure 7.12. Cluster-based thinking can help guide policies in science and technology, education and training, and promotion of exports and foreign investment, among others. A location's best chance of attracting foreign investment and promoting exports, for example, lies in its existing or emerging clusters.

A cluster orientation highlights the fact that more parts of government have an influence on competitiveness, often not recognized within gov-

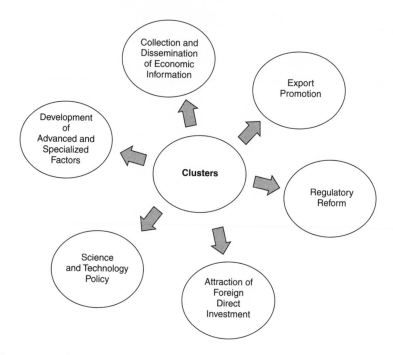

Figure 7.12   Clusters and Economic Policy

ernment itself. Cluster theory clarifies the impacts on competitive posi-tion of government policies and makes needed actions more operational. Effective solutions often require collaboration among different parts of government. (See the insert "Microclusters in Catalonia" for an example.)

In some locations, government agencies that relate to business have begun to organize themselves internally to align with local clusters. In Arizona, for example, the Department of Commerce now develops staff as experts on particular clusters, in contrast to a past focus on individual foreign countries (for example, Canada or Japan). A cluster orientation in government also provides a mechanism through which officials can become better informed about the practical costs and benefits of policies and better motivated to make policies and government organizations more cost effective. Ongoing cluster assessments represent a powerful tool for identifying and validating economy-wide policy deficiencies and for finding practical solutions. A problem that surfaces in several different clusters clearly should be a priority.

Finally, cluster thinking also highlights the important roles of government at a number of geographic levels. The traditional focus of economic policy has been at the national level, where many aspects of the general business environment are best addressed. Recently, globalization has focused attention on worldwide multilateral institutions. State, metropolitan region, and local governments, however, also significantly influence the general business environment in a location. At the cluster level, these influences often dominate, and consideration of clusters should represent an important component of state and local economic policy.

Each level of government exerts an important influence on the overall business environment and on clusters. National policies should set minimum standards while pushing public investment choices down to smaller geographic levels, and they should avoid centralization and rigidities that obstruct policies tailored for implementation at the state and local level.[32] Economic development programs should increasingly involve parallel efforts at multiple geographic levels. In New Zealand, for example, cluster development began at the national level but has spread to the state and local level. Almost three-quarters of all local economic development agencies in New Zealand have adopted the identification and upgrading of clusters as an integral part of their activities.[33]

Finally, while far less common, influences on productivity—and clusters themselves—sometimes cross national borders. Coordination among transportation systems, energy networks, and other areas among neighboring countries can benefit productivity in ways that go well beyond customs unions and free trade zones. Groups of neighboring countries, then, also have a joint role to play in formulating economic policy. Figure 7.13 illustrates the broadening geographic units of policy analysis important in modern competition.

The Corporate Role in Cluster Development

The existence of clusters suggests that much of a company's potential to achieve competitive advantage, both in operational effectiveness and in establishing a unique strategy, lies outside the company and even outside the industry. The presence of a well-developed cluster provides

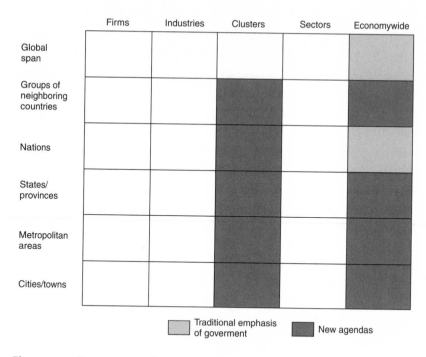

Figure 7.13 Government Influences on Competitiveness

powerful benefits to productivity and to the capacity for innovation that are difficult for firms based elsewhere to match. Often, for a given field, only a few locations in the world can achieve such an environment.

Even though clusters offer tangible competitive benefits, the first reaction of managers is often to be wary of them. There are concerns that the expansion of a cluster will invite unwanted competition and drive up the costs of employees and inputs. Managers have nightmare visions of losing valued employees to rivals or spinoffs. As their understanding of the cluster concept grows, however, managers realize that many cluster participants do not directly compete. Although a company may face competition for employees and other inputs, the presence of the cluster expands their supply. The net access to specialized skills, services, technology, and information in a cluster often increases. Any increases in competition comes with cluster benefits in productivity, flexibility, and innovation.

Cluster theory suggests new tasks and roles for companies. Cluster analysis must become part of competitive assessments, along with company and industry analysis. Private sector roles in cluster upgrading can be found in all parts of the diamond, as shown in Figure 7.14. Improving factor conditions provides the most obvious example, with efforts possible in enhancing the supply of appropriately trained personnel, the quality and appropriateness of local university research activities, the creation of specialized physical infrastructure, and the supply of cluster-specific information. Ongoing relationships with government bodies and local institutions, such as utilities, schools, and research groups, are necessary to attain these benefits. There is also a role for private investment by cluster participants to establish common specialized infrastructure, such as port or handling facilities, satellite communication links, and testing laboratories. Often such investments can be made and administered through third parties, for example, universities or trade associations.

In the area of related and supporting industries, firms have a role in attracting suppliers, services, and complementary-product producers to the cluster, as well as in forming supplier businesses to fill gaps. Joint

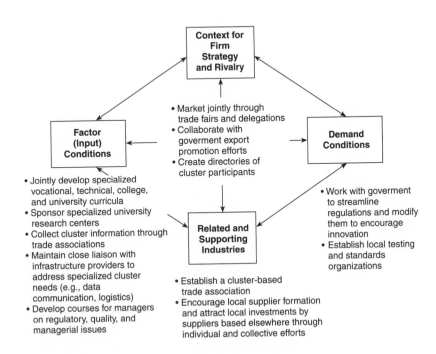

Figure 7.14   Private Sector Influences on Cluster Upgrading

ventures are sometimes used to establish local capability in essential supporting industries.

The need for cluster participants to inform and prod government to address the constraints or weaknesses under its control cuts across all parts of the diamond. Individual departments or units of government that impact the cluster must be engaged and educated on the effect of regulations and policies and on the quality of government services. An open, constructive dialogue must replace self-serving lobbying or paternalism in these relationships.

THE ROLE OF TRADE ASSOCIATIONS AND COLLECTIVE BODIES

Individual companies can independently influence cluster development, and cluster pioneers or leading firms often play this role because they gain major benefits. Given the important externalities and public goods involved in clusters, however, informal networks and formal trade associations, consortia, and other collective bodies often become necessary and appropriate. Trade associations representing all or most cluster participants can command greater attention and achieve greater influence than can individual members, and an association or collective body (for example, a joint research center or testing laboratory) creates a vehicle for cost sharing.

Many trade associations do little more than lobby government, compile some statistics, and host social functions. The opportunity for associations to enhance cluster competitiveness, however, is much greater. Associations or collective bodies institutionalize cluster linkages. In addition to providing a neutral forum for identifying common needs, constraints, and opportunities, associations can serve as focal points for efforts to address them. Associations often take the lead in organizing national and international fairs and delegations; they create training programs in conjunction with local institutions, manage purchasing consortia, establish university-based research programs and testing facilities, collect cluster-related information, offer forums on common managerial problems, investigate solutions to environmental issues, and pursue many other common interests. These activities are in addition to performance of the traditional task of interfacing with local, state, and national government, guiding regulatory reform, and representing the cluster with other business groups.

Associations fulfill especially important functions for clusters consisting of many small- and medium-sized firms (for example, tourism, apparel, or agriculture). Such clusters have a particularly great need for a collective body to take on scale-sensitive functions. In the Netherlands, for example, grower cooperatives built the specialized auction and handling facilities that constitute one of the Dutch flower cluster's greatest competitive advantages. The Dutch Flower Council and the Association of Dutch Flower Growers Research Groups, in which most growers participate, have taken on other functions as well, such as marketing and applied research.

At times, cluster-based trade associations may not exist. Or, existing associations may be too narrow, including industry participants but not suppliers, companies in related industries, or local institutions. Existing trade organizations may be national rather than local in scope. National associations have been the norm, as most associations have seen their primary role as lobbying government, with the national government viewed as most important. National associations, however, are rarely effective in addressing many of the training, infrastructure, and other issues most important to cluster productivity. Another typical pattern among a location's business organizations is chambers of commerce, roundtables, or councils cutting across the entire economy or large parts of it. Once again, these inevitably focus primarily on government lobbying and general business issues. Cluster-based associations are also needed. In other cases, several associations may be present that would be more useful if combined or at least coordinated. Given individuals' and companies' limited time and money for participation in associations, the more integrated the efforts of various groups, the better.

Surprisingly often, cluster participants never meet, and there is little public or government recognition of the cluster's significance to the local economy. Both situations existed in the Massachusetts medical-devices cluster. Where absent, the formation of associations should be part of a location's economic development agenda. In Massachusetts, this effort was undertaken by the Governor's Council on Economic Growth and Technology. This private-sector advisory body, composed of leaders from firms, universities, and other entities, convened a series of task forces to examine Massachusetts clusters that led to the formation of new and permanent associations where they did not yet exist, as in telecommunications and medical devices.

CORPORATE LOCATION

Globalization and the ease of transportation and communication have led to a surge of outsourcing, with companies relocating many facilities to locations with low wages, low taxes, and low utility costs. Outsourcing some activities to tap lower cost inputs can indeed reduce locational disadvantages. Cluster theory, however, suggests a more complex view of corporate locational choices: Corporate location involves far more than simply building offices or factories.

First, cluster theory suggests that locational choices should weigh overall productivity potential, not just input costs or taxes. In locating activities, the aim is low total cost. Locations with low wages and low taxes, however, often lack efficient infrastructure, available suppliers, timely maintenance, and other conditions that clusters offer. Logistical costs and costs of introducing new models may be substantial. Many companies have discovered that such productivity disadvantages can be more than offsetting. Yet the effects of low wages, low taxes, and low utility costs are easy to measure up front, while productivity costs remain hidden and unanticipated.

Locating in an existing or developing cluster, then, often involves lower total systems cost and greatly improved capacity for innovation. A shift back toward clusters is beginning among companies who once believed in the cost savings of highly dispersed activities. This trend is evident in choices of international locations (with activities being moved back to places such as the United States) and locations within nations (with clusters gaining in appeal over remote Sun Belt or other sites).

Second, firms must capture the cost advantages of spreading activities across locations while *also* harnessing advantages of clusters. (See Chapter 8 for a full treatment of global strategy, or, more broadly, of competition across locations.) The determinants of location differ markedly for various activities. For activities such as assembly plants, manufacture of stable, labor-intensive components, and software translation, locational choices often should be driven by factor cost and market access. For what I term "home base" activities, however, the basis for choice should be very different. Home base activities are those involved in the creation and renewal of the firm's product, processes, and services. This includes activities, such as fabrication of frequently redesigned components, that involve substantial, ongoing changes.

The location of home base activities should be heavily driven by total systems cost and by innovation potential. Clusters usually provide conditions favorable for innovation. Home base activities should sometimes move to locations outside the company's nation of principal ownership or the nation containing its corporate headquarters—if a more vibrant cluster exists elsewhere. This rule applies especially to product lines, but also to entire business units. The siting of regional headquarters should also involve consideration of clusters, not just of tax considerations or the convenience of executives.

Cluster thinking also underscores the desirability of moving groups of linked activities to the same place rather than spreading them across numerous states and nations. Grouping in this way lowers total system costs, eases sharing of internal information, facilitates and spreads innovation, creates critical mass for supporting company infrastructure and facilities, and extends deeper roots into local clusters that increase the ability to capture externalities and spillovers.

Finally, activities located in places isolated from other firms in the same field require firms to begin building a cluster. The process calls for wooing suppliers, encouraging local institutions to make supporting investments, and finding ways to build the local stock of specialized inputs. Corporate location, then, is not something to be delegated to operations departments but is part of overall strategy.

Organizing Cluster Development Initiatives

Numerous cluster-related initiatives—to organize participants, assess advantages and disadvantages, and catalyze public and private action—have arisen at the national, state, and city levels, as illustrated by the examples in Table 7.1. Some relatively recent efforts have begun to develop initiatives around clusters that cross the borders of neighboring

Table 7.1   Examples of Cluster Initiatives*

Multi-Country Regions	Nations	Regions/States/ Provinces	Cities/ Metropolitan Areas
Central America	Andorra	Arizona	Bogota
Middle East	Bermuda	Atlantic region	Charlotte
	Bolivia	(Canada)	Christchurch
	Bulgaria	Basque Region	Long Island
	Canada	(Spain)	Minneapolis
	Colombia	California	Rotterdam
	Costa Rica	Catalonia	Silicon Valley
	Denmark	Connecticut	Sonoma, CA
	Egypt	Chihuahua	Tampa
	El Salvador	Massachusetts	Wellington
	Finland	Minnesota	Worcester, MA
	Hong Kong	North Carolina	
	India	Ohio	
	Israel	Oregon	
	Jordan	Scotland	
	Malaysia	Quebec	
	Morocco		
	Northern Ireland		
	Norway		
	Netherlands		
	New Zealand		
	Panama		
	Portugal		
	Peru		
	Republic of Ireland		
	South Africa		
	Sweden		
	Tatarstan		
	Venezuela		

*Citations of the published output of many of these initiatives appear in the references at the end of this chapter.

countries in Central America and in the Middle East, a practice that would benefit other regions, as well.

Cluster initiatives provide a new way of organizing economic development efforts that go beyond traditional efforts to reduce the cost of doing business and enhance the overall business environment. Efforts focusing on clusters draw firms to become much more interested and engaged than in broad, economy-wide efforts that must necessarily gravitate to general issues, such as tax policy and export promotion. Business-government-university dialogue tends to take place on a more concrete level, making action possible. Cluster initiatives can not only bring focus to discussions of government policy, but can reveal and help address issues within the private sector, as well.[34]

One cluster initiative is profiled in the insert "Microclusters in Catalonia." Similar profiles of other efforts in Arizona, Chihuahua, the Netherlands, and New Zealand are available.[35]

These and other successful cluster initiatives have a number of common characteristics:

- *A shared understanding of competitiveness and the role of clusters in competitive advantage.* Productivity and innovation, not low wages, low taxes, or a devalued currency, are the definition of competitiveness. Participants understand the influences that bear on productivity and how clusters enhance it. Roles for both business and government are well understood, and not confused with market distortion or with picking winners. Early and ongoing communication and discussion educates cluster participants about competitiveness and helps to shift mindsets. In addition to government and businesses, other constituencies share the understanding of competitiveness. Labor unions and non-governmental organizations that may fear lost jobs, lower pay, and watered-down regulations concerning safety, working conditions, and environmental impact are brought to recognize that competitiveness depends on productivity, which supports rising wages, and on an improved quality of life.

- *A focus on removing obstacles and easing constraints to cluster upgrading.* Explicit, upfront discussion of goals at the beginning of a cluster initiative and regular reinforcement of those goals helps overcome the urge to seek subsidies or limit competition. The presence of suppliers and customers in the cluster process provides a natural check to these tendencies. Some participants may cling to the status quo and may join the cluster initiative only to influence its efforts in that direction. Successful cluster initiatives remain alert against these tendencies.

• *A structure that embraces all clusters in a nation or state.* Setting priorities among clusters is not only bad economics, it disenfranchises large parts of the private sector. Successful cluster initiatives include traditional clusters, such as agriculture and tourism, and even declining clusters. They include emerging clusters as well as established ones. To avoid misguided attempts at creating clusters that have no assets on which to build, emerging clusters should have a demonstrable local foundation and a base of firms that have met a market test. Practical considerations may require the sequencing of cluster projects, but early clusters where work is undertaken should involve a representative spectrum of the types of clusters present (for example, a traditional cluster, an emerging cluster and a declining cluster) and should strive to demonstrate the value of the cluster approach. Careful choices early on help disseminate the concepts and processes to clusters that will be included in later initiatives.

• *Appropriate cluster boundaries.* By definition, clusters include industries and institutions with important linkages or spillovers, rather than broad sectors (for example, manufacturing or high tech) or individual industries (for example, plastic machinery or Italian restaurants). Cluster boundaries should reflect economic reality, not necessarily political boundaries. In the Atlantic provinces of Canada, for example, several clusters cross provincial borders, and the cluster initiative there was structured accordingly.

• *Wide involvement of cluster participants and associated institutions.* Cluster initiatives should include firms of all sizes, as well as representatives of all important constituencies. Excluding individuals, even (or especially) difficult ones, invites opposition. While any effort will have its share of the skeptical, parochial, self-serving, and opportunistic, the most successful cluster initiatives make an effort to reach out and educate them. Individuals who then choose not to participate have less ground for criticizing or opposing recommendations. Ultimately, cluster initiatives must carry on with those who are willing to work to improve conditions for all.

• *Private-sector leadership.* Active government participation in a private-led effort, rather than an initiative controlled by government, will have a better chance of success. Companies can usually better identify the obstacles and constraints in their path, as well as the opportunities, than can government. Letting the private sector lead also reduces the initiative's political content, while taking advantage of the private sector's often superior implementation ability. Cluster initiatives should be as nonpartisan as possible and remain independent of any party or administration's political agenda. Legislators and the executive branch, the opposition parties, and those in power must all be involved. Ideally, the cluster initiative will take place through an entity *independent* of government. Otherwise, promising efforts may be dropped when a new government takes office.[36]

• *Close attention to personal relationships.* In itself, the presence of an established or emerging cluster does not guarantee functioning cluster linkages. Many of the benefits of clusters flow from the personal relationships which facilitate linkages, foster open communication, and build trust. Information is essential to productivity, and relationships that improve its flow will endure and even strengthen after a cluster project ends. Instigating communications is the essence of successful cluster initiatives. Neutral facilitators often help with this where trust is lacking and relationships are undeveloped. From the outset, major efforts will be required to ensure efficient and regular communication, both internal and external. Successes should be widely publicized.

• *A bias towards action.* Cluster initiatives must be motivated by the desire to achieve results; they should not be driven by academic institutions, think tanks, or government agencies that see research as an end in itself. Diagnosis and a broad vision for the future must be combined with concrete, active steps. Strong, senior champions are needed in both government and the private sector. Entrepreneurial leadership and the involvement of opinion leaders characterize virtually all successful initiatives.

• *Institutionalization.* Cluster upgrading is a long-term process that must have a life beyond a one-shot effort. It requires institutionalization of concepts, relationships, and linkages among constituencies. In the private sector, new or revitalized trade associations often take leading roles in the continuing upgrading of clusters. In government, cluster upgrading can be institutionalized by appropriately organizing government agencies, organization through the gathering and dissemination of economic statistics, and by controlling the structure and membership of business advisory groups.

Summary

A cluster is a system of interconnected firms and institutions the whole of which is greater than the sum of the parts. Clusters play an important role in competition, and these raise important implications for companies, governments, universities, and other institutions in an economy.

Clusters represent a new and complementary way of understanding an economy, organizing economic development, and setting public policy. Understanding the state of clusters in a location provides important insights into the productive potential of its economy and the constraints on its future development. Paradoxically, then, the most enduring competitive advantages in a global economy will often be local.

Microclusters in Catalonia

History

Catalonia, one of Spain's seventeen autonomous regions, accounts for 13 percent of the national population but almost 20 percent of its GDP and about 40 percent of its industrial exports. In December 1989, Antoni Subirà was appointed Catalonia's Minister of Industry, Trade and Commerce. Soon after, he obtained a manuscript copy of *The Competitive Advantage of Nations* and circulated several chapters within the ministry. With Spain facing entry into the European Common Market in 1992, Subirà sought to develop a new approach to industrial policy in Catalonia. He chose clusters as a central element.

Since then, approximately twenty Catalan clusters have been studied in detail. As of 1997, clusters continued to be used in Catalonia as the main methodology for assessing the region's industrial competitiveness and for identifying areas in which the government could improve the environment for companies.

Actors

Initially, Subirà asked Professors Eduard Ballarin and Josep Faus from IESE, a top business school based in Barcelona, to apply the cluster methodology to the study of Catalonia's industry. Their preliminary work set the stage for a larger report, prepared together with Monitor Company, a consulting firm.[a] The report offered an overall diagnosis of Catalonia's strengths and weaknesses and was well received. It defined groups of clusters (for example, mass-market consumption goods) and provided some general guidelines about what was needed to enhance their competitive advantage.

Subirà decided to take this work one step further and to study discrete clusters in more detail. Already-existing capabilities within the Ministry of Industry, Trade and Commerce were reorganized, and a local consulting firm—CLUSTER Competitiveness—was asked to lead a series of cluster initiatives. Each study involved companies, suppliers, trade associations, business schools, universities, and many government departments.

Cluster Definition

Catalan clusters included wooden toys, agricultural machinery, jewelry, leather, knitting, processed meats, publishing, consumer electronics, and furniture.[b] Specific clusters were defined relatively narrowly. In furniture, for example, three separate clusters were isolated in different parts of Catalonia, each competing in different segments and facing different challenges. Estimates indicate that Catalonia has more than one hundred such narrowly defined clusters, or microclusters.

Each microcluster study included firms, suppliers, universities, and a wide range of other interested participants. Cluster boundaries and participation emerged as a result of the study process. Self-selection was the rule: All firms interested in participating were considered part of the cluster.

All clusters were viewed as equally desirable. For practical reasons, however, cluster studies were sequenced. Some clusters were initially much better organized than others. One goal of the process was to establish effective trade organizations to serve each cluster.

Process of Change

The cluster studies in Catalonia took place in three stages. In the first, the cluster's problems and opportunities were identified and the basic concepts of cluster upgrading, such as the goal of enhancing rather than suppressing competition, were laid out. At times, the study revealed a view of the cluster's problems that differed from that presented by conventional wisdom. Members of the Catalan leather-tanning cluster, for example, had attributed their decline in competitiveness to the laxity of environmental regulations in LDCs.[c] Research revealed, however, that the environmental regulations of their most significant rivals, the Italians, were, in fact, more stringent than those in Catalonia. As a result, Catalan leather tanners who had previously been asking for a relaxation of government environmental legislation decided to set up a joint cleaning and tanning plant and an R&D center. The cluster process convinced them that caring for the environment would actually improve their competitiveness.

The second stage of the study process involved the attempt to achieve a consensus vision of the cluster's future that would unite all participants and facilitate change. In the third stage, cluster participants created strategies and action steps for fulfilling the vision. Specific individuals were identified to lead the action initiatives.

Results

The cluster process equipped the Catalan government with the knowledge it needed to influence Spanish national policy more effectively. More importantly, however, it resulted in a new and more productive dialogue between government and business within Catalonia. Previously, broad, sector-wide organizations had sought general measures, such as subsidies and tax cuts. The cluster process allowed businesses to assess competitive position in specific, operational terms. Companies requested more specific and pro-competitive government support, such as help in establishing research laboratories or promoting foreign trade. Participants agreed that the competitive advantage of the region's industries had clearly benefited from taking a cluster perspective.

The cluster approach helped numerous firms (many of them small and medium sized) to think more strategically about their problems. Examples of resulting initiatives included the transfer of a leather research center from the Universidad de Barcelona to a location near the leather cluster in Igualada; a series of seminars that helped textile producers make the transition from a production to a retailing focus; and a project for developing a common subassembly facility to serve the local Honda, Yamaha, and Derbi motorcycle factories. Some clusters initially lacked effective associations (for example, the furniture cluster in Montsia); others were part of organizations that represented a too broad constituency (for example, lathe operators); still others had ineffective associations (for example, the leather tanners' cluster in Igualada). Following the cluster effort, new and more cluster-specific associations were created and old associations were revived.

Catalan government policies shifted toward cluster upgrading: improving the market access of clusters; facilitating foreign direct investment; introducing product certification programs; and instituting policies for upgrading technology. Based on cluster studies, for example, the government provided assistance for a cork research and applications center in Parafrugell (currently developing an international standard for cork quality). In follow-up discussions, however, some firms expressed the view that the best service provided by the government was the stimulation of dialogue among cluster participants.

In one of the major benefits of the cluster process, government officials were transformed into an informed audience for firms. The dialogue among various agencies and departments within the Catalan government also increased and coordination improved.

Catalonia's experience offers many lessons about applying cluster

methodology. First, one of the major benefits of convening a cluster is to explore common opportunities, not just discuss common problems. Second, leaders stressed the value to the cluster process of keeping a low profile; limiting publicity during the early stages helped avoid creating premature, unrealistic expectations and helped minimize formation of political and other opposition. Third, the particular leaders that emerged in a given cluster had much to do with its success in improving. Finally, the cluster initiative benefited greatly from the close and aggressive support and follow-up by Minister Subirà, who, with his business training and orientation, insulated the process from politics.

---

a. See Monitor Company (1992).

b. See Conejos, et al. (1997).

c. See Rodriguez, Prats, Enright, and Ballarin (1995).

NOTES

1. For a recent example, see Cairncross (1997).

2. See Enright (1993B) for examples illustrating clusters' varying geographic scope.

3. Enright (1993C) offers an interesting discussion of how to draw cluster boundaries.

4. While industry analysis properly involves suppliers, channels, and customers, cluster analysis widens the scope considerably to include chains or related industries at all levels, as well as a wide range of institutions.

5. The case of Italy, where such clusters are quite common, helped spawn a literature on industrial districts. Industrial districts are a special case of clusters.

6. The literature about such cases uses a number of alternate terms, such as *technopoles* and *science cities*. See A. Advani (1997) for one example.

7. See Porter (1990), Chapters 3 and 4.

8. See Harrison, Kelley, and Gant (1996) for a good summary. Static agglomeration economies consist of a local concentration of customers (or downstream firms) suffi-

cient to permit suppliers to achieve economies of scale in production or distribution, great enough for local firms to amass sufficient demand to warrant the provision (usually by or via local governments) of specialized infrastructure, and large enough to realize a specialized local division of labor. So-called dynamic agglomeration economies consist of advantages in terms of technological learning and improvement.

9. Stigler (1951). For a more recent re-statement, see Krugman (1991B).

10. An extensive literature has explored these advantages, including Pascal and McCall (1980), Angel (1990), Rauch (1993), and Glaeser and Maré (1994).

11. Adams and Jaffe (1996), for example, found that the influence of parent firm R&D on plant-level productivity diminishes with geographic distance.

12. Saxenian (1994) describes the workings of the remarkable information flow within Silicon Valley.

13. For a model capturing some of these elements, see Stahl (1982).

14. See Monitor Company (1994).

15. Enright (1990).

16. Strong empirical support exists for the spillover effects among firms and between universities and firms in R&D and innovation. Jaffe, Trajtenberg, and Henderson (1993) show geographic localization of knowledge spillovers. Audretsch and Feldman (1996) find a strong association between the importance of new knowledge and spatial clustering. Harrison, Kelley, and Gant (1996) also highlight the geographic dimension of innovation.

17. For an example drawn from the Swiss watch industry, see Glasmeier (1991).

18. Enright (1990), building on Porter (1990), provides the foundational treatment of the role of geographic concentration. See also Enright (1993A).

19. See, for example, von Hippel (1988), Case (1992), and Rogers (1995).

20. See Porter and Caves (1977).

21. See, for example, Burt (1997); Granovetter (1985); Henton, Melville, and Walesh (1997); Nohria (1992); Perrow (1992); Putnam, Leonard, and Naneth (1993); Fukuyama (1995); and Harrison and Weiss (1998).

22. Some empirical research is beginning to explore the effect of clustering on the rate of growth of cities. Glaeser et al. (1992) and Henderson, Kuncoro, and Turner (1995) find support for a positive association.

23. I use the term *exports* to apply to industries that compete outside a geographic area, even if destined for another state and not a foreign country. Note that most exports actually move to other locations, while other exporting industries (mainly services) attract outside customers to the home location.

24. See Ingham (1995).

25. More efforts are under way to bring cluster thinking into the mainstream of economic development. Cluster development has become a core approach in the World Bank's Private Sector Development Department, for example. See also Fairbanks and Lindsay (1997B) and Rosenfeld (1997).

26. Interesting recent work by economic geographers explores the synthesis between globalization and location. See Cox (1997) and Storper (1997).

27. My book *The Competitive Advantage of Nations* (1990) contains the basic treatment of the life cycle of clusters. Many other cluster studies provide some

historical perspective, as well. A particularly detailed historical analysis of the development of an array of Swedish clusters is contained in Porter, Sölvell, and Zander (1993). See also van der Linde (1992) and Hernesniemi, Lammi, and Ylä-Anttila (1996).

28. See Metropolitan Council (1995B).

29. For some interesting examples, see Rosenfeld (1997).

30. See Rosenfeld (1996B).

31. My research team has created a classification that regroups all SIC and SITC industries into clusters; this system is designed to serve as a consistent starting point for statistical research, recognizing that local modifications will usually be needed. The classification is available from the author.

32. See Markusen (1995B) and Porter (1995A).

33. See Ffowcs-Williams (1996) and Mitchell (1997).

34. See Waits (1996) for a discussion of the cluster approach taken in Arizona. See Jacobs and de Man (1996) for a discussion of some of the practical considerations that arise when formulating cluster-based economic policies and strategies.

35. Contact the author for more information.

36. See Andorra, Govern d', *Andorra Pla Estratègic* (1993).

Bibliography

General References

Abrams, M. "Emerging Clusters in Regional Economies." Paper presented at the Technopolis '97 conference, Ottawa, Canada, September 1997.

Adams, J., and A. Jaffe. "Bounding the Effects of R&D: An Investigation Using Matched Establishment-Firm Data." *Rand Journal of Economics* 27, no. 4 (1996):700–721.

Advani, A. "Industrial Clusters: A Support System for Small and Medium Sized Enterprises." Private Sector Development Department, occasional paper no. 32, The World Bank, April 1997.

Amin, A., and N. Thrift. "Neo-Marshallian Nodes in Global Networks." *International Journal of Urban and Regional Research* 16, no. 4 (1992):571–587.

Andorra, Govern d'. *Andorra Pla Estratègic.* Govern d'Andorra, 1993.

Angel, D. "New Firm Formation in the Semiconductor Industry: Elements of a Flexible Manufacturing System." *Regional Studies* 24, no. 3 (1990):211–221.

Arthur, P. "Industry Location Patterns and the Importance of History." Technical paper no. 84, Center for Economic Policy Research, Stanford University, Stanford, Calif., 1986.

Audretsch, D., and M. Feldman. "Innovative Clusters and the Industry Life Cycle." Discussion paper no. 1161, Centre for Economic Policy Research, London, 1995.

———. "R&D Spillovers and the Geography of Innovation and Production." *American Economic Review* 86, no. 3 (1996):630–640.

Babiec, J., with M. Fairbanks. *Pink Sand: Strategies for Tourism Clusters in the Age of Competitive Advantage.* Cambridge, Mass.: Monitor Company, in press.

Bartik, T. "Business Location Decisions in the United States: Estimates of the Effects of Unionization, Taxes, and Other Characteristics of States." *Journal of Business and Economic Statistics* 3, no. 1 (1985):14–22.

Becattini, G. "The Marshallian Industrial District as a Socio-Economic Notion." In *Industrial Districts and Inter-Firm Cooperation in Italy*, edited by F.

Pyke, G. Becattini and W. Sengenberger. Geneva: International Institute for Labour Studies, 1990.

Becattini, G., ed. *Mercato e Forze Locali: Il Distretto Industriale.* Bologna: Il Mulino, 1987.

———. *Modelli locali di Sviluppo.* Bologna: Il Mulino, 1989.

Becker, G., and K. Murphy. "The Division of Labor, Coordination Costs and Knowledge." *Quarterly Journal of Economics* 107, no. 4 (1992):1137–1160.

Beckmann, M., and J. F. Thisse. "The Location of Production Activities." In *Handbook of Regional and Urban Economics,* Vol. 1, edited by P. Nijkamp, Chapter 2. Amsterdam: Elsevier Science, 1987.

Benabou, R. "Workings of a City: Location, Education and Production." *Quarterly Journal of Economics* 108, no. 3 (1993):619–652.

Bengt-Åke, L., ed. *National Systems of Innovation: Towards a Theory of Innovation and Interactive Learning.* London: Pinte, 1992.

Bergman, E., E. Feser, and S. Sweeney. "Targeting North Carolina Manufacturing: Understanding the State's Economy Through Industrial Cluster Analysis." University of North Carolina Institute for Economic Development, Chapel Hill, North Carolina, 1996.

Breault, R. "The Evolution of Clusters or Structured Economic Development Regions and Their Future." Breault Research Organization, Inc., Tucson, Arizona, 1997.

Breault, R., ed. *Global Networking of Regional Optics Clusters.* Denver, Colo.: The International Society for Optical Engineering, 1996.

Burt, R. "The Contingent Value of Social Capital." *Administrative Science Quarterly* 42, no. 2 (1997):339–365.

Cairncross, F. *The Death of Distance: How the Communications Revolution Will Change Our Lives.* Boston, Mass.: Harvard Business School Press, 1997.

Carlton, D. "The Location and Employment Decisions of New Firms: An Econometric Analysis with Discrete and Continuous Exogenous Variables." *Review of Economics and Statistics* 65, no. 3 (1983):440–449.

Case, A. "Neighborhood Influence and Technological Change." *Regional Science and Urban Economics* 22, no. 4 (1992):491–508.

Ciccone, A., and R. Hall. "Productivity and the Density of Economic Activity." *American Economic Review* 86, no. 1 (1996):54–70.

Cimoli, M., and G. Dosi. "Technological Paradigms, Patterns of Learning and Development: An Introductory Roadmap." *Journal of Evolutionary Economics* 5, no. 3 (1995):243–268.

Conejos, J., E. Duch, J. Fontrodona, J. M. Hernández, A. Luzárraga, and E. Terré. *Cambio Estratégico y Clusters en Cataluña.* Barcelona: Gestión 2000, 1997.

Cox, K. R. "Globalization and the Politics of Distribution: A Critical Assessment." In *Spaces of Globalization: Reasserting the Power of the Local,* edited by K. R. Cox. New York: Guilford, 1997.

Cox, K. R., ed. *Spaces of Globalization: Reasserting the Power of the Local.* New York: Guilford, 1997.

Davis, D., and D. Weinstein. "Does Economic Geography Matter for International Specialization?" Working paper 5706, National Bureau of Economic Research, Cambridge, Mass., 1996.

———. "Economic Geography and Regional Production Structure: An Empirical Investigation." Working paper 6093, National Bureau of Economic Research, Cambridge, Mass., 1997.

Dodge, W. R. "Regional Excellence: Governing Together to Compete Globally and Flourish Locally." Washington, D.C.: National League of Cities, 1996.

Doeringer, B., and D. G. Terkla. "Business Strategy and Cross-Industry Clusters." *Economic Development Quarterly* 9, no. 3 (1995):225–237.

Dosi, G., R. Giannetti, and P. Toninelli. *Technology and Enterprise in Historical Perspective.* Oxford: Oxford University Press, 1992.

DRI/McGraw-Hill. *America's Clusters.* Conference Building Industry Clusters, DRI/McGraw-Hill, Lexington, Mass., 1995.

DRI/McGraw-Hill and FOCS. *Le Maroc Compétitif: A Cluster Development Initiative in Morocco.* Washington, D.C.: DRI/McGraw-Hill and FOCS, 1996.

Ellison, G., and E. Glaeser. "Geographic Concentration in U.S. Manufacturing Industries: A Dartboard Approach." *Journal of Political Economy* 105, no. 5 (1997):889–927.

Englmann, F., and U. Walz. "Industrial Centers and Regional Growth in the Presence of Local Inputs." *Journal of Regional Science* 35 (1995):3–27.

Enright, M. "The Determinants of Geographic Concentration in Industry." Working paper 93-052, Division of Research, Harvard Business School, Boston, Mass., 1993 (A).

———. "The Geographic Scope of Competitive Advantage." In *Stuck in the Region? Changing Scales of Regional Identity,* edited by E. Dirven, J. Groenewegen and S. van Hoof, 87–102. Utrecht: Netherlands Geographical Studies 155, 1993(B).

———. "Geographical Concentration and Industrial Organization." Ph.D. diss., Harvard University, 1990.

————. "Organization and Coordination in Geographically Concentrated Industries." In *Coordination and Information: Historical Perspectives on the Organization of Enterprise,* edited by D. Raff and N. Lamoreux, 103–142. Chicago: University of Chicago Press, 1995.

————. "Regional Clusters and Economic Development: A Research Agenda." Paper presented at the Conference on Regional Clusters and Business Networks, Fredericton, New Brunswick, November 1993 (C).

————. "Why Local Clusters Are the Way to Win the Game." *World Link* 5, no. 4 (1992):24–25.

Enright, M., and R. Weder. *Studies in Swiss Competitive Advantage.* Bern: European Academic Publishers, 1995.

Eriksson, A. "Emerging Clusters in Regional Economies." Paper presented at the Technopolis '97 Conference, Ottawa, Canada, September 1997.

Fairbanks, M., and S. Lindsay. "Choosing Prosperity: An Agenda for Emerging Markets." *Economic Reform Today.* Washington, D.C.: Center for International Private Enterprise, 1997 (A).

————. *Plowing the Sea: Nurturing the Hidden Sources of Growth in the Developing World.* Boston: Harvard Business School Press, 1997 (B).

Feldman, M. "An Examination of the Geography of Innovation." *Industrial and Corporate Change* 2, no. 3 (1993):451–470.

————. *The Geography of Innovation.* Dordrecht: Kluwer Academic Publishers, 1994.

Ffowcs-Williams, I. "Hard and Soft Networks: Helping Firms Cooperate for Export Growth." *New Zealand Strategic Management* 2, no. 2 (1996):30–36.

————. "Stimulating Local Clusters." Paper prepared for the Workshop for Practitioners in Cluster Formation, Chihuahua, Mexico, November 1997.

Fitzgerald, R., ed. *The Competitive Advantage of Far Eastern Business.* Studies in Far Eastern Business No. 1. Essex, Great Britain: Frank Cass, 1994.

Fujita, M., and J. F. Thisse. "Economics of Agglomeration." *Journal of the Japanese and International Economies* 10, no. 4 (1996):339–378.

Fukuyama, F. *Trust: The Social Virtues and the Creation of Prosperity.* New York: Free Press, 1995.

Gabszewicz, J., and J. F. Thisse. "Spatial Competition and the Location of Firms." In *Location Theory,* edited by J. Gabszewicz, J. F. Thisse, M. Fujita, and U. Schweizer, 1–71. Chur (Switzerland): Harwood Academic, 1986.

Gagné, P., M. Lefevre, and G. Tremblay. *The Québec Industrial Atlas.* Montreal: Publi-Relais, 1993.

Gertler, M. "Between the Global and the Local: The Spatial Limits to Productive Capital." In *Spaces of Globalization: Reasserting the Power of the Local,* edited by K. R. Cox. New York: Guilford, 1997.

Giarratani, F. "Nurture the Symbiosis Between Economics and Regional Science (It's Worth the Trouble)." *International Regional Science Review* 17, no. 3 (1994):343–346.

Giersch, H. "Economic Union Between Nations and the Location of Industries." *Review of Economic Studies* 17 (1949):87–97.

Glaeser, E. "Cities, Information, and Economic Growth." *Cityscape: A Journal of Policy Development and Research* 1, no. 1 (1994):9–47.

Glaeser, E., H. Kallal, J. Scheinkman, and A. Shleifer. "Growth in Cities." *Journal of Political Economy* 100, no. 6 (1992):1126–1152.

Glaeser, E., and D. Maré. "Cities and Skills." Working paper 4728, National Bureau of Economic Research, 1994.

Glaeser, E., J. Scheinkman, and A. Shleifer. "Economic Growth in a Cross-Section of Cities." Working paper 5013, National Bureau of Economic Research, 1995.

Glasmeier, A. "Factors Governing the Development of High Tech Industry Agglomerations: A Tale of Three Cities." *Regional Studies* 22, no. 4 (1988):287–301.

———. "High-Tech Industries and the Regional Division of Labor." *Industrial Relations* 25, no. 2 (1986):197–211.

———. "The Role of Merchant Wholesalers in Industrial Agglomeration Formation." *Annals of the Association of American Geographers* 80, no. 3 (1990):394–417.

———. Technological Discontinuities and Flexible Production Networks: The Case of Switzerland and the World Watch Industry." *Research Policy* 20, no. 5 (1991):469–485.

Glasmeier, A., and R. Leichenko. "From Free Market Rhetoric to Free Market Reality: The Future of the U.S. South in an Era of Globalization." *International Journal of Urban and Regional Research* 20, no. 4 (1996):601–615.

Glasmeier, A., J. Thompson, and A. Kays. "The Geography of Trade Policy: Trade Regimes and Location Decisions in the Textile and Apparel Complex." *Transactions of British Geographers* 18 (Spring 1993):19–35.

Goldstein, G., and T. Gronberg. "Economies of Scale and Economies of Agglomeration." *Journal of Urban Economics* 16, no. 1 (1984):91–104.

Gotchev, A., ed. *The Competitiveness of Bulgarian Export Industries.* Sofia: Albatross, 1997.

Granovetter, M. "Economic Action and Social Structure: The Problem of Embeddedness." *American Journal of Sociology* 91 (1985):481–510.

Hagstrom, P. "Unshackling Corporate Geography." *Human Geography.* Geografiska Anneler, Series B, vol. 72, B(1990):3–12.

Hall, P., and A. Markusen. *Silicon Landscapes.* Boston: Allen and Unwin, 1985.

Hanson, G. "Agglomeration, Dispersion, and the Pioneer Firm." *Journal of Urban Economics* 39, no. 3 (1996):255–281.

Harris, C. "The Market as a Factor on the Localization of Industry in the United States." *Annals of the Association of American Geographers* 64 (1954):315–348.

Harrison, B. "Industrial Districts: Old Wine in New Bottles?" *Regional Studies* 26 (1992):469–483.

Harrison, B., M. Kelley, and J. Gant. "Innovative Firm Behavior and Local Milieu: Exploring the Intersection of Agglomeration, Firm Effects, Industrial Organization, and Technological Change." *Economic Geography* 72, no. 3 (1996):233–258.

Harrison, B., and M. Weiss. *Workforce Development Networks.* Thousand Oaks, Calif.: Sage, 1998.

Henderson, V. "Ways to Think About Urban Concentration: Neoclassical Urban Systems versus the New Economic Geography." *International Regional Science Review* 19, no. 1-2 (1996):31–36.

———. "Where Does an Industry Locate?" *Journal of Urban Economics* 35, no. 1 (1994):83–104.

Henderson, V., A. Kuncoro, and M. Turner. "Industrial Development in Cities." *Journal of Political Economy* 103, no. 5 (1995):1067–1090.

Henton, D., J. Melville, and K. Walesh. *Grassroots Leaders for a New Economy.* San Francisco: Jossey-Bass, 1997.

Hernesniemi, H., M. Lammi, and P. Ylä-Anttila. *Advantage Finland: The Future of Finnish Industries.* Helsinki: ETLA, Taloustieto Oy, 1996.

Hill, E., and Z. Austrian. "Creating Competitive Industries in Northeast Ohio by Strengthening Industrial Clustering Behavior within the Region." Proposal to The Greater Cleveland Growth Association and Cleveland Tomorrow, 1996.

Hirschman, A. *The Strategy of Economic Development.* New Haven: Yale University Press, 1958.

Hyvärinen, J., and J. Borsos. *Emerging Estonian Industrial Transformation: Towards a Dual Industrial Strategy for Estonia.* Helsinki: ETLA, Taloustieto Oy, 1994.

Ingham, V. "The Competitiveness of Argentina: From Sheltered Markets to Global Rivalry." Ph.D. diss., Tufts University, 1995.

Isard, W. *Location and Space-Economy.* Cambridge, Mass.: MIT Press, 1956.

Jacobs, D., P. Boekholt, and W. Zegveld. *De Economische Kracht van Nederland: een toepassing van Porters benadering van de concurrentiekracht van landen.* SMO-Boek, TNO-Beleidsstudies. S-Gravenhage: Stichting Maatschappij en Onderneming, 1990.

Jacobs, D., and M. W. de Jong. "Industrial Clusters and the Competitiveness of the Netherlands: Empirical and Conceptual Issues." *De Economist* 140, no. 2 (1992):233–252.

Jacobs, D., and A. P. de Man. "Clusters, Industrial Policy and Firm Strategy: A Menu Approach." *Technology Analysis and Strategic Management* 8, no. 4 (1996):425–437.

Jaffe, A., M. Trajtenberg, and R. Henderson. "Geographic Localization of Knowledge Spillovers as Evidenced by Patent Citations." *Quarterly Journal of Economics* CVIII, no. 3 (1993):577–598.

Krugman, P. *Development, Geography, and Economic Theory.* Cambridge, Mass.: MIT Press, 1995.

———. "Increasing Returns and Economic Geography." *Journal of Political Economy* 99, no. 3 (1991A):483–499.

———. *Strategic Trade Policy and the New International Economics.* Cambridge, Mass.: MIT Press, 1986.

———. *Trade and Geography.* Cambridge, Mass.: MIT Press, 1991(B).

Leymaire, S., and J. Tripier. *Maroc: Le Prochain Dragon.* Paris: Karthala, 1993.

Lloyd, P., and P. Dicken. *Location in Space.* London: Harper & Row, 1977.

Lösch, A. *The Economics of Location.* New Haven: Yale University Press, 1954.

McCann, Philip. "Logistics Costs and the Location of the Firm: A One-Dimensional Comparative Static Approach." *Location Science* 4, no. 1/2 (1996):101–116.

———. "On Regional Science: Some Thoughts From a Recent Observer." *International Regional Science Review* 18, no. 2 (1995A):249–252.

———. "Rethinking the Economics of Location and Agglomeration." *Urban Studies* 32, no. 3 (1995B):563–577.

Mair, A. "Strategic Localization: The Myth of the Postnational Enterprise." In *Spaces of Globalization: Reasserting the Power of the Local,* edited by K. R. Cox. New York: Guilford, 1997.

Markusen, A. "Growing Pains: Thoughts on Theory, Method, and Politics for a Regional Science of the Future." *International Regional Science Review* 17, no. 3 (1995A):319–326.

———. "The Interaction Between Regional and Industrial Policies: Evidence from Four Countries." In *Proceedings of The World Bank Annual Conference on Development Economics 1994*, Supplement to The World Bank Economic Review and The World Bank Research Observer, edited by Michael Bruno and Boris Pleskovic. Washington, D.C.: The International Bank for Reconstruction and Development/The World Bank, 1995(B).

———. *Profit Cycles, Oligopoly, and Regional Development*. Cambridge, Mass.: MIT Press, 1985.

Marshall, Alfred. *Industry and Trade*. 3d ed. London: Macmillan, 1920.

———. *Principles of Economics*. 8th ed. London: Macmillan, 1920.

Metropolitan Council. *Twin Cities Industry Cluster Study*. Minneapolis/St. Paul, Minn.: Metropolitan Council, 1995.

Ministry of Economic Affairs. *Economie met open grenzen*. The Hague: Sdu, 1990.

———. *Kennis in beweging*. The Hague: Sdu, 1995.

Mitchell, C. "Identifying and Stimulating Clusters: A Local Initiative with National Import." *Firm Connections* 5, no. 5 (1997):11–12.

Monitor Company. *The Competitiveness of Portugal: Building Self-Confidence*. Cambridge, Mass.: Monitor Company, 1994(A).

———. *Creación de la ventaja para Colombia*. Bogotá, Colombia: Colombia Camara de Comercio de Bogotá, 1994(B).

———. *La estrategia competitiva para Bogotá*. Bogotá, Colombia: Colombia Camara de Comercio de Bogotá, 1995(A).

———. *Estudi Sobre els Avantatges Competitius de Catalunya*. Cambridge, Mass.: Monitor Company, 1992.

———. *El valle del cauca de cara al mundo*. Cali, Colombia: Camara de comercio de Cali, 1995(B).

Nadvi, K., and H. Schmitz. "Industrial Clusters in Less Developed Countries: Review of Research Experiences and Research Agenda." Discussion paper 339, Institute of Development Studies, University of Sussex, U. K., 1994.

Nelson, R., ed. *National Innovation Systems, A Comparative Analysis*. New York: Oxford University Press, 1993.

Nohria, N. "Information and Search in the Creation of New Business Ventures: The Case of the 128 Venture Group." In *Networks and Organizations:*

Structure, Form and Action, edited by N. Nohria and R. Eccles. Boston: Harvard Business School Press, 1992.

Oakey, R. "High Technology Industry and Agglomeration Economies." In *Silicon Landscapes,* edited by P. Hall and A. Markusen, 94–117. Boston: Allen & Unwin, 1985.

Pari Sabety, J., and J. Griffin. "Pro-Competitive Alliances: New Vehicles for Regional, State and Community Based Economic Development." *Economic Development Review* 14, no. 2 (1996):2–6.

Pascal, A., and J. McCall. "Agglomeration Economies, Search Costs, and Industrial Location." *Journal of Urban Economics* 8, no. 3 (1980):383–388.

Perrow, C. "Small-Firm Networks." In *Networks and Organizations: Structure, Form and Action,* edited by N. Nohria and R. Eccles. Boston: Harvard Business School Press, 1992.

Piore, M., and C. Sabel. *The Second Industrial Divide.* New York: Basic Books, 1984.

Porter, M. "Comment on 'Interaction Between Regional and Industrial Policies: Evidence from Four Countries,' by Markusen." In *Proceedings of The World Bank Annual Conference on Development Economics 1994,* Supplement to The World Bank Economic Review and The World Bank Research Observer, edited by Michael Bruno and Boris Pleskovic, 303–307. Washington, D.C.: The International Bank for Reconstruction and Development/The World Bank, 1995(A).

———. "Competitive Advantage, Agglomeration Economies, and Regional Policy." *International Regional Science Review* 19, nos. 1 & 2 (1996):85–94.

———. "The Competitive Advantage of the Inner City." *Harvard Business Review* 73, no. 3 (1995B):55–71.

———. *The Competitive Advantage of Nations.* New York: Free Press, 1990.

———. "The Role of Location on Competition." *Journal of the Economics of Business* 1, no. 1 (1994):35–39.

Porter, M., and J. Armstrong. "Canada at the Crossroads." *Business Quarterly* 56, no. 4 (1992):6–10.

Porter, M., S. Borner, R. Weder, and M. Enright. *Internationale Wettbewerbsvorteile: Ein Strategisches Konzept fur die Schweiz.* Frankfurt/New York: Campus Verlag, 1991.

Porter, M., and R. Caves. "From Entry Barriers to Mobility Barriers: Conjectural Decisions and Contrived Deterrence to New Competition." *Quarterly Journal of Economics* (1977):241–262.

Porter, M., G. Crocombe, and M. Enright. *Upgrading New Zealand's Competitive Advantage.* Auckland: Oxford University Press, 1991.

Porter, M., Ö. Sölvell, and I. Zander. *Advantage Sweden*, 2d ed. Stockholm, Sweden: Norstedts Juridik, 1993.

Porter, M., H. Takeuchi, and M. Sakakibara. *Two Japans: Competitive Advantage and Disadvantage of the Japanese Economy*, in press.

Pade, H. *Voekst og dynamik I dansk erhvervsliv*. København: Danmarks Internationale Koncurrenceevne, Schultz, 1991.

Preer, R. *The Emergence of Technopolis: Knowledge-Intensive Technologies and Regional Development*. New York: Praeger, 1992.

Puga, D. "The Rise and Fall of Regional Inequalities." Discussion paper 314, Centre for Economic Performance, London School of Economics, U.K., 1996.

Puga, D., and A. Venables. "The Spread of Industry: Spatial Agglomeration in Economic Development." *The Journal of the Japanese and International Economies* 10, no. 4 (1996):440–464.

Putnam, R. D., R. Leonardi, and R. Y. Nanetti. *Making Democracy Work: Civic Traditions in Modern Italy*. Princeton, N.J.: Princeton University Press, 1993.

Pyke, F., G. Becattini, and W. Sengenberger, eds. *Industrial Districts and Interfirm Cooperation in Italy*. Geneva: International Institute for Labour Studies, 1990.

Pyke, F., and W. Sengenberger, eds. *Industrial Districts and Local Economic Regeneration*. Geneva: International Institute for Labour Studies, 1992.

Quah, D. "Regional Convergence Clusters Across Europe." Discussion paper 1286, Centre for Economic Policy Research, London, 1996.

Rauch, J. "Productivity Gains from Geographic Concentration of Human Capital: Evidence from the Cities." *Journal of Urban Economics* 34, no. 3 (1993):380–400.

Rivera-Batiz, F. "Increasing Returns, Monopolistic Competition, and Agglomeration Economies in Consumption and Production." *Journal of Regional Science and Urban Economics* 18 (1988):125–153.

Rodriguez, M. D., M. Prats, M. Enright, and E. Ballarin. "The Catalan Leather Industry." Case 9-795-105. Boston: Harvard Business School, 1995.

Rogers, E. M. *Diffusion of Innovations*. 4th ed. New York: Free Press, 1995.

Rosenfeld, S. "Bringing Business Clusters into the Mainstream of Economic Development." *European Planning Studies* 5, no. 1 (1997):3–23.

———. *Industrial-Strength Strategies, Regional Business Clusters, and Public Policy*. Washington, D.C.: The Aspen Institute Rural Economic Policy Program, 1995.

————. "Overachievers, Business Clusters that Work: Prospects for Regional Development." Paper presented at The Graylyn Center, Winston-Salem, North Carolina, May 1996(A).

————. "United States: Business Clusters." In *Networks of Enterprises and Local Development*, 179–202. Paris: OECD, 1996(B).

Saxenian, A. "The Cheshire Cat's Grin: Innovation, Regional Development and the Cambridge Case." Working paper 497, Institute of Urban and Regional Development, University of California, Berkeley, 1989.

————. *Regional Advantage: Culture and Competition in Silicon Valley and Route 128.* Cambridge, Mass.: Harvard University Press, 1994.

Schmitz, H. "Small Shoemakers and Fordist Giants: Tale of a Supercluster." *World Development* 23, no. 1 (1995):9–28.

Scotchmer, S., and J. F. Thisse. "Space and Competition: A Puzzle." *Annals of Regional Science* 26 (1992):269–286.

Scott, A. "The Aerospace-Electronics Industrial Complex of Southern California: The Formative Years, 1940–1960." *Research Policy* 20, no. 5 (1991):439–456.

————. "Industrial Organization and Location: Division of Labor, the Firm, and Spatial Process." *Economic Geography* 63 (1987):214–231.

Sears, G. "Technopole Survey: Interviews with Community Leaders." Paper presented at the Technopolis '97 Conference, Ottawa, Canada, September 1997.

Stahl, K. "Differentiated Products, Consumer Search, and Locational Oligopoly." *Journal of Industrial Economics* 31, no. 1/2 (1982):97–114.

Steinbock, D. *The Competitive Advantage of Finland: From Cartels to Competition?* Helsinki: ETLA, Taloustieto Oy, 1998.

Sternberg, E. "The Sectoral Cluster in Economic Development Policy: Lessons from Rochester and Buffalo," *Economic Development Quarterly* 5, no. 4 (1991):342–356.

Stigler, G. "The Division of Labor Is Limited by the Extent of the Market." *Journal of Political Economy* 59, no. 3 (1951):185–193.

Storper, M. "Territories, Flows, and Hierarchies in the Global Economy." In *Spaces of Globalization: Reasserting the Power of the Local*, edited by K. R. Cox. New York: Guilford Press, 1997.

Storper, M., and R. Salais. *The Regional World: Territorial Development in the Global Economy.* New York: Guilford Press, 1997(A).

————. *Worlds of Production: The Action Frameworks of the Economy.* Cambridge, Mass.: Harvard University Press, 1997(B).

Swyngedouw, E. "Neither Global Nor Local: 'Glocaliation' and the Politics of Scale." In *Spaces of Globalization: Reasserting the Power of the Local,* edited by K. R. Cox, 137–166. New York: Guilford Press, 1997.

Tyson, L. *Who's Bashing Whom? Trade Conflict in High-Technology Industries.* Washington, D. C.: Institute for International Economics, 1992.

Ullring, S. "Challenges in International Shipping." Paper presented at the Massachusetts Institute of Technology, Cambridge, Mass., January 1995.

van den Bosch, F. A. J., and A. P. de Man. "Government's Impact on the Business Environment and Strategic Management." *Journal of General Management* 19, no. 3 (1994):50–59.

————, eds. *Perspectives on Strategy: Contributions of Michael E. Porter.* Dordrecht: Kluwer Academic Publishers, 1997.

van der Linde, C. *The Competitive Advantage of Germany.* Ph.D. diss., University of St. Gallen, 1991.

————. *Deutsche Wettbewerbsvorteile.* Düsseldorf: Econ, 1992.

von Hippel, E. *The Sources of Innovation.* New York: Oxford University Press, 1988.

Voyer, R. "Can High-Tech Clusters be Created?" Paper presented at the Technopolis '97 Conference, Ottawa, Canada, September 1997.

————. "Emerging High-Technology Industrial Clusters in Brazil, India, Malaysia, and South Africa." Paper presented at the Technopolis '97 Conference, Ottawa, Canada, September 1997.

Waits, M. J. "State of Cluster-Based Economic Development in Arizona." In *Global Networking of Regional Optics Clusters,* edited by R. Breault, 1–10. Denver, Colo.: The International Society for Optical Engineering, 1996.

Waits, M. J., and G. Howard. "Industry Clusters: A Multipurpose Tool for Economic Development." *Economic Development Commentary* 20, no. 3 (1996):5–11.

Weber, A. *Theory of the Location of Industries,* trans. Carl J. Friedrich. Chicago: University of Chicago Press, 1929.

Zieminski, J., and J. Warda. "What Makes Technopoles Tick: A Corporate Perspective." Paper presented at the Technopolis '97 Conference, Ottawa, Canada, September 1997.

Cluster-Based Reports and Case Studies

Appalachia

"Exports, Competitiveness, and Synergy in Appalachian Industry Clusters: A Report to the Appalachian Regional Commission." Regional Technology Strategies, Inc., Chapel Hill, N.C., February 1997.

Arizona

Arizona Optics Industry Association. "Arizona Optics Industry Resource Directory and Industry Analysis." Arizona Optics Industry Association, Tucson, Ariz., May 1996.

"New Foundations for Arizona's Future: Defining Economic Development for the 1990s." Governor's Strategic Partnership for Economic Development, 1990.

"Greater Tucson Strategic Economic Plan." Greater Tucson Economic Council, Tucson, Ariz., July 1996.

"Greater Tucson Legislative Agenda." Greater Tucson Strategic Partnership for Economic Development, Tucson, Ariz., January 1997.

Brazil

Chadha, S., M. Harrison, R. Parsley, and V. Serra. "The Brazilian Financial Cluster." Student report prepared for Seminar on Competition and Competitiveness, Harvard Business School, Boston, Mass., May 1997.

California

Alexander, R., R. Arney, N. Black, E. Frost, and A. Shivananda. "The California Wine Cluster." Student report prepared for Seminar on Competition and Competitiveness, Harvard Business School, Boston, Mass., May 1997.

Center for Economic Competitiveness. "An Economy at Risk." Menlo Park, Calif.: Center for Economic Competitiveness, SRI International, 1992.

Evans, D., N. Hugh, T. Kazinos, and P. Teague. "The Hollywood Filmed Entertainment Cluster." Student report prepared for Seminar on Competition and Competitiveness, Harvard Business School, Boston, Mass., May 1997.

Joint Venture, Silicon Valley Network. "Blueprint for a Twenty-first Century Community." San Jose, Calif.: Joint Venture, Silicon Valley Network, Phase II Report, June 1993.

––––––. "The Joint Venture Way: Lessons for Regional Rejuvenation." San Jose, Calif.: Joint Venture, Silicon Valley Network, 1995.

————. "Joint Venture's Index of Silicon Valley: Measuring Progress Toward a Twenty-first Century Community." San Jose, Calif.: Joint Venture, Silicon Valley Network, 1995, 1996, 1997. [An annual publication.]

Canada

Porter, M., and Monitor Company. "Canada at the Crossroads: The Reality of a New Competitive Environment." Ottawa: Business Council on National Issues and the Government of Canada, 1991.

Central America

Andrade, M., A. Espejel, D. Lazarus, V. Silhy, and M. Velasco. "Textiles and Apparel in Central America." Student report prepared for Seminar on Competition and Competitiveness, Harvard Business School, Boston, Mass., May 1997.

Connecticut

Department of Economic and Community Development. "Connecticut: The International State." Department of Economic and Community Development International Strategic Plan, Hartford, Conn., 1991.

Chandra, R., R. Becherer, D. Young, and A. De Maria. "Review of the CONNECT Program Progress and the Connecticut Photonics Cluster." In *Global Networking of Regional Optics Clusters*, edited by R. Breault, 63–69. Bellingham, Wash.: The International Society for Optical Engineering, 1996.

Ireland

Industrial Policy Review Group. "A Time for Change: Industrial Policy for the 1990s." Dublin: The Stationery Office, 1992.

O'Malley, E., K. A. Kennedy, and R. O'Donnell. *Report to the Industrial Policy Review Group on the Impact of the Industrial Development Agencies.* Dublin: The Stationery Office, 1992.

Massachusetts

Porter, M., and Monitor Company. "The Competitive Advantage of Massachusetts." Boston, Mass.: Office of the Secretary of State, 1991.

Porter, M., R. Wayland, and C. J. Grogan, in collaboration with Challenge to Leadership. "Toward a Shared Economic Vision for Massachusetts." December 1992.

Minnesota

Metropolitan Council. "The Financial Services Cluster of the Twin Cities: A Follow-Up to the Twin Cities Industry Cluster Study." Minneapolis/St. Paul: Metropolitan Council, October 1995(A).

———. "Twin Cities Industry Cluster Study." Minneapolis/St. Paul: Metropolitan Council, 1995(B).

"Southeastern Minnesota Industrial Cluster Study." The Initiative Fund of Southeastern and South Central Minnesota, Owatonna, Minn., September 1996.

Morocco

DRI/McGraw-Hill and FOCS. *Le Maroc Compétitif: A Cluster Development Initiative in Morocco.* Washington, D.C.: DRI/McGraw Hill and FOCS, September 1996.

———. *Le Maroc Compétitif: Plan d'Action Stratégique.* Washington, D.C.: DRI/McGraw Hill and FOCS, November 1996.

Netherlands

Ministry of Economic Affairs. *Economie met Open Grenzen.* The Hague: Sdu, 1990.

———. *Kennis is Beweging.* The Hague: Sdu, 1995.

New York City

Aslett, M., J. Kondo, S. Pannu, K. Park, and A. Rodriguez. "New York Fashion: Recommendations from a Global Cluster Analysis." Student report prepared for Seminar on Competition and Competitiveness, Harvard Business School, Boston, Mass., May 1997.

Beauchamp, C., D. Bodor, M. Capur, E. Kuo, and T. Shoeb. "Multimedia in Manhattan." Student report prepared for Seminar on Competition and Competitiveness, Harvard Business School, Boston, Mass., May 1997.

New Zealand

Graduate School of Business and Government Management. *Partnership and Enterprise: Putting Porter into Practice.* Auckland: GMBGM Special Report Series No. 3, 1991.

Northern Ireland

Northern Ireland Growth Challenge. *North Ireland Growth Challenge: Interim Summary of Progress.* Northern Ireland Growth Challenge, Belfast, Northern Ireland, May 1995.

Pennsylvania

Pittsburgh High Technology Council and Southwestern Pennsylvania Industrial Resource Center. "Thinking Differently About the Region: Southwestern Pennsylvania's Manufacturing and Technology Assets." Pittsburgh: Pittsburgh High Technology Council and Southwestern Pennsylvania Industrial Resource Center, 1994.

Portugal

Forum para a Competitividade. *A Competitividade da Economia Portuguesa.* Lisboa: Forum para a Competitividade, 1995.

Ministério da Industria e Energia. *O Projecto Porter: A aplicaçao a Portugal 1993/1994.* Lisboa: Ministério da Industrio e Energia, 1995.

Monitor Company, under the direction of M. Porter. "Construir as Vantagens Competitivas de Portugal." Lisboa: Forum para a Competitividade, 1994.

CHAPTER 8

Competing Across Locations

Enhancing Competitive
Advantage Through a
Global Strategy

Michael E. Porter

ONE OF THE MOST POWERFUL forces affecting companies since World War II has been the globalization of competition. We have seen transport and communication costs fall, the flow of information and technology across borders increase, national infrastructures grow more similar, and trade and investment barriers ease. The result has been marked growth in international trade and investment. In an ever-widening range of industries a global, as opposed to a domestic, strategy is a necessity.

Unsurprisingly, as the globalization of competition has become more apparent, research and corporate practice in international strategy has taken on greater prominence. Thinking about international strategy has focused by and large on the power of the multinational company to create competitive advantage through globalness. A global strategy, involving operations spread among many countries, has been seen as a powerful means of reaping economies of scale, assimilating and responding to international market needs, and efficiently assembling resources such

This article draws on an earlier article, "Global Competition and the Localization of Competitive Advantage," written with Rebecca E. Wayland, published in *Proceedings of the Integral Strategy Collegium*, Graduate School of Business, Indiana University (Greenwich, Connecticut: JAI Press, 1995). The article benefited from research by Hernan Cristerna and joint work with Michael Enright, of the University of Hong Kong, and Örjan Sölvell and Ivo Zander, both of Stockholm School of Economics. I am also grateful for the helpful comments offered by David Collis and Hans Thorelli.

as capital, labor, raw materials, and technology from around the world. Authors as diverse as Ohmae, Reich, and Bartlett and Ghoshal see the global firm as transcending national boundaries. The national identity of a corporation must be replaced, in this view, by a strategic paradigm that knows no borders.

When considering the globalization of competition, however, one must confront an apparent paradox: Although companies do indeed compete globally and inputs such as raw materials, capital, and scientific knowledge now move freely around the world, strong evidence shows that location continues to play a crucial role in competitive advantage. First, striking differences persist in the economic performance of nations and of states and cities within nations. Second, in a wide variety of industries, the world's leading competitors are all based in one or two countries; this tendency is especially marked if *industry* is defined narrowly in terms meaningful for setting strategy and if industries are excluded in which government policy heavily distorts competition. This geographic concentration of competitive advantage appears not only in established industries such as automobiles and machine tools but also in new industries such as software, biotechnology, and advanced materials. Third, global companies have indeed dispersed activities to many countries, but they continue to concentrate in one location a critical mass of their most important activities for competing in each of their major product lines or businesses. Interestingly, however, these "home bases," as I call them, are not all located in the home country or even in the same country.

This article aims to reconcile these seemingly divergent perspectives into a framework for understanding the nature of international competition and the shift from domestic to global strategy in particular businesses. In creating competitive advantage, global strategy must integrate the roles of both location and a global network of activities. To bring the framework to life, I employ extended examples drawn from three premier global competitors: the Novo-Nordisk Group, based in Denmark; Hewlett-Packard, based in the United States; and Honda, based in Japan. (See the insert "Case Studies of Three Global Competitors.") This article concludes by examining how its framework can be employed to develop a concrete global strategy for a particular business.

While the discussion here frames the issues in terms of global competition, the principles can be applied much more generally. The same

Case Studies of Three Global Competitors

To bring life to this discussion of global strategy, I have drawn on the international activities of three prototypical global corporations. For each of these successful international leaders, headquartered variously in Europe, Japan, and the United States, profiles of their international operations probe the international configuration and coordination of their activities.

• *Novo-Nordisk Group (Novo)*. Headquartered in Denmark, Novo is the world's leading exporter of insulin and industrial enzymes.[a] Novo generates more than 90 percent of its revenues outside its home country and has strong positions in Europe, the United States, and Japan. Data for 1991 show that 27 percent of its employees were based outside Denmark and 19 percent of its total assets were located outside Europe. Novo had seven R&D locations and nine production sites outside Denmark. The company distributes its products in one hundred countries and had its own marketing subsidiaries in forty-three countries. Novo sourced animal pancreases, a key raw material for insulin, in more than twenty countries. It also sourced its capital from around the world, funding 83 percent of its short-term debt and 54 percent of its long-term debt in currencies other than the Danish kroner. The company was listed on the London and the New York stock exchanges.

• *Honda*. Headquartered in Japan, Honda is one of the world's leading producers of automobiles and is the world leader in motorcycles.[b] Honda generated 61 percent of its revenues outside Japan in 1991 and held particularly strong market positions in Asia and North America. It based 22 percent of its employees and 39 percent of its total assets outside Japan, maintained production and assembly facilities in thirty-nine countries, and distributed its automobiles and motorcycles in 150 countries. Inputs and capital were sourced worldwide; the company was listed on the Tokyo and the New York stock exchanges.

• *Hewlett-Packard (HP)*. Headquartered in the United States, HP is the world's largest and most diversified manufacturer of electronic measurement and testing equipment as well as a leader in other products such as printers, medical instruments, and computers.[b] HP generated 54 percent of its revenues outside the United States in 1991. It based 38 percent of its 93,000 employees and 50 percent of its total assets outside the United States and operated 600 sales and support offices and distributorships in 110 countries. It was listed on the London, Paris, Tokyo, Frankfurt, Stuttgart, Switzerland, and Pacific stock exchanges.

Globalization has led each of these firms to spread activities extensively around the world. Hewlett-Packard's location philosophy is instructive. HP locates low-skilled manufacturing activities with high direct-labor content in low-cost areas, at an estimated savings of 40 to 75 percent compared to U.S. locations. Some component assembly and manufacturing for personal computers (PCs), for example, is conducted in Singapore, and electronic component manufacturing is conducted in Malaysia. Hewlett-Packard also locates some medium-skilled activities in lower-cost countries; for example, some product and process engineering activities (such as manufacturing cost reduction programs) are conducted at the PC manufacturing facilities in Singapore, process engi-

neering for some new electronic component products has been transferred to the manufacturing plant in Malaysia, and some software coding and maintenance has been subcontracted to countries such as India, China, Eastern Europe, and the former Soviet Union, where college-educated programmers work for 40 to 60 percent lower wages than those in the United States.

---

a. Information on Novo draws on Enright (1989) and field research.
b. The profiles of Honda and of Hewlett-Packard are based on Porter and Wayland (1995). Most figures are taken from 1991 annual reports and other corporate filings.

framework applies in examining *competition across locations* at any level—cities, states, regions, or even groups of neighboring countries. The same thought process can be used by a local competitor seeking to compete nationally or by a national competitor seeking to compete regionally.

A General Framework for Global Strategy

Most issues in competitive strategy are the same for domestic and global companies; in both cases, success is a function of the attractiveness of the industries in which the firm competes and of the firm's relative position in those industries.[1] The firm's performance within the industry depends on its competitive advantages (or disadvantages) vis-à-vis its rivals. Competitive advantage is manifested either in lower costs than those of rivals or in the ability to differentiate and command a premium price that exceeds the extra cost of differentiating. Some competitive advantages arise because of differences in operational effectiveness, but the most sustainable advantages come from occupying a unique competitive position. Both domestic and global companies must understand the structure of their industry, identify their sources of competitive advantage, and analyze competitors.

"Global" strategy, then, refers to the special issues that arise when firms compete across nations. The need for a global strategy depends on the nature of international competition in a particular industry. There is not one single pattern of international competition, but many. Not all industries require a global strategy. The nature of international competition in industries can be arrayed along a spectrum. At one end are *multidomestic* industries, present in many countries (even every country) but industries in which competition takes place on a country-by-country basis with little or no linkage. Examples include most types of retailing, metal fabrication, construction, and many services. Indeed, numerous industries are regional within nations or even local. At the other end of the spectrum are truly *global industries*, in which competition in different countries is linked because a firm's position in a given country significantly affects its position elsewhere. Prominent examples are commercial aircraft, consumer electronics, and many types of industrial machinery.

In multidomestic industries, there is no need for a global strategy. Here, the international strategy should be a series of distinct domestic strategies. Country operating units should be given wide latitude and autonomy. In global industries, however, firms must create integrated strategies involving all countries simultaneously. Just because a firm is multinational, therefore, does not mean that it has or should have a global strategy. The essential question in global strategy is this: When and how is the international whole more than the sum of the domestic parts?

To understand the underpinnings of competitive advantage and what a global strategy might contribute requires that what a firm does is disaggregated into its *value chain* (see Figure 8.1).[2] A firm competing in a particular business performs an array of discrete but interrelated economic activities; for example, it assembles products, its salespeople make sales visits, it processes orders, it recruits and trains, staff and it purchases inputs. All activities normally involve some procedures or routines, human resources, physical assets, enabling technologies, and the creation and use of information. A firm's "strengths," "competencies,"

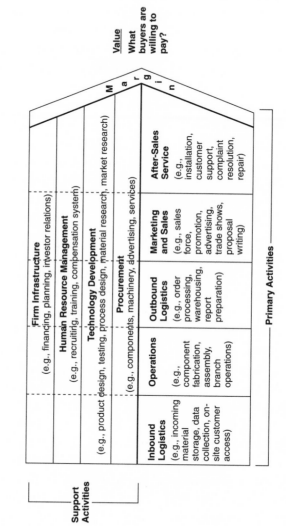

Figure 8.1 The Value Chain

"capabilities," and "resources,"—common phrases in discussions of strategy—can best be understood in terms of the particular activities to which they apply.

The value chain groups a firm's activities into several categories, distinguishing between those directly involved in producing, marketing, delivering, and supporting a product or service; those that create, source, and improve inputs and technology; and those performing overarching functions such as raising capital or overall decisionmaking. Within each of these categories appears an array of discrete activities or economic/ organizational processes, at the level of field repair, inbound materials receiving and storage, billing, and reviewing and rewarding employees. The particular activities performed depend at least partly on the business.

Activities form the basic foundation of competitive advantage in either cost or differentiation. As noted above, competitive advantage results when a firm has the ability to perform the required activities at a collectively lower cost than rivals or to perform some activities in unique ways that create non-price buyer value and support a premium price. Creating buyer value depends, in turn, on how a firm influences the activities of its channels and end-users.

Competitive advantage in activities can arise from both operational effectiveness and strategy. Operational effectiveness refers to performing given or similar activities at the state of best practice. This includes the use of the most cost-effective purchased inputs, managerial practices, and the like. Part of the need for a global strategy is to enhance operational effectiveness through such things as global sourcing and transfer of knowledge.

A firm's strategy defines its particular configuration of activities and how they fit together. Different strategic positions involve tailoring activities to produce particular product/service varieties, to address the special needs of particular customer groups, or to access most efficiently certain types of customers. Broadly targeted competitors seek to gain advantages by sharing activities across an array of industry segments. Narrowly targeted competitors (which I term *focusers*) seek advantage by tailoring activities to the needs of one (or a few) particular segment(s). Global strategy also bears on strategic positioning by affecting the trade-offs underlying a position or the ability to tailor activities to it.

The value chain provides the basic tool to highlight the strategy issues unique to a global strategy. Both domestic firms and global firms have value chains. The domestic (or multidomestic) company performs all the activities in the home (or in each) country. What distinguishes a global strategy, however, is the latitude to spread parts of the value chain among countries. The basic choices can be grouped into two areas:

1. *Configuration:* Configuration focuses on *where* each of the activities in a firm's value chain are located; assembly can be in one country, for example, and product R&D in another. Moreover, a given activity can occur in one location or be dispersed to many.
2. *Coordination:* Coordination focuses on the nature and extent to which dispersed activities are *coordinated* in a network or remain *autonomous,* that is, tailored to local circumstances.

Any firm that competes internationally must sell in many countries. Some activities, such as many of those involved in sales and distribution, necessarily are tied to the customer's location. A firm seeking to sell in a country must either establish its own marketing and sales and physical distribution activities there or rely on others (for example, distributors or joint venture partners). Other activities in the value chain, however, can be uncoupled from the customer, giving the international firm discretion over the number and location of such activities. In multidomestic strategy, the company performs the entire value chain in each country, and each country subsidiary has near or complete autonomy to tailor the activities to the country. In a global strategy, the company selectively locates activities in different countries and coordinates among them to harness and extend the competitive advantage of the network.

CONFIGURATION

The international configuration of a firm's activities creates competitive advantage through the choice of *where* to locate each activity and the *number of sites.* One motivation for locating an activity is *comparative advantage* in performing the activity, such as a location with the most cost-effective pool of raw materials or people. Some multinational software firms locate software debugging and program maintenance activities in India, for example, to access low-cost but good-quality programmers. Because the location with comparative advantage varies by activity, the global firm has the potential to gain the benefits of arbitraging comparative advantages across locations.

A second and less understood motivation for the choice of location is *competitive* or *productivity advantage*. Here, as will be discussed further, activities or groups of activities are located in the countries with the most attractive environments for innovation and productivity growth.

Choice of location includes deciding not only where to locate but how many sites to maintain. The firm might *concentrate* an activity in one location to serve the world or *disperse* the activity to several or many locations. By concentrating an activity, firms may gain economies of scale or may progress rapidly down the learning curve. Concentrating a group of linked activities in one location may also allow a firm to better coordinate among them. Dispersing activities to a number of locations, in contrast, may be justified by the need to minimize transportation and storage costs, hedge against the risks of a single activity site, tailor activities sensitive to local market differences, facilitate learning about country and market conditions that can be transmitted to headquarters, or respond to local government pressure or incentives to locate in a country in order to sell or produce there.

The global firm should disperse only those activities necessary to obtain these benefits, and no more. Both efficiency and the ease of innovation are enhanced, other things being equal, if as many activities as possible are co-located. This minimizes coordination and transshipment costs. Sometimes, a firm must disperse one activity to a country in order to gain the ability (or permission from local government) to concentrate other activities elsewhere. Establishing local assembly plants in a variety of countries, for example, may allow a company to import scale-sensitive components into each of the countries and thus to concentrate more scale-sensitive component production elsewhere. The particular activities to be dispersed should be those incurring the least sacrifice in terms of economies of scale or learning and requiring the least close coordination with other activities.

COORDINATION

A global strategy can also contribute to competitive advantage by coordinating activities across locations. Coordinating methods, technology, and output decisions across dispersed activities contributes a number of potential competitive advantages. These include the ability to respond to shifting comparative advantages (for example, raw materials prices or exchange rates); to share learning among countries; to reinforce the corporate brand reputation for mobile buyers who encounter the firm in different places (for example, McDonald's or Coca-Cola); to differentiate with or more efficiently serve multinational buyers who simultaneously deal with several of the firm's country units; to bargain more effectively with governments by using the carrot and stick of expanding or contracting local operations; or to respond more cost effectively to competitive threats by choosing the location at which to do battle. Some of these benefits relate to operational effectiveness, while others reinforce a company's unique position. Successful coordination is important to gaining the benefits of dispersing activities. These potential advantages of coordination are weighed against the benefits of allowing each dispersed unit to act autonomously and tailor its activities to local circumstances. An international strategy involving high levels of autonomy for dispersed units is favored where local needs and conditions vary, all customers are local, or few economies of scale are present. In practice, the balance between coordination and autonomy varies by activity.

A number of forms of coordination across locations are possible, including setting common standards, exchanging information, and allocating responsibility among sites. Coordination that involves allocating responsibilities across countries, such as assigning worldwide responsibility for producing particular models to different locations, can unleash economies of scale. Coordination involving information exchange reaps the benefits of worldwide learning. Coordination, then, can allow a firm to realize the advantages of dispersing its activities; conversely, the failure to coordinate activities can lessen those advantages. A central issue in coordination is how and where information, technology, and other knowledge gained from disparate locations becomes integrated into and reflected in products, processes, and other activities. The home base performs these essential functions.

Coordination across geographically dispersed locations involves daunting organization challenges, among them those of language and cultural differences and of aligning individual managers' and subsidiaries' incentives with those of the global enterprise as a whole. Some forms of coordination, such as allocating responsibilities for component production to different locations, require less ongoing interchange than others.

PATTERNS OF GLOBAL STRATEGY

Some competitive advantages of a global strategy arise from location; others arise from the overall global network and the way it is managed. Every global strategy normally begins with some kind of advantage in location, reflected in the company's competitive position. This advantage allows the firm to penetrate international markets and to overcome the inherent disadvantages of competing in another country. Without some asymmetry among firms based in different countries, competition will remain multidomestic.

The initial location-based advantages are extended and supplemented through a global network. The advantages of other locations can also be tapped by dispersing activities. Global competition has not one but many patterns, depending on the particular activities concentrated or dispersed, the location of various activities, and how activities are coordinated. In multidomestic industries, industry structure favors a highly dispersed configuration in which each country contains virtually the entire value chain. In such industries, strong benefits follow from allowing country units nearly full strategic autonomy. Competition in an industry globalizes when the competitive advantages of a global network are substantial enough to overcome the local focus and local knowledge of domestic or country-centered competitors.

Global strategy thus takes many forms. The particular global strategy utilized by McDonald's in the fast food industry differs a good deal from that of Intel in the microprocessor industry or Boeing in commercial aircraft. Figure 8.2, which sketches Citibank's global strategy in retail banking, illustrates this. As in many service businesses, Citibank disperses many activities, including branch operations, marketing, and even many forms of processing. Active coordination occurs on image,

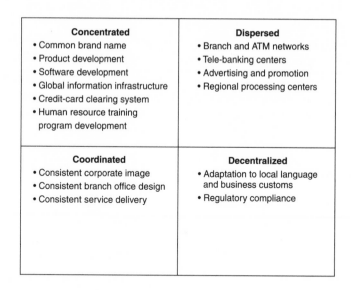

Concentrated	Dispersed
• Common brand name • Product development • Software development • Global information infrastructure • Credit-card clearing system • Human resource training program development	• Branch and ATM networks • Tele-banking centers • Advertising and promotion • Regional processing centers
Coordinated • Consistent corporate image • Consistent branch office design • Consistent service delivery	**Decentralized** • Adaptation to local language and business customs • Regulatory compliance

Figure 8.2   Citicorp: Global Configuration and Coordination in Retail Banking

branch design, and service standards, however, and local autonomy is narrowly drawn.

Firms can play a major role in shaping the benefits and costs of a global versus a domestic strategy. Firms can redefine competition through strategic innovations that increase the advantages of a global strategy or that reduce its disadvantages. Becton Dickinson, for example, created worldwide demand for disposable syringes in favor of reusable glass syringes. Partly by being the first mover, Becton Dickinson emerged as the world leader. Other firms have triggered globalization by pioneering new approaches to competing that increased economies of scale or by inventing product designs or production processes that reduced the cost of tailoring products to differing country needs. Many global industry leaders have emerged because they were early to perceive and act on these levers. Theodore Levitt's 1983 work on the globalization of markets is typically seen as arguing the merits of world products.[3] Yet often unrecognized is the essay's more important emphasis on the ability of the firm to *create* world products by pioneering new approaches to segmentation and marketing rather than by passively responding to preexisting needs.

Location and Global Competition

The globalization of competition allows firms to gain competitive advantages independent of location by coordinating activities across a wide range of countries. Globalization has not eliminated the importance of location in competition, however. In hundreds of industries that have been studied, including services and newly emerging fields such as software, advanced materials, and biotechnology, the world leaders are typically headquartered in just a few countries and sometimes in only one country.[4] The three case studies of companies presented in the insert "Case Studies of Three Global Competitors" all fit this rule. Honda is not the only Japanese success story in the automotive and motorcycle industries: Nine of the world's automobile companies and the four dominant global motorcycle companies are all based in Japan. Similarly, Hewlett-Packard is not the only successful U.S. firm in its industries: U.S. firms are preeminent in workstations, PCs, medical instruments, and test and instrumentation equipment. Two Denmark-based companies, merged into Novo-Nordisk only in 1989, dominated insulin exports. Novo is also a world leader in industrial enzymes, a field in which other Danish firms compete as well.

The geographic concentration of leading firms *within* nations demonstrates the importance of location to competition even more clearly. The United States presents a particularly interesting example. Despite free trade among the states, a common language and laws, and great similarities across states along many dimensions, successful competitors in particular businesses are far from evenly distributed. Publishing concentrates heavily in New York City; movies and television production, in Hollywood; office furniture, in western Michigan; pharmaceuticals, in Philadelphia and New Jersey; hosiery and home furnishings, in North Carolina; artificial hips and joints, in Indiana: Countless other examples could be added.[5] A similar pattern of geographic concentration can be found, in varying degrees, in every advanced nation.[6]

A close look at the configuration and coordination of activities in global companies also reveals the strong influence of location, including Novo, Hewlett-Packard, and Honda. Accounts emphasizing the widespread geographic dispersion of activities by multinationals can be misleading. Company diversification often means extensive foreign activities, but these may span many entirely different product areas. In a given business, activities are far less dispersed.

A more important distinction in assessing geographic dispersion is that between the *types* of activities located in different countries. International firms tend to concentrate their most sophisticated activities in a single country—often, though less so over time, in their home country. Novo markets its insulin products around the world and sources some inputs globally, but it conducts the most strategically important activities in the value chain—all production and core product and process R&D—in Denmark. Honda has extensive worldwide manufacturing and distribution, but Japan remains the home base for strategy, design, and the production of Honda's most sophisticated components, including all core engine research. Hewlett-Packard's operations encompass more than sixteen thousand product lines sold around the world, yet it concentrates worldwide responsibility (HP refers to this as "worldwide re") for each product line, including core manufacturing, R&D, and decision making, in one particular location.

Additional evidence comes from Asea Brown Boveri (ABB), often cited as the prototype of a company with no national identity.[7] ABB has multiple operations located throughout the world, but it bases global responsibility for establishing business strategy, selecting product development priorities, and allocating production among countries in each product line in a particular geographic location. Leadership for power transformers is based in Germany, for example; electric drives in Finland; and process automation in the United States. Moreover, multinationals seem to be relocating headquarters of particular businesses from one nation to another with increasing frequency.

COMPARATIVE ADVANTAGE VS. COMPETITIVE ADVANTAGE

The apparent paradox between the globalization of competition and a strong national or even local role in competitive advantage can be resolved by recognizing that the paradigm that governs the competition among locations has shifted from *comparative advantage* to the broader notion of *competitive advantage*.

Comparative advantage due to lower factor costs (for example, labor, raw materials, capital, or infrastructure) or size still exists, but it no longer confers competitive advantage in most industries nor supports high wages. Globalization now allows firms to match comparative advantages by sourcing inputs such as raw materials, capital, and even generic scientific knowledge from anywhere and to disperse selective activities overseas to take advantage of low-cost labor or capital. The global firm must do these things to attain operational effectiveness. Failure to disperse activities to access comparative advantages will lead to a competitive *dis*advantage, but doing so yields the firm no advantage.

Similarly, the size of the home market is far less important than the ability to penetrate the much larger world market. Moreover, advancing technology has given firms the capacity to reduce, nullify, or circumvent many weaknesses in comparative advantage. Japanese firms, for example, have prospered in many industries, despite the high local costs of energy and land, by pioneering energy-saving and space-saving innovations such as lean production. New technology also diminishes economies of scale,[8] while vertical integration now gives way to greater outsourcing to specialized suppliers.

The competitive advantage of locations arises not from the availability of low cost inputs or size per se, but from superior productivity in using inputs: Basic inputs create competitive disadvantages, not advantages. The enduring advantages of a location come from providing an environment in which firms can operate productively and continuously innovate and upgrade their ways of competing to more sophisticated levels, thereby allowing rising productivity. Innovation refers not only to technology in the narrow sense but also to ways of marketing, product positioning, and providing service. The most dynamic and innovative companies in such locations can outpace their rivals elsewhere, even entrenched competitors enjoying low-cost factors or economies of scale in older methods of operating. In productivity competition, firms spread activities globally to source inputs and access markets but competitive advantage arises from a process of innovation and productivity growth heavily localized at the firm's "home base" for a particular product line: the location of its strategy development, core product and process R&D, and a critical mass of the firm's sophisticated production (or service provision).[9] At the home base reside the essential skills and technology; it is the integration site for inputs and information sourced from global activities; and the most productive jobs are located there.

The location of a firm's owners or of its corporate headquarters becomes far less significant than the location of the home-based activities for each strategically distinct business.

THE COMPETITIVE ADVANTAGE OF LOCATIONS

The competitive advantages of a location lie in the quality of the environment it provides for achieving high and rising levels of productivity in a particular field. While we tend to think of the sources of competitive advantage as primarily arising within a company, a company's potential for advantage and many of the necessary inputs resides in its proximate environment. Only this can explain why so many successful companies in particular fields emerge in the same country and even in the same region within a country.

My research has highlighted four aspects of a national (and state or local) environment that define the context for growth and innovation and productivity: factor (input) conditions; the context for strategy and rivalry; demand conditions; and related and supporting industries. These four areas, which I collectively term the *diamond*, help explain why companies based in particular locations can achieve consistent innovation and upgrading in particular fields (see Figure 8.3). Diamond theory is treated in greater detail in Chapters 6 and 7. Here I sketch an outline designed to lay the foundation for discussing global strategy.[10]

Factor (Input) Conditions. Factors of production are the basic inputs to competition; they include land, labor, capital, physical infrastructure, commercial or administrative infrastructure, natural resources, and scientific knowledge. The notion of comparative advantage normally refers to the cost and availability of inputs. General purpose inputs, such as sound roads and ports or a cadre of college-educated employees, are necessary to avoid a competitive disadvantage, but they are no longer sufficient for gaining a locational advantage.

The advantages of a location for productivity competition arise instead from high quality inputs and especially from *specialized* inputs, such as pools of skills, applied technology, physical infrastructure, regulatory regimes, legal processes, information, and sources of capital tailored to

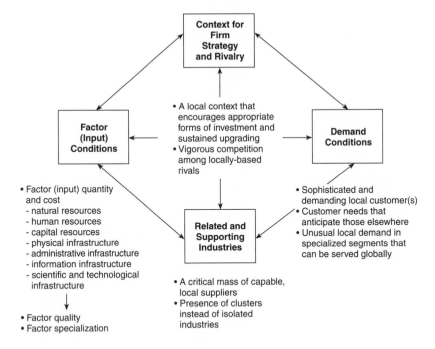

Figure 8.3   Sources of Locational Competitive Advantage

the needs of particular industries. In the United States, for example, preeminence in software rests on a unique concentration of highly trained programmers and other computer science professionals, unparalleled research programs in computer-related disciplines, an efficient body of rules governing software licensing and use, and well-developed and expert sources of risk capital for software firms (many American venture capital firms specialize in software). Hewlett-Packard benefits from some of these advantages in its computer-related businesses. Nations and regions do not inherit the most important factors of production for sophisticated competition; they must create them. This, in turn, depends on the local presence and quality of specialized institutions in education, training, research, data collection, and other areas. Such institutions become a potent source of locational advantage.

More paradoxical as a locational advantage is the role of selective *disadvantages* in basic inputs, such as high costs of land or local raw material shortages. These can lead to competitive advantages because they trigger innovation and/or stimulate the development of specialized institutions. In Holland, for example, a poor climate and land shortages have led to innovations in such areas as greenhouse cultivation methods, breeding technology, and handling techniques for cut flowers, a product for which the Dutch hold more than 60 percent of world exports. Conversely, in locations with abundant labor, cheap debt capital, and bountiful natural resources, firms tend to use these resources less productively, raising their vulnerability to more productive competitors based elsewhere.

The presence of pools of specialized inputs, and the institutions that create and renew them, become an external advantage or collective asset of a location. This public good builds up over time through cumulative investment by many firms, institutions, and government entities. The presence of the external advantage obviates the need for individual companies to bear the internal costs. While a company may be able to gain access to some of the locational assets through global sourcing, many are hard to access from a distance.

Context for Strategy and Rivalry. Locations have advantages in productivity competition if the context of rules, social norms, and incentives there foster sustained investment in forms appropriate to a particular industry. Forms of investment include not only fixed assets but R&D, training, and market development.

The tax system, intellectual property rules, and the stability of the macroeconomic and political environment clearly influences the investment climate in a location. Corporate ownership and governance rules also have an important influence. The American system of venture capital and public offerings constitutes a major advantage in array of industries, for example, while institutional ownership and frequent trading make it more difficult for American companies to compete in lower growth, longer life-cycle fields. Cultural factors can sometimes raise or lower the prestige of various occupations and fields and thereby the investment devoted to them.

The intensity of local rivalry forms another major dimension of the competitive context in a location. Combined with a favorable investment climate, local rivalry is perhaps the most potent advantage of a location. Firms can rarely succeed abroad, for example, unless they have competed with some capable rivals at home. Honda, for example, faces competition from eight other Japanese auto companies, all of which compete internationally. Rivalry among a group of locally-based competitors heightens pressure to innovate and upgrade. Relative performance comparisons among local rivals stimulates rapid improvement. Local rivals, faced with comparable input costs and access to the home market, are forced to seek other ways to compete. In locations with a poor investment climate, rivalry can degenerate to price cutting. Where local conditions support investment, however, rivalry fosters upgrading. Since no firm can comfortably dominate the home market, rivals are forced to compete internationally.[11] Novo, for example, was pushed to export early because it had a strong Danish rival; most other insulin producers were effectively national monopolies. Intense local rivalry creates a situation where individual companies have difficulty staying ahead for long, but the entire local industry progresses more rapidly than competitors based elsewhere.[12]

Demand Conditions. A third type of locational advantage arises from the character of the local market. Advantage arises from having sophisticated and demanding local customers, or customers with unusually intense needs for specialized varieties also in demand elsewhere. Sophisticated, demanding buyers pressure companies to meet high standards, provide a window into evolving customer needs, and prod companies to innovate and move to more advanced segments. Home customers are particularly valuable if their needs anticipate or shape those of other nations, thereby providing "early-warning indicators" of global market trends. Local demand also creates advantages when it highlights industry segments ignored elsewhere. In productivity competition, the character of home demand is far more important than its size.

Home demand conditions reflect local needs, sophistication levels, purchasing power, and even cultural affinities for particular products. Government policies can directly and indirectly influence demand conditions in a variety of ways, such as product, safety, and environmental regulations mandating certain attributes of products or processes. Strict environmental or energy-efficiency standards can stimulate innovation and productivity improvement, for example, if standards are flexible enough to accommodate new methods.[13]

The advantages of home demand are rooted in information and incentives difficult to obtain from a distance. Local customers offer high visibility, ease in communication, and the opportunity for joint working relationships. All three of the global leaders discussed in the insert above benefit from sophisticated demand at home. Novo, for example, sells to perhaps the most sophisticated group of medical specialists in the treatment of diabetes in the world and operates in the context of a national health care system providing generous reimbursement for new treatments.

Related and Supporting Industries. The final type of locational advantages in productivity competition arises from the local presence of capable specialized suppliers and related industries. Proximity to local suppliers of the specialized components, machinery, and services and related firms is not necessary to gain access to inputs, which can be sourced globally. Instead, the advantage arises from efficiency, knowledge, and the ease of innovation.

The presence of capable local suppliers reduces the often considerable transaction cost and delay of importing and dealing with distant vendors and facilitiates repair and problem solving. Companies also have more discretion in choosing appropriate levels of vertical integration. The presence of capable local firms in related fields further contributes to efficiency by making it easier to gain complementarities in R&D, distribution, and marketing.

The efficiency gains from local suppliers and related industries are often less significant, however, than the benefits in terms of innovation and dynamism. Nearby suppliers and firms in related businesses foster the rapid flow of information, scientific collaboration, and joint development efforts. Speed and flexibility in introducing new products increase because companies can readily farm out parts of the process. More broadly, companies can more readily influence their suppliers' technical efforts and serve as test sites for new developments, accelerating the pace of innovation. Honda benefited from a strong local supplier network in both automobiles and motorcycles, as did HP in all its principal businesses. Novo enjoyed particular advantages from the presence in Denmark of related fields, such as brewing and dairy products, which employed related technology, skills, and machinery.

As with demand advantages, the benefits of home-based suppliers and related industries for innovation are difficult to replicate from a distance. Highly applied technology and specialized skills are difficult to codify, accumulate, and transfer. Global sourcing works best for raw materials, standard components, and general purpose equipment and machinery with little need for associated information and technical exchange. Here, foreign sourcing involves lower transaction costs and little impact on the innovation process, although it may reduce flexibility.

The importance of local suppliers and firms in related fields, coupled with local demand conditions, underlies the fundamental role of *clusters* of interconnected industries. An extensive discussion of clusters is the subject of Chapter 7. Clusters include specialized suppliers, service providers, downstream (for example, channel or customer) industries, information providers, infrastructure providers, and firms in related fields. Associated institutions such as trade associations, standards-setting agencies, and university departments constitute part of the cluster as well. The cluster represents a collective asset, creating an environment in which firms can easily and efficiently assemble knowledge, skills, and inputs. This raises productivity and speeds the rate of innovation.

THE DIAMOND AS A LOCAL SYSTEM

Together, the four types of location-based advantages in the diamond constitute a dynamic system more important than its parts. The effect on productivity of one part of the diamond depends on the state of the other parts. Vigorous local rivalry stimulates productivity growth—provided that the local context supports investment (context for strategy and rivalry) and that local buyers seek quality products (demand conditions). Otherwise, rivalry can degenerate into destructive price cutting. Similarly, improving the supply of skilled engineers (factor conditions) will not boost productivity unless firms invest in R&D and process improvements and an adequate supplier base supports innovation-based strategies. Serious weakness in any part of the diamond will constrain an industry's potential for productivity growth.

Given appropriate institutional and other linkages, the four types of location advantages are strongly reinforcing. Vigorous domestic rivalry contributes, for example, to the development of unique pools of specialized skills and technology. The presence of a number of rivals encourages local institutions, such as universities, colleges, and training providers, to adapt and support the industry's distinctive needs. Active local rivalry also promotes the formation and upgrading of local supplier industries, which find a ready local market.

The processes of cluster formation and upgrading are not inevitable. The health of the feedback loops depend on the strength of local relationships, the openness of information flow, and the mutual responsiveness of the various firms and institutions. The intensity of local rivalry and the climate for investment play particularly important roles because they have much to do with whether firms act. Some locations are far better organized to facilitate improvement and upgrading than others. Because of the cumulative and self-reinforcing nature of the diamond and the time required to build specialized institutions, knowledge, and a critical mass of firms, normally only a small number of locations will favor competition in a particular business. Foreign firms and specialized suppliers will be drawn to invest in these locations. Often, these newcomers are relocating from weaker diamonds. In pharmaceuticals, for example, the Philadelphia/New Jersey diamond attracts substantial investment by German, Swiss, British, and Japanese pharmaceutical firms because of its superior demand conditions and excellent access to specialized factors. Finally, individuals with good ideas and specialized skills will be drawn to these locations as well because they offer the greatest excitement and rewards. The cycle is interrupted only when major technological changes invalidate past skills, suppliers, and other local advantages or when pressures to upgrade dissipate because local rivalry is eliminated or buyer sophistication lags.

Competition is becoming increasingly national and global, then, but the crucial sources of competitive advantage often remain local. They reside in critical masses of highly specialized and interconnected skills, applied technologies, firms, suppliers, and institutions in particular locations.[14] While the advantages of locations for input cost competition can be easily tapped through global networks, the advantages of a location for productivity competition require proximity. Anything that can be sourced from a distance or via a global network becomes accessible to rivals and ceases to be a robust source or competitive advantage. The important location advantages increasingly lie in local things—knowledge relationships, motivation—that distant rivals cannot match.

Competing Across Locations: From Local to Global Strategy

We are now in a position to bring together the competitive advantages of global networks and the competitive advantages of locations into an integrated conception of global strategy. Competing across locations involves a series of choices that will be illustrated using our three company examples: Novo, Hewlett-Packard, and Honda.

Build Globalization on the Foundation of a Unique Competitive Position. A global (or multilocation) strategy must begin with a unique competitive position that results in a clear competitive advantage. A company will not be able to overcome the barriers to penetrating unfamiliar markets unless it brings a meaningful advantage in either cost or differentiation to the table. Novo, for example, was a clear differentiator in the insulin industry. It pioneered high purity insulins, led in purity and in insulin delivery technology, and sought scientific excellence through its research institute, affiliated diabetes hospital, and hosting of international medical meetings. Novo's differentiation allowed it to make headway in selling its product to doctors and health authorities in each new country whose market it entered.

A corollary to this principle is that companies should globalize first in those businesses and product lines where they have the most unique advantages. These product areas present the greatest odds of international competitive success.

Penetrate International Markets with a Consistent Positioning. Internationalization opens up huge and growing international markets. A global strategy requires a patient, long-term campaign to enter every significant foreign market while maintaining and leveraging the company's unique strategic positioning. Novo-Nordisk, Honda, and HP all followed this approach. The portion of the foreign market available, given a company's particular strategy, will vary from country to country, depending on local purchasing power and the array of local needs (this can guide the order of entering country markets). Maintaining a consistent strategy from country to country, however, will reinforce a company's competitive advantage. Over time, the target market of a company's strategy will often grow, based on economic development in the country as well as efforts to educate the market about the benefits of a company's unique offering.

Efforts to internationalize based on opportunistic modifications of a company's competitive positioning from country to country rarely succeed. Neither does making a string of acquisitions of differently positioned companies, unless these companies are maintained as separate entities or, alternatively, repositioned to align them with the company's strategy and integrated. Without a consistent position, the company lacks a real competitive advantage, and its reputation does not cumulate. Moreover, efforts to integrate activities across countries will often be frustrated or ineffective.

Properly conceived, geographic expansion remains one of the best ways to grow without compromising a company's distinctive strategy. Expanding globally with a consistent position should reinforce a company's advantages. In contrast, broadening the strategy within existing markets runs the risk of compromising the company's uniqueness. One of the greatest barriers to the success of firms based in smaller countries is the perceived need to serve all segments and offer all varieties to capture the limited market opportunity. Instead, the imperative should be to stay focused and pursue the much larger international opportunity.

Establish a Clear Home Base for Each Distinct Business. A firm must have a clear home base for competing in each strategically distinct business. (The location of overall *corporate headquarters* is less significant, and can reflect historical factors or convenience.) The home base for a business is the location where strategy is set, core product and process technology is created and maintained, and a critical mass of sophisticated production and service activities reside. A coordinating center is not enough. Co-locating a critical mass of such activities at one location fosters rapid progress by allowing easier communication, better cross-functional coordination, and more rapid decision making. Firms are also better placed to capture the productivity and innovation benefits of the local cluster because these cut across many activities. The home base should have clear worldwide responsibility for the business unit and should serve as the coordinating and integrating point for inputs, production activities, information, and technology sourced elsewhere.

The home base should be located in the nation or region with the most favorable diamond for the particular business. This will provide the best environment for innovation and productivity growth. The most favorable home base may not necessarily be the country of ownership. Novo, Hewlett-Packard, and Honda each has a clear home base for each of its major businesses. Denmark serves as the home base of Novo's insulin business (and of both Novo's and Nordisk's insulin businesses prior to the merger). Even though 95 percent of sales is generated outside Denmark, all insulin purification facilities, which comprise the most critical activities in production process, are based in Denmark. Denmark's large pig-farming industry initially provided all of the crucial raw material, pig pancreases. Insulin purification requires not only a large investment but also highly specialized machinery, skilled technicians, and quality-control systems. Denmark is home to suppliers of critical machinery and other specialized production inputs, in part because of its strong position in the dairy and beer industries, which utilize related technologies and skills. All of Novo's core product and process R&D is also conducted in Denmark, which is the location of an array of world-class diabetes research institutes and two leading diabetes hospitals. The demand conditions for insulin in Denmark are also advanced. The country's generous health care system provided early funding for new diabetes testing and treatments. Danish doctors not only examine patients but also conduct and monitor programs that train diabetes patients in eating and cooking habits. Novo-Nordisk personnel interact directly with hospital doctors to gain quick feedback on the success of new products and on emerging issues facing diabetics.

Honda's home base for both motorcycles and automobiles is in Japan, where most of Honda's sophisticated activities are conducted. Japan accounts for 76 percent of Honda's production capacity in motorcycles and 68 percent of its automobile production. Foreign production plants are primarily assembly facilities, employing sophisticated parts from Japan. Honda's Japanese motorcycle plants have an average capacity of 396,000 units, for example, compared to 75,000 for those located elsewhere. R&D is even more concentrated: All core engine research and 95 percent of R&D employees and are located in Japan. R&D personnel based outside Japan must undergo two years' training at the Tochigi Research Center in Tokyo before beginning work in their native country.

Hewlett-Packard, which is far more diversified than Novo or Honda, also has a clear home base for each business. Worldwide responsibility for each product line—including core research, the most sophisticated production activities, and decision making—are concentrated in a particular location. The United States hosts 43 percent of HP's physical space dedicated to marketing but 77 percent of the space dedicated to manufacturing, R&D, and administration. At the home base, engineers with specialized expertise are designated worldwide experts; they transfer their knowledge either electronically or through periodic trips to subsidiaries. Regional subsidiaries take responsibility for some process-oriented R&D, product localization, and local marketing.

Leveraged Product-Line Home Bases at Different Locations. As a firm's product range broadens, the home bases for some product lines may best be located in different countries. A firm should specialize its international activity by assigning lead product line responsibility to the country with the most favorable home diamond in that particular segment. This approach is far superior to replicating production and R&D activities for a wide product line in several countries, an inefficient approach that dulls innovation. Instead, each major subsidiary should specialize in models for which it has the most favorable diamond, and serve those segments worldwide. Instead of dispersing activities individually, groups of activities comprising product-line home bases should be located in countries with locational advantage.

Hewlett-Packard provides an interesting example of these notions. HP locates many product line home bases outside the United States. It concentrates inkjet printer operations in Vancouver, British Columbia, for example, with localization for regional markets and assembly in

Barcelona (Spain). Worldwide responsibility for a new line of compact inkjet printers is based in Singapore. This product line combines printer technology transferred from Vancouver with Asian expertise in designing space-saving office products. Within the United States, HP similarly concentrates product line responsibility. It bases responsibility for personal computers and workstations in California (home to almost all of the world's leading personal computer and workstation firms) and medical instruments in Massachusetts (which has an extraordinary concentration of world-renowned research hospitals and numerous leading medical instrument companies).

Honda's home base for automobiles has been entirely in Japan; however, Honda has begun the process of creating a product-line home base for station wagons in the United States. Adapted from a sedan designed and engineered in Japan, the Accord station wagon was conceived, designed, and developed in the United States. The United States, considered the most advanced market for station wagons, has a well-established network of station wagon component suppliers. Honda's California R&D design facility created the models and life-size mock-ups of the wagon; the Ohio R&D facility fabricated the metal prototype; and major production tooling, including stamping dies, was made by American Honda Engineering. Honda has stated that the United States will become its world headquarters for station wagons and that U.S. designers and engineers will continue to develop and upgrade the product. American Honda also has worldwide responsibility for development of a two-door Civic coupe.[15] By the end of the 1990s, American Honda plans to export 70,000 automobiles from the United States to more than twenty countries.

Disperse Activities to Extend Home Base Advantages. While the home base is the location of core activities, other activities can and should be dispersed to extend the company's competitive position. Each activity in the value chain should be systematically examined for these opportunities, which will take one of the following three forms.

- **Sourcing comparative advantages.** Inputs not integral to the innovation process, such as low skilled assembly labor, raw materials, general purpose components or capital, can and must be sourced from the most cost-effective location. In this way, the global competitor harnesses the input cost advantages of various locations. The global competitor can thus exploit the comparative advantage of many locations, while nullifying the cost disadvantages of its home base.

- **Securing or improving foreign market access.** Locating selected activities near the market signals commitment to foreign customers and may allow a company to better address local needs and tailor offerings to local preferences. To this aim, many companies disperse some R&D activities to support product adaptation and compliance with local regulations. Modern flexible manufacturing systems and the increased power of information and communications technologies, however, work to lessen the need to dispersed activities to support local tailoring. Greater harmonization of technical standards and diminishing trade barriers have the same effect. Customization to serve local needs can often be most easily accomplished from a single facility.

  Some activities may need to be dispersed not to enhance competitiveness but in order to respond to actual or threatened government mandates. Much Japanese auto and consumer electronics assembly in the United States, for example, reflects such considerations. When a firm must respond to government pressures, it should disperse some less scale-sensitive activities or activities requiring less coordination and integration with others. The goal should be to deal with government mandates at the least possible sacrifice to efficiency and especially to the rate of innovation.

- **Selectively tapping competitive advantages at other locations.** The home base rarely offers all valuable expertise and promising technologies, no matter how favorable the location. To gain access to their benefits, global competitors can locate activities in other centers of innovation. When tapping the capabilities of other diamonds, however, the home base must be supplemented, not replicated or replaced. The firm's ultimate aim should be to improve capabilities in important skills or technologies at home in order to facilitate more rapid innovation. Relying too heavily on advantages sourced elsewhere threatens the capacity to innovate.

Overall, firms should disperse *only* those activities needed to achieve these three classes of benefits.

Novo illustrates all these motivations in different activities in the value chain. In procurement, Novo sources its traditional raw material, pig pancreases, from twenty countries. Worldwide sourcing not only allows access to larger supplies but hedges risk and allows Novo to capitalize on favorable price and currency fluctuations in particular farming countries. To access low cost capital, Novo funds 83 percent of its long-term debt in currencies other than the Danish kroner and taps foreign equity markets, including the United States. To facilitate market access and lower transportation costs, and, in several cases, to deal with government barriers, Novo has dispersed four insulin processing plants to France, South Africa, Japan, and the United States. These plants—the only Novo production facilities outside Denmark— are not full-scale production sites but units that dilute concentrated insulin crystals imported from Denmark and then package products for final sale. Dispersing these less scale-sensitive processing plants saves modestly on transport costs. More importantly, however, it has allowed Novo to continue to concentrate its more scale- and skill-dependent primary production in Denmark. In marketing and sales, Novo has established marketing joint ventures with local companies in a number of countries to improve access to local medical communities and government health care systems. Finally, in R&D, Novo has established a limited number of highly specialized research centers outside Denmark to tap particular skills or technologies not available at home. Zymotech, based in Seattle, Washington, was acquired to access expertise in genetic engineering (a U.S. strength). A Japanese research facility was established as well. After repeated delays in gaining regulatory approval in Denmark, Novo established a genetically engineered insulin production facility in Japan, where approval was more rapid. Novo has not ceded this core technology to its foreign operations, however. Novo's own genetic engineering capabilities have been expanded in Denmark. The company transfers the knowledge acquired in the United States and Japan back to its Danish home base and has established genetic insulin production there as well.

Honda has also dispersed activities for all three reasons. Automobiles are assembled in eleven countries and motorcycles in thirty countries, to reduce transportation and tariff costs and to source lower-cost labor. To ensure continued market access in the face of rising concern over Japanese automobile imports, Honda has invested more than $2 billion in facilities in the United States: two assembly plants; a manufacturing facility for engines, transmissions, and suspension parts; an engineering center; and an R&D facility. Honda's U.S. activities enjoy lower operating costs and focus on adaptation of products and processes to the U.S. market. Innovation remains centered in Japan. Finally, Honda taps styling expertise available in California and high performance design capabilities in Germany, via small, local design centers that transfer knowledge back to the Japanese home base, where it is incorporated into model development.

Coordinate and Integrate Dispersed Activities. Unlocking the competitive advantage from dispersed activities requires that activities be coordinated globally. Coordination ensures consistency and reinforcement across countries, to enhance differentiation. Coordination is also necessary to allow learning and technology gained from dispersed activities to be integrated at the home base.

The particular advantages of coordination in its various forms were described earlier. All three of our example companies exhibit these benefits, but Novo's case is particularly interesting. In raw material procurement, Novo's sourcing is dispersed to twenty countries, but coordinated centrally to take advantage of price and currency shifts. In marketing, all subsidiaries, agents, and distributors use consistent promotional materials, and Novo trains them in consistent selling approaches. Novo works hard to ensure a common image worldwide and reinforces it with periodic sponsorship of physicians' conferences on diabetes in Denmark.

Coordinating across disparate country locations, however, raises formidable organizational challenges. Language, culture, and distance work against communication and common ways of thinking. Country subsidiaries have a natural tendency to want autonomy, and to extensively tailor their activities to local circumstances. Successful global competitors overcome these challenges in a variety of ways. First, they establish clear positioning and a well understood concept for global strategy. Second, subsidiary managers recognize the overall global position as a difficult to match source of advantage in their particular country. Thus, they are careful to tailor local activities in ways that do not undermine the global strategy. Third, information and accounting systems are made consistent worldwide, right down to part numbers and client codes, facilitating operational coordination, the exchange of information comparisons across locations, and making appropriate tradeoffs. Fourth, the company makes active efforts to encourage personal relationships and the exchange of learning among subsidiary managers, both to foster mutual understanding and to give coordination a human face. Finally, any company that seeks a global strategy must put in place an incentive system that weights overall contribution to the company in addition to subsidiary performance.[16]

Preserve National Identity in Business Units. A firm's national identity in a particular business is not something to overcome, as some observers have suggested, but something to preserve. Competitive advantage in a business often arises from distinctive attributes of a firm's home environment; location places an imprint on the firm and shapes its method of competing. Foreign customers value national identity and culture, and the company characteristics they connote. Most Americans, for example, appreciate German cars because *German* has come to connote high standards of design, performance, and craftsmanship, not because German car companies have become "American" or "global."

When accessing foreign markets, a firm must adapt—in the sense that it tailors its product to local needs and shows sensitivity to local business practices. Yet the company should not lose its distinctive positioning and identity, which should, indeed, be nurtured and inculcated in foreign subsidiaries. At Honda, for example, managers hired to run international subsidiaries train for two years at the Japanese headquarters before assuming their responsibilities.

Alliances as Enabling Devices for Globalization, but Not as Strategy. Once a company understands how to configure its global network in a business, alliances with firms based elsewhere can be a means of more effectively or more rapidly achieving the desired configuration. Alliances are a means to build a network of dispersed activities not an end, and can make activities outside the home base more effective. Market access, for example, can often be enhanced by a local partner. The ability to source inputs or to tap advanced skills and technologies in a new location may require a partner's well-established presence. Alliances, however, can blur a company's positioning and get in the way of a consistent positioning in every market. They complicate coordination and can slow innovation.

The best alliances are highly selective: They focus on particular activities and on obtaining a particular competitive benefit. Novo, for example, formed joint ventures with a variety of firms to gain access to particular national markets. Broad alliances, covering many activities and markets, tend to stunt a company's own development. They inhibit or relieve the sense of urgency about building the brand or developing the firm's own products. The best alliances are often transitional devices, assisting a firm to build on its strengths and to learn. In the long run, the partners may go their separate ways or upgrade the alliance to a full merger. A firm cannot rely on a partner for assets crucial to its competitive advantage.[17]

Business Extension in Industries and Segments with Location Advantages. A location's competitive advantages provide a means for identifying the industries in which a firm can gain a unique competitive advantage vis-à-vis rivals based elsewhere, as well as those industry segments where the home-base environment provides the greatest benefits. New business development should concentrate in these areas.

The new paradigm of productivity competition raises cautions about extensive vertical integration. Vertical integration consumes resources and creates inflexibilities, and should be restricted to activities tightly connected to the overall strategy. Elsewhere, a company may be better served by developing strong relationships with local suppliers of specialized machinery and inputs.

Diversification should proceed along cluster lines. By diversifying, companies will better leverage not only their own internal assets but also the unique assets of locations to which they have special access, such as suppliers, research centers, and skill pools. HP's diversification from measurement and test equipment into information systems and medical instruments has followed these principles, in each case involving a field in which the United States has unique strengths. Novo's move from insulin to industrial enzymes also followed cluster lines, as did Honda's diversification from motorcycles to automobiles. Innovations often originate at the interstices between industries and clusters, when related technologies and skills are combined. To get its start in automobiles, for example, Honda drew on its small-engine technology expertise, nurtured in motorcycle manufacture. It combined this with assets in the Japanese automobile cluster, including a strong supplier base and demand conditions encouraging compact designs and energy efficiency.

Upgrade the Home Bases. An important part of a firm's competitive advantage in a business clearly resides in the local environment where that business is based, not merely within the firm itself. Without a fundamentally healthy home base, a business's capacity for productivity growth and rapid innovation will diminish. The firm will be unable to assemble the resources, skills, technologies, and information most essential to competitive advantage. While dispersing sophisticated production or outsourcing critical components and machinery can often offset home base weaknesses and improve performance in the short run, the firm's ability to innovate over the long run will be threatened.

The presence of external competitive advantages adds new and often unfamiliar dimensions to a company's strategic agenda. Firms should support specialized training programs and should promote university research in areas relevant to their particular business. Local suppliers should be nurtured and upgraded (depending heavily on distant suppliers nullifies a potential competitive advantage). Firms must guide and pressure local infrastructure providers to meet their needs and ensure that government regulations enhance productivity. Industry associations can play an important role in sponsoring training programs, research on standards and enabling technologies, and the collection of market information. Chapter 7 provides a more extensive discussion of these opportunities. Unfortunately, few companies see their local environment as a vital competitive resource. In the United States, for example, many companies take their suppliers for granted and see education and training as the responsibility of government.

The example of Novo illustrates how global leaders take an active role in upgrading their home environment. Before the merger of Nordisk and Novo, Nordisk established the Nordic Insulin Fund (in 1926) to support insulin research projects in Scandinavia and the Steno Memorial Hospital (in 1932) as a center for research and treatment of diabetes. Novo founded the Hvidore Diabetes Hospital soon after and later (in 1957) founded the Hagedoorn Research Institute to conduct basic research on diabetes. The Novo Research Institute was created (in 1964) to investigate the causes and origins of diabetes. Today, the Steno Diabetes Center and Hvidore Diabetes Hospital treat 6,000 diabetes patients and conduct 25,000 diabetes consultations each year. Novo also sponsors international conferences on diabetes in Denmark, bringing together local experts and specialists from around the world.[18]

The history of the Danish insulin industry illustrates the power of active local rivalry to motivate continual innovation. The companies recognized one of the risks of their merger as the possibility that, while achieving some efficiencies, it would undermine dynamism. The parent company hopes to address this and other risks by keeping the two operations separate. The broader principle, however, remains: The presence of local rivals creates advantages. Seeking to eliminate local competition, under most circumstances, is a misguided effort.

Relocate the Home Base if Necessary. If the vitality of a firm's home base for a particular business deteriorates because of lagging customer sophistication, a requirement for new types of suppliers, ineffective local institutions, or for other reasons, the first response should be to upgrade at home. If such efforts are exhausted without success, however, a firm may need to shift its home base to a more favorable location. This is perhaps the ultimate manifestation of global competition.

Shifts of home bases from country to country occur with increasing frequency in multinational companies. As global competition exposes companies to the world's best rivals and nullifies traditional comparative advantages in access to capital, raw materials, and labor, the penalty of an unfavorable home diamond increases. Yet, the decision to relocate a home base must be approached reluctantly, because it entails becoming accepted as a true insider in a new location and a new culture.

Firms rarely shift an entire company's home base. Instead, they relocate the home base of particular product lines or business segments. One common catalyst (and enabler) of such shifts is acquisition of a foreign firm already established in a more vibrant location. Such acquisitions provide the critical mass for new home bases, which, over time, gain increasing worldwide responsibility in particular segments or businesses. Nestlé, for example, has relocated the world headquarters for its confectionery business to England, associating it with the acquired Rowntree MacIntosh company. England, with its sweet-toothed consumers, sophisticated retailers, advanced advertising agencies, and highly competitive media companies, constitutes a more dynamic environment for competing in mass-market candy than Switzerland. Similarly, Nestlé has moved its headquarters for bottled water to France, the most competitive location in that industry.

Although each of our example companies, Novo, Hewlett-Packard, and Honda, continues to enjoy a strong home diamond in its principal businesses, not all firms are so fortunate. The Canadian manufacturer Northern Telecom, for example, has relocated the home base for its digital central-office switching equipment from Canada to the United States.[19] Northern Telecom manufactured and installed the first local digital switch, the DMS-10, in the United States in 1977. The subsequent AT&T divestiture and mandate for equal access reconfigured the U.S. diamond for telecommunications service and equipment and led Northern Telecom to expand its U.S. operations dramatically. By 1991, the company had relocated its world headquarters for central-office switching to the United States. It now conducts all R&D activities for this product line in the United States, with a work force of more than one thousand employees. Virtually all of the company's central-office switching manufacturing is also conducted in North Carolina.

The rationale behind Northern Telecom's move to the United States can be seen in the strength of the U.S. telecommunications equipment diamond. Compared to Canada, the United States presents a unique array of highly specialized factors, including sophisticated software engineering and world-class university research programs in computer science and telecommunications. American buyers and end-users are among the most sophisticated in the world, and the existence of twenty to twenty-five major independent U.S. switch buyers leads to intense competition that encourages Northern Telecom's customers to continuously upgrade their central-office switching capabilities. American firms in integrated circuit manufacturing and systems-level software design provide strong capabilities in related industries. The openness of the U.S. market to foreign rivals further intensifies the local rivalry within the U.S. market. (In telecommunications equipment, governments have tended to protect local markets and support monopoly suppliers.)

In another interesting example, Wesson (1993) describes Hyundai's shift of its home base in personal computers from Korea to Silicon Valley, when it discovered that it simply could not "keep up" from a Korean location. With all competitors sourcing low-cost parts internationally, crucial competitive imperatives were the rapid introduction of new models that met evolving customer needs and the ability to successfully access evolving distribution channels. In these areas, the United States was far ahead of other locations. Traditionally, foreign direct investment (FDI) has been seen as exploiting home base advantages. Wesson employs statistical evidence to confirm the prevalence of home-base *seeking* FDI, that is, FDI directed at accessing the sophisticated advantages of other locations, even to the extent of relocating the firm's home base elsewhere.

Competing Globally from a Developing Country

Developing countries have become a growing part of the international economy, and many firms based in developing countries are exporters. The platform of a developing country, however, raises some particular issues for the move to a global strategy.

The basic challenge is to shift from comparative advantage to competitive advantage. Most firms based in developing countries have internationalized through exports of resource- or labor-intensive commodities or via OEM agreements with multinationals that rest on resource labor costs. Such exports have been primarily directed to advanced economies. Opportunities to expand into other developing markets, including neighboring countries, have been limited by similarities in factor conditions and circumscribed by protectionist government policies.

Moving beyond the traditional modes of internationalization requires that firms based in developing countries create distinctive strategies. Without their own product or service varieties, production methods, or reputations, they find it difficult to penetrate foreign markets. At the same time, firms must extend their value chains to include international distribution, marketing, sourcing, and ultimately production. The best opportunities for true international strategies emanating from developing countries often lie within the region and with other like economies. While exports to advanced economies based on comparative advantage can continue, firms must take advantage of the opening of neighboring markets to build regional networks. The challenge becomes one of building distinctive product varieties and production methods while gaining knowledge and control of international marketing and distribution. Over time, the firm must build innovative capacity sufficient to enter more and more advanced markets based on competitive rather than comparative advantage.

Integrating Location and Global Competition

Since the 1950s, globalization has exerted an ever-increasing influence on competitive strategy. Aggregate statistics confirm the popular view that firms have become increasingly global in their sales and operations. The traditional role of comparative advantage has been superseded, and it is tempting to conclude that many corporations now transcend national boundaries.

Deeper investigation reveals, however, a striking localization of competitive advantage. This apparent paradox can be explained by recognizing the new paradigm of international competition which makes productivity and innovation paramount. Firms must harness the comparative advantages from many locations to avoid a disadvantage. Firms' advantages over others, however, often lie in their locations' competitive advantage for raising productivity. This paradigm must guide a new generation of thinking about global strategy, one that integrates localization and globalization in wholly new ways.

Localization was once seen as a necessary evil to be balanced against the compelling benefits of a global strategy. Instead, the home base location should be seen as the root of competitive advantage. Global strategies can extend this advantage through dispersing activities to source comparative advantages, access markets, or tap particular skills or technologies. To play this role, however, dispersed activities must be coordinated. This new synthesis, which recognizes the complex role of location in competitive advantage, will drive competition in the coming decades.

NOTES

1. See Porter (1980).
2. See Porter (1985).
3. See Theodore Levitt, "Globalization of Markets," *Harvard Business Review* 61, no. 3 (1983): 92–102.
4. See, for example, Porter (1990); Crocombe, Enright, and Porter (1991); and Sölvell, Zander, and Porter (1991).
5. See Figure 7-5 in Chapter 7.
6. See also Enright (1993 and 1994).
7. See Cristerna (1993).
8. See, for example, Jaikumar and Upton (1993).
9. This group of activities, which varies in composition from industry to industry, will be termed *home-based activities* or *core activities.*
10. See also Porter (1990).
11. Thomas (1993) confirms this result in pharmaceuticals, where firms facing local rivals (and strict product approval regulation, see below) are the most innovative.
12. Some observers have cited collaboration rather than competition as an important basis of competitiveness, referring most often to Japan and to the industrial districts of Italy. This view confuses *vertical* collaboration with buyers, suppliers, and local institutions, which diamond theory stresses, with *horizontal* collaboration among competitors. Horizontal collaboration is rare in successful Japanese and Italian industries (*keiretsu,* for example, do not contain direct competitors).
13. See, for example, Porter and van der Linde (1995).
14. See also Kogut (1991). Such location-based advantages are inconsistent with Reich's (1991) views of mobile resources, information, and technology. Reich's notion of symbolic analyst zones, which focuses only on skilled employees, attempts to bridge this inconsistency.
15. Honda's movement toward greater local content relates to its establishment of new product-line home bases.
16. For a useful discussion of other organizational issues in global companies, see Bartlett and Ghoshal (1989).
17. For further discussion, see Porter and Fuller (1986) and Porter and Ghemawat (1986).
18. Enright (1989).
19. Wesson (1993) discusses the Northern Telecom case.

Bibliography

Bartlett, C. A., and S. Ghoshal. *Managing Across Borders: The Transnational Solution.* Boston: Harvard Business School Press, 1989.

Cristerna, H. "The Role of Home-Based Advantages in Global Expansion: Five Case Studies." Unpublished MBA research report, Harvard Business School, Boston, Mass., 1993.

Crocombe, G. T., M. J. Enright, and M. E. Porter. *Upgrading New Zealand's Competitive Advantage.* Auckland, New Zealand: Oxford University Press, 1991.

Enright, M. J. "The Determinants of Geographic Concentration in Industry." Working paper 93-052, Harvard Business School, Boston, Mass., 1993.

————. "Novo Industri." Case 9-389-148. Boston: Harvard Business School, 1989.

————. "Organization and Coordination in Geographically Concentrated Industries." In *Coordination and Information: Historical Perspectives on the Organization of Enterprise,* edited by Naomi R. Lamoreaux and Daniel G. M. Raff (Chicago: University of Chicago Press/NBER, 1994).

Jaikumar, R., and D. M. Upton. "The Coordination of Global Manufacturing." In *Globalization, Technology, and Competition: The Fusion of Computers and Telecommunications in the 1990s,* edited by S. P. Bradley, J. A. Hausman, and R. L. Nolan. Boston: Harvard Business School Press, 1993.

Kogut, B. "Country Capabilities and the Permeability of Borders." *Strategic Management Journal* (Summer 1991), 33–47.

Porter, M. E. "Competition in Global Industries: A Conceptual Framework." In *Competition in Global Industries,* edited by M. E. Porter. Boston: Harvard Business School Press, 1986.

————. *Competitive Advantage: Creating and Sustaining Superior Performance.* New York: Free Press, 1985.

————. *The Competitive Advantage of Nations.* New York: Free Press, 1990.

————. *Competitive Strategy: Techniques for Analyzing Industries and Competitors.* New York: Free Press, 1980.

Porter, M. E., and M. B. Fuller. "Coalitions and Global Strategy." In *Competition in Global Industries,* edited by M. E. Porter. Boston: Harvard Business School Press, 1986.

Porter, M. E., and P. Ghemawat. "Patterns of International Coalition Activity." In *Competition in Global Industries,* edited by M. E. Porter. Boston: Harvard Business School Press, 1986.

Porter, M. E., and C. van der Linde. "Green and Competitive: Ending the Stalemate." *Harvard Business Review* 73, no. 5 (1995): 120–134.

Porter, M. E., and R. E. Wayland. "Global Competition and the Localization of Competitive Advantage." Published in the proceedings of the Integral Strategy Collegium, Graduate School of Business, Indiana University. Greenwich, CT: JAI Press, 1995.

Reich, R. B. "Who Is Us?" *Harvard Business Review* 68, no. 1 (1990): 53–64.

Sölvell, Ö., I. Zander, and M. E. Porter. *Advantage Sweden.* Stockholm, Sweden: Norstedts, 1991.

Thomas, L. G. "Spare the Road and Spoil the Industry: Vigorous Regulation and Vigorous Competition Promote International Competitive Advantage." Working paper, Emory University, Atlanta, Georgia, 1993.

Wesson, T. "The Determinants of Foreign Direct Investment in U.S. Manufacturing Industries." Ph.D. diss., Harvard Business School, 1993.

Part III Competitive Solutions to Societal Problems

CHAPTER 9

Green and Competitive

Ending the Stalemate

Michael E. Porter

Claas van der Linde

THE NEED FOR REGULATION to protect the environment gets widespread but grudging acceptance: widespread because everyone wants a livable planet, grudging because of the lingering belief that environmental regulations erode competitiveness. The prevailing view is that there is an inherent and fixed trade-off: ecology versus the economy. On one side of the trade-off are the *social* benefits that arise from strict environmental standards. On the other are industry's *private* costs for prevention and cleanup—costs that lead to higher prices and reduced competitiveness. With the argument framed this way, progress on environmental quality has become a kind of arm-wrestling match. One side pushes for tougher standards; the other tries to roll them back. The balance of power shifts one way or the other depending on the prevailing political winds.

This static view of environmental regulation, in which everything except regulation is held constant, is incorrect. If technology, products, processes, and customer needs were all fixed, the conclusion that regulation must raise costs would be inevitable. But companies operate in the real world of dynamic competition, not in the static world of much

The authors are grateful to Benjamin C. Bonifant, Daniel C. Esty, Donald B. Marron, Jan Rivkin, Nicolaj Siggelkow, and R. David Simpson for their extremely helpful comments; to the Management Institute for Environment and Business for joint research; and to Reed Hundt for ongoing discussions that have greatly benefited the thinking behind this article.

September–October 1995

economic theory. They are constantly finding innovative solutions to pressures of all sorts—from competitors, customers, and regulators.

Properly designed environmental standards can trigger innovations that lower the total cost of a product or improve its value. Such innovations allow companies to use a range of inputs more productively—from raw materials to energy to labor—thus offsetting the costs of improving environmental impact and ending the stalemate. Ultimately, this enhanced *resource productivity* makes companies more competitive, not less.

Consider how the Dutch flower industry has responded to its environmental problems. Intense cultivation of flowers in small areas was contaminating the soil and groundwater with pesticides, herbicides, and fertilizers. Facing increasingly strict regulation on the release of chemicals, the Dutch understood that the only effective way to address the problem would be to develop a closed-loop system. In advanced Dutch greenhouses, flowers now grow in water and rock wool, not in soil. This lowers the risk of infestation, reducing the need for fertilizers and pesticides, which are delivered in water that circulates and is reused.

The tightly monitored closed-loop system also reduces variation in growing conditions, thus improving product quality. Handling costs have gone down because the flowers are cultivated on specially designed platforms. In addressing the environmental problem, then, the Dutch have innovated in ways that have raised the productivity with which they use many of the resources involved in growing flowers. The net result is not only dramatically lower environmental impact but also lower costs, better product quality, and enhanced global competitiveness. (See the insert "Innovating to Be Competitive: The Dutch Flower Industry.")

Innovating to Be Competitive: The Dutch Flower Industry

The Dutch flower industry is responsible for about 65 percent of world exports of cut flowers—an astonishing figure given that the most important production inputs in the flower business would seem to be land and climate. Anyone who has been to the Netherlands knows its disadvantages on both counts. The Dutch have to reclaim land from the sea, and the weather is notoriously problematic.

How can the Dutch be the world's leaders in the flower business when they lack comparative advantage in the traditional sense? The answer, among other reasons, is that they have innovated at every step in the value chain, creating technology and highly specialized inputs that enhance resource productivity and offset the country's natural disadvantages.

In selling and distribution, for example, the Netherlands has five auction houses custom designed for the flower business. Carts of flowers are automatically towed on computer-guided paths into the auction room. The buying process occurs in a few seconds. Buyers sit in an amphitheater, and the price on the auction clock moves down until the first buyer signals electronically. That buyer's code is attached to the cart, which is routed to the company's shipping and handling area. Within a few minutes, the flowers are on a truck to regional markets or in a specialized, precooled container on their way to nearby Schiphol airport. Good airports and highway systems may be plentiful elsewhere, too. But the Netherlands' innovative, spe-cialized infrastructure is a competitive advantage. It leads to very high productivity. It is so successful that growers from other countries actually fly flowers there to be processed, sold, and reexported.

Paradoxically, having a *shortage* of general-purpose or more basic inputs can sometimes be turned into an advantage. If land were readily available and the climate more favorable, the Dutch would have competed the same way other countries did. Instead they were forced to innovate, developing a high-tech system of year-round greenhouse cultivation. The Dutch continually improve the unique, specialized technology that creates high resource productivity and underpins their competitiveness.

In contrast, an abundance of labor and natural resources or a lack of environmental pressure may lead a country's companies to spend the national resources unproductively. Competing based on cheap inputs, which could be used with less productivity, was sufficient in a more insular, less global economy. Today, when emerging nations with even cheaper labor and raw materials are part of the global economy, the old strategy is unsustainable.

This example illustrates why the debate about the relationship between competitiveness and the environment has been framed incorrectly. Policy makers, business leaders, and environmentalists have focused on the static cost impacts of environmental regulation and have ignored the more important offsetting productivity benefits from innovation. As a result, they have acted too often in ways that unnecessarily drive up costs and slow down progress on environmental issues. This static mind-set has thus created a self-fulfilling prophecy leading to ever more costly environmental regulation. Regulators tend to set regulations in ways that deter innovation. Companies, in turn, oppose and delay regulations instead of innovating to address them. The whole process has spawned an industry of litigators and consultants that drains resources away from real solutions.

Pollution = Inefficiency

Are cases like the Dutch flower industry the exception rather than the rule? Is it naïve to expect that reducing pollution will often enhance competitiveness? We think not, and the reason is that pollution often is a form of economic waste. When scrap, harmful substances, or energy forms are discharged into the environment as pollution, it is a sign that resources have been used incompletely, inefficiently, or ineffectively. Moreover, companies then have to perform additional activities that add cost but create no value for customers: for example, handling, storage, and disposal of discharges.

The concept of resource productivity opens up a new way of looking at both the full systems costs and the value associated with any product. Resource inefficiencies are most obvious within a company in the form of incomplete material utilization and poor process controls, which result in unnecessary waste, defects, and stored materials. But there also are many other hidden costs buried in the life cycle of the product. Packaging discarded by distributors or customers, for example, wastes resources and adds costs. Customers bear additional costs when they use products that pollute or waste energy. Resources are lost when products that contain usable materials are discarded and when customers pay—directly or indirectly—for product disposal.

Environmental improvement efforts have traditionally overlooked these systems costs. Instead, they have focused on pollution control through better identification, processing, and disposal of discharges or waste—costly approaches. In recent years, more advanced companies and regulators have embraced the concept of pollution prevention, sometimes called source reduction, which uses such methods as material substitution and closed-loop processes to limit pollution before it occurs.

But, although pollution prevention is an important step in the right direction, ultimately companies must learn to frame environmental improvement in terms of resource productivity.[1] Today managers and regulators focus on the actual costs of eliminating or treating pollution. They must shift their attention to include the opportunity costs of pollution—wasted resources, wasted effort, and diminished product value to the customer. At the level of resource productivity, environmental improvement and competitiveness come together.

This new view of pollution as resource inefficiency evokes the quality revolution of the 1980s and its most powerful lessons. Today we have little trouble grasping the idea that innovation can improve quality while actually lowering cost. But as recently as fifteen years ago, managers believed there was a fixed trade-off. Improving quality was expensive because it could be achieved only through inspection and rework of the "inevitable" defects that came off the line. What lay behind the old view was the assumption that both product design and production processes were fixed. As managers have rethought the quality issue, however, they have abandoned that old mind-set. Viewing defects as a sign of inefficient product and process design—not as an inevitable by-product of manufacturing—was a breakthrough. Companies now strive to build quality into the entire process. The new mind-set unleashed the power of innovation to relax or eliminate what companies had previously accepted as fixed trade-offs.

Like defects, pollution often reveals flaws in the product design or production process. Efforts to eliminate pollution can therefore follow the same basic principles widely used in quality programs: Use inputs more efficiently, eliminate the need for hazardous, hard-to-handle materials, and eliminate unneeded activities. In a recent study of major process changes at ten manufacturers of printed circuit boards, for example, pollution-control personnel initiated thirteen of thirty-three major changes. Of the thirteen changes, twelve resulted in cost reduction, eight in quality improvements, and five in extension of production capabilities.[2] It is not surprising that total quality management (TQM) has become a source of ideas for pollution reduction that can create offsetting benefits. The Dow Chemical Company, for example, explicitly identified the link between quality improvement and environmental performance by using statistical-process control to reduce the variance in processes and to lower waste.

Innovation and Resource Productivity

To explore the central role of innovation and the connection between environmental improvement and resource productivity, we have been collaborating since 1991 with the Management Institute for Environment and Business (MEB) on a series of international case studies of industries and sectors significantly affected by environmental regulation: pulp and paper, paint and coatings, electronics manufacturing, refrigerators, dry cell batteries, and printing inks. (See Table 9.1.) The data clearly show that the costs of addressing environmental regulations can be minimized, if not eliminated, through innovation that delivers other competitive benefits. We first observed the phenomenon in the course of our research for a study of national competitiveness, *The Competitive Advantage of Nations* (The Free Press, 1990).

Consider the chemical sector, where many believe that the ecology-economy trade-off is particularly steep. A study of activities to prevent waste generation at twenty-nine chemical plants found innovation offsets that enhanced resource productivity. Of 181 of these waste prevention activities, only one resulted in a net cost increase. Of the seventy activities with documented changes in product yield, sixty-eight reported increases; the average for twenty initiatives documented with specific data was 7 percent. These innovation offsets were achieved with surprisingly low investments and very short payback times. One-quarter of the forty-eight initiatives with detailed capital cost information required no capital investment at all; of the thirty-eight initiatives with data on the payback period, nearly two-thirds recouped their initial investments in six months or less. The annual savings per dollar spent on source reduction averaged three dollars and forty-nine cents for the twenty-seven activities for which this information could be calculated. The study also found that the two main motivating factors for source reduction activities were waste disposal costs and environmental regulation.

Table 9.1   Environmental Regulation Has Competitive Implications

Sector/Industry	Environmental Issues	Innovative Solutions	Innovation Offsets
Pulp and paper	Dioxin released by bleaching with chlorine	Improved cooking and washing processes Elimination of chlorine by using oxygen, ozone, or peroxide for bleaching Closed-loop processes (still problematic)	Lower operating costs though greater use of by-product energy sources 25% initial price premium for chlorine-free paper
Paint and coatings	Volatile organic compounds (VOCs) in solvents	New paint formulations (low-solvent-content paints, water-borne paints) Improved application techniques Powder or radiation-cured coatings	Price premium for solvent-free paints Improved coatings quality in some segments Worker safety benefits Higher coatings-transfer efficiency Reduced coating costs through materials savings
Electronics manufacturing	Volatile organic compounds (VOCs) in cleaning agents	Semiaqueous, terpene-based cleaning agents Closed-loop systems No-clean soldering where possible	Increase in cleaning quality and thus in product quality 30% to 80% reduction in cleaning costs, often for one-year payback periods Elimination of an unnecessary production step
Refrigerators	Chlorofluorocarbons (CFCs) used as refrigerants Energy usage Disposal	Alternative refrigerants (propane-isobutane mix) Thicker insulation Better gaskets Improved compressors	10% better energy efficiency at same cost 5% to 10% initial price premium for "green" refrigerator
Dry cell batteries	Cadmium, mercury, lead, nickel, cobalt, lithium, and zinc releases in landfills or to the air (after incineration)	Rechargeable batteries of nickel-hydride (for some applications) Rechargeable lithium batteries (now being developed)	Nearly twice as efficient at same cost Higher energy efficiency Expected to be price competitive in the near future
Printing inks	VOCs in petroleum inks	Water-based inks and soy inks	Higher efficiency, brighter colors, and better printability (depending on application)

Sources: Benjamin C. Bonifant, Ian Ratcliffe, and Claas van der Linde.

Innovation in response to environmental regulation can fall into two broad categories. The first is new technologies and approaches that minimize the cost of dealing with pollution once it occurs. The key to these approaches often lies in taking the resources embodied in the pollution and converting them into something of value. Companies get smarter about how to process toxic materials and emissions into usable forms, recycle scrap, and improve secondary treatment. For example, at a Rhône-Poulenc plant in Chalampe, France, nylon by-products known as diacids used to be incinerated. Rhône-Poulenc invested 76 million francs and installed new equipment to recover and sell these diacids as additives for dyes and tanning and as coagulation agents. The new recovery process has generated annual revenues of about 20.1 million francs. New de-inking technologies developed by Massachusetts-based Thermo Electron Corporation, among others, are allowing more extensive use of recycled paper. Molten Metal Technology of Waltham, Massachusetts, has developed a cost-saving catalytic extraction method to process many types of hazardous waste.

The second and far more interesting and important type of innovation addresses the root causes of pollution by improving resource productivity in the first place. Innovation offsets can take many forms, including more efficient utilization of particular inputs, better product yields, and better products. (See the insert "Environmental Improvement Can Benefit Resource Productivity.") Consider the following examples.

Resource productivity improves when less costly materials are substituted or when existing ones are better utilized. Dow Chemical's California complex scrubs hydrochloric gas with caustic to produce a wide range of chemicals. The company used to store the wastewater in evaporation ponds. Regulation called for Dow to close the evaporation ponds by 1988. In 1987, under pressure to comply with the new law, the company redesigned its production process. It reduced the use of caustic soda, decreasing caustic waste by 6,000 tons per year and hydrochloric acid waste by eighty tons per year. Dow also found that it could capture a portion of the waste stream for reuse as a raw material in other parts of the plant. Although it cost only $250,000 to implement, the process gave Dow an annual savings of $2.4 million.[3]

3M also improved resource productivity. Forced to comply with new regulations to reduce solvent emissions by 90 percent, 3M found a way

Environmental Improvement Can Benefit Resource Productivity

Process Benefits

• materials savings resulting from more complete processing, substitution, reuse, or recycling of production inputs

• increases in process yields

• less downtime through more careful monitoring and maintenance

• better utilization of by-products

• conversion of waste into valuable forms

• lower energy consumption during the production process

• reduced material storage and handling costs

• savings from safer workplace conditions

• elimination or reduction of the cost of activities involved in discharges

or waste handling, transportation, and disposal

• improvements in the product as a by-product of process changes (such as better process control)

Product Benefits

• higher quality, more consistent products

• lower product costs (for instance, from material substitution)

• lower packaging costs

• more efficient resource use by products

• safer products

• lower net costs of product disposal to customers

• higher product resale and scrap value

to avoid the use of solvents altogether by coating products with safer, water-based solutions. The company gained an early-mover advantage in product development over competitors, many of whom switched significantly later. The company also shortened its time to market because its water-based product did not have to go through the approval process for solvent-based coatings.[4]

3M found that innovations can improve process consistency, reduce downtime, and lower costs substantially. The company used to produce adhesives in batches that were then transferred to storage tanks. One bad batch could spoil the entire contents of a tank. Lost product, downtime, and expensive hazardous-waste disposal were the result. 3M developed a new technique to run rapid quality tests on new batches. It reduced hazardous wastes by 110 tons per year at almost no cost, yielding an annual savings of more than $200,000.[5]

Many chemical-production processes require an initial start-up period after production interruptions in order to stabilize output and bring it within specifications. During that time, only scrap material is produced. When regulations raised the cost of waste disposal, Du Pont was motivated to install higher-quality monitoring equipment, which in turn reduced production interruptions and the associated production start-ups. Du Pont lowered not only its waste generation but also cut the amount of time it wasn't producing anything.[6]

Process changes to reduce emissions and use resources more productively often result in higher yields. As a result of new environmental standards, Ciba-Geigy Corporation reexamined the waste-water streams at its dye plant in Tom's River, New Jersey. Engineers made two changes to the production process. First, they replaced sludge-creating iron with a less harmful chemical conversion agent. Second, they eliminated the release of a potentially toxic product into the wastewater stream. They not only reduced pollution but also increased process yields by 40 percent, realizing an annual cost savings of $740,000. Although that part of the plant was ultimately closed, the example illustrates the role of regulatory pressure in process innovation.

Process innovations to comply with environmental regulation can even improve product consistency and quality. In 1990, the Montreal Protocol and the U.S. Clean Air Act required electronics companies to eliminate ozone-depleting chlorofluorocarbons (CFCs). Many companies used them as cleaning agents to remove residues that occur in the manufacture of printed circuit boards. Scientists at Raytheon confronted the regulatory challenge. Initially, they thought that complete elimination of CFCs would be impossible. After research, however, they found an alternate cleaning agent that could be reused in a closed-loop system. The new method improved average product quality—which the old CFC-based cleaning agent had occasionally compromised—while also lowering operating costs. Responding to the same regulation, other researchers identified applications that did not require any cleaning at all and developed so-called no-clean soldering technologies, which lowered operating costs without compromising quality. Without environmental regulation, that innovation would not have happened.

Innovations to address environmental regulations can also lower product costs and boost resource productivity by reducing unnecessary packaging or simplifying designs. A 1991 law in Japan set standards to make products easier to recycle. Hitachi, along with other Japanese appliance producers, responded by redesigning products to reduce disassembly time. In the process, it cut back the number of parts in a washing machine by 16 percent and the number of parts in a vacuum cleaner by 30 percent. Fewer components made the products easier not only to disassemble but also to assemble in the first place. Regulation that requires such recyclable products can lower the user's disposal costs and lead to designs that allow a company to recover valuable materials more easily. Either the customer or the manufacturer who takes back used products reaps greater value.

Although such product innovations have been prompted by regulators instead of by customers, world demand is putting a higher value on resource-efficient products. Many companies are using innovations to command price premiums for "green" products and to open up new market segments. Because Germany adopted recycling standards earlier than most other countries, German companies have first-mover advantages in developing less packaging-intensive products, which are both lower in cost and sought after in the marketplace. In the United States, Cummins Engine Company's development of low-emissions diesel engines for such applications as trucks and buses—innovation that U.S. environmental regulations spurred—is allowing it to gain position in international markets where similar needs are growing.

These examples and many others like them do not prove that companies always can innovate to reduce environmental impact at low cost. However, they show that there are considerable opportunities to reduce pollution through innovations that redesign products, processes, and methods of operation. Such examples are common in spite of companies' resistance to environmental regulation and in spite of regulatory standards that often are hostile to innovative, resource-productive solutions. The fact that such examples are common carries an important message: Today a new frame of reference for thinking about environmental improvement is urgently needed.

Do We Really Need Regulation?

If innovation in response to environmental regulation can be profitable—if a company can actually offset the cost of compliance through improving resource productivity—why is regulation necessary at all? If such opportunities exist, wouldn't companies pursue them naturally and wouldn't regulation be unnecessary? That is like saying there will rarely be ten-dollar bills to be found on the ground because someone already will have picked them up.

Certainly, some companies do pursue such innovations without, or in advance of, regulation. In Germany and Scandinavia, where both companies and consumers are very attuned to environmental concerns, innovation is not uncommon. As companies and their customers adopt the resource productivity mind-set and as knowledge about innovative technologies grows, there may well be less need for regulation over time in the United States.

But the belief that companies will pick up on profitable opportunities without a regulatory push makes a false assumption about competitive reality—namely, that all profitable opportunities for innovation have already been discovered, that all managers have perfect information about them, and that organizational incentives are aligned with innovating. In fact, in the real world, managers often have highly incomplete information and limited time and attention. Barriers to change are numerous. The Environmental Protection Agency's Green Lights program, which works with companies to promote energy-saving lighting, shows that many ten-dollar bills are still waiting to be picked up. In one audit, nearly 80 percent of the projects offered paybacks within two years or less, and yet the companies considering them had not taken action.[7] Only after companies joined the program and benefited from the EPA's information and cajoling were such highly profitable projects implemented.

We are now in a transitional phase of industrial history in which companies are still inexperienced in handling environmental issues creatively. Customers, too, are unaware that resource inefficiency means that they must pay for the cost of pollution. For example, they tend to see discarded packaging as free because there is no separate charge for it and no current lower-cost alternative. Because there is no direct way to recapture the value of the wasted resources that customers already have paid for, they imagine that discarding used products carries no cost penalty for them.

Regulation, although a different type than is currently practiced, is needed for six major reasons:

- To create pressure that motivates companies to innovate. Our broader research on competitiveness highlights the important role of outside pressure in overcoming organizational inertia and fostering creative thinking.

- To improve environmental quality in cases in which innovation and the resulting improvements in resource productivity do not completely offset the cost of compliance; or in which it takes time for learning effects to reduce the overall cost of innovative solutions.

- To alert and educate companies about likely resource inefficiencies and potential areas for technological improvement (although government cannot know better than companies how to address them).

- To raise the likelihood that product innovations and process innovations in general will be environmentally friendly.

- To create demand for environmental improvement until companies and customers are able to perceive and measure the resource inefficiencies of pollution better.

- To level the playing field during the transition period to innovation-based environmental solutions, ensuring that one company cannot gain position by avoiding environmental investments. Regulation provides a buffer for innovative companies until new technologies are proven and the effects of learning can reduce technological costs.

Those who believe that market forces alone will spur innovation may argue that total quality management programs were initiated without regulatory intervention. However, TQM came to the United States and Europe through a different kind of pressure. Decades earlier, TQM had been widely diffused in Japan—the result of a whole host of government efforts to make product quality a national goal, including the creation of the Deming Prize. Only after Japanese companies had devastated them in the marketplace did Americans and Europeans embrace TQM.

The Cost of the Static Mind-Set

Regulators and companies should focus, then, on relaxing the trade-off between environmental protection and competitiveness by encouraging innovation and resource productivity. Yet the current adversarial climate drives up the costs of meeting environmental standards and circumscribes the innovation benefits, making the trade-off far steeper than it needs to be.

To begin with, the power struggle involved in setting and enforcing environmental regulations consumes enormous amounts of resources. A 1992 study by the Rand Institute for Civil Justice, for example, found that 88 percent of the money that insurers paid out between 1986 and 1989 on Superfund claims went to pay for legal and administrative costs, whereas only 12 percent was used for actual site cleanups.[8] The Superfund law may well be the most inefficient environmental law in the United States, but it is not the only cause of inefficiency. We believe that a substantial fraction of environmental spending as well as of the revenues of environmental products and services companies relates to the regulatory struggle itself and not to improving the environment.

One problem with the adversarial process is that it locks companies into static thinking and systematically pushes industry estimates of the costs of regulation upward. A classic example occurred during the debate in the United States on the 1970 Clean Air Act. Lee Iacocca, then executive vice president of the Ford Motor Company, predicted that compliance with the new regulations would require huge price increases for automobiles, force U.S. production to a halt by 1975, and severely damage the U.S. economy. The 1970 Clean Air Act was subsequently enacted, and Iacocca's dire predictions turned out to be wrong. Similar stories are common.

Static thinking causes companies to fight environmental standards that actually could enhance their competitiveness. Most distillers of coal tar in the United States, for example, opposed 1991 regulations requiring substantial reductions in benzene emissions. At the time, the only solution was to cover the tar storage tanks with costly gas blankets. But the regulation spurred Aristech Chemical Corporation of Pittsburgh, Pennsylvania, to develop a way to remove benzene from tar in the first processing step, thereby eliminating the need for gas blankets. Instead of suffering a cost increase, Aristech saved itself $3.3 million.

Moreover, company mind-sets make the costs of addressing environmental regulations appear higher than they actually are. Many companies do not account for a learning curve, although the actual costs of compliance are likely to decline over time. A recent study in the pulp-and-paper sector, for example, found the actual costs of compliance to be four dollars to five dollars and fifty cents per ton, whereas original industry estimates had been as high as sixteen dollars and forty cents.[9] Similarly, the cost of compliance with a 1990 regulation controlling sulfur dioxide emissions is today only about half of what analysts initially predicted, and it is heading lower. With a focus on innovation and resource productivity, today's compliance costs represent an upper limit.

There is legitimate controversy over the benefits to society of specific environmental standards. Measuring the health and safety effects of cleaner air, for example, is the subject of ongoing scientific debate. Some believe that the risks of pollution have been overstated. But whatever the level of *social* benefits proves to be, the *private* costs to companies are still far higher than necessary.

Good Regulation versus Bad

In addition to being high-cost, the current system of environmental regulation in the United States often deters innovative solutions or renders them impossible. The problem with regulation is not its strictness. It is the way in which standards are written and the sheer inefficiency with which regulations are administered. Strict standards can and should promote resource productivity. The United States' regulatory process has squandered this potential, however, by concentrating on cleanup instead of prevention, mandating specific technologies, setting compliance deadlines that are unrealistically short, and subjecting companies to unnecessarily high levels of uncertainty.

The current system discourages risk taking and experimentation. Liability exposure and the government's inflexibility in enforcement, among other things, contribute to the problem. For example, a company that innovates and achieves 95 percent of target emissions reduction while also registering substantial offsetting cost reductions is still 5 percent out of compliance and subject to liability. On the other hand, regulators would reward it for adopting safe but expensive secondary treatment. (See the insert "Innovation-Friendly Regulation.")

Just as bad regulation can damage competitiveness, good regulation can enhance it. Consider the differences between the U.S. pulp-and-paper sector and the Scandinavian. Strict early U.S. regulations in the

---

Innovation-Friendly Regulation

Regulation, properly conceived, need not drive up costs. The following principles of regulatory design will promote innovation, resource productivity, and competitiveness:

Focus on outcomes, not technologies. Past regulations have often prescribed particular remediation technologies, such as catalysts or scrubbers for air pollution. The phrases "best available technology" (BAT) and "best available control technology" (BACT) are deeply rooted in U.S. practice and imply that one technology is best, discouraging innovation.

Enact strict rather than lax regulation. Companies can handle lax regulation incrementally, often with end-of-pipe or secondary treatment solutions. Regulation, therefore, needs to be stringent enough to promote real innovation.

Regulate as close to the end user as practical, while encouraging upstream solutions. This will normally allow more flexibility for innovation in the end product and in all the production and distribution stages. Avoiding pollution entirely or, second best, mitigating it early in the value chain is almost always less costly than late-stage remediation or cleanup.

Employ phase-in periods. Ample but well-defined phase-in periods tied to industry-capital-investment cycles will allow companies to develop innovative resource-saving technologies rather than force them to implement expensive solutions hastily, merely patching over problems. California imposed such short compliance deadlines on its wood-furniture industry that many manufacturers chose to leave the state rather than add costly control equipment.

Use market incentives. Market incentives such as pollution charges and deposit-refund schemes draw attention to resource inefficiencies. In addition, tradable permits provide continuing incentives for innovation and encourage creative use of technologies that exceed current standards.

Harmonize or converge regulations in associated fields. Liability exposure in the United States leads companies to stick to safe, BAT approaches, and inconsistent regulation on alternative technologies deters beneficial innovation. For example, one way to eliminate refrigerator cooling agents suspected of damaging the ozone layer involves replacing them with small amounts of propane and butane. But narrowly conceived safety regulations covering these gases seem to have impeded development of the new technology in the United States, while several leading European companies are already marketing the new products.

Develop regulations in sync with other countries or slightly ahead of them. It is important to minimize possible competitive disadvantages relative to foreign companies that are not yet subject to the same standard. Developing regulations slightly ahead of other countries will also maximize export potential in the pollution-control sector by raising incentives for innovation. When standards in the United States lead world developments, domestic companies get opportunities for valuable early-mover advantages. However, if standards are too far ahead of, or too different in character from, those that are likely to apply to foreign competitors, industry may innovate in the wrong directions.

Make the regulatory process more stable and predictable. The regulatory process is as important as the standards. If standards and phase-in periods are set and accepted early enough and if regulators commit to keeping standards in place for, say, five years, industry can lock in and tackle root-cause solutions instead of hedging against the next twist or turn in government philosophy.

Require industry participation in setting standards from the beginning. U.S. regulation differs sharply from European in its adversarial approach. Industry should help in designing phase-in periods, the content of regulations, and the most effective regulatory process. A predetermined set of information requests and interactions with industry representatives should be a mandatory part of the regulatory process. Both industry and regulators must work toward a climate of trust because industry needs to provide genuinely useful information and regulators need to take industry input seriously.

Develop strong technical capabilities among regulators. Regulators must understand an industry's economics and what drives its competitiveness. Better information exchange will help avoid costly gaming in which ill-informed companies use an array of lawyers and consultants to try to stall the poorly designed regulations of ill-informed regulators.

approvals. Potential and actual litigation creates uncertainty and consumes resources. Mandatory arbitration procedures or rigid arbitration steps before litigation would lower costs and encourage innovation.

Minimize the time and resources consumed in the regulatory process itself. Time delays in granting permits are usually costly for companies. Self-regulation with periodic inspections would be more efficient than requiring formal

For an extended discussion of the ways in which environmental regulation should change, see Michael E. Porter and Claas van der Linde, "Toward a New Conception of the Environment-Competitiveness Relationship," Journal of Economic Perspectives 9, no. 4 (fall 1995).

1970s were imposed without adequate phase-in periods, forcing companies to adopt best available technologies quickly. At that time, the requirements invariably meant installing proven but costly end-of-pipe treatment systems. In Scandinavia, on the other hand, regulation permitted more flexible approaches, enabling companies to focus on the production process itself, not just on secondary treatment of wastes. Scandinavian companies developed innovative pulping and bleaching technologies that not only met emission requirements but also lowered operating costs. Even though the United States was the first to regulate, U.S. companies were unable to realize any first-mover advantages because U.S. regulations ignored a critical principle of good environmental regulation: Create maximum opportunity for innovation by letting industries discover how to solve their own problems.

Unfortunately for the U.S. pulp-and-paper industry, a second principle of good regulation was also ignored: Foster continuous improvement; do not lock in on a particular technology or the status quo. The Swedish regulatory agency took a more effective approach. Whereas the United States mandated strict emissions goals and established very tight compliance deadlines, Sweden started out with looser standards but clearly communicated that tougher ones would follow. The results were predictable. U.S. companies installed secondary treatment systems and stopped there. Swedish producers, anticipating stricter standards, continually incorporated innovative environmental technologies into their normal cycles of capacity replacement and innovation.

The innovation-friendly approach produced the residual effect of raising the competitiveness of the local equipment industry. Spurred by Scandinavian demand for sophisticated process improvements, local pulp-and-paper-equipment suppliers, such as Sunds Defibrator and Kamyr, ultimately made major international gains in selling innovative pulping and bleaching equipment.

Eventually, the Scandinavian pulp-and-paper industry was able to reap innovation offsets that went beyond those directly stemming from regulatory pressures. By the early 1990s, producers realized that growing public awareness of the environmental problems associated with pulp-mill effluents was creating a niche market. For a time, Scandinavian companies with totally chlorine-free paper were able to command significant price premiums and serve a rapidly growing market segment of environmentally informed customers.

Implications for Companies

Certainly, misguided regulatory approaches have imposed a heavy burden on companies. But managers who have responded by digging in their heels to oppose all regulation have been shortsighted as well. It is no secret that Japanese and German automobile makers developed lighter and more fuel-efficient cars in response to new fuel consumption standards, while the less competitive U.S. car industry fought such standards and hoped they would go away. The U.S. car industry eventually realized that it would face extinction if it did not learn to compete through innovation. But clinging to the static mind-set too long cost billions of dollars and many thousands of jobs.

To avoid making the same mistakes, managers must start to recognize environmental improvement as an economic and competitive opportunity, not as an annoying cost or an inevitable threat. Instead of clinging to a perspective focused on regulatory compliance, companies need to ask questions such as What are we wasting? and How could we enhance customer value? The early movers—the companies that can see the opportunity first and embrace innovation-based solutions—will reap major competitive benefits, just as the German and Japanese car makers did. (See the insert "The New Environmentalists.")

At this stage, for most companies, environmental issues are still the province of outsiders and specialists. That is not surprising. Any new management issue tends to go through a predictable life cycle. When it first arises, companies hire outside experts to help them navigate. When practice becomes more developed, internal specialists take over. Only after a field becomes mature do companies integrate it into the ongoing role of line management.

Many companies have delegated the analysis of environmental problems and the development of solutions to outside lawyers and environmental consultants. Such experts in the adversarial regulatory process, who are not deeply familiar with the company's overall technology and operations, inevitably focus on compliance rather than innovation. They invariably favor end-of-pipe solutions. Many consultants, in fact, are associated with vendors who sell such technologies. Some companies are in the second phase, in which environmental issues are assigned to inter-

---

The New Environmentalists

Environmentalists can foster innovation and resource productivity by speaking out for the right kind of regulatory standards and by educating the public to demand innovative environmental solutions. The German section of Greenpeace, for example, noted in 1992 that a mixture of propane and butane was safer for cooling refrigerators than the then-prevalent cooling agents—hydrofluorocarbons or hydrochlorofluorocarbons—that were proposed as replacements for chlorofluorocarbons. Greenpeace for the first time in its history began endorsing a commercial product. It ac-

tually ran an advertising campaign for a refrigerator designed by Foron, a small refrigerator maker on the verge of bankruptcy. The action was greatly leveraged by extensive media coverage and has been a major reason behind the ensuing demand for Foron-built propane-butane refrigerators and the switch that the established refrigerator producers in Germany later made to the same technology.

Environmental organizations can support industry by becoming sources of information about best practices that may not be well known outside of a few pioneering companies. When it realized that German magazine publishers and readers alike were unaware of the much improved quality of chlorine-free paper, Greenpeace Germany issued a magazine printed on chlorine-free paper. It closely resembled the leading German political weekly, *Der Spiegel*, and it encouraged readers to demand that publishers switch to chlorine-free paper. Shortly after, *Der Spiegel* and several other large magazines did indeed switch. Other environmental organizations could shift some resources away from litigation to focus instead on funding and disseminating research on innovations that address environmental problems.

Among U.S. environmental groups, the Environmental Defense Fund (EDF) has been an innovator in its willingness to promote market-based regulatory systems and to work directly with industry. It supported the sulfur-dioxide trading system that allows companies either to reduce their own emissions or to buy emissions allowances from companies that have managed to exceed their reduction quotas at lower cost. The EDF-McDonald's Waste Reduction Task Force, formed in 1990, led to a substantial redesign of McDonald's packaging, including the elimination of the polystyrene-foam clamshell. EDF is now working with General Motors on plans to remove heavily polluting cars from the road and with Johnson & Johnson, McDonald's, NationsBank, The Prudential Insurance Company of America, Time Warner, and Duke University to promote the use of recycled paper.

Source: Benjamin C. Bonifant and Ian Ratcliffe, "Competitive Implications of Environmental Regulation in the Pulp and Paper Industry," working paper, Management Institute for Environment and Business, Washington, D.C., 1994.

nal specialists. But these specialists—for example, legal, governmental-affairs, or environmental departments—lack full profit responsibility and are separate from the line organization. Again, the result is almost always narrow, incremental solutions.

If the sorts of process and product redesigns needed for true innovation are even to be considered, much less implemented, environmental strategies must become an issue for general management. Environmental impact must be embedded in the overall process of improving productivity and competitiveness. The resource-productivity model, rather than the pollution-control model, must govern decision making.

How can managers accelerate their companies' progress toward a more competitive environmental approach? First, they can measure their direct and indirect environmental impacts. One of the major reasons that companies are not very innovative about environmental problems is ignorance. A large producer of organic chemicals, for example, hired a consultant to explore waste reduction opportunities in its 40 waste streams. A careful audit uncovered 497 different waste streams—the company had been wrong by a factor of more than ten.[10] Our research indicates that the act of measurement alone leads to enormous opportunities to improve productivity.

Companies that adopt the resource-productivity framework and go beyond currently regulated areas will reap the greatest benefits. Companies should inventory all unused, emitted, or discarded resources or packaging. Within the company, some poorly utilized resources will be held within plants, some discharged, and some put in dumpsters. Indirect resource inefficiencies will occur at the level of suppliers, channels, and customers. At the customer level, resource inefficiencies show up in the use of the product, in discarded packaging, and in resources left in the used-up product.

Second, managers can learn to recognize the opportunity cost of under-utilized resources. Few companies have analyzed the true cost of toxicity, waste, and what they discard, much less the second-order impacts that waste and discharges have on other activities. Fewer still look beyond the out-of-pocket costs of dealing with pollution to the opportunity cost of the resources they waste or the productivity they forgo. There are scarcely any companies that think about customer value and the opportunity cost of wasted resources at the customer level.

Many companies do not even track environmental spending carefully, and conventional accounting systems are ill equipped to measure under-utilized resources. Companies evaluate environmental projects as discrete, stand-alone investments. Straightforward waste- or discharge-reduction investments are screened using high hurdle rates that presume the investments are risky—leaving ten-dollar bills on the ground. Better information and evaluation methods will help managers reduce environmental impact while improving resource productivity.

Third, companies should create a bias in favor of innovation-based, productivity-enhancing solutions. They should trace their own and their customers' discharges, scrap, emissions, and disposal activities back into company activities to gain insight about beneficial product design, packaging, raw material, or process changes. We have been struck by the power of certain systems solutions: Groups of activities may be reconfigured, or substitutions in inputs or packaging may enhance utilization and potential for recovery. Approaches that focus on treatment of discrete discharges should be sent back to the organization for rethinking.

Current reward systems are as anti-innovation as regulatory policies. At the plant level, companies reward output but ignore environmental costs and wasted resources. The punishment for an innovative, economically efficient solution that falls short of expectations is often far greater than the reward for a costly but "successful" one.

Finally, companies must become more proactive in defining new types of relationships with both regulators and environmentalists. Businesses need a new mind-set. How can companies argue shrilly that regulations harm competitiveness and then expect regulators and environmentalists to be flexible and trusting as those same companies request time to pursue innovative solutions?

The World Economy in Transition

It is time for the reality of modern competition to inform our thinking about the relationship between competitiveness and the environment. Traditionally, nations were competitive if their companies had access to the lowest cost inputs—capital, labor, energy, and raw materials. In industries relying on natural resources, for example, the competitive companies and countries were those with abundant local supplies. Because technology changed slowly, a comparative advantage in inputs was enough for success.

Today globalization is making the notion of comparative advantage obsolete. Companies can source low-cost inputs anywhere, and new, rapidly emerging technologies can offset disadvantages in the cost of inputs. Facing high labor costs at home, for example, a company can automate away the need for unskilled labor. Facing a shortage of a raw material, a company can find an alternative raw material or create a synthetic one. To overcome high space costs, Japanese companies pioneered just-in-time production and avoided storing inventory on the factory floor.

It is no longer enough simply to have resources. Using resources productively is what makes for competitiveness today. Companies can improve resource productivity by producing existing products more efficiently or by making products that are more valuable to customers—products customers are willing to pay more for. Increasingly, the nations and companies that are most competitive are not those with access to the lowest-cost inputs but those that employ the most advanced technology and methods in using their inputs. Because technology is constantly changing, the new paradigm of global competitiveness requires the ability to innovate rapidly.

This new paradigm has profound implications for the debate about environmental policy—about how to approach it, how to regulate, and how strict regulation should be. The new paradigm has brought environmental improvement and competitiveness together. It is important to use resources productively, whether those resources are natural and physical or human and capital. Environmental progress demands that companies innovate to raise resource productivity—and that is precisely what the new challenges of global competition demand. Resisting innovation that reduces pollution, as the U.S. car industry did in the 1970s, will lead not only to environmental damage but also to the loss of competitiveness in the global economy. Developing countries that stick with resource-wasting methods and forgo environmental standards because they are "too expensive" will remain uncompetitive, relegating themselves to poverty.

How an industry responds to environmental problems may, in fact, be a leading indicator of its overall competitiveness. Environmental regulation does not lead inevitably to innovation and competitiveness or to higher productivity for all companies. Only those companies that innovate successfully will win. A truly competitive industry is more likely to take up a new standard as a challenge and respond to it with innovation. An uncompetitive industry, on the other hand, may not be oriented toward innovation and thus may be tempted to fight all regulation.

It is not at all surprising that the debate pitting the environment against competitiveness has developed as it has. Indeed, economically destructive struggles over redistribution are the norm in many areas of public policy. But now is the time for a paradigm shift to carry us forward into the next century. International competition has changed dramatically over the last few decades. Senior managers who grew up at a time when environmental regulation was synonymous with litigation will see increasing evidence that environmental improvement is good business. Successful environmentalists, regulatory agencies, and companies will reject old trade-offs and build on the underlying economic logic that links the environment, resource productivity, innovation, and competitiveness.

NOTES

1. One of the pioneering efforts to see environmental improvement this way is Joel Makower's *The E-Factor: The Bottom-Line Approach to Environmentally Responsible Business* (New York: Times Books, 1993).

2. Andrew King, "Improved Manufacturing Resulting from Learning from Waste: Causes, Importance, and Enabling Conditions," working paper, Stern School of Business, New York University, New York, 1994.

3. Mark H. Dorfman, Warren R. Muir, and Catherine G. Miller, *Environmental Dividends: Cutting More Chemical Wastes* (New York: INFORM, 1992).

4. Don L. Boroughs and Betsy Carpenter, "Helping the Planet and the Economy," *U.S. News and World Report* 110, no. 11, March 25, 1991, p. 46.

5. John H. Sheridan, "Attacking Wastes and Saving Money. . .Some of the Time," *Industry Week*, February 17, 1992, p. 43.

6. Gerald Parkinson, "Reducing Wastes Can Be Cost-Effective," *Chemical Engineering* 97, no. 7, July 1990, p. 30.

7. Stephen J. DeCanio, "Why Do Profitable Energy-Saving Projects Languish?" working paper, Second International Research Conference of the Greening of Industry Network, Cambridge, Massachusetts, 1993.

8. Jan Paul Acton and Lloyd S. Dixon, "Superfund and Transaction Costs: The Experiences of Insurers and Very Large Industrial Firms," working paper, Rand Institute for Civil Justice, Santa Monica, California, 1992.

9. Norman Bonson, Neil McCubbin, and John B. Sprague, "Kraft Mill Effluents in Ontario," report prepared for the Technical Advisory Committee, Pulp and Paper Sector of MISA, Ontario Ministry of the Environment, Toronto, March 29, 1988, p. 166.

10. Parkinson, p. 30.

CHAPTER 10

The Competitive Advantage of the Inner City

Michael E. Porter

THE ECONOMIC DISTRESS of America's inner cities may be the most pressing issue facing the nation. The lack of businesses and jobs in disadvantaged urban areas fuels not only a crushing cycle of poverty but also crippling social problems, such as drug abuse and crime. And, as the inner cities continue to deteriorate, the debate on how to aid them grows increasingly divisive.

The sad reality is that the efforts of the past few decades to revitalize the inner cities have failed. The establishment of a sustainable economic base—and with it employment opportunities, wealth creation, role models, and improved local infrastructure—still eludes us despite the investment of substantial resources.

Past efforts have been guided by a social model built around meeting the needs of individuals. Aid to inner cities, then, has largely taken the form of relief programs such as income assistance, housing subsidies, and food stamps, all of which address highly visible—and real—social needs.

The research that this article is based on would not have been possible without the generous support of the Harvard Business School and the assistance of many individuals. Whitney Tilson, Michael Marubio, and Barbara Paige were integrally involved in preparing this article. I would also like to thank the many M.B.A. students from both the Harvard Business School and other schools who have been involved in the research effort that made this article possible.

May–June 1995

Programs aimed more directly at economic development have been fragmented and ineffective. These piecemeal approaches have usually taken the form of subsidies, preference programs, or expensive efforts to stimulate economic activity in tangential fields such as housing, real estate, and neighborhood development. Lacking an overall strategy, such programs have treated the inner city as an island isolated from the surrounding economy and subject to its own unique laws of competition. They have encouraged and supported small, subscale businesses designed to serve the local community but ill equipped to attract the community's own spending power, much less *export* outside it. In short, the social model has inadvertently undermined the creation of economically viable companies. Without such companies and the jobs they create, the social problems will only worsen.

The time has come to recognize that revitalizing the inner city will require a radically different approach. While social programs will continue to play a critical role in meeting human needs and improving education, they must support—and not undermine—a coherent economic strategy. The question we should be asking is how inner city-based businesses and nearby employment opportunities for inner city residents can proliferate and grow. A sustainable economic base *can* be created in the inner city, but only as it has been created elsewhere: through private, for-profit initiatives and investment based on economic self-interest and genuine competitive advantage—not through artificial inducements, charity, or government mandates.

We must stop trying to cure the inner city's problems by perpetually increasing social investment and hoping for economic activity to follow. Instead, an economic model must begin with the premise that inner city businesses should be profitable and positioned to compete on a regional, national, and even international scale. These businesses should be capable not only of serving the local community but also of exporting goods and services to the surrounding economy. The cornerstone of such a model is to identify and exploit the competitive advantages of inner cities that will translate into truly profitable businesses.

Our policies and programs have fallen into the trap of redistributing wealth. The real need—and the real opportunity—is to create wealth.

Toward a New Model: Location and Business Development

Economic activity in and around inner cities will take root if it enjoys a competitive advantage and occupies a niche that is hard to replicate elsewhere. If companies are to prosper, they must find a compelling competitive reason for locating in the inner city. A coherent strategy for development starts with that fundamental economic principle, as the contrasting experiences of the following companies illustrate.

Alpha Electronics (the company's name has been disguised), a twenty-eight-person company that designed and manufactured multimedia computer peripherals, was initially based in lower Manhattan. In 1987, the New York City Office of Economic Development set out to orchestrate an economic "renaissance" in the South Bronx by inducing companies to relocate there. Alpha, a small but growing company, was sincerely interested in contributing to the community and eager to take advantage of the city's willingness to subsidize its operations. The city, in turn, was happy that a high-tech company would begin to stabilize a distressed neighborhood and create jobs. In exchange for relocating, the city provided Alpha with numerous incentives that would lower costs and boost profits. It appeared to be an ideal strategy.

By 1994, however, the relocation effort had proved a failure for all concerned. Despite the rapid growth of its industry, Alpha was left with only eight of its original twenty-eight employees. Unable to attract high-quality employees to the South Bronx or to train local residents, the company was forced to outsource its manufacturing and some of its design work. Potential suppliers and customers refused to visit Alpha's offices. Without the city's attention to security, the company was plagued by theft.

What went wrong? Good intentions notwithstanding, the arrangement failed the test of business logic. Before undertaking the move, Alpha and the city would have been wise to ask themselves why none of the South Bronx's thriving businesses was in electronics. The South Bronx as a location offered no specific advantages to support Alpha's business, and it had several disadvantages that would prove fatal. Isolated from the lower Manhattan hub of computer-design and software companies, Alpha was cut off from vital connections with customers, suppliers, and electronic designers.

In contrast, Matrix Exhibits, a $2.2 million supplier of trade-show exhibits that has thirty employees, is thriving in Atlanta's inner city. When Tennessee-based Matrix decided to enter the Atlanta market in 1985, it could have chosen a variety of locations. All the other companies that create and rent trade-show exhibits are based in Atlanta's suburbs. But the Atlanta World Congress Center, the city's major exhibition space, is just a six-minute drive from the inner city, and Matrix chose the location because it provided a real competitive advantage. Today Matrix offers customers superior response time, delivering trade-show exhibits faster than its suburban competitors. Matrix benefits from low rental rates for warehouse space—about half the rate its competitors pay for similar space in the suburbs—and draws half its employees from the local community. The commitment of local police has helped the company avoid any serious security problems. Today Matrix is one of the top five exhibition houses in Georgia.

Alpha and Matrix demonstrate how location can be critical to the success or failure of a business. Every location—whether it be a nation, a region, or a city—has a set of unique local conditions that underpin the ability of companies based there to compete in a particular field. The competitive advantage of a location does not usually arise in isolated companies but in clusters of companies—in other words, in companies that are in the same industry or otherwise linked together through customer, supplier, or similar relationships. Clusters represent critical masses of skill, information, relationships, and infrastructure in a given field. Unusual or sophisticated local demand gives companies insight into customers' needs. Take Massachusetts's highly competitive cluster of information-technology industries: it includes companies specializing in semiconductors, workstations, supercomputers, software, networking equipment, databases, market research, and computer magazines.

Clusters arise in a particular location for specific historical or geo-graphic reasons—reasons that may cease to matter over time as the cluster itself becomes powerful and competitively self-sustaining. In successful clusters such as Hollywood, Silicon Valley, Wall Street, and Detroit, several competitors often push one another to improve products and processes. The presence of a group of competing companies contributes to the formation of new suppliers, the growth of companies in related fields, the formation of specialized training programs, and the emergence of technological centers of excellence in colleges and universities. The clusters also provide newcomers with access to expertise, connections, and infrastructure that they in turn can learn and exploit to their own economic advantage.

If locations (and the events of history) give rise to clusters, it is clusters that drive economic development. They create new capabilities, new companies, and new industries. I initially described this theory of location in *The Competitive Advantage of Nations* (Free Press, 1990), applying it to the relatively large geographic areas of nations and states. But it is just as relevant to smaller areas such as the inner city. To bring the theory to bear on the inner city, we must first identify the inner city's competitive advantages and the ways inner city businesses can forge connections with the surrounding urban and regional economies.

The True Advantages of the Inner City

The first step toward developing an economic model is identifying the inner city's true competitive advantages. There is a common misperception that the inner city enjoys two main advantages: low-cost real estate and labor. These so-called advantages are more illusory than real. Real estate and labor costs are often higher in the inner city than in suburban and rural areas. And even if inner cities were able to offer lower-cost labor and real estate compared with other locations in the United States, basic input costs can no longer give companies from relatively prosperous nations a competitive edge in the global economy. Inner cities would inevitably lose jobs to countries like Mexico or China, where labor and real estate are far cheaper.

Only attributes that are unique to inner cities will support viable businesses. My ongoing research of urban areas across the United States identifies four main advantages of the inner city: strategic location, local market demand, integration with regional clusters, and human resources. Various companies and programs have identified and exploited each of those advantages from time to time. To date, however, no systematic effort has been mounted to harness them.

Inner cities are located in what *should* be economically valuable areas. They sit near congested high-rent areas, major business centers, and transportation and communications nodes. As a result, inner cities can offer a competitive edge to companies that benefit from proximity to downtown business districts, logistical infrastructure, entertainment or tourist centers, and concentrations of companies.

For example, Boston's food processing and distribution industry gains a competitive edge from its inner city location in Newmarket Square (see Figure 10.1). The industry consists of such businesses as seafood importers, meat processors, bakeries, and food distributors. Because they are near downtown Boston, these businesses can make rapid deliveries, and downtown buyers have a convenient location at which to purchase goods. Land, although more costly than in the suburbs, is cheaper in the inner city than it is downtown, and zoning regulations permit food processing operations. Newmarket Square has excellent access to trucking as well as sea and air transport, which provides it with a particular competitive advantage in the export of seafood. The combination of those factors has produced a dense concentration of processors, caterers, truckers, wholesalers, distributors, and other suppliers in the inner city.

Although the location of Boston's food processing cluster has historic roots that predate the modern inner city, examples of newly formed companies underscore how critical an advantage proximity can be. Consider the catering supplier Be Our Guest. Founded in 1984, the company rents linens, party equipment, and other hard goods associated with the catering business. Located in Boston's inner city neighborhood of Roxbury, the company enjoys immediate and easy access to downtown Boston. As a result, it is able to offer a higher level of service to customers than its competitors can. To reinforce its service strategy, Be Our Guest maintains sufficient inventory levels to meet peaks in demand. Today the company has thirty-six full-time employees and annual sales of $1.2 million.

In Boston and Los Angeles, it is striking how many of the businesses that have remained in the inner city in the face of numerous difficulties are ones for which location matters. For example, both cities have a concentration of logistics and storage businesses. Advances in transpor-

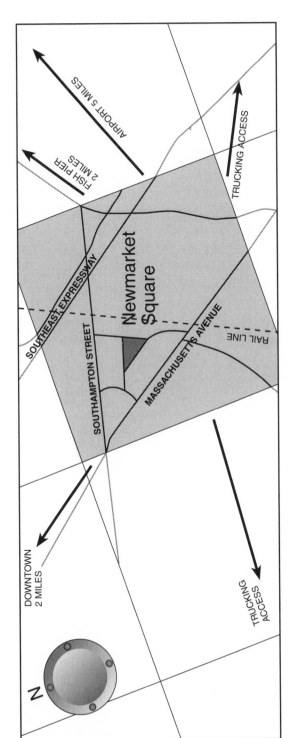

Figure 10.1 The Competitive Advantage of Newmarket Square

tation and communications may have reduced the importance of location for some kinds of businesses. However, the increasing importance of regional clusters and of such concepts as just-in-time delivery, superior customer service, and close partnerships between customers and suppliers are making location more critical than ever before.

There is significant potential, then, for expanding the inner-city business base by building on the advantage of strategic location. Among the initial prospects are location-sensitive industries now situated elsewhere, nearby companies and industries that face space constraints, and back-office or support functions amenable to relocation or outsourcing. Consider Boston's Longwood medical area, a huge concentration of world-class health care facilities. Longwood is located near the inner city neighborhoods of Roxbury and Jamaica Plain. Today such activities as laundry services, building maintenance, and just-in-time delivery of supplies are performed in-house or by suburban vendors. But, because of Longwood's proximity to the inner city, activities like these could be shifted to businesses based in Roxbury or Jamaica Plain—especially if basic infrastructure such as roads could be improved.

LOCAL MARKET DEMAND

The inner city market itself represents the most immediate opportunity for inner-city-based entrepreneurs and businesses. At a time when most other markets are saturated, inner city markets remain poorly served—especially in retailing, financial services, and personal services. In Los Angeles, for example, retail penetration per resident in the inner city compared with the rest of the city is 35 percent in supermarkets, 40 percent in department stores, and 50 percent in hobby, toy, and game stores.

The first notable quality of the inner city market is its size. Even though average inner city incomes are relatively low, high population density translates into an immense market with substantial purchasing power. Boston's inner city, for example, has an estimated total family income of $3.4 billion. Spending power per acre is comparable with the rest of the city despite a 21 percent lower average household income level than in the rest of Boston, and, more significantly, higher than in the surrounding suburbs. In addition, the market is young and growing rapidly, owing in part to immigration and relatively high birth rates.

A handful of forward-looking entrepreneurs have recognized the opportunities for profit and growth in this large, underdeveloped market and have opened retail outlets in the inner city. Chicago's historic retailer Goldblatt Brothers found new life after bankruptcy with a strategy built on inner city stores. In 1981, the company closed all its stores but six profitable ones located in the inner city. Focusing on cash-and-carry items and offering goods at closeout prices, Goldblatt Brothers has re-emerged as a competitive retailer. Today the company has fourteen stores, most of which are located in Chicago's inner city. Similarly, Stop & Shop and Purity Supreme are opening new stores in the inner city of Boston.

Another important quality of the inner city market is its character. Most products and services have been designed for white consumers and businesses. As a result, product configurations, retail concepts, entertainment, and personal and business services have not been adapted to the needs of inner city customers. Although microsegmentation has been slow to come to the inner city, it holds promise for creating thriving businesses.

Inner city consumers, in fact, represent a major growth market of the future, and companies based in the inner city have a unique ability to understand and address their needs. For example, Miami-based, Latino-owned CareFlorida has rapidly expanded its HMO business by tailoring its marketing to Latino customers. And Detroit's Universal Casket has grown to $3 million in sales by focusing on African-American-owned funeral homes. Many of the largest and most enduringly successful minority-owned (although not necessarily inner city-based) businesses have drawn their advantages from serving inner city residents' cultural and ethnic needs in fields such as food products (Parks Sausage and Brooks Sausages); beauty care (Soft Sheen, Proline, Dudley, Luster Products, and Johnson Products); and media (Essence, Earl Graves, Johnson Publishing, and Black Entertainment Television). Although inner city businesses need not be limited to serving local needs, this kind of focused strategy is one way to gain a clear competitive advantage over established businesses such as Procter & Gamble, Safeway, and Levi Strauss.

More important, businesses catering to local demand have the potential to expand beyond the inner city and become major players. Companies can target and sell not only to their own local communities but also to similar communities nationally and even internationally. Consider

Americas' Food Basket, a Cuban-owned supermarket based in Boston's inner city. In its second year of operation, the company has reached sales of $8 million annually and is profitable. It has developed a product mix that satisfies local demand better than mainstream supermarkets do. Its management's strong relationship with the community has reduced security problems and employee turnover. Unlike other nearby mom-and-pop stores, Americas' Food Basket has developed a partnership with a leading national wholesaler that provides goods and financing at competitive rates. As a result, its selection, prices, and service are far superior to those of smaller competitors. More important, Americas' Food Basket shows signs of becoming a major regional business by seeking ways to export its goods to the surrounding region. It is currently expanding into wholesaling with a start-up called Selmac Corporation. Selmac will supply mainly Latino products to Americas' Food Basket and to small *bodegas* throughout the inner city and the surrounding region. It also plans to bid on contracts to supply wholesale food services to schools, prisons, and other institutions throughout Massachusetts.

Tailored retailing concepts in a broad range of areas such as food, clothing, pharmaceuticals, toys, books, and restaurants could also set off a chain reaction of opportunities: Companies create demand for new types of products, which in turn creates new opportunities for manufacturers of specialized products. For example, tailored supermarkets are increasing the demand for established ethnic food producers and distributors such as Goya Foods, a supplier of Latino foods with annual sales of approximately $500 million. Such stores also represent a critical distribution channel for recent start-ups such as Glory Foods, which sells canned foods targeted at African-American consumers.

The most intriguing attribute of the inner city market is its potential to be a leading indicator of major nationwide trends. The tastes and sensibilities of inner city communities are cutting-edge in a number of respects and often become mainstream. Popular music is one example. Or consider Parks Sausage, based in Baltimore, Maryland, which developed its food products for African-American consumers but has found a receptive market nationally. Today it is competing head-to-head with Jimmy Dean Sausage, the industry leader.

Ultimately, what will attract the inner city consumer more than anything else is a new breed of company that is not small and high-cost but a professionally managed major business employing the latest in technology, marketing, and management techniques. This kind of company, much more than exhortation, will attract spending power and recycle capital within the inner city community.

INTEGRATION WITH REGIONAL CLUSTERS

The most exciting prospects for the future of inner city economic development lie in capitalizing on nearby regional clusters: those unique-to-a-region collections of related companies that are competitive nationally and even globally. For example, Boston's inner city is next door to world-class financial-services and health-care clusters. South Central Los Angeles is close to an enormous entertainment cluster and a large logistical-services and wholesaling complex.

The ability to access competitive clusters is a very different attribute— and one much more far-reaching in economic implication—than the more generic advantage of proximity to a large downtown area with concentrated activity. Competitive clusters create two potential advantages. The first is for business formation. Companies providing supplies, components, and support services could be created to take advantage of the inner city's proximity to multiple nearby customers in the cluster. For example, Detroit-based Mexican Industries has emerged as one of the most respected suppliers of head rests, arm rests, air bags, and other auto parts by forging close relationships with General Motors, Ford, Chrysler, and Volkswagen of America. Last year, the company had more than 1,000 employees, most of whom live in the inner city, and revenues of more than $100 million. Bing Steel, a fifty-four-person company with $57 million in sales, has made similar connections, supplying flat roll steel and coils to the auto industry.

The second advantage of these clusters is the potential they offer inner city companies to compete in downstream products and services. For example, an inner city company could draw on Boston's strength in financial services to provide services tailored to inner city needs—such as secured credit cards, factoring, and mutual funds—both within and outside the inner city in Boston and elsewhere in the country. Boston Bank of Commerce (BBOC) is a trusted local institution in the inner city with strong ties to the community. It has many small nonprofit customers, such as the Dimock Community Health Center in Roxbury, which has a $1 million endowment. There are many nonprofit organizations like

Dimock whose funds are sitting idle in low-interest savings accounts because they lack the investment savvy and size to attract sophisticated money managers. In total, however, such organizations represent a significant pool of capital. BBOC sees an opportunity here to take advantage of the trust it enjoys within the community and the proximity of world-class asset managers in the city's nearby financial services cluster. The company is developing a product to do asset management for nonprofits in its service area; it will pool funds from its clients and then subcontract their management to companies in the nearby cluster.

Few of these opportunities are currently being pursued. Most of today's inner city businesses either have not been export oriented, selling only within the local community rather than outside it, or have seen their opportunities principally in terms defined by government preference programs. Consequently, networks and relationships with surrounding companies are woefully underdeveloped. New private sector initiatives will be needed to make these connections and to increase inner city entrepreneurs' awareness of their value. Integration with regional clusters is potentially the inner city's most powerful and sustainable competitive advantage over the long term. It also provides tremendous leverage for development efforts: By focusing on upgrading existing and nascent clusters, rather than on supporting isolated companies or industries, public and private investments in training, infrastructure, and technology can benefit multiple companies simultaneously.

HUMAN RESOURCES

The inner city's fourth advantage takes on a number of deeply entrenched myths about the nature of its residents. The first myth is that inner city residents do not want to work and opt for welfare over gainful employment. Although there is a pressing need to deal with inner city residents who are unprepared for work, most inner city residents are industrious and eager to work. For moderate-wage jobs (six to ten dollars per hour) that require little formal education (for instance, warehouse workers, production-line workers, and truck drivers), employers report that they find hardworking, dedicated employees in the inner city. For example, a company in Boston's inner city neighborhood of Dorchester bakes and decorates cakes sold to supermarkets throughout the region. It attracts and retains area residents at seven to eight dollars per hour (plus contributions to pensions and health insurance) and has almost 100 local employees. The loyalty of its labor pool is one of the factors that has allowed the bakery to thrive.

Admittedly, many of the jobs currently available to inner city residents provide limited opportunities for advancement. But the fact is that they are jobs; and the inner city and its residents need many more of them close to home. Proposals that workers commute to jobs in distant suburbs—or move to be near those jobs—underestimate the barriers that travel time and relative skill level represent for inner city residents. Moreover, in deciding what types of businesses are appropriate to locate in the inner city, it is critical to be realistic about the pool of potential employees. Attracting high-tech companies might make for better press, but it is of little benefit to inner city residents. Recall the contrasting experiences of Alpha Electronics and Matrix Exhibits. In the case of Alpha, there was a complete mismatch between the company's need for highly skilled professionals and the available labor pool in the local community. In contrast, Matrix carefully considered the available workforce when it established its Atlanta office. Unlike the Tennessee headquarters, which custom-designs and creates exhibits for each client, the Atlanta office specializes in rentals made from prefabricated components—work requiring less-skilled labor, which can be drawn from the inner city. Given the workforce, low-skill jobs are realistic and economically viable: they represent the first rung on the economic ladder for many individuals who otherwise would be unemployed. Over time, successful job creation will trigger a self-reinforcing process that raises skill and wage levels.

The second myth is that the inner city's only entrepreneurs are drug dealers. In fact, there is a real capacity for legitimate entrepreneurship among inner city residents, most of which has been channeled into the provision of social services. For instance, Boston's inner city has numerous social service providers as well as social, fraternal, and religious organizations. Behind the creation and building of those organizations is a whole cadre of local entrepreneurs who have responded to intense local demand for social services and to funding opportunities provided by government, foundations, and private sector sponsors. The challenge is to redirect some of that talent and energy toward building for-profit businesses and creating wealth.

The third myth is that skilled minorities, many of whom grew up in or near inner cities, have abandoned their roots. Today's large and growing pool of talented minority managers represents a new generation of potential inner city entrepreneurs. Many have been trained at the nation's leading business schools and have gained experience in the nation's leading companies. Approximately 2,800 African Americans and 1,400 Hispanics graduate from M.B.A. programs every year compared with only a handful twenty years ago. Thousands of highly trained minorities are working at leading companies such as Morgan Stanley, Citibank, Ford, Hewlett-Packard, and McKinsey & Company. Many of these managers have developed the skills, network, capital base, and confidence to begin thinking about joining or starting entrepreneurial companies in the inner city. Two Harvard Business School graduates, for example, have launched Delray Farms with the aim of creating a national chain of small inner city supermarkets that focus on produce and other perishables. Backed by significant private-equity capital, Delray Farms is operating its first store in Chicago and is planning to open six new stores within a year.

The Real Disadvantages of the Inner City

The second step toward creating a coherent economic strategy is addressing the very real disadvantages of locating businesses in the inner city. The inescapable fact is that businesses operating in the inner city face greater obstacles than those based elsewhere. Many of those obstacles are needlessly inflicted by government. Unless the disadvantages are addressed directly, instead of indirectly through subsidies or mandates, the inner city's competitive advantages will continue to erode.

LAND

Although vacant property is abundant in inner cities, much of it is not economically usable. Assembling small parcels into meaningful sites can be prohibitively expensive and is further complicated by the fact that a number of city, state, and federal agencies each control land and fight over turf. For example, development of the Jeffrey Plaza shopping center in Chicago's South Side required government efforts over eight years to assemble twenty-one contiguous parcels. Similarly, attempts to rebuild South Central Los Angeles after the 1992 riots have been hampered because only nine of 200 vacant or underutilized properties are larger than one acre. (By comparison, Wal-Mart requires four to six acres for a single store.) Once assembled, an inner city site often requires expensive demolition, environmental cleanup, and extensive litigation. Private developers and banks tend to avoid sites with even a hint of environmental problems because of punitive liability laws.

BUILDING COSTS

The cost of building in the inner city is significantly higher than in the suburbs because of the costs and delays associated with logistics, negotiations with community groups, and strict urban regulations: restrictive zoning, architectural codes, permits, inspections, and government-required union contracts and minority set-asides. Ironically, despite the desperate need for new projects, construction in inner cities is far more regulated than it is in the suburbs—a legacy of big city politics and entrenched bureaucracies.

More damaging than regulatory costs is the uncertainty that the regulatory process creates for potential investors. Managers interviewed in Boston, Los Angeles, and Chicago expressed frustration with the three-year to five-year waiting periods necessary to obtain the numerous permit and site approvals required to build, expand, or improve facilities. Undeniably, the wait is expensive; but the uncertainty about whether an application will be approved or when a ruling will be made makes forming a financial strategy nearly impossible.

OTHER COSTS

Compared with the suburbs, inner cities have high costs for water, other utilities, workers' compensation, health care, insurance, permitting and other fees, real estate and other taxes, OSHA compliance, and neighborhood hiring requirements. For example, Russer Foods, a manufacturing company located in Boston's inner city, operates a comparable plant in upstate New York. The Boston plant's expenses are 55 percent higher for workers' compensation, 50 percent higher for family medical insurance, 166 percent higher for unemployment insurance, 340 percent higher for water, and 67 percent higher for electricity. High costs like these drive away companies and hold down wages. Some costs, such as those for workers' compensation, apply to the state or region as a whole. Others, such as real estate taxes, apply citywide. Still others, such as property insurance, are specific to the inner city. All are devastating to maintaining fragile inner city companies and to attracting new businesses.

It is an unfortunate reality that many cities—because they have a greater proportion of residents dependent on welfare, Medicaid, and other social programs—require higher government spending and, as a result, higher corporate taxes. The resulting tax burden feeds a vicious cycle—driving out more companies while requiring even higher taxes from those that remain. Cities have been reluctant to challenge entrenched bureaucracies and unions, as well as inefficient and outdated government departments, all of which unduly raise city costs.

Finally, excessive regulation not only drives up building and other costs but also hampers almost all facets of business life in the inner city, from putting up an awning over a shop window to operating a pushcart to making site improvements. Regulation also stunts inner city entrepreneurship, serving as a formidable barrier to small and start-up companies. Restrictive licensing and permitting, high licensing fees, and archaic safety and health regulations create barriers to entry into the very types of businesses that are logical and appropriate for creating jobs and wealth in the inner city.

SECURITY

Both the reality and the perception of crime represent profound impediments to urban economic development. First, crime against property raises costs. For example, the Shops at Church Square, an inner city strip shopping center in Cleveland, Ohio, spends two dollars per square foot more than a comparable suburban center for a full-time security guard, increased lighting, and continuous cleaning—raising overall costs by more than 20 percent. Second, crime against employees and customers creates an unwillingness to work in and patronize inner city establishments and restricts companies' hours of operation. Fear of crime ranks among the most important reasons why companies opening new facilities failed to consider inner city locations and why companies already located in the inner city left. Currently, police devote most of their resources to the security of residential areas, largely overlooking commercial and industrial sites.

INFRASTRUCTURE

Transportation infrastructure planning, which today focuses primarily on the mobility of residents for shopping and commuting, should consider equally the mobility of goods and the ease of commercial transactions. The most critical aspects of the new economic model—the importance of the location of the inner city, the connections between inner city businesses and regional clusters, and the development of export-oriented businesses—require the presence of strong logistical links between inner city business sites and the surrounding economy. Unfortunately, the business infrastructure of the inner city has fallen into disrepair. The capacity of roads, the frequency and location of highway on-ramps and off-ramps, the links to downtown, and the access to railways, airports, and regional logistical networks are inadequate.

EMPLOYEE SKILLS

Because their average education levels are low, many inner city residents lack the skills to work in any but the most unskilled occupations. To make matters worse, employment opportunities for less-educated workers have fallen markedly. In Boston between 1970 and 1990, for example, the percentage of jobs held by people without high school diplomas dropped from 29 percent to 7 percent, while those held by college graduates climbed from 18 percent to 44 percent. And the unemployment rate for African-American men aged sixteen to sixty-four with less than a high school education in major northeastern cities rose from 19 percent in 1970 to 57 percent in 1990.

MANAGEMENT SKILLS

The managers of most inner city companies lack formal business training. That problem, however, is not unique to the inner city; it is a characteristic of small businesses in general. Many individuals with extensive work histories but little or no formal managerial training start businesses. Inner city companies without well-trained managers experience a series of predictable problems that are similar to those that affect many small businesses: weaknesses in strategy development, market segmentation, customer-needs evaluation, introduction of information technology, process design, cost control, securing or restructuring financing, interaction with lenders and government regulatory agencies, crafting business plans, and employee training. Local community colleges often offer management courses, but their quality is uneven, and entrepreneurs are hard-pressed for time to attend them.

CAPITAL

Access to debt and equity capital represents a formidable barrier to entrepreneurship and company growth in inner city areas.

First, most inner city businesses still suffer from poor access to debt funding because of the limited attention that mainstream banks paid them historically. Even in the best of circumstances, small-business lending is only marginally profitable to banks because transaction costs are high relative to loan amounts. Many banks remain in small-business lending only to attract deposits and to help sell other more profitable products.

The federal government has made several efforts to address the inner city's problem of debt capital. As a result of legislation like the Community Reinvestment Act, passed in order to overcome bias in lending, banks have begun to pay much more attention to inner city areas. In Boston, for example, leading banks are competing fiercely to lend in the inner city—and some claim to be doing so profitably. Direct financing efforts by government, however, have proved ineffective. The proliferation of government loan pools and quasi-public lending organizations has produced fragmentation, market confusion, and duplication of overhead. Business loans that would provide scale to private sector lenders are siphoned off by these organizations, many of which are high-cost, bureaucratic, and risk-averse. In the end, the development of high-quality private sector expertise in inner city business financing has been undermined.

Second, equity capital has been all but absent. Inner city entrepreneurs often lack personal or family savings and networks of individuals to draw on for capital. Institutional sources of equity capital are scarce for minority-owned companies and have virtually ignored inner city business opportunities.

ATTITUDES

A final obstacle to companies in the inner city is antibusiness attitudes. Some workers perceive businesses as exploitative, a view that guarantees poor relations between labor and management. Equally debilitating are the antibusiness attitudes held by community leaders and social activists. These attitudes are the legacy of a regrettable history of poor treatment of workers, departures of companies, and damage to the environment. But holding on to these views today is counterproductive. Too often, community leaders mistakenly view businesses as a means of directly meeting social needs; as a result, they have unrealistic expectations for corporate involvement in the community. For example, some businesses interested in locating in Boston's inner city decided against it because of demands to build playgrounds, fund scholarships, and cede control of hiring and training to community-based organizations. Such demands on existing and potential businesses rarely help the community; instead, they drive businesses—and jobs—to other locations.

Demanding linkage payments and contributions and stirring up antibusiness sentiment are political tools that brought questionable results in the past when owners had less discretion about where they chose to locate their companies. In today's increasingly competitive business environment, such tactics will serve only to stunt economic growth.

Changing Roles and Responsibilities for Inner City Development

Overcoming the business disadvantages of the inner city as well as building on its inherent advantages will require the commitment and involvement of business, government, and the nonprofit sector. Each will have to abandon deeply held beliefs and past approaches. Each must be willing to accept a new model for the inner city based on an economic rather than a social perspective. The private sector, not government or social service organizations, must be the focus of the new model. (See Table 10.1.)

THE NEW ROLE OF THE PRIVATE SECTOR

The economic model challenges the private sector to assume the leading role. First, however, it must adopt new attitudes toward the inner city. Most private sector initiatives today are driven by preference programs or charity. Such activities would never stand on their own merits in the marketplace. It is inevitable, then, that they contribute to growing cynicism. The private sector will be most effective if it focuses on what it does best: creating and supporting economically viable businesses built on true competitive advantage. It should pursue four immediate opportunities as it assumes its new role.

Table 10.1 Inner City Economic Development

New Model	Old Model
Economic: create wealth	Social: redistribute wealth
Private sector	Government and social service organizations
Profitable businesses	Subsidized businesses
Integration with the regional economy	Isolation from the larger economy
Companies that are export oriented	Companies that serve the local community
Skilled and experienced minorities engaged in building businesses	Skilled and experienced minorities engaged in the social service sector
Mainstream, private sector institutions enlisted	Special institutions created
Inner city disadvantages addressed directly	Inner city disadvantages counterbalanced with subsidies
Government focused on improving the environment for business	Government involved directly in providing services or funding

Create and expand business activity in the inner city. The most important contribution companies can make to inner cities is simply to do business there. Inner cities hold untapped potential for profitable businesses. Companies and entrepreneurs must seek out and seize those opportunities that build on the true advantages of the inner city. In particular, retailers, franchisers, and financial services companies have immediate opportunities. Franchises represent an especially attractive model for inner city entrepreneurship because they provide not only a business concept but also training and support.

Businesses can learn from the mistakes that many outside companies have made in the inner city. One error is the failure of retail and service businesses to tailor their goods and services to the local market. The needs and preferences of the inner city market can vary greatly— something that companies like Goldblatt Brothers have recognized. The Chicago retailer understands that its inner city customers buy to meet immediate needs, and it has tailored its retail merchandise and purchasing planning to its customers' buying habits. For example, unlike most stores, which stock winter coats in the fall, Goldblatt Brothers stocks its coats in the winter.

Another common mistake is the failure to build relationships within the community and to hire locally. Hiring local residents builds loyalty from neighborhood customers, and local employees of retail and service businesses can help stores customize their products. Evidence suggests that companies that were perceived to be in touch with the community had far fewer security problems, whether or not the owners lived in the community. For example, Americas' Food Basket hires locally and is widely viewed as a good citizen of the community. As a result, management reports that it has not had to hire a security guard and that neighbors often call if they witness anything amiss.

Companies have discovered a number of other effective tactics for dealing with security. For instance, large concentrations of businesses spread security costs and reinforce perceptions of safety. MetroTech, a back-office operations complex serving nearby Wall Street, is located in a high-poverty and high-crime area near the federal buildings in downtown Brooklyn. The developers created an 18-acre campus that could support 4 million to 8 million square feet of office space. The complex is so large that tenants pay only 33 cents per square foot for twenty-four-hour private security. Because transportation infrastructure adds to perceptions of safety in traveling to and from business locations, MetroTech enlisted the city government to renovate the local subway stations and to locate a police branch near the site. Crime has been insignificant, and MetroTech is fully occupied by leading financial institutions.

In other cases, companies have organized themselves into associations to increase the effectiveness of security and to spread costs. The associations work closely with the police department and with members of the community to identify and address security problems. In some cities, special neighborhood-managed tax-assessment districts—such as New York City's many Business Improvement Districts—have been established to provide funds for supplemental security protection and other services.

Establish business relationships with inner city companies. By entering into joint ventures or customer-supplier relationships, outside companies will help inner city companies by encouraging them to export and by forcing them to be competitive. In the long run, both sides will benefit. For example, AB&W Engineering, a Dorchester-based metal fabricator, has built a close working relationship with General Motors. GM has given AB&W management assistance and a computerized ordering system and has referred a lot of new business to AB&W. In turn, AB&W has become a high-performing and reliable supplier. Such relationships, based not on charity but on mutual self-interest, are sustainable ones; every major company should develop them.

Redirect corporate philanthropy from social services to business-to-business efforts. Countless companies give many millions of dollars each year to worthy inner-city social-service agencies. But philanthropic efforts will be more effective if they also focus on building business-to-business relationships that, in the long run, will reduce the need for social services.

First, corporations could have a tremendous impact on training. The existing system for job training in the United States is ineffective. Training programs are fragmented, overhead intensive, and disconnected from the needs of industry. Many programs train people for nonexistent jobs in industries with no projected growth. Although reforming training will require the help of government, the private sector must determine how and where resources should be allocated to ensure that the specific employment needs of local and regional businesses are met. Ultimately, employers, not government, should certify all training programs based on relevant criteria and likely job availability.

Training programs led by the private sector could be built around industry clusters located in both the inner city (for example, restaurants, food service, and food processing in Boston) and the nearby regional economy (for example, financial services and health care in Boston). Industry associations and trade groups, supported by government incentives, could sponsor their own training programs in collaboration with local training institutions.

Programs that help inner city residents with the school-to-work transition could also take advantage of regional clusters. Project ProTech in Boston lets high school students compete for apprentice-like positions in the health care cluster. The program mixes classroom work and internship training during the school year and over the summer, beginning in the junior year of high school. Project ProTech is currently expanding to include other clusters, such as utilities and financial services.

Second, the private sector could make an equally substantial impact by providing management assistance to inner city companies. As with training, current programs financed or operated by the government are inadequate. Outside companies have much to offer companies in the inner city: talent, know-how, and contacts. One approach to upgrading management skills is to emphasize networking with companies in the regional economy that either are part of the same cluster (customers, suppliers, and related businesses) or have expertise in needed areas. An inner city company could team up with a partner in the region who provides management assistance; or a consortium of companies with a required expertise, such as information technology, could provide assistance to inner city businesses in need of upgrading their systems.

Professional associations could develop advisory programs for inner city managers. Business schools could develop and teach custom-designed short and practical executive programs or assist inner city companies through field studies programs. The Harvard Business School, for example, offers a for-credit course that matches teams of M.B.A.

students with inner city companies. We are encouraging the development of such programs elsewhere.

Adopt the right model for equity capital investments. The investment community—especially venture capitalists—must be convinced of the viability of investing in the inner city. There is a small but growing number of minority-oriented equity providers (although none specifically focus on inner cities). A successful model for inner city investing will probably not look like the familiar venture-capital model created primarily for technology companies. Instead, it may resemble the equity funds operating in the emerging economies of Russia or Hungary—investing in such mundane but potentially profitable projects as supermarkets and laundries. Ultimately, inner-city-based businesses that follow the principles of competitive advantage will generate appropriate returns to investors—particularly if aided by appropriate incentives, such as tax exclusions for capital gains and dividends for qualifying inner city businesses.

THE NEW ROLE OF GOVERNMENT

To date, government has assumed primary responsibility for bringing about the economic revitalization of the inner city. Existing programs at the federal, state, and local levels designed to create jobs and attract businesses have been piecemeal and fragmented at best. Still worse, these programs have been based on subsidies and mandates rather than on marketplace realities. Unless we find new approaches, the inner city will continue to drain our rapidly shrinking public coffers.

Undeniably, inner cities suffer from a long history of discrimination. However, the way for government to move forward is not by looking behind. Government can assume a more effective role by supporting the private sector in new economic initiatives. It must shift its focus from direct involvement and intervention to creating a favorable environment for business. This is not to say that public funds will not be necessary. But subsidies must be spent in ways that do not distort business incentives, focusing instead on providing the infrastructure to support genuinely profitable businesses. Government at all levels should focus on four goals as it takes on its new role.

Direct resources to the areas of greatest economic need. The crisis in our inner cities demands that they be first in line for government assistance. This may seem an obvious assertion. But the fact is that many programs in areas such as infrastructure, crime prevention, environmental cleanup, land development, and purchasing preference spread funds across constituencies for political reasons. For example, most transportation infrastructure spending goes to creating still more attractive suburban areas. In addition, a majority of preference-program assistance does not go to companies located in low-income neighborhoods.

Investments that boost the economic potential of inner cities must receive priority. For example, Superfund cleanup dollars should go to sites in high-unemployment inner city areas before they go to low-unemployment suburban sites. Infrastructure improvements should go to making inner city areas more attractive business locations. And crime prevention resources should go to high-crime inner city areas. Spending federal, state, and local money in that way will have the added benefit of easing critical social problems, thus reducing social service spending.

Unfortunately, the qualifying criteria for current government assistance programs are not properly designed to channel resources where they are most needed. Preference programs support business based on the race, ethnicity, or gender of their owners rather than on economic need. In addition to directing resources away from the inner city, such race-based or gender-based distinctions reinforce inappropriate stereotypes and attitudes, breed resentment, and increase the risk that programs will be manipulated to serve unintended populations. Location in an economically distressed area and employment of a significant percentage of its residents should be the qualification for government assistance and preference programs. Shifting the focus to economic distress in this way will help enlist all segments of the private sector in the solutions to the inner city's problems.

Increase the economic value of the inner city as a business location. In order to stimulate economic development, government must recognize that it is a part of the problem. Today its priorities often run counter to business needs. Artificial and outdated government-induced costs must be stripped away in the effort to make the inner city a profitable location for business. Doing so will require rethinking policies and programs in a wide range of areas. There is early evidence that self-inflicted regulatory costs can be overcome. Consider the success of the Indianapolis Regulatory Study Commission in Indiana. In two short years, Indianapolis ended its taxi monopoly, streamlined its building permitting process, and eliminated a wide range of needless regulations.

Indeed, there are numerous possibilities for reform. Imagine, for example, policy aimed at eliminating the substantial land and building cost penalties that businesses face in the inner city. Ongoing rent subsidies run the risk of attracting companies for which an inner city location offers no other economic value. Instead, the goal should be to provide building-ready sites at market prices. A single government entity could be charged with assembling parcels of land and with subsidizing demolition, environmental cleanup, and other costs. The same entity could also streamline all aspects of building—including zoning, permitting, inspections, and other approvals.

That kind of policy would require further progress on the environmental front. A growing number of cities—including Detroit, Chicago, Indianapolis, Minneapolis, and Wichita, Kansas—have successfully developed so-called brownfield urban areas by making environmental cleanup standards more flexible depending on land use, indemnifying land owners against additional costs if contamination is found on a site after a cleanup, and using tax-increment financing to help fund cleanup and redevelopment costs.

Government entities could also develop a more strategic approach to developing transportation and communications infrastructures, which would facilitate the fluid movement of goods, employees, customers, and suppliers within and beyond the inner city. Two projects in Boston are prime examples: first, a new exit ramp connecting the inner city to the nearby Massachusetts Turnpike, which in turn connects to the surrounding region and beyond; and a direct access road to the harbor tunnel, which connects to Logan International Airport. Though inexpensive, both projects are stalled because the city does not have a clear vision of their economic importance.

Deliver economic development programs and services through mainstream, private sector institutions. There has been a tendency to rely on small community-based nonprofits, quasi-governmental organizations, and special-purpose entities, such as community development banks and specialized small-business investment corporations, to provide capital and business-related services. Social service institutions have a role, but it is not this. With few exceptions, nonprofit and government organizations cannot provide the quality of training, advice, and support to substantial companies that mainstream, private sector organizations can. Compared with private sector entities such as commercial banks and venture capital companies, special-purpose institutions and nonprofits are plagued by high overhead costs; they have difficulty attracting and retaining high-quality personnel, providing competitive compensation, or offering a breadth of experience in dealing with companies of scale.

Consider access to capital. Government must help create the conditions necessary for private, mainstream financial institutions to lend and invest profitably in inner city businesses. Efforts to eliminate discrimination are vital but are not sufficient. Financing in the inner city must be profitable, or private sector institutions will never have the enthusiasm to develop it aggressively. Some conventional lenders claim that the reason they have not found inner city loans profitable is not higher default rates, as is commonly assumed, but the high transaction costs of finding and actually making inner city loans. Government should address those costs head on through better information and relaxed paperwork requirements and regulations. In addition, it could provide direct incentives, giving banks a transaction fee rather than a loan guarantee for closing a qualifying inner-city-based business loan. Such an approach would encourage banks to make and maintain good loans, instead of forcing capital into bad loans to fill lending quotas based on race, ethnicity, or gender.

The most important way to bring debt and equity investment to the inner city is by engaging the private sector. Resources currently going to government or quasi-public financing would be better channeled through other private financial institutions or directed at recapitalizing minority-owned banks focusing on the inner city, provided that there were matching private sector investors. Minority-owned banks that have superior knowledge of the inner city market could gain a competitive advantage by developing business-lending expertise in inner city areas.

As in lending, the best approach to increase the supply of equity capital to the inner cities is to provide private sector incentives consistent with building economically sustainable businesses. One approach would be for both federal and state governments to eliminate the tax on capital gains and dividends from long-term equity investments in inner-city-based businesses or subsidiaries that employ a minimum percentage of inner city residents. Such tax incentives, which are based on the premise of profit, can play a vital role in speeding up private sector investment. Private sector sources of equity will be attracted to inner city investment only when the creation of genuinely profitable businesses is encouraged.

Align incentives built into government programs with true economic performance. Aligning incentives with business principles should be the goal of every government program. Most programs today would fail such a test. For example, preference programs in effect guarantee companies a market. Like other forms of protectionism, they dull motivation and retard cost and quality improvement. A 1988 General Accounting Office report found that within six months of graduating from the Small Business Association's purchasing preference program, 30 percent of the companies had gone out of business. An additional 58 percent of the remaining companies claimed that the withdrawal of the SBA's support had had a devastating impact on business. To align incentives with economic performance, preference programs should be rewritten to require an increasing amount of non-set-aside business over time.

Direct subsidies to businesses do not work. Instead, government funds should be used for site assembly, extra security, environmental cleanup, and other investments designed to improve the business environment. Companies then will be left to make decisions based on true profit.

THE NEW ROLE OF COMMUNITY-BASED ORGANIZATIONS

Recently, there has been renewed activity among community-based organizations (CBOs) to become directly involved in business development. CBOs can, and must, play an important supporting role in the process. But choosing the proper strategy is critical, and many CBOs will have to change fundamentally the way they operate. While it is difficult to make a general set of recommendations to such a diverse group of organizations, four principles should guide community-based organizations in developing their new role.

Identify and build on strengths. Like every other player, CBOs must identify their unique competitive advantages and participate in economic development based on a realistic assessment of their capabilities, resources, and limitations. Community-based organizations have played a much-needed role in developing low-income housing, social programs, and civic infrastructure. However, while there have been a few notable successes, the vast majority of businesses owned or managed by CBOs have been failures. Most CBOs lack the skills, attitudes, and incentives to advise, lend to, or operate substantial businesses. They were able to master low-income housing development, in which there were major public subsidies and a vacuum of institutional capabilities. But, when it comes to financing and assisting for-profit business development, CBOs simply can't compete with existing private sector institutions.

Moreover, CBOs naturally tend to focus on community entrepreneurship: small retail and service businesses that are often owned by neighborhood residents. The relatively limited resources of CBOs, as well as their focus on relatively small neighborhoods, is not well-suited to developing the more substantial companies that are necessary for economic vitality.

Finally, the competitive imperatives of for-profit business activity will raise inevitable conflicts for CBOs whose mission rests with the community. Turning down local residents in favor of better-qualified outside entrepreneurs, supporting necessary layoffs or the dismissal of poorly performing workers, assigning prime sites for business instead of social uses, and approving large salaries to successful entrepreneurs and managers are only a handful of the necessary choices. Given these organizations' roots in meeting the social needs of neighborhoods, it will be difficult for them to put profit ahead of their traditional mission.

Work to change workforce and community attitudes. Community-based organizations have a unique advantage in their intimate knowledge of and influence within inner city communities, and they can use that advantage to help promote business development. CBOs can help create a hospitable environment for business by working to change community and workforce attitudes and acting as a liaison with residents to quell unfounded opposition to new businesses. When BayBank wanted to open a new branch in Dorchester, for example, a local community development corporation was instrumental in smoothing relations with a few vocal critics who could have delayed the project or even driven the bank away.

Create work-readiness and job-referral systems. Community-based organizations can play an active role in preparing, screening, and referring employees to local businesses. A pressing need among many inner city residents is work-readiness training, which includes communication, self-development, and workplace practices. CBOs, with their intimate knowledge of the local community, are well equipped to provide this service in close collaboration with industry. The Urban League of Eastern Massachusetts, for example, has taken up the challenge in its new Employment Resource Center. The center provides workers with basic training as well as instruction on specific topics, such as customer-service and interviewing skills and written and oral communication.

CBOs can also help inner city residents by actively developing screening and referral systems. Admittedly, some inner-city-based businesses do not hire many local residents. The reasons are varied and complex but seem to revolve around a few bad experiences that owners have had with individual employees and their work attitudes, absenteeism, false injury claims, or drug use. A study of the impoverished Red Hook neighborhood in Brooklyn points to the importance of social networks—networks that are often lacking in inner cities—as informal job referral systems.[1] The study found that a local development corporation, the South Brooklyn LDC, played an important role in helping local residents get jobs by developing relationships with nearby businesses and screening and referring employees to them.

Facilitate commercial site improvement and development. Community-based organizations (especially community development corporations) can also leverage their expertise in real estate and act as a catalyst to facilitate environmental cleanup and the development of commercial and industrial property. For example, the Codman Square Neighborhood Development Corporation in Boston was part of a group including the

Boston Public Facilities Department, local merchants, and the local health center that encouraged 36 businesses to move into a depressed neighborhood. The group used its considerable community organizing talent to help merchants form an association to identify the neighborhood's needs as well as barriers to meeting them. It negotiated with the police to increase patrols in the area and pushed the mayor's office to board up abandoned buildings and to rid the area of trash and abandoned cars. After bringing together many different constituencies, it led a campaign to encourage businesses to locate in the neighborhood.

Overcoming Impediments to Progress

This economic model provides a new and comprehensive approach to reviving our nation's distressed urban communities. However, agreeing on and implementing it will not be without its challenges. The private sector, government, inner city residents, and the public at large all hold entrenched attitudes and prejudices about the inner city and its problems. These will be slow to change. Rethinking the inner city in economic rather than social terms will be uncomfortable for many who have devoted years to social causes and who view profit and business in general with suspicion. Activists accustomed to lobbying for more government resources will find it difficult to embrace a strategy for fostering wealth creation. Elected officials used to framing urban problems in social terms will be resistant to changing legislation, redirecting resources, and taking on recalcitrant bureaucracies. Government entities may find it hard to cede power and control accumulated through past programs. Local leaders who have built social service organizations and merchants who have run mom-and-pop stores could feel threatened by the creation of new initiatives and centers of power. Local politicians schooled in old-style community organizing and confrontational politics will have to tread unfamiliar ground in facilitating cooperation between business and residents.

These changes will be difficult ones for both individuals and institutions. Nonetheless, they must be made. The private sector, government, and community-based organizations all have vital new parts to play in revitalizing the economy of the inner city. Businesspeople, entrepreneurs, and investors must assume a lead role; and community activists, social service providers, and government bureaucrats must support them. The time has come to embrace a rational economic strategy and to stem the intolerable costs of outdated approaches.

NOTES

1. See Philip Kasinitz and Jan Rosenberg, "Why Enterprise Zones Will Not Work: Lessons from a Brooklyn Neighborhood," *City Journal*, Autumn 1993, pp. 63–69.

CHAPTER 11

Redefining Competition in Health Care

Michael E. Porter

Elizabeth Olmsted Teisberg

THE U.S. HEALTH CARE SYSTEM HAS REGIS-
tered unsatisfactory performance in both costs and quality over many
years. While this might be expected in a state-controlled sector, it is
nearly unimaginable in a competitive market—and in the United States,
health care is largely private and subject to more competition than
virtually anyplace else in the world.

In healthy competition, relentless improvements in processes and
methods drive down costs. Product and service quality rise steadily.
Innovation leads to new and better approaches, which diffuse widely and
rapidly. Uncompetitive providers are restructured or go out of business.
Value-adjusted prices fall, and the market expands. This is the trajectory
common to all well-functioning industries—computers, mobile communications, banking, and many others.

Health care could not be more different. Costs are high and rising,
despite efforts to reduce them, and these rising costs cannot be explained
by improvements in quality. Quite the opposite: Medical services are
restricted or rationed, many patients receive care that lags currently
accepted procedures or standards, and high rates of preventable medical
error persist. There are wide and inexplicable differences in costs and
quality among providers and across geographic areas. Moreover, the
differences in quality of care last for long periods because the diffusion
of best practices is extraordinarily slow. It takes, on average, 17 years

---

June 2004

for the results of clinical trials to become standard clinical practice. Important constituencies in health care view innovation as a problem rather than a crucial driver of success. Taken together, these outcomes are inconceivable in a well-functioning market. They are intolerable in health care, with life and quality of life at stake.

We believe that competition is the root of the problem with U.S. health care performance. But this does not mean we advocate a state-controlled system or a single-payer system; those approaches would only make matters worse. On the contrary, competition is also the solution, but the nature of competition in health care must change. Our research shows that competition in the health care system occurs at the wrong level, over the wrong things, in the wrong geographic markets, and at the wrong time. Competition has actually been all but eliminated just where and when it is most important.

There is no villain here. Poor public-policy choices have contributed to the problem, but so have the bad choices made by health plans, hospitals, and the employers who buy their services. Decades of "reform" have failed, and attempts to reform will continue to fail until we finally get the right kind of competition working (see the insert "How Reform Went Wrong").

How Reform Went Wrong

Attempts to reform the U.S. health care system have failed because they have been based on the wrong diagnosis of the problem.

These reform efforts have not resulted in meaningful competition at the level of specific diseases and conditions—the level at which value is created in medicine. With competition at the wrong level, all the system participants—consumers, providers, employers, and insurers—have acted counterproductively. Some historical perspective appears in the figure, "The Evolution of Reform Models."

The managed care era was focused largely on cost; reformers treated health care as if it were a commodity. To cut their expenses, payers shifted costs and aggressively pursued bargaining power. Providers did the same. Services were rationed, and there were few true improvements in efficiency. Ironically, costs continued to rise.

In reaction to managed care, reformers tried to give patients more legal rights. Those efforts ended up saddling health care providers with extra regulatory layers—and increased costs. Requiring hospitals and doctors to adhere to a patients' bill of rights did eliminate some of the more egregious examples of cost-driven rationing by providers, but it also left untouched the fundamental cause of providers' behavior—namely, competition structured to compel players to focus on cost. Costs rose even higher.

When their attempts to fix the system through legal and regulatory means proved futile, reformers began to focus on consumer choice—a good topic to examine, but subscribers' choice of health plan is not the choice that really matters. Consumers today have little choice about providers and treatments and are in no position to make informed decisions given the limited information available to them.

Recent thinking on health care reform has migrated to improving quality and reducing medical errors. Employer consortia are attempting to improve hospital practices by requiring that facilities, for instance, enter treatment orders into a computerized system, maintain appropriate coverage in intensive care units and emergency rooms, and meet volume thresholds for some referrals. These are useful requirements, but they do not change the underlying incentives for zero-sum competition. Similarly, employer-proposed "pay for performance" initiatives will help in the near term to get more providers to comply with current accepted medical standards. But this will not be enough to reform the system because the incentives are to conform to specific processes, not to achieve real results. Effective incentives need to be tied to goals rather than means.

Some recently proposed reforms will even exacerbate zero-sum competition. For instance, some employer groups advocate "system to system" competition, in which physicians are forced to commit to one closed network or another. This actually limits competition at the level of diseases and treatments while accentuating the power of a few full-line systems to completely avoid competing at this level. Meanwhile, other proposed reforms, such as the migration of some consumers from Medicare to private insurance and the purchase of prescription drugs from Canada, are not reforms at all. Shifting Medicare patients to a private system that is not working is not a solution. And buying drugs from Canada is the system's latest attempt to shift costs rather than create value.

Missing in the discussion about health care reform is an understanding of the role competition plays in driving quality, safety, and efficiency improvements and the type of competition that will best do so. If the objective is to create value, then competition to improve outcomes and increase efficiency in specific medical conditions is essential. Getting the level of competition right will reduce error and encourage the spread of new, excellent practices. Reform must focus on the rules, incentives, information, and strategies that will enable positive-sum competition where it counts—at the level of individual diseases and treatments.

The Evolution of Reform Models

PAST

objective: **reduce costs, avoid costs**

Focus was on **costs, bargaining power, and rationing.**

System characterized by:

- cost shifting among patients, providers, physicians, payers, employers, and the government
- limits on access to services
- bargained down prices for drugs and services
- prices unrelated to the economics of delivering care

Focus was on **legal recourse and regulation.**

System characterized by:

- patients' rights
- detailed rules for system participants
- increased reliance on the legal system

PRESENT

objective: **enable choice, reduce errors**

Focus is on **choice of health plan.**

System characterized by:

- competition among health plans
- information on health plans
- financial incentives for patients

Focus is on **provider and hospital practices.**

System characterized by:

- online order entry
- Six Sigma practices
- appropriate ER staffing
- volume thresholds for complex referrals
- mandatory guidelines
- "pay for performance" when standards of care are used

FUTURE

objective: **increase value**

Focus should be on **the nature of competition.**

System characterized by:

- competition at the level of specific diseases and conditions
- distinctive strategies by payers and providers
- incentives to increase value rather than shift costs
- information on providers' experiences, outcomes, and prices
- consumer choice

The health care system can achieve stunning gains in quality and efficiency. And employers, the major purchasers of health care services, could lead the transformation.

Zero-Sum Competition

In any industry, competition should drive up value for customers over time as quality improves and costs fall. It is often argued that health care is different because it is complex; because consumers have limited information; and because services are highly customized. Health care undoubtedly has these characteristics, but so do other industries where competition works well. For example, the business of providing customized software and technical services to corporations is highly complex, yet, when adjusted for quality, the cost of enterprise computing has fallen dramatically over the last decade.

Health care competition, by contrast, has become zero sum: The system participants divide value instead of increasing it. In some cases, they may even erode value by creating unnecessary costs. Zero-sum competition in health care is manifested in several ways: First, it takes the form of cost shifting rather than fundamental cost reduction. Costs are shifted from the payer to the patient, from the health plan to the hospital, from the hospital to the physician, from the insured to the uninsured, and so on. Passing costs from one player to another, like a hot potato, creates no net value. Instead, gains for one participant come at the expense of others—and frequently with added administrative costs.

Second, zero-sum competition involves the pursuit of greater bargaining power rather than efforts to provide better care. Health plans, hospital groups, and physician groups have consolidated primarily to gain more clout and to cut better deals with suppliers or customers. But the quality and efficiency gains from consolidation are quite modest.

Third, zero-sum competition restricts choice and access to services instead of making care better and more efficient. As the system is currently structured, health plans make money by refusing to pay for services and by limiting subscribers' and physicians' choices. Health plans and care providers restrict patients' access to medical innovations or limit the services that are covered. Many health plans pay hospitals a set amount per admission for a given ailment rather than for a full treatment cycle. This creates an incentive for hospitals to use cheaper treatments rather than more effective, innovative ones—and if patients consequently must be readmitted, the hospitals are paid again.

Fourth, zero-sum competition relies on the court system to settle disputes. Yet lawsuits compound the problem. They actually raise costs directly (through legal fees and administrative expenses) and indirectly (through the practice of unnecessary, defensive medicine)—none of which creates value for patients. Moreover, of the billions of dollars that doctors and hospitals pay annually for malpractice insurance, less than 30% goes to injured patients or their families.

What Happened?

Zero-sum competition in health care is the consequence of a series of unfortunate strategic choices made by nearly all the actors in the system—encouraged, and in some cases reinforced, by bad incentives introduced through government regulation. These include:

THE WRONG LEVEL OF COMPETITION

The most fundamental and unrecognized problem in U.S. health care today is that competition operates at the wrong level. It takes places at the level of health plans, networks, and hospital groups. It should occur in the prevention, diagnosis, and treatment of individual health conditions or co-occurring conditions. It is at this level that true value is created—or destroyed—disease by disease and patient by patient. It is here where huge differences in cost and quality persist. And it is here where competition would drive improvements in efficiency and effectiveness, reduce errors, and spark innovation. Yet competition at the level of individual health conditions is all but absent.

The fundamental economics of health care are driven at the level of diseases or conditions. Numerous studies show that when physicians or teams treat a high volume of patients who have a particular disease or condition, they create better outcomes and lower costs. (For more on this concept, see figure 11.1.") The renowned Texas Heart Institute (THI), for example, prides itself on having surgical costs that are one-third to one-half lower than those of other academic medical centers despite taking on the most difficult cases and using the newest technologies. Because of its specialization, THI attracts the most complex and demanding patients, whose needs produce even more rapid learning. In health care, as in most industries, cost and quality can improve simultaneously as providers prevent errors, boost efficiency, and develop expertise. As we have learned in many businesses, "doing it right the first time" not only improves outcomes but can dramatically cut costs. The trade-off between cost and quality in health care, then, is significantly reduced by competition at the right level.

Competition at the level of individual diseases and conditions is getting even more important as medical research reveals that diagnoses and treatments should be increasingly specialized. Prostate cancer, for

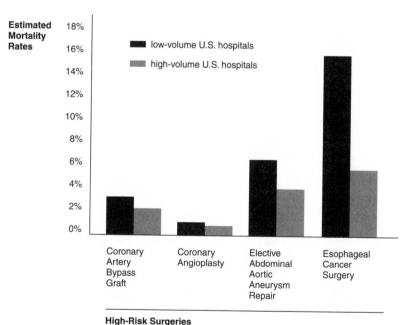

High-Risk Surgeries

Source: John D. Birkmeyer, *Leapfrog Patient Safety Standards: The Potential Benefits of Universal Adoption*, November 2000.

Figure 11.1 Experience Matters
The more experience physicians and teams have in treating patients with a particular disease or condition, the more likely they are to create better outcomes—and, ultimately, realize lower costs. By performing particular procedures over and over, teams increase their learning opportunities and thereby reduce mortality rates.

example, is now understood to be six different diseases that respond to different treatments. Providers should compete to be the best at addressing a particular set of problems, and patients should be free to seek out the providers with the best track records given their unique circumstances. In the current environment, where patients' treatments are determined by the networks they are in, network providers are all but guaranteed the business.

THE WRONG OBJECTIVE

Competition at the wrong level has been exacerbated by pursuit of the wrong objective: reducing cost. Even worse, the objective has often not been to reduce the total cost of health care but to reduce the cost that is borne by the system's intermediaries—health plans or employers. The right goal is to improve value (quality of health outcomes per dollar expended), and value can only be measured at the disease and treatment level. Competing on cost alone makes sense only in commodity businesses, where all sellers are more or less the same. Clearly, that is not true in health care. Yet that perverse assumption—which neither buyers nor sellers really believe—underlies the behavior of the system participants. Payers, employers, and even providers pay insufficient attention to achieving better outcomes and improving value over time, which are what really matter.

THE WRONG FORMS OF COMPETITION

Instead of competing to increase value at the level of individual diseases or conditions, the players in health care have entered into four unhealthy kinds of competition, all of which have unhappy consequences. One is the annual competition among health plans to sign up subscribers. Because of strong network restrictions, however, signing up for a health plan blocks most of the competition at the level of diseases and treatments. And because the commitment between the subscriber and the health plan is for just one year, both payers and employers are motivated to engage in short-term thinking rather than invest in practices and therapies that will improve value over time.

Another form of unproductive competition occurs when providers compete to be included in health plan networks by giving deep discounts to payers and employers that have large patient populations. There is little or no economic rationale for such discounts. It does not cost less to treat a patient employed by a large company than a patient who is self-employed. Health care delivery does not become more efficient from treating twice as many patients with a random distribution of diseases; patients are still treated one at a time and according to their particular circumstances. Large discounts in return for increased overall patient flow simply shift revenue from providers to health plans or to large employers. This creates artificial benefits for large groups and shifts costs to small groups, unaffiliated individuals, patients seeking out-of-network care, and the uninsured—with little, if any, compensating value. Such cost shifting ultimately drives up overall costs—even to large groups—by increasing the number of uninsured patients who must be treated in expensive settings (emergency rooms, for instance) and hence the amount of free care that must be subsidized.

Providers also compete to see who can form the largest, most powerful group, able to offer a complete array of services. Here, too, there are few efficiencies to be gained, apart from modest opportunities to share overhead. Hospital mergers often result in two departments in the same specialty rather than one department, even when the facilities are close to one another. Provider groups are formed not to create value but to boost bargaining power vis-à-vis health plans and other system participants. Throughout Florida, for example, large hospital networks have won price increases far above the rate of inflation and unconnected to any improvements made in quality of care after threatening to cut off one of the region's largest health plans. And because their referrals are heavily skewed toward affiliated physician groups and institutions, large provider groups further limit competition at the level of diseases and treatments.

Finally, there is always a squabble over who pays. This struggle takes many forms. Providers and payers try to shift costs to each other. Payers raise rates on subscribers who become ill. Providers boost their list prices so Medicare discounts will not cut so deep. Patients seek coverage for optional or cosmetic care. And employers allow health plans to deny payment to their employees. All of this is costly. None of it creates value for patients.

THE WRONG GEOGRAPHIC MARKET

Competition should force providers to equal or exceed the value created by the best in their region or even nationally. For the most part, however, health care competition is local. Such competition insulates mediocre providers from market pressures and inhibits the spread of best practices and innovations. Throughout the United States, there is an almost three-fold variation in annual costs per Medicare enrollee—from less than $3,000 per patient in some areas to more than $8,500 in others. According to studies by Dartmouth Medical School's John Wennberg and the school's Center for the Evaluative Clinical Sciences, the higher costs are not associated with better medical outcomes and cannot be explained by differences in age, sex, race, rates of illness (which affect the need for care) or cost of living (which affects the cost of delivering care). These studies did find, as have several others, major differences across regions in outcomes and in delivery of care at the disease or treatment level. Such differences are sustained by the absence of competition.

Localized competition is institutionalized by health plan policies that require subscribers to pay most of the costs of out-of-network care—discouraging them from seeking providers outside their immediate area—or that penalize physicians for making out-of-network referrals. Medicare, for its part, computes HMO capitation payments at the county level, creating little incentive for hospitals in different counties to compete, even if they are only a few miles apart. Localized competition is also the result of habit, inertia, and information; as a matter of course, physicians refer their patients to nearby doctors—even their Medicare patients, who have no geographic restrictions.

Though many health care services should be provided locally, health care competition should take place regionally, or even nationally, especially for more complex or uncommon conditions. In this way, all providers would be subject to competitive pressures to improve. And providers treating less common conditions, drawing from a wider area, could serve enough patients to develop the expertise and efficiency that come with repeated experience and learning.

An ideal health care system would encourage close working relationships between local providers (for most routine and emergency services and follow-up care) and a wide array of leading providers (for definitive diagnoses, treatment strategies, and complex procedures in certain areas). These relationships would speed up the diffusion of state-of-the-art clinical care and would help to increase quality and efficiency throughout the system—but they are often resisted today.

THE WRONG STRATEGIES AND STRUCTURE

Although value is created by developing deep expertise and tailored facilities in a set of areas where providers can truly excel, most hospitals and networks have instead pursued wide service lines to negotiate better with health plans. Hospitals and physician groups have broadened their services by merging with or acquiring other institutions, resulting in roughly 700 hospital mergers between 1996 and 2000 and very high levels of local industry concentration. In North Carolina, for instance, only 18 of 100 counties had multiple hospital systems in 2000. Rivalry is severely limited as a result.

This reduction in competition produces few offsetting benefits. As we have discussed, consolidation has led to few efficiencies. Nor is it at all clear that quality is better when the breadth of services is wider. Though some patients have multiple diseases, focused institutions can easily cope with this. The M.D. Anderson Cancer Center in Houston, for example, has staff cardiologists but does not maintain a full-line cardiology practice. When difficult cases arise or heart surgery is required, the physicians at M.D. Anderson consult with outside colleagues or refer their cancer patients to leading cardiac centers.

THE WRONG INFORMATION

Information is integral to competition in any well-functioning market. It allows buyers to shop for the best value and forces sellers to compare themselves to rivals. In health care, though, the information really needed to support value-creating competition has been largely absent or suppressed. There is plenty of information about things that have a modest impact on value—health plan coverage and subscriber satisfaction surveys, for instance. But much more relevant is information about providers' experiences and outcomes in treating particular conditions. Even this basic information is unavailable. For example, most hospitals and physicians do not even provide data on how many patients with a particular diagnosis or condition they have treated. Instead, available information about medical experiences and outcomes is largely word-of-mouth, even among physicians, and may be unsupported by evidence.

There have been efforts to collect the right kind of information—among them, Cleveland Health Quality Choice, the Pennsylvania Health Care Cost Containment Council, and New York State's Cardiac Surgery Reporting System. But these have been small-scale experiments. Providers argue that data on the outcomes of treatments—appropriately risk-adjusted to reflect the complexity or severity of the patients' initial conditions—are complex and difficult to measure in meaningful ways. Indeed, the collection of outcome information has been actively opposed by some system participants—sometimes for good reasons (the difficulty of performing risk adjustments, for instance) and sometimes for not so good reasons (fear of comparison and accountability, for instance).

Some observers have tried to discredit the attempts that have been made so far to collect relevant information. But these experiments demonstrate both the critical value of having the right information and the feasibility of developing it. In Cleveland, the information collected was not disseminated to patients or referring doctors. Employers, faced with short-term cost pressures, did not use the data to select high-quality providers. Patients and doctors were left in the dark. Meanwhile, in New York, information was collected on risk-adjusted mortality rates following cardiac bypass surgeries performed statewide, and the data were made more widely available. In response to the data, cardiac surgery groups pursued process improvements, and some hospitals revoked the privileges of cardiac surgeons with low volume and high mortality rates. After four years of published data, New York had the lowest risk-adjusted mortality following bypass surgery of any state in the country.

Encouraging competition at the level of specific diseases or conditions will speed the development of the right kind of information. For instance, insurer Preferred Global Health (PGH) helps its subscribers choose among the world-class providers and treatments it offers for the 15 critical diseases it covers. To find the highest-quality providers, PGH identifies those with the most experience in the most advanced treatments, documents their effectiveness and outcomes, and asks them to participate in quality-improvement processes. PGH's experience belies the argument that there is too little information available for meaningful consumer choice in health care. America cannot afford to wait for perfect information to be developed before it can be disseminated. Nothing will drive improvements in information faster than making the existing data widely available.

THE WRONG INCENTIVES FOR PAYERS

Health insurers should be rewarded for helping their customers learn about and obtain care with the best value; for simplifying administrative processes; and for making participants' lives easier. Instead, payers benefit financially from enrolling healthy people and from raising premiums for or denying coverage to sick people. Payers have incentives to complicate billing; they can shift costs by issuing incomprehensible or inaccurate invoices and by delaying or disputing payment. They also have incentives to shift costs or reduce services by putting roadblocks between patients and care providers, restricting patients' access to expensive treatments and most out-of-network treatments. (Although out-of-network care is not inherently more expensive, hospitals charge out-of-network patients list prices that may be twice as high as negotiated in-network prices. The difference between the amount the payer will reimburse and the artificially high list prices essentially makes out-of-network care prohibitively expensive for many patients.) Finally, payers benefit from slowing down innovations that do not show immediate, short-term cost savings. All these incentives reinforce zero-sum competition and work against value creation in health care.

A single-payer system, which has been proposed, would end the practice of excluding high-risk subscribers. But it would only exacerbate all the other skewed incentives by eliminating competition at the level of health plans and giving the payer more bargaining power with which to shift costs to providers, patients, and employers. A single payer would have greater incentive to reduce its costs by restricting or rationing services and by slowing the diffusion of innovation. The only real solution is to change these incentives and open up competition, not to make health insurance a government monopoly.

THE WRONG INCENTIVES FOR PROVIDERS

Providers should be rewarded for competing regionally and nationally to deliver the best-value care for particular conditions or diseases. Instead,

providers' incentives, just like the payers' incentives, reinforce zero-sum
competition in health care. Hospitals and physicians have incentives to
not refer patients to other providers who may be more experienced or
to make referrals only within their network. Reimbursement practices
encourage physicians to spend less time with patients, discharge them

**The Features of ZERO-SUM
Competition in Health Care**

The Wrong Level of Competition
Competition is among health plans,
hospitals, and networks.

The Wrong Objective
Cost reduction; participants try to reduce
their own costs by transferring them to
someone else without reducing the total cost.

The Wrong Forms of Competition
Competition is to sign up healthy subscribers.
Methods include discounting prices to large
payers and groups, consolidating to increase
bargaining power, and shifting costs.

The Wrong Geographic Market
Competition is local.

The Wrong Strategies and Structure
Participants build full-line services, form
closed networks, consolidate with others
(thereby reducing rivalry), and match their
competitors.

The Wrong Information
Information is about health plans and
subscribers' satisfaction surveys.

The Wrong Incentives for Payers
Payers try to attract healthy subscribers
and raise rates for unhealthy subscribers.
They restrict treatments and out-of-network
services, shift costs to providers and
patients, and slow down innovation.

The Wrong Incentives for Providers
Providers offer every service, but often below
prevailing medical standards. They refer
patients within the network, if at all; spend
less time with patients and discharge them
quickly; and practice defensive medicine.

Figure 11.2   Pitfalls and Potential: An Overview of What's Plaguing U.S. Health Care
In any industry, competition should drive up value for consumers over time. In health
care, competition is zero sum—value is divided (sometimes destroyed) instead of
increased. The system can change if the participants strive for positive-sum
competition.

quickly, and readmit them if there is a problem. While many physicians resist the pressure to undertreat their patients, this conflict between good medicine and economic self-interest demoralizes physicians and slows the diffusion of best practices.

The threat of malpractice suits creates opposing incentives for physicians to overtest, overtreat, and overrefer their patients. Unfortunately,

---

The Features of POSITIVE-SUM Competition in Health Care

The Right Level of Competition
Competition is to prevent, diagnose, and treat specific diseases or combinations of conditions.

The Right Objective
Improve value—quality per expended dollars over time.

The Right Forms of Competition
Competition is to create value at the level of diseases or conditions by developing expertise, reducing errors, increasing efficiency, and improving outcomes.

The Right Geographic Market
Competition is at the regional or national level.

The Right Strategies and Structure
Participants define their distinctiveness by offering services and products that create unique value. The system has many focused competitors.

The Right Information
Information is about providers, treatments, and alternatives for specific conditions.

The Right Incentives for Payers
Payers help subscribers find the best-value care for specific conditions. They simplify billing and administrative processes and pay bills promptly.

The Right Incentives for Providers
Providers succeed by developing areas of excellence and expertise. They measure and enhance quality and efficiency. They eradicate mistakes; they get it right the first time. They meet, exceed, and improve standards.

The Ingredients for Change

No Restrictions to Competition and Choice
- No preapprovals for referrals or treatments
- No network restrictions
- Strict antitrust enforcement against collusion, excessive concentration, and unfair practices
- Meaningful co-payments and medical savings accounts with high deductibles, all of which will give consumers incentives to seek good value

Accessible Information
- Appropriate information on treatments and alternatives is formally collected and widely disseminated.
- Information about providers' experience in treating particular diseases and conditions is made available immediately.
- Risk-adjusted outcome data are developed and continually enhanced.
- Some information is standardized nationally to enable comparisons.

Transparent Pricing
- Provider sets a single price for a given treatment or procedure.
- Different providers set different prices.
- Price estimates are made available in advance to enable comparison.

Simplified Billing
- One bill per hospitalization or per period of chronic care
- Payer has legal responsibility for medical bills of paid-up subscribers.

Nondiscriminatory Insurance
- No re-underwriting
- Assigned risk pools for those who need them
- Required health plan coverage, which would create equity and value throughout the system

Treatment Coverage
- National list of minimum required coverage
- Additional coverage results from competition, not litigation.

Fewer Lawsuits
- More information means more disclosure of risks and better-informed choices by patients.
- Lawsuits address use of obsolete treatments and carelessness.

these incentives to overtreat do not cancel out the reimbursement incentives to undertreat. Instead, the result is less effective clinical practice and mountains of paperwork that drain doctors' time. Worse still, the threat of malpractice suits creates risks for providers who try to learn from bad outcomes by measuring and analyzing them. Ironically, while technology has made knowledge diffusion faster and easier than ever before, the social and economic structures of the health care sector work against the rapid dissemination of learning.

Positive-Sum Competition

In a healthy system, competition at the level of diseases or treatments becomes the engine of progress and reform. Improvement feeds on itself. For that process to begin, however, the locus of competition has to shift from "Who pays?" to "Who provides the best value?" Getting there will require changes in the strategies of providers and payers and in the behaviors of employers purchasing health plans. In addition, some important system infrastructure needs to be put in place—rules and regulations that shift the incentives and create the right types of information. (See figure 11.2) Let's look at each needed reform in turn.

PROVIDER STRATEGIES: DISTINCTIVENESS

Under positive-sum competition, providers would not attempt to match competitors' every move. Instead, they would develop clear strategies around unique expertise and tailored facilities in those areas where they can become distinctive. Most hospitals would retain a wide array of service areas, but they would not try to be all things to everyone. In most businesses, it is common sense to develop products and services that create unique value. For many hospitals, developing uniqueness is a significant change in mind-set and deciding what *not* to do is an even more radical idea.

NO RESTRICTIONS TO CHOICE

Under positive-sum competition, all restrictions to choice at the disease or treatment level would disappear, including network restrictions and approvals of referrals. Reasonable co-pays and large deductibles combined with medical savings accounts would let patients take some financial responsibility for their choices. But co-pays would be the same inside and outside of the network. Antitrust authorities would scrutinize system participants so that one hospital system or health plan did not unfairly dominate an important market.

TRANSPARENT PRICING

Prices would be posted and readily available. Providers would charge the same price to any patient for addressing a given medical condition, regardless of the patient's group affiliation. Providers could and would set different prices from their competitors, but that pricing would not vary simply because one patient was insured by Aetna, another covered by Blue Cross, and another self-insured. Payers could negotiate, but price changes would have to benefit all patients, not just their own. The cost of treating a medical condition has nothing to do with who the patient's employer or insurance company is.

Price discrimination not related to costs imposes huge burdens on the system today. Having multiple prices drives up administrative costs. Patients covered by the public sector are subsidized by private-sector patients. And within the private sector, patients in large groups are subsidized by the uninsured, members of small groups, and out-of-network patients, who pay list prices. Artificially high list prices make more patients unable to pay, driving up uncompensated care expenses, which leads to ever higher list prices and bigger discounts for large groups. The price disincentives for care outside of the network stifle competition, which in turn slows quality and efficiency improvements that would otherwise benefit all patients. Without service-by-service competition, costs spiral ever higher while quality lags. The cost of dysfunctional competition far outweighs any short-term advantages system participants get from price discrimination—even for those firms that currently get the biggest discounts.

Paradoxically, the most practical way to eliminate price differentials for favored groups might be to temporarily institutionalize them. The federal government could limit the spread between the most discounted price and the highest price charged by a provider for any service and then reduce this spread each year over a five-year period. Ending the price anomalies would put a short-run burden on the biggest beneficiaries of the current system—master cost shifters like Medicare and the largest health plans. But over time, all participants would benefit from the enormous improvements in value and efficiency.

SIMPLIFIED BILLING

A fundamental function of pricing is to convey information to consumers and competitors. Current billing practices obscure that information. Unnecessarily complex billing contributes to cost shifting, drives up administrative costs, and makes price and value comparisons virtually impossible. Under positive-sum competition, providers would have to issue a single bill for each service bundle, or for each time period in treating chronic conditions, rather than a myriad of bills for each discrete service. Many other industries have solved the problem of how to issue a single bill for customized services; among them aerospace, construction, auto repair, and consulting. A competitive health care industry could figure it out, too. Competing providers would also figure out how to give price estimates in advance of service. Such estimates would not only improve consumer choice but would also spur providers to learn about their real costs.

The other major source of billing problems is that currently, the patient bears the legal responsibility for bills, even with fully paid-up insurance. In positive-sum competition, payers would bear full legal responsibility for the medical bills of paid-up subscribers. If providers bill once and payers cannot shift costs to patients or providers, much of the confusion in billing will end.

ACCESSIBLE INFORMATION

Under positive-sum competition, both the providers and the consumers of health care would get the information they need to make decisions about care. The government or a broad consortium of employers could jump-start the collection and dissemination process by agreeing on a standard set of information that would be collected nationally on a regular basis. Indeed, medical information is not unlike the corporate disclosures overseen by the SEC. The benefits of national comparisons are compelling and will unleash a tidal wave of improvements in quality and efficiency.

An obvious—and relatively uncontroversial—starting point would be to collect information on specific providers' experience with given diseases, treatments, and procedures. The data would be made publicly available after a waiting period during which providers could correct any errors. Over time, information about providers' risk-adjusted medical outcomes also would need to be collected and disseminated, allowing consumers to evaluate the providers' areas of expertise. This information would be specific to particular diseases or medical conditions, not aggregated across different areas of medical practice. A productive system would also collect or disseminate pricing information, enabling comparisons for specific treatments or procedures.

NONDISCRIMINATORY INSURANCE UNDERWRITING

Two anomalies mar the pricing of health plans. First, people who are included in large risk pools (such as those who work for big companies) can get a reasonably priced health plan even if someone in the family has medical risks. But those without access to such a pool (such as people who work for small firms or are self-employed) will pay very high prices if a family member has medical risks. Realistic reform efforts need to assume that health care coverage will continue to come mostly from employers. However, risk-pooling solutions need to be developed for those who are self-employed, employed by small firms, employed part-time, or unemployed. For example, smaller companies are joining consortia for health plan purchases. For high-risk people unable to buy health plans, assigned risk pools, like those used in automobile insurance, will need to be developed.

In addition, people in small groups or with individual insurance policies face the likelihood that their premiums will rise sharply if someone in the family actually develops an expensive medical condition, even if the family has paid premiums for years without making large claims. This practice, known as "re-underwriting," negates the purpose of health insurance and must be eliminated.

FEWER LAWSUITS

Malpractice litigation and the associated defensive medical practices inflict huge costs on everyone, and they have done little to raise the quality of health care. Indeed, the threat of malpractice creates incentives for physicians and hospitals to hide their mistakes rather than own up to and eliminate them. Standards for malpractice litigation need to change. Lawsuits are appropriate only in cases of truly bad medical practice, such as negligence, the use of obsolete treatments, or carelessness, not when a patient had a bad outcome despite receiving appropriate, up-to-date treatment. With better information and no restrictions on choice, many lawsuits will be averted. The money spent on enabling information and choice is an investment in removing billions of dollars of administrative and legal costs from the system.

NATIONAL LIST OF MINIMUM COVERAGE

The current system of individual negotiation and litigation over coverage is expensive. A better system would mandate a minimum level of coverage with a national list (such as the one used in the Federal Employees Health Benefits Program). Health plans could choose to cover more services and treatments for competitive reasons, but they could not be forced to do so by lawsuits. This change would refocus health care expenditures from malpractice premiums to delivery of care for more people.

PAYER STRATEGIES: CHOICE AND EFFICIENCY

Positive-sum competition would induce payers to compete to create value, not just to minimize cost. They would simplify billing and administrative processes. They would serve subscribers by identifying treatment alternatives and providers with excellent outcomes. They would help subscribers to know when and where it is appropriate to travel outside of their immediate areas for quality care. (Some payers have begun to post information about treatments and providers on their Web sites, but the information is often only about those treatments and providers within a small radius around the subscriber's ZIP code.) The best payers would be able to recommend effective disease-management options for subscribers with chronic conditions. Competition would shift to providing information and excellent service. Attempts to limit patients' choices or to control physicians' behavior would end.

ACCELERATING THE TRANSFORMATION

Two other steps would accelerate the transformation in health care—one a transitional change and the other a larger, more controversial one. The transitional step, with major symbolic importance, would be the creation of a short-term mechanism to encourage the diffusion of promising new approaches to care that are initially expensive. One model would be for Medicare, traditionally slow to adopt new treatments, to create an Adoption of Innovation Fund to support the spread of promising FDA-approved therapies to patients. Providers, working with technology suppliers, pharmaceutical companies, and payers, would compete to win the funding under well-defined standards for institutional review and informed patient consent. In time, such a fund may not be needed as positive-sum competition takes hold. As a transitional device, however, it would speed treatments toward lower cost and wider adoption.

The larger, more controversial step would be for the government to require health coverage for all, with subsidies for low-income people. With required health care coverage, everyone would be a paying customer concerned with the value of health care. While subsidies to low-income people would drive up health care expenditures, there would be offsetting cost savings and revenues. The huge cost of free care would be eliminated, and providers would no longer have to raise their prices to cover it. Cost savings would result from more care delivered at the right time rather than after complications have developed, and in cost-effective settings rather than in emergency rooms. Additional revenues would come from people who can afford coverage but who choose not to buy it and become part of the uncompensated care pool if they become ill or injured.

Employers Should Lead the Way

Companies have a lot at stake in how the U.S. health care system performs. Businesses' health care costs have outpaced inflation in 13 of the last 17 years, reaching more than $6,200 per employee in 2003. Double-digit increases the last three years, projected to continue in 2004, have caught senior management's attention. A Hewitt Associates study of 622 major U.S. companies found that 96% of CEOs and CFOs are significantly or critically concerned about health care costs for 2004, and 91% voiced the same concern for the impact health care costs will have on their employees.

As major purchasers of health care services, employers have the clout to insist on change. (See the insert "Deeper Diagnosis.") Unfortunately, they have also been part of the problem. In buying health care services, companies have forgotten some basic lessons about how competition works and how to buy intelligently. Ignoring differences in quality, companies have bought health plans based on price rather than value. They have delegated the management of their health plans to parties whose incentives were not well aligned with the companies' attempts to maximize value or with the well-being of employees. Hence, employers have become unwitting conspirators in a troubled system.

They should have known better. Few products or services are really commodities—especially not complex services like providing quality health care. The relevant standard should be value, not cost. Companies know that experience and expertise simultaneously improve quality and reduce cost. They know that innovation is crucial to progress, not an expense to be suppressed. And they know that relevant information is essential to good decision making.

Some employers have started to purchase health care services differently. And consortia like the Leapfrog Group (a coalition of 150 public and private organizations that provide health care benefits) are working to improve the quality of health care; Leapfrog's focus is on reducing the high incidence of errors in U.S. medical care. These efforts are important, but they will be even more effective when they focus on the power of competition. Rather than approve hospitals or tell them how to run their operations, employers need to insist that choice and information be made truly available at the level of specific diseases and treatments so that patients and referring physicians can choose providers that use efficient, state-of-the-art methods of care. Leapfrog is moving in this direction with its efforts to promote regional referrals for high-risk surgeries to highly experienced providers. Honeywell is also moving in this direction by hiring Consumer's Medical Resource, a decision-support service that provides independent information on diagnoses and treatments to employees.

The newest employer initiatives, known as "pay for performance," set higher reimbursement rates for providers that comply with specified standards of medical care. These measures aim to prevent subpar care by encouraging widespread use of well-established standards that are too often ignored. Pay for performance could be an important transitional measure until experience and outcome data are widely available. However, it is an inadequate long-term solution because it rewards providers for following mandated practices, not for achieving excellent (risk-adjusted) outcomes. The system will improve much faster if providers face competitive pressure to produce truly good results, patient by patient and condition by condition.

By setting new expectations for health plans and providers and by purchasing health care services differently, employers can realize the power of positive-sum competition in health care. (Figure 11.3 outlines what employers should demand from their health plans.) Most employers resist the idea of an end to volume discounts, but these discounts contribute to the vicious cycle of cost increases and cost shifting in

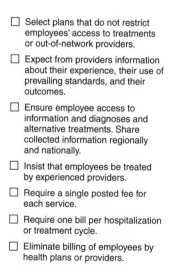

☐ Select plans that do not restrict employees' access to treatments or out-of-network providers.

☐ Expect from providers information about their experience, their use of prevailing standards, and their outcomes.

☐ Ensure employee access to information and diagnoses and alternative treatments. Share collected information regionally and nationally.

☐ Insist that employees be treated by experienced providers.

☐ Require a single posted fee for each service.

☐ Require one bill per hospitalization or treatment cycle.

☐ Eliminate billing of employees by health plans or providers.

Figure 11.3   What Employers Can Do Immediately

health care. If employers take the lead in creating productive health care competition, insisting that competition take place at the right level, firms and their employees will benefit from the increased value of services and the broader information available. Pursued seriously, such changes would radically alter the health care system, instigating a transformation of historic proportions. The system can be fixed.

Deeper Diagnosis

Improved health care delivery should be a top priority for corporate managers. Yet most companies continue to depend on government and industry "experts," whose reform efforts during the past decade have failed to create effective competition in health care. In "Fixing Competition in U.S. Health Care," professors Michael E. Porter and Elizabeth Olmsted Teisberg explain what's wrong with the system from a business perspective and what changes will be required to improve the value equation. This report features in-depth analyses and comprehensive facts and figures gleaned from the authors' exhaustive research. For more information, visit http://hcreport.hbr.org.

Part IV Strategy, Philanthropy, and Corporate Social Responsibility

CHAPTER 12

Philanthropy's New Agenda

Creating Value

Michael E. Porter

Mark R. Kramer

DURING THE PAST TWO DECADES, the number
of charitable foundations in the United States has doubled, while the
value of their assets has increased more than 1,100%. Foundations now
hold over $330 billion in assets and contribute over $20 billion annually
to educational, humanitarian, and cultural organizations of all kinds.
No other country in the world can claim such substantial and widespread
commitment to philanthropy and volunteerism. But are we, as a society,
realizing the full fruits of this commitment?

Grant-giving foundations are intermediaries between the individual
donors who fund them and the various social enterprises that they, in
turn, support. But if foundations serve only as passive middlemen, as
mere conduits for giving, then they fall far short of their potential and
of society's high expectations.

Foundations can and should lead social progress. They have the potential to make more effective use of scarce resources than either individual
donors or the government. Free from political pressures, foundations
can explore new solutions to social problems with an independence that
government can never have. And compared with individual donors,
foundations have the scale, the time horizon, and the professional management to create benefits for society more effectively.

Whether foundations are fulfilling their potential, however, is an open
question. Not enough foundations think strategically about how they

November 1999

can create the most value for society with the resources they have at their disposal. Little effort is devoted to measuring results. On the contrary, foundations often consider measuring performance to be unrelated to their charitable mission.

If foundations are to survive and thrive in the new century, those attitudes and practices must change. True, foundations are created by the generosity of private individuals. But compared with direct giving, foundations are strongly favored through tax preferences. When individuals contribute to a foundation, then, they cross an important line. Some of the money that foundations give away belongs, in a sense, to all of us. That is why we look to foundations to achieve a social impact disproportionate to their spending. We look to them to create real value for society.

Foundations must rise to this challenge sooner rather than later. Despite the dramatic increase in the number and wealth of foundations, the resources available for solving society's problems are scarcer than ever. Using those limited resources most effectively has immense social value, and foundations are uniquely suited to do so. But they cannot as long as their founders, trustees, and staff are unwilling to rethink what they do and how they do it. Satisfied with their historic agenda of doing good, too few foundations work strategically to do better. The time has come to embrace a new agenda, one with a commitment to creating value.

An Obligation to Create Value

When a donor gives money to a social enterprise, all of the money goes to work creating social benefits. When a donor gives money to a foundation, most of the gift sits on the sidelines. On average, foundations donate only 5.5% of their assets to charity each year, a number slightly above the legal minimum of 5%. The rest is invested to create financial, not social, returns. (Only .01% of foundation investment portfolios is invested to support philanthropic purposes.) Most of the $330 billion currently held by foundations, then, represents a future benefit to society, one that will be realized only when the money is finally given away.

We rarely stop to think about the differences between direct giving to operating charities and donations through foundations, but they are striking. When an individual contributes $100 to a charity, the nation loses about $40 in tax revenue, but the charity gets $100, which it uses to provide services to society. The immediate social benefit, then, is 250% of the lost tax revenue. When $100 is contributed to a foundation, the nation loses the same $40. But the immediate social benefit is only the $5.50 per year that the foundation gives away—that is, less than 14% of the forgone tax revenue.

Of course, the foundation will continue to pay out 5.5% of principal for many years to come. Even so, there is a substantial cost in holding so much money aside. At a 10% discount rate, for example, the present value of the foundation's cumulative contributions after five years is only $21. After 100 years, it is still only $55. Compare that with the $100 contributed directly to the provider of social services in year one.

Regardless of the discount rate one chooses, the fact remains that we as a nation pay up front for deferred social benefits. The whole donation gets the tax break, not just the small part that is spent. Since foundations also pay almost no taxes on the appreciation of their assets, the forgone tax revenue grows even larger. Over the past decade, when the stock market has been strong, the United States has forgone tax revenue of 75 cents for every dollar foundations gave to social enterprises.

Moreover, when philanthropy is channeled through foundations, two additional layers of costs are added. First, foundations have their own administrative costs, estimated at between $2 billion and $3 billion per year. Second, a heavy administrative burden is imposed on grantees complying with the foundations' sometimes detailed and protracted application and reporting procedures. Such costs are very real.

Foundations, then, are an expensive way to allocate dollars to social enterprises. This is not to say that foundations cannot contribute far greater value than their added tax and administrative costs. They can. Nor do we mean to imply that the government would spend tax revenues as well as foundations do, or for the same purposes. What we are saying is that as a nation, we make a substantial investment in foundation philanthropy—one well worth making if foundations meet their obligation to perform.

How, then, can foundations increase the social impact of their work enough to compensate for their costs? At its best, a foundation brings to social problems more than money and the passion of its good intentions. The permanence of a foundation's asset base means that it has an appropriately long time horizon in which to tackle social issues and develop expertise in its field. Thus foundation dollars can achieve greater social impact than the same monies spent by either private donors or the government. That is what we mean when we challenge foundations to create value.

Creating Value Through Others

The vast majority of foundations work through others by giving grants. (Only a small number of operating foundations provide social services themselves.) Grant-making foundations purchase social benefits from the organizations they support. However, anyone, including private donors and the government, could purchase the same benefits with the same dollars. Foundations create value when their activities generate social benefits that go beyond the mere purchasing power of their grants. They can do so in four ways. The first two are relatively well known but are rarely practiced systematically. The last two are far more powerful but far less common. All four can create value, but there is a clear hierarchy of ascending impact. Each successive approach leverages a foundation's special assets—resources, expertise, independence, and time horizon—more than the preceding one, as the focus of activity shifts from the individual recipient to the overall social sector. (See Figure 12.1.)

1. SELECTING THE BEST GRANTEES

The process of value creation here is straightforward. Like investment advisers in the business world, foundations can use their expertise to channel resources to their most productive uses within the social sector by funding organizations that are the most cost effective or that address urgent or overlooked problems. For example, of the many organizations that seek funding for programs aimed at reducing the high school dropout rate, a foundation can select the most effective one. Thus its dollar will earn a higher social return than a dollar given less knowledgeably by

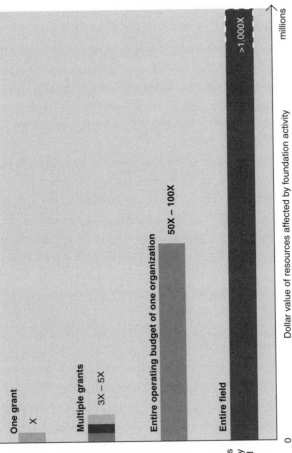

1. Selecting the best grantees
Each dollar will earn a higher
social return than a dollar given
by a less knowledgeable donor.

2. Signaling other funders
By attracting other donors, a
foundation effectively improves
the return on a larger pool of
philanthropic resources.

**3. Improving the performance
of grant recipients**
Helping a grantee to improve its
own capabilities increases its
overall effectiveness as an
organization and thus improves
the return on all the money
it spends.

**4. Advancing the state of
knowledge and practice**
Such agenda-setting work makes
every dollar spent in the field—by
philanthropists, government, and
other organizations—more
productive.

One grant
X

Multiple grants
3X – 5X

Entire operating budget of one organization
50X – 100X

Entire field
>1,000X

millions

0   Dollar value of resources affected by foundation activity

Figure 12.1   Foundations Create Value in Four Ways
Each successive approach leverages a foundation's special assets more than the preceding one as the pool of resources
affected grows from a single grant to an entire field.

an individual donor. In this way, choosing recipients and allocating funds is itself a source of value.

While most foundations recognize evaluation and selection as their primary tasks, few operate systematically to measure their own performance in order to improve the return on their future allocations. One notable exception is the Colorado Trust, a foundation that specializes in two areas: accessible and affordable health care and the strengthening of families.

The Colorado Trust is unusual in its focus on improving its own selection process by analyzing results and then incorporating that knowledge into its future decisions. For every initiative the trust underwrites, it evaluates not only the grantee's performance but also its own effectiveness. Was the trust's strategy for the initiative based on sound assumptions? How good were the criteria used to select grantees? By asking such questions systematically, the trust works to become more effective with each successive round of funding.

2. SIGNALING OTHER FUNDERS

The second way to create value is a logical extension of the first. If a foundation is skilled at evaluating and selecting charities, it can magnify the value it creates by taking the additional steps of educating and attracting other donors (especially those lacking the foundation's expertise in the area). By so doing, it effectively improves the return on a larger pool of philanthropic resources.

Attracting other funders by offering matching grants is one form of signaling, yet even it is rarely used—representing only 4% of all grants. Beyond matching grants, foundations can actively help grantees to raise additional resources and can educate other funders to improve their own selection procedures. The prevailing culture of independence among foundations, however, continues to be a barrier to such learning and the improved performance that could result from it.

3. IMPROVING THE PERFORMANCE OF GRANT RECIPIENTS

Foundations can create still more value if they move from the role of capital provider to the role of fully engaged partner, thereby improving the grantee's effectiveness as an organization. The value created in this way extends beyond the impact of one grant: it raises the social impact of the grantee in all that it does and, to the extent that grantees are willing to learn from one another, it can increase the effectiveness of other organizations as well.

Affecting the overall performance of grant recipients is important because foundation giving represents only about 3% of the nonprofit sector's total income. By helping grantees to improve their own capabilities, foundations can affect the social productivity of more resources than just their slice of the whole. Working directly with grantees to improve performance is thus a more powerful use of scarce resources than selecting grantees or signaling other funders.

Nonprofits operate without the discipline of the bottom line in the delivery of services, though they do compete for contributions. As a result, they lack strong incentives to measure and manage their performance. Foundations can not only encourage them to do so but also bring to bear their objectivity as well as their own and outside expertise to help grantees identify and address weaknesses.

Consider the David and Lucile Packard Foundation. It spends $12 million a year assisting nonprofits in management, planning, restructuring, and staff development. One grant, for example, was used to teach an environmental organization how to be more effective at marketing and fund-raising. The Intercultural Center for the Study of Deserts and Oceans (CEDO) is a Mexican-American partnership that promotes sustainable use of the desert and upper gulf region of California. CEDO succeeded in bringing attention—and tourists—to the area, but it lacked the marketing expertise to benefit from the increased tourism. The Packard Foundation's grant paid for marketing consultants who taught CEDO how to turn tourists into members, creating an ongoing revenue stream for CEDO far greater than the Foundation's $50,000 grant.

The Echoing Green Foundation, created by venture capitalist Ed Cohen, gives $1.4 million a year to improve the performance of the nonprofit sector even more broadly. It invests in social entrepreneurs, individuals with the drive and vision to catalyze social change. It aims to build a community of public-service leaders who share their experience, knowledge, and energy with one another. To date, Echoing Green has funded more than 300 fellows who not only pursue their own projects but also visit with one another to share best practices. The lessons learned are recorded, distributed to all grantees, and made publicly available.

The range of ways in which foundations can assist nonprofits goes well beyond making management-development grants. Foundations can become fully engaged partners, providing advice, management assistance, access to professional service firms, clout, and a host of other non-cash resources. Improving the performance of grant recipients often requires foundations to work closely with grantees. It also requires the willingness to engage for the long term. Foundations are capable of both.

In the fall of 1998, for example, the Charles and Helen Schwab Family Foundation in San Mateo, California, joined with the Peninsula Community Foundation and the Sobrato Foundation in a $2 million, two-year initiative to address internal issues of management and growth at 16 local family-service agencies. Every eight weeks for the life of the project, foundation staff members meet with all 16 agency directors. Management experts are brought in to address relevant topics. As a result of the group discussions, three of the grantees have decided that they can operate more efficiently if they merge, and foundation staff has worked closely with them to accomplish the merger. Because technology management has surfaced as a major issue, the foundations have researched and funded technology needs at several of the agencies.

4. ADVANCING THE STATE OF KNOWLEDGE AND PRACTICE

Foundations can create the greatest value by funding research and a systematic progression of projects that produce more effective ways to address social problems. At its best, such work results in a new framework that shapes subsequent work in the field—making every dollar spent by philanthropists, government, and other organizations more productive.

Foundations are uniquely positioned to study a field in depth. They can set a new agenda and change both public sentiment and government policy. The green revolution, for example, had its roots in research sponsored jointly by the Ford and Rockefeller Foundations in the late 1950s and early 1960s. Concerned with world hunger and population growth, the two foundations created research institutes that developed new strains of wheat and rice that doubled and tripled crop output per acre.

Within six years, India doubled its rice production, and Mexico, once an importer of wheat, became an exporter. Nigeria and Colombia created their own research institutes modeled on the foundations' research. The Rockefeller Foundation subsequently disseminated its results to organizations from 28 developing countries. Altogether, many millions of the world's poorest people benefited from the knowledge created by those two foundations.

Studies by the Carnegie Foundation have had a similarly powerful impact on education in the United States over the last 95 years. In 1904, Carnegie funded research by Abraham Flexner on the state of medical education, which revealed a widespread lack of standards. This study revolutionized the teaching of medicine in the United States. Over the next 20 years, nearly half of the medical schools in existence were closed, and the model curriculum that Flexner proposed still serves as the basis for medical training across the country.

The Carnegie Foundation subsequently funded hundreds of studies in the field of education, first in other areas of professional education, such as law, engineering, and business. In each field, the research influenced the spread of new and standardized models of education.

In 1967, the Carnegie Commission on Higher Education set the model for requirements in liberal arts undergraduate education that most universities follow today. Carnegie also studied and promoted standardized testing and is responsible for creating the Educational Testing Service in Princeton, New Jersey.

It is work of this kind—not only pursuing knowledge breakthroughs and establishing pilot projects but also pushing them through to fruition—that we tend to associate with foundations of an earlier era. Today some foundations are carrying out activities with such potentially high impact. The Pew Charitable Trust, for example, recently created the Pew Center on Global Climate Change to study global warming, educate the public, and coordinate international negotiations.

Despite cutbacks in government funding for social programs, foundations can still create enormous value by advancing the state of knowledge and practice in the social sector. Unfortunately, too few take this path.

Foundations Need Strategy

In practice, the four approaches to creating value—selecting grantees, signaling others, improving the performance of nonprofits, and creating and disseminating new ideas—are mutually reinforcing, and their benefits are cumulative. The more foundations are able to improve the performance of social enterprises, create new knowledge, and influence larger public and private sector efforts, the greater will be their impact.

But the ability to create value in any of these four ways requires a real strategy. Unfortunately, the word "strategy" has been so overused in the foundation world that it has become almost meaningless. "Strategic giving" now refers to almost any grant made with some purpose in mind. Rarely does a foundation's strategy serve—as it does in business—as a definition of its distinctiveness and a discipline that dictates every aspect of the organization's operations.

In business, a company's strategy lays out how it will create value for its customers by serving a specific set of needs better than any of its competitors. A company must either produce equivalent value at a lower cost than rivals or produce greater value for comparable cost. It can do so only if it stakes out a unique positioning or a distinctive way of competing that is tailored to the kind of value it has chosen to deliver. (To learn more about the fundamentals of strategy, see Michael E. Porter, "What Is Strategy?" HBR November–December 1996.)

The goals of philanthropy may be different, but the underlying logic of strategy is still the same. Instead of competing in markets, foundations are in the business of contributing to society by using scarce philanthropic resources to their maximum potential. A foundation creates value when it achieves an equivalent social benefit with fewer dollars or creates greater social benefit for comparable cost.

In both cases—business and philanthropy—strategy means embracing the following principles:

I. THE GOAL IS SUPERIOR PERFORMANCE IN A CHOSEN ARENA

For a foundation to achieve superior performance, its activities, investments, and grants, taken together, would achieve greater social impact per dollar expended than any other organization tackling the same objective. Aiming for superior performance is not a matter of self-aggrandizement or zero-sum competition among foundations. It is the best way for foundations to raise their overall contribution to society.

In practice, of course, precise, apples-to-apples measures of peer performance among foundations are hard to come by. But that doesn't mean that foundations should abandon the goal of superior performance. At the very least, a foundation can measure its own performance over time, challenging itself to continual improvement. The Ewing Marion Kauffman Foundation, for example, has taken the reduction in high school dropout rates as a primary objective of its Youth Development division. Over ten years of constant experimentation and careful evaluation, the Kauffman Foundation has fundamentally changed its approach because it has learned that community partnerships and the attention of caring adults is more powerful than direct educational reform. As a result, it has been able to redirect its funding to achieve greater results with the same dollars and to demonstrate superior performance.

A foundation should also measure its own success by the performance of the organizations that it funds. This view is not widely held today. However, because grant-making foundations can create value only through others, they must accept responsibility for the success or failure of their grantees. For a foundation to be successful, its roster of grantees, taken as a group, should perform consistently better than average. Of course, not every grant will succeed—progress usually requires taking calculated risks. But superior social performance per dollar of funding should be the aim.

As a starting point, it is important that foundations accept the legitimacy of the goal of superior performance. Then they must be committed to measuring results and acting on what they learn.

2. STRATEGY DEPENDS ON CHOOSING A UNIQUE POSITIONING

No organization can achieve superior performance if it tries to be all things to all people. The starting point for strategy is to limit the number of social challenges the foundation addresses. A foundation must determine where it will make its impact and how.

Consider the Avina Foundation, created in 1993 by the Swiss philanthropist Stephan Schmidheiny. Avina works in the environmental field—that is where it seeks to have its impact. However, limiting grants to one or two fields is not the same as having a strategy. Within the broad category of environmental work, Avina pursues a more pointed target: sustainable development in Latin America. Of all the ways to foster sustainable development, Avina has chosen to promote environmentally friendly business practices. Avina is thus very clear about both dimensions of positioning—where it will make its impact and how.

Because the most effective philanthropy is driven by motivated, knowledgeable, and passionate people working on issues they care about, choosing the right positioning involves understanding the foundation's culture—its values, history, and often the priorities of its original donor or current trustees. Ultimately, positioning revolves around asking the question, How can our foundation create the greatest value, given everything we know about our foundation's culture, passions, expertise, and resources, about what other funders have done or are doing, and about the problems we wish to address?

Consider again the Charles and Helen Schwab Foundation, which is positioned to strengthen the organizational capacity and management of human-service and family-service organizations. This choice of how to make an impact was influenced by the trustees' appreciation of the importance of sound management, but even more by staff investigation within the field, which showed that very few funders provide this kind of support. Positioning thus reflects both personal values and a realistic assessment of opportunities, strengths, and weaknesses.

3. STRATEGY RESTS ON UNIQUE ACTIVITIES

Every major activity of the foundation—its selection process; the size, mix, and duration of its grants; the composition and roles of its staff and board; the types of nonmonetary support it provides grantees; and its evaluation and reporting procedures—must then be tailored to its positioning.

In the field of education, the Philanthropic Ventures Foundation in Oakland, California, for example, focuses on grassroots funding. In 1995, PVF created the Teacher Resource Grants program. Working within the large field of education, PVF chose a specialized positioning appropriate to its small size. PVF provides inexpensive but badly needed classroom materials to teachers in its region—materials that are useless if they don't arrive quickly, when the teacher needs them.

PVF notified more than 6,000 teachers that grants of up to $1,500 would be available for classroom materials, field trips, or teacher training courses. (After a year of experience, PVF lowered the ceiling to $500 per grant.) Teachers refer to the program as the "faxgrant program" because the foundation takes requests by fax, and then sends an answer within one hour of receipt and a check within 24 hours.

Since its positioning is to help under-resourced teachers and it makes thousands of small grants, the Philanthropic Ventures Foundation developed a no-paperwork rule, freeing teachers from time-consuming grant applications. PVF finds that an elaborate process around the receipt, investigation, consideration, and funding of grant requests is not necessary in its chosen area.

PVF is a perfect example of a foundation that tailored its activities to create value. Only by doing things differently from others, in a way that is linked tightly to what the foundation seeks to accomplish, can it achieve greater impact with the same grant dollars or enable its grantees to be more successful. Tailoring activities to strategy is the way a foundation institutionalizes and reinforces its distinctive strengths.

4. EVERY POSITIONING REQUIRES TRADE-OFFS

To achieve excellence at what it does, a foundation must forgo opportunities in other approaches and in other fields. Deciding what not to do is the acid test of whether a foundation (or any organization, for that matter) has a strategy.

For the Philanthropic Ventures Foundation, that means saying no to many interesting opportunities in education. It means saying no to large concentrated grants or multiyear initiatives that might create model programs, train teachers differently, or even affect public policy. Such grants would require not only a different allocation of funds but also different staffing and a different operating model geared toward research and deliberation. The point is not that one goal is more worthy than another; it is that positioning requires trade-offs.

This aspect of strategy is particularly difficult for foundations. So many organizations clamor for their help, every grant seems to do some good, and there is so little accountability for results. It is hard to resist the pressure to oblige a trustee or a colleague. Even foundations that start out in one field find themselves drawn into many others. But if superior performance is the goal, making trade-offs is essential.

The State of Current Practice

There has been no comprehensive study documenting foundation practices or the effectiveness of foundation giving. However, available data paint a picture that is far from the approach we are advocating. Strategy demands focus, yet foundations generally spread their resources—both money and people—too thin. A fragmented pattern of giving and the constant pressure of responding to individual grant requests leaves little time for developing expertise, assisting grantees, or examining social problems in depth. Staff members are frequently trapped by the tyranny of the grant cycle, with barely the time to write up pending grant requests between board meetings. (See figure 12.2.)

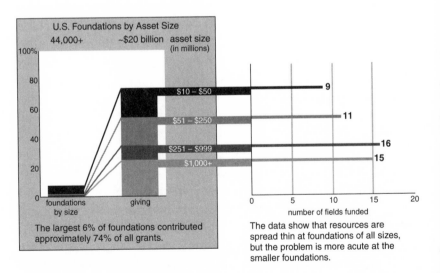

Figure 12.2 Resources are scattered . . . across too many fields . . . across staffs spread too thin . . . across too many small grants.

The average foundation, for example, makes grants in ten unrelated fields every year, where fields are such broadly defined areas as education and health care. Fewer than 9% of foundations make 75% or more of their grants in a single field, and only 5% focus more than 90% of their grants in one field. Such scattered giving is inconsistent with a clear strategic positioning.

Nor do the data suggest that many foundations are taking advantage of their unique ways to create value. Among the largest foundations, with assets in excess of $1 billion, each professional employee handles approximately seven grants per year (and up to 100 times as many grant requests). There are, on average, just three professional employees for every field in which the foundation makes grants. Staff at the largest foundations may well have sufficient time and expertise to evaluate grants, but it is hard to see how even the most dedicated staff could have much time to assist grantees. The smaller the foundation, the more stretched the staff. Among the hundreds of foundations with $50 million to $250 million in assets, there are five times as many grants per professional, and an average of two staff members handle grants in 11 unrelated fields. The smallest foundations often rely on the volunteer efforts of trustees, making it almost certain that many decisions are reached with little formal evaluation at all.

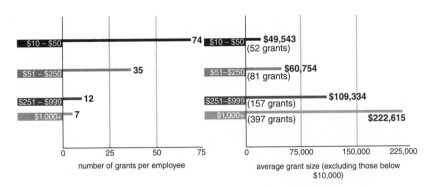

Source: The Foundation Center, based on a sample of 1,000 foundations giving at least $1 million in 1997 and excluding grants below $10,000.

Figure 12.2 Continued

Those broad metrics also suggest that foundations are not using the more powerful forms of value creation beyond selection. Foundations rarely contribute resources other than financial support. Only 2.2% of foundation grants were designated to improve the grantees' performance. Ninety-five percent of all foundation grants are for one year. Although one-year grants are sometimes awarded for several years in a row, there is little evidence that foundations exploit the opportunity to work more closely with grantees over extended periods of time to improve their performance. Foundations, which should be able to take the long view, tend to focus on grant making quarter-to-quarter.

Finally, while foundations express a strong interest in innovation and advancing the state of knowledge about society's problems, very few fund studies that explore the relative effectiveness of different approaches to a given problem. Only 8.8% of foundation grants went to research, and most of that was in basic medical and scientific areas. Funding studies or data collection is rare, and foundations generally see them as less desirable than current social services.

Instead of funding research, many foundations seek to promote innovation through seed grants that are designed to establish and support specific new programs. There is little benefit, however, in starting new initiatives if they do not survive and grow. Too often foundations overlook projects aimed at fostering the growth and replication of new initiatives, or they fail to support the grantee over an appropriately long time span. They rarely do the up-front research and the postevaluation needed to ascertain if their programs have been successful and have continued to thrive after the initial period of seed grant support.

In some ways, however, the overall failure to evaluate the results of foundation grants is the most telling danger sign of all. Almost no money is set aside for program evaluation. Many foundations are ambivalent about whether funds should be spent on evaluation and whether assessing the performance of past grants can improve future grant making. This ambivalence about evaluation is reinforced by the performance criteria used to judge foundation staff. These tend to emphasize the paper trail of pregrant analysis and recommendations and give little credit for achieving the real-world results that motivated the grant in the first place. Program evaluation, therefore, has only a downside: failure risks censure, but success adds no reward.

The evaluations that do take place are often problematic in three ways. First, they are limited to reports as to whether the money was spent as intended (*output* evaluation); they do not attempt to measure social impact (*outcome* evaluation). Second, many of the evaluations are done by the grant recipients themselves, who invariably seek further support from the foundation. How objective and reliable are these reports likely to be? Third, even in the few cases where the social impact of a program is measured by an outside consultant, it is usually assessed at the single grantee level, in isolation from the foundation's other grants. Therefore, it does not reflect the foundation's success in reaching its overall goals.

Certainly, evaluation may at times be costly and complex. But given clear goals at the outset, it is always possible. The criteria to evaluate a job-training program will differ from those used to evaluate a funding program for young artists. But meaningful criteria can be established for both.

Consider the San Francisco-based Roberts Enterprise Development Fund, which focuses on creating employment for the homeless and indigent. Working closely with its grantee Rubicon Programs, REDF developed 25 criteria that not only measure the success of job-training programs but also help Rubicon to manage the programs more effectively. In addition to the most obvious criteria—changes in employment stability, wages, and job skills—REDF and Rubicon found that related factors such as substance abuse and even qualitative factors such as the trainees' own assessments of their success in reaching personal goals were all meaningful measures of outcomes the program was trying to achieve.

Without evaluation, a foundation will never know whether or not it has been successful. The most basic premise of strategy—striving for superior performance—is violated if performance is not measured.

Addressing the New Agenda

How can foundations begin down the path we have outlined? A number of foundations, including those operating under the new rubric of venture philanthropy, are already moving in the direction outlined here. But none that we have encountered has gone all the way. Putting these elements together into a coherent whole will require developing a strategy, aligning operations with that strategy, and revising the foundation's governance so that the strategy can be monitored effectively. Responsibility for such change lies ultimately with the trustees and directors, who are the fiduciaries accountable for the use of the foundation's (and society's) funds.

To develop a strategy, the place to start is positioning. This always requires systematic thought and research into important social challenges that are not being addressed well by others. The goal is not necessarily to identify the most important problem, since many are important. What matters is how effectively the foundation can contribute to its solution.

Second, a foundation can learn from prior efforts within its chosen area of funding. Do current socioeconomic trends favor one approach over another? What are other organizations doing in the field? Can the work of this foundation reinforce or complement theirs? Can we uncover root causes of the problem?

Third, what unique strengths will enable this foundation to create value most effectively in its field? Part of the answer to this question comes from examining objectively where the foundation has made the greatest impact in the past. It also comes from a realistic assessment of weaknesses.

Scale plays an important role in the choice of strategy. A foundation needs enough resources to pursue its particular way of creating value. Larger foundations may well have the scale to work in more than one field. If they choose to do so, each area must have its own strategy and tailored operations. All foundations, however, can create more value by putting a greater proportion of their resources to work. This means stepping up the rate of giving in their chosen fields and investing a portion of their investment portfolios to support their philanthropic work.

Once the foundation has chosen a strategy, it can begin to realign its operations. A foundation, like any enterprise, is a collection of many activities. Each activity—how proposals are solicited, for example, and how grantees are supported—must be tailored to the chosen strategy.

A particularly important aspect of operational alignment is the development of measures to help the foundation know whether or not it has been successful.

Operating strategically will require most foundations to rethink their governance systems. Change will be difficult in an environment where the pressure of processing grants and getting the money out the door extends beyond the staff to the boardroom. Today boards of all but the very largest foundations discuss and approve specific grant allocations at their meetings. Without goals or strategy, they have no way to delegate the grant selection process to staff and no framework through which to evaluate their experience. The Chicago-based Crown Foundation, in an effort to break this cycle, considers grant requests at only two of its quarterly board meetings each year; the other two are reserved for discussing policy, reviewing performance, and studying issues in more depth. Boards need to move away from the operating function of approving grants to focus on setting strategy and evaluating outcomes.

With goals, a strategy, and evaluation mechanisms in place, staff could have greater independence to make grant decisions themselves on a more timely and flexible basis. At the Colorado Trust, the board considers and approves multiyear, multimillion-dollar initiatives that have clearly defined goals and a clearly articulated strategy. Once the board sets the framework, program staff has the authority to make individual grants for the life of the initiative. Staff members, then, have greater responsibility and more freedom to make decisions on individual grants, and the board has the time to study the field, set overall strategies, and assess staff performance.

For those who care deeply about social problems and work tirelessly to make a difference, current foundation practices not only diminish effectiveness, they inevitably reduce the satisfaction that donors, staff, and trustees derive from their work. Scattered funding, arm's-length relationships with grantees, and a lack of awareness of outcomes necessarily create a divide between the foundation and the ultimate results of its work. Acting strategically is much more difficult. But for trustees and staff alike, it will be far more rewarding as well.

Improving the performance of philanthropy would enable foundations to have a much greater impact on society. Foundations could play a leading role in changing the culture of social sector management. They could spearhead the evolution of philanthropy from private acts of conscience into a professional field. Until foundations accept their accountability to society and meet their obligation to create value, they exist in a world where they cannot fail. Unfortunately, they also cannot truly succeed.

CHAPTER 13

The Competitive Advantage of Corporate Philanthropy

Michael E. Porter

Mark R. Kramer

CORPORATE PHILANTHROPY IS in decline. Charitable contributions by U.S. companies fell 14.5% in real dollars last year, and over the last 15 years, corporate giving as a percentage of profits has dropped by 50%. The reasons are not hard to understand. Executives increasingly see themselves in a no-win situation, caught between critics demanding ever higher levels of "corporate social responsibility" and investors applying relentless pressure to maximize short-term profits. Giving more does not satisfy the critics—the more companies donate, the more is expected of them. And executives find it hard, if not impossible, to justify charitable expenditures in terms of bottom-line benefit.

This dilemma has led many companies to seek to be more strategic in their philanthropy. But what passes for "strategic philanthropy" today is almost never truly strategic, and often it isn't even particularly effective as philanthropy. Increasingly, philanthropy is used as a form of public relations or advertising, promoting a company's image or brand through cause-related marketing or other high-profile sponsorships. Although it still represents only a small proportion of overall corporate charitable expenditures, U.S. corporate spending on cause-related marketing jumped from $125 million in 1990 to an estimated $828 million in 2002. Arts sponsorships are growing, too—they accounted for an additional $589 million in 2001. While these campaigns do provide much-needed support to worthy causes, they are intended as much to

December 2002

increase company visibility and improve employee morale as to create social impact. Tobacco giant Philip Morris, for example, spent $75 million on its charitable contributions in 1999 and then launched a $100 million advertising campaign to publicize them. Not surprisingly, there are genuine doubts about whether such approaches actually work or just breed public cynicism about company motives. (See the insert "The Myth of Strategic Philanthropy.")

The Myth of Strategic Philanthropy

Few phrases are as overused and poorly defined as "strategic philanthropy." The term is used to cover virtually any kind of charitable activity that has some definable theme, goal, approach, or focus. In the corporate context, it generally means that there is some connection, however vague or tenuous, between the charitable contribution and the company's business. Often this connection is only semantic, enabling the company to rationalize its contributions in public reports and press releases. In fact, most corporate giving programs have nothing to do with a company's strategy. They are primarily aimed at generating goodwill and positive publicity and boosting employee morale.

Cause-related marketing, through which a company concentrates its giving on a single cause or admired organization, was one of the earliest practices cited as "strategic philanthropy," and it is a step above diffuse corporate contributions. At its most sophisticated, cause-related marketing can improve the reputation of a company by linking its identity with the admired qualities of a chosen nonprofit partner or a popular cause. Companies that sponsor the Olympics, for example, gain not only wide exposure but also an association with the pursuit of excellence. And by concentrating funding through a deliberate selection process, cause-related marketing has the potential to create more impact than unfocused giving would provide.

However, cause-related marketing falls far short of truly strategic philanthropy. Its emphasis remains on publicity rather than social impact. The desired benefit is enhanced goodwill, not improvement in a company's ability to compete. True strategic giving, by contrast, addresses important social and economic goals simultaneously, targeting areas of competitive context where the company and society both benefit because the firm brings unique assets and expertise.

Given the current haziness surrounding corporate philanthropy, this seems an appropriate time to revisit the most basic of questions: Should corporations engage in philanthropy at all? The economist Milton Friedman laid down the gauntlet decades ago, arguing in a 1970 *New York Times Magazine* article that the only "social responsibility of business" is to "increase its profits." "The corporation," he wrote in his book *Capitalism and Freedom*, "is an instrument of the stockholders who own it. If the corporation makes a contribution, it prevents the individual stockholder from himself deciding how he should dispose of his funds." If charitable contributions are to be made, Friedman concluded, they should be made by individual stockholders—or, by extension, individual employees—and not by the corporation.

The way most corporate philanthropy is practiced today, Friedman is right. The majority of corporate contribution programs are diffuse and unfocused. Most consist of numerous small cash donations given to aid local civic causes or provide general operating support to universities and national charities in the hope of generating goodwill among employees, customers, and the local community. Rather than being tied to well-thought-out social or business objectives, the contributions often reflect the personal beliefs and values of executives or employees. Indeed, one of the most popular approaches—employee matching grants—explicitly leaves the choice of charity to the individual worker. Although aimed at enhancing morale, the same effect might be gained from an equal increase in wages that employees could then choose to donate to charity on a tax-deductible basis. It does indeed seem that many of the giving decisions companies make today would be better made by individuals donating their own money.

What about the programs that are at least superficially tied to business goals, such as cause-related marketing? Even the successful ones are hard to justify as charitable initiatives. Since all reasonable corporate expenditures are deductible, companies get no special tax advantage for spending on philanthropy as opposed to other corporate purposes. If cause-related marketing is good marketing, it is already deductible and does not benefit from being designated as charitable.

But does Friedman's argument always hold? Underlying it are two implicit assumptions. The first is that social and economic objectives are separate and distinct, so that a corporation's social spending comes at the expense of its economic results. The second is the assumption that corporations, when they address social objectives, provide no greater benefit than is provided by individual donors.

These assumptions hold true when corporate contributions are unfocused and piecemeal, as is typically the case today. But there is another, more truly strategic way to think about philanthropy. Corporations can use their charitable efforts to improve their *competitive context*—the quality of the business environment in the location or locations where they operate. Using philanthropy to enhance context brings social and economic goals into alignment and improves a company's long-term business prospects—thus contradicting Friedman's first assumption. In addition, addressing context enables a company not only to give money but also to leverage its capabilities and relationships in support of charitable causes. That produces social benefits far exceeding those provided by individual donors, foundations, or even governments. Context-focused giving thus contradicts Friedman's second assumption as well.

A handful of companies have begun to use context-focused philanthropy to achieve both social and economic gains. Cisco Systems, to take one example, has invested in an ambitious educational program— the Cisco Networking Academy—to train computer network administrators, thus alleviating a potential constraint on its growth while providing attractive job opportunities to high school graduates. By focusing on social needs that affect its corporate context and utilizing its unique attributes as a corporation to address them, Cisco has begun to demonstrate the unrealized potential of corporate philanthropy. Taking this new direction, however, requires fundamental changes in the way companies approach their contribution programs. Corporations need to rethink both *where* they focus their philanthropy and *how* they go about their giving.

Where to Focus

It is true that economic and social objectives have long been seen as distinct and often competing. But this is a false dichotomy; it represents an increasingly obsolete perspective in a world of open, knowledge-based competition. Companies do not function in isolation from the society around them. In fact, their ability to compete depends heavily on the circumstances of the locations where they operate. Improving education, for example, is generally seen as a social issue, but the educational level of the local workforce substantially affects a company's potential competitiveness. The more a social improvement relates to a company's business, the more it leads to economic benefits as well. In establishing its Networking Academy, for example, Cisco focused not on the educational system overall, but on the training needed to produce network administrators—the particular kind of education that made the most difference to Cisco's competitive context. (For a more detailed look at that program, see the insert "The Cisco Networking Academy.")

The Cisco Networking Academy

Cisco Systems' Networking Academy exemplifies the powerful links that exist between a company's philanthropic strategy, its competitive context, and social benefits. Cisco, the leading producer of networking equipment and routers used to connect computers to the Internet, grew rapidly over the past decade. But as Internet use expanded, customers around the world encountered a chronic shortage of qualified network administrators, which became a limiting factor in Cisco's—and the entire IT industry's—continued growth. By one estimate, well over 1 million information technology jobs remained unfilled worldwide in the late 1990s. While Cisco was well aware of this constraint in its competitive context, it was only through philanthropy that the company found a way to address it.

The project began as a typical example of goodwill-based giving: Cisco contributed networking equipment to a high school near its headquarters, then expanded the program to other schools in the region. A Cisco engineer working with the schools realized, however, that the teachers and administrators lacked the training to manage the networks once they were installed. He and several other Cisco engineers volunteered to develop a program that would not only donate equipment but also train teachers how to build, design, and maintain computer networks. Students began attending these courses and were able to absorb the information successfully. As Cisco expanded the program, company executives began to realize that they could develop a Web-based distance-learning curriculum to train and certify secondary- and postsecondary-school students in network administration, a program that might have a much broader social and economic impact. The Networking Academy was born.

Because the social goal of the program was tightly linked to Cisco's specialized expertise, the company was able to create a high-quality curriculum rapidly and cost-effectively, creating far more social and economic value than if it had merely contributed cash and equipment to a worthy cause. At the suggestion of the U.S. Department of Education, the company began to target schools in "empowerment zones," designated by the federal government as among the most economically challenged communities in the country. The company also began to include community colleges and midcareer training in the program. More recently, it has worked with the United Nations to expand the effort to developing countries, where job opportunities are particularly scarce and networking skills particularly limited. Cisco has also organized a worldwide database of employment opportunities for academy graduates, creating a more efficient job market that benefits its cluster as well as the graduates and the regions in which they live.

Cisco has used its unique assets and expertise, along with its worldwide presence, to create a program that no other educational institution, government agency, foundation, or

corporate donor could have designed as well or expanded as rapidly. And it has amplified the impact by signaling other corporations in its cluster. Other companies supplemented Cisco's contributions by donating or discounting products and services of their own, such as Internet access and computer hardware and software. Several leading technology companies also began to recognize the value of the global infrastructure Cisco had created, and, rather than create their own Web-based learning programs, they partnered with Cisco. Companies such as Sun Microsystems, Hewlett-Packard, Adobe Systems, and Panduit expanded the academy curriculum by sponsoring courses in programming, IT essentials, Web design, and cabling. Because the project was linked to Cisco's business, it could gain the support of other companies in its cluster and use their contributions effectively.

Although the program is only five years old, it now operates 9,900 academies in secondary schools, community colleges, and community-based organizations in all 50 states and in 147 countries. The social and economic value that has been created is enormous. Cisco estimates that it has invested a total of $150 million since the program began. With that investment, it has brought the possibility of technology careers, and the technology itself, to men and women in some of the most economically depressed regions in the United States and around the world. More than 115,000 students have already-graduated from the two-year program, and 263,000 students are currently enrolled, half of them outside the United States. The program continues to expand rapidly, with 50 to 100 new academies opening every week. Cisco estimates that 50% of academy graduates have found jobs in the IT industry, where the average salary for a network administrator in the United States is $67,000. Over the span of their careers, the incremental earnings potential of those who have already joined the workforce may approach several billion dollars.

To be sure, the program has benefited many free riders—employers around the world who gain access to highly skilled academy graduates and even direct competitors. But as the market-leading provider of routers, Cisco stands to benefit the most from this improvement in the competitive context. Through actively engaging others, Cisco has not had to bear the full cost of the program. Not only has Cisco enlarged its market and strengthened its cluster, but it has increased the sophistication of its customers. Through these tangible improvements in competitive context, and not just by the act of giving, Cisco has attracted international recognition for this program, generating justified pride and enthusiasm among company employees, goodwill among its partners, and a reputation for leadership in philanthropy.

In the long run, then, social and economic goals are not inherently conflicting but integrally connected. Competitiveness today depends on the productivity with which companies can use labor, capital, and natural resources to produce high-quality goods and services. Productivity depends on having workers who are educated, safe, healthy, decently housed, and motivated by a sense of opportunity. Preserving the environment benefits not only society but companies too, because reducing pollution and waste can lead to a more productive use of resources and help produce goods that consumers value. Boosting social and economic conditions in developing countries can create more productive locations for a company's operations as well as new markets for its products. Indeed, we are learning that the most effective method of addressing many of the world's pressing problems is often to mobilize the corporate sector in ways that benefit both society and companies.

That does not mean that every corporate expenditure will bring a social benefit or that every social benefit will improve competitiveness. Most corporate expenditures produce benefits only for the business, and charitable contributions unrelated to the business generate only social benefits. It is only where corporate expenditures produce simultaneous social and economic gains that corporate philanthropy and shareholder interests converge, as illustrated in figure 13.1. The highlighted area shows where corporate philanthropy has an important influence on a company's competitive context. It is here that philanthropy is truly strategic.

Competitive context has always been important to strategy. The availability of skilled and motivated employees; the efficiency of the local infrastructure, including roads and telecommunications; the size and sophistication of the local market; the extent of governmental regulations—such contextual variables have always influenced companies' ability to compete. But competitive context has become even more critical as the basis of competition has moved from cheap inputs to superior productivity. For one thing, modern knowledge- and technology-

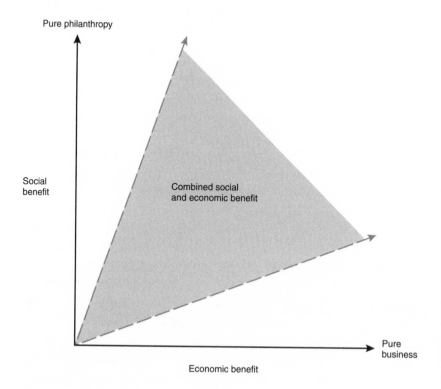

Figure 13.1   A Convergence of Interests

based competition hinges more and more on worker capabilities. For another, companies today depend more on local partnerships: They rely on outsourcing and collaboration with local suppliers and institutions rather than on vertical integration; they work more closely with customers; and they draw more on local universities and research institutes to conduct research and development. Finally, navigating increasingly complex local regulations and reducing approval times for new projects and products are becoming increasingly important to competition. As a result of these trends, companies' success has become more tightly intertwined with local institutions and other contextual conditions. And the globalization of production and marketing means that context is often important for a company not just in its home market but in multiple countries.

A company's competitive context consists of four interrelated elements of the local business environment that shape potential productivity: factor conditions, or the available inputs of production; demand conditions; the context for strategy and rivalry; and related and supporting industries. This framework is summarized in figure 13.2 and described in detail in Michael E. Porter's *The Competitive Advantage of Nations*. Weakness in any part of this context can erode the competitiveness of a nation or region as a business location.

Some aspects of the business environment, such as road systems, corporate tax rates, and corporation laws, have effects that cut across all industries. These general conditions can be crucial to competitiveness in developing countries, and improving them through corporate philanthropy can bring enormous social gains to the world's poorest nations. But often just as decisive, if not more, are aspects of context that are specific to a particular *cluster*—a geographic concentration of interconnected companies, suppliers, related industries, and specialized institutions in a particular field, such as high-performance cars in Germany or software in India. Clusters arise through the combined influence of all four elements of context. They are often prominent features of a region's economic landscape, and building them is essential to its development, allowing constituent firms to be more productive, making innovation easier, and fostering the formation of new businesses.

Philanthropic investments by members of a cluster, either individually or collectively, can have a powerful effect on the cluster's competitiveness and the performance of all of its constituent companies.

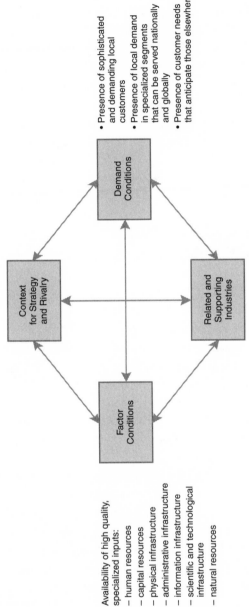

Figure 13.2 The Four Elements of Competitive Context

Philanthropy can often be the most cost-effective way—and sometimes the only way—to improve competitive context. It enables companies to leverage not only their own resources but also the existing efforts and infrastructure of nonprofits and other institutions. Contributing to a university, for example, may be a far less expensive way to strengthen a local base of advanced skills in a company's field than developing training in-house. And philanthropy is amenable to collective corporate action, enabling costs to be spread over multiple companies. Finally, because of philanthropy's wide social benefits, companies are often able to forge partnerships with nonprofit organizations and governments that would be wary of collaborating on efforts that solely benefited a particular company.

Influencing Competitive Context

By carefully analyzing the elements of competitive context, a company can identify the areas of overlap between social and economic value that will most enhance its own and its cluster's competitiveness. Consider each of the four elements of context and how companies have influenced them through philanthropy in ways that have improved their long-term economic prospects.

FACTOR CONDITIONS

Achieving high levels of productivity depends on the presence of trained workers, high-quality scientific and technological institutions, adequate physical infrastructure, transparent and efficient administrative processes (such as company registration or permit requirements), and available natural resources. All are areas that philanthropy can influence.

Charitable giving can, for example, improve education and training. DreamWorks SKG, the film production company, recently created a program to train low-income students in Los Angeles in skills needed to work in the entertainment industry. Each of the company's six divisions is working with the Los Angeles Community College District, local high schools, and after-school programs to create a specialized curriculum that combines classroom instruction with internships and mentoring. The social benefit is an improved educational system and better employment opportunities for low-income residents. The economic benefit is greater availability of specially trained graduates. Even though relatively few of them will join DreamWorks itself, the company also gains by strengthening the entertainment cluster it depends on.

Philanthropic initiatives can also improve the local quality of life, which benefits all citizens but is increasingly necessary to attract mobile employees with specialized talents. In 1996, SC Johnson, a manufacturer of cleaning and home-storage products, launched "Sustainable Racine," a project to make its home city in Wisconsin a better place in which to live and work. In partnership with local organizations, government, and residents, the company created a communitywide coalition focused on enhancing the local economy and the environment. One project, an agreement among four municipalities to coordinate water and sewer treatment, resulted in savings for residents and businesses while reducing pollution. Another project involved opening the community's first charter school, targeting at-risk students. Other efforts focused on economic revitalization: Commercial vacancy rates in downtown Racine have fallen from 46% to 18% as polluted sites have been reclaimed and jobs have returned for local residents.

Philanthropy can also improve inputs other than labor, through enhancements in, say, the quality of local research and development institutions, the effectiveness of administrative institutions such as the legal system, the quality of the physical infrastructure, or the sustainable development of natural resources. Exxon Mobil, for example, has devoted substantial resources to improving basic conditions such as roads and the rule of law in the developing countries where it operates.

DEMAND CONDITIONS

Demand conditions in a nation or region include the size of the local market, the appropriateness of product standards, and the sophistication of local customers. Sophisticated local customers enhance the region's competitiveness by providing companies with insight into emerging customer needs and applying pressure for innovation. For example, the advanced state of medical practice in Boston has triggered a stream of innovation in Boston-based medical device companies.

Philanthropy can influence both the size and quality of the local market. The Cisco Networking Academy, for instance, improved demand conditions by helping customers obtain well-trained network administrators. In doing so, it increased the size of the market and the sophistication of users—and hence users' interest in more advanced solutions. Apple Computer has long donated computers to schools as a means of introducing its products to young people. This provides a clear social benefit to the schools while expanding Apple's potential market and turning students and teachers into more sophisticated purchasers. Safeco, an insurance and financial services firm, is working in partnership with nonprofits to expand affordable housing and enhance public safety. As home ownership and public safety increased in its four test markets, insurance sales did too, in some cases by up to 40%.

CONTEXT FOR STRATEGY AND RIVALRY

The rules, incentives, and norms governing competition in a nation or region have a fundamental influence on productivity. Policies that encourage investment, protect intellectual property, open local markets to trade, break up or prevent the formation of cartels and monopolies, and reduce corruption make a location a more attractive place to do business.

Philanthropy can have a strong influence on creating a more productive and transparent environment for competition. For example, 26 U.S. corporations and 38 corporations from other countries have joined to support Transparency International in its work to disclose and deter corruption around the world. By measuring and focusing public attention on corruption, the organization helps to create an environment that rewards fair competition and enhances productivity. This benefits local citizens while providing sponsoring companies improved access to markets.

Another example is the International Corporate Governance Network (ICGN), a nonprofit organization formed by major institutional investors, including the College Retirement Equities Fund (TIAA-CREF) and the California Public Employees Retirement System, known as CalPERS, to promote improved standards of corporate governance and disclosure, especially in developing countries. ICGN encourages uniform global accounting standards and equitable shareholder voting procedures. Developing countries and their citizens benefit as improved governance and disclosure enhance local corporate practices, expose unscrupulous local competitors, and make regions more attractive for foreign investment. The institutional investors that support this project also gain better and fairer capital markets in which to invest.

RELATED AND SUPPORTING INDUSTRIES

A company's productivity can be greatly enhanced by having high-quality supporting industries and services nearby. While outsourcing from distant suppliers is possible, it is not as efficient as using capable local suppliers of services, components, and machinery. Proximity enhances responsiveness, exchange of information, and innovation, in addition to lowering transportation and inventory costs.

Philanthropy can foster the development of clusters and strengthen supporting industries. American Express, for example, depends on travel-related spending for a large share of its credit card and travel agency revenues. Hence, it is part of the travel cluster in each of the countries in which it operates, and it depends on the success of these clusters in improving the quality of tourism and attracting travelers. Since 1986, American Express has funded Travel and Tourism Academies in secondary schools, training students not for the credit card business, its core business, nor for its own travel services, but for careers in other travel agencies as well as airlines, hotels, and restaurants. The program, which includes teacher training, curriculum support, summer internships, and industry mentors, now operates in ten countries and more than 3,000 schools, with more than 120,000 students enrolled. It provides the major social benefits of improved educational and job opportunities for local citizens. Within the United States, 80% of students in the program go on to college, and 25% take jobs in the travel industry after graduation. The economic gains are also substantial, as local travel clusters become more competitive and better able to grow. That translates into important benefits for American Express.

The Free Rider Problem

When corporate philanthropy improves competitive context, other companies in the cluster or region, including direct competitors, often share the benefits. That raises an important question: Does the ability of other companies to be free riders negate the strategic value of context-focused philanthropy? The answer is *no*. The competitive benefits reaped by the donor company remain substantial, for five reasons:

- Improving context mainly benefits companies based in a given location. Not all competitors will be based in the same area, so the company will still gain an edge over the competition in general.

- Corporate philanthropy is ripe for collective activity. By sharing the costs with other companies in its cluster, including competitors, a company can greatly diminish the free rider problem.

- Leading companies will be best positioned to make substantial contributions and will in turn reap a major share of the benefits. Cisco, for example, with a leading market share in networking equipment, will benefit most from a larger, more rapidly growing market.

- Not all contextual advantages are of equal value to all competitors. The more tightly corporate philanthropy is aligned with a company's unique strategy—increasing skills, technology, or infrastructure on which the firm is especially reliant, say, or increasing demand within a specialized segment where the company is strongest—the more disproportionately the company will benefit through enhancing the context.

- The company that initiates corporate philanthropy in a particular area will often get disproportionate benefits because of the superior reputation and relationships it builds. In its campaign to fight malaria in African countries, for example, Exxon Mobil not only improves public health. It also improves the health of its workers and contractors and builds strong relationships with local governments and nonprofits, advancing its goal of becoming the preferred resource-development partner.

A good example of how a company can gain an edge even when its contributions also benefit competitors is provided by Grand Circle Travel. Grand Circle, the leading direct marketer of international travel for older Americans, has a strategy based on offering rich cultural and educational experiences for its customers. Since 1992, its corporate foundation has given more than $12 million to historical preservation projects in locations that its customers like to visit, such as the Foundation of Friends of the Museum and Ruins of Ephesus in Turkey and the State Museum of Auschwitz-Birkenau in Poland. Other tours travel the same routes and so benefit from Grand Circle's donations. Through its philanthropy, however, Grand Circle has built close relationships with the organizations that maintain these sites and can provide its travelers with special opportunities to visit and learn about them. Grand Circle thus gains a unique competitive advantage that distinguishes it from other travel providers.

How to Contribute

Understanding the link between philanthropy and competitive context helps companies identify *where* they should focus their corporate giving. Understanding the ways in which philanthropy creates value highlights *how* they can achieve the greatest social and economic impact through their contributions. As we will see, the where and the how are mutually reinforcing.

In "Philanthropy's New Agenda: Creating Value" (HBR November–December 1999), we outlined four ways in which charitable foundations can create social value: selecting the best grantees, signaling other funders, improving the performance of grant recipients, and advancing knowledge and practice in the field. These efforts build on one another: Increasingly greater value is generated as a donor moves up the ladder from selecting the right grantees to advancing knowledge. (See figure 13.3.) The same principles apply to corporate giving, pointing the way to how corporate philanthropy can be most effective in enhancing competitive context. Focusing on the four principles also ensures that corporate donations have greater impact than donations of the same magnitude by individuals.

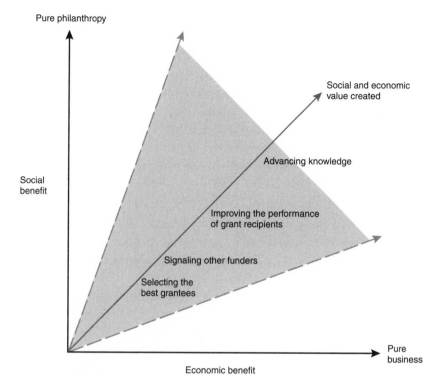

Figure 13.3   Maximizing Philanthropy's Value

SELECTING THE BEST GRANTEES

Most philanthropic activity involves giving money to other organizations that actually deliver the social benefits. The impact achieved by a donor, then, is largely determined by the effectiveness of the recipient. Selecting a more effective grantee or partner organization will lead to more social impact per dollar expended.

Selecting the most effective grantees in a given field is never easy. It may be obvious which nonprofit organizations raise the most money, have the greatest prestige, or manage the best development campaigns, but such factors may have little to do with how well the grantees use contributions. Extensive and disciplined research is usually required to select those recipients that will achieve the greatest social impact.

Individual donors rarely have the time or expertise to undertake such serious due diligence. Foundations are far more expert than individuals, but they have limited staff. Corporations, on the other hand, are well positioned to undertake such research if their philanthropy is connected to their business and they can tap into their internal capabilities, particularly the financial, managerial, and technical expertise of employees. Whether through their own operations or those of their suppliers and customers, corporations also often have a presence in many communities across a country or around the world. This can provide significant local knowledge and the ability to examine and compare the operation of nonprofits firsthand.

In some cases, a company can introduce and support a particularly effective nonprofit organization or program in many of the locations in which it operates. Grand Circle Travel, for example, uses its 15 overseas offices to identify historical preservation projects to fund. FleetBoston Financial assembles teams of employees with diverse management and financial skills to examine the inner-city economic development organizations that its foundation supports. The teams visit each nonprofit, interview management, review policies and procedures, and report to the corporate foundation on whether support should be continued and, if so, where it should be directed. This level of attention and expertise is substantially greater than most individual donors, foundations, or even government agencies can muster.

SIGNALING OTHER FUNDERS

A donor can publicize the most effective nonprofit organizations and promote them to other donors, attracting greater funding and thus creating a more effective allocation of overall philanthropic spending.

Corporations bring uniquely valuable assets to this task. First, their reputations often command respect, becoming imprimaturs of credibility for grantees. Second, they are often able to influence a vast network of entities in their cluster, including customers, suppliers, and other partners. This gives them far greater reach than individual donors or even most nonprofits and foundations. Third, they often have access to communication channels and expertise that can be used to disseminate information widely, swiftly, and persuasively to other donors.

Signaling other funders is especially important in corporate philanthropy because it mitigates the free rider problem. Collective social investment by participants in a cluster can improve the context for all players, while reducing the cost borne by each one. By leveraging its relationships and brand identity to initiate social projects that are also funded by others, a corporation improves the cost-benefit ratio. The Cisco Networking Academy draws support from numerous technology companies in Cisco's cluster as well as educational systems and governments throughout the world, all of which benefit from the graduates' success. American Express's Travel and Tourism Academies depend on the help of more than 750 travel cluster partners who bear part of the cost and reap part of the benefit. Different companies will bring different strengths to a given philanthropic initiative. By tapping each company's distinctive expertise, the collective investment can be far more effective than a donation by any one company.

IMPROVING THE PERFORMANCE OF GRANT RECIPIENTS

By improving the effectiveness of nonprofits, corporations create value for society, increasing the social impact achieved per dollar expended. While selecting the right grantee improves society's return on a single contribution, and signaling other funders improves the return on multiple contributions, improving grantee performance can increase the return on the grantee's total budget.

Unlike many other donors, corporations have the ability to work directly with nonprofits and other partners to help them become more effective. They bring unique assets and expertise that individuals and foundations lack, enabling them to provide a wide range of nonmonetary assistance that is less costly and more sophisticated than the services most grantees could purchase for themselves. And because they typically make long-term commitments to the communities in which they operate, corporations can work closely with local nonprofits over the extended periods of time needed for meaningful organizational improvement. By operating in multiple geographical areas, moreover, companies are able to facilitate the transfer of knowledge and operational improvements among nonprofits in different regions or countries. Contextual issues within a particular industry or cluster will often be similar across different locations, increasing a company's ability to add and derive value in multiple regions.

By tying corporate philanthropy to its business and strategy, a company can create even greater social value in improving grantee performance than other donors. Its specialized assets and expertise, after all, will be most useful in addressing problems related to its particular field. DreamWorks' film production expertise helped it design the educational curriculum necessary to help inner-city students in Los Angeles get jobs in the entertainment industry. The Cisco Networking Academy utilized the special expertise of Cisco employees.

FleetBoston Financial took similar advantage of its corporate expertise in launching its Community Renaissance Initiative. Recognizing that its major markets were in older East Coast cities, Fleet decided to focus on inner-city economic revitalization as perhaps the most important way to improve its context. Fleet combined its philanthropic contributions with its expertise in financial services, such as small business services, inner-city lending, home mortgages, and venture capital. The bank's foundation identified six communities where the bank had a presence, the economic need was great, and strong community-based organizations could be identified as reliable partners: Brooklyn and Buffalo, New York; Lawrence, Massachusetts; New Haven, Connecticut; and Camden and Jersey City, New Jersey. The foundation committed $725,000 to each city, building a coalition of local community, business, and government organizations to work on a set of issues identified by the community as central to its revitalization. Bank personnel provided technical advice and small business financing packages to local companies as well as home mortgages and home-buyer education programs. The foundation also attracted $6 million from private and municipal sources, greatly amplifying its own $4.5 million investment.

Another example is America Online, which has unique capabilities in managing Internet access and content. Working closely with educators, AOL developed AOL@School, a free, easy-to-use, noncommercial site tailored by grade level to students, administrators, and teachers. This service improves the classroom experience for hundreds of thousands of students nationally by giving them access to enrichment and reference tools while providing lesson plans and reference materials for teachers. Through this program, AOL has been able to leverage its specialized expertise, more than just its donations, to assist in improving secondary school performance more rapidly and cost-effectively than could most other organizations. In the process, it has improved both the long-term demand for its services and the talent needed to provide them.

ADVANCING KNOWLEDGE AND PRACTICE

Innovation drives productivity in the nonprofit sector as well as in the commercial sector. The greatest advances come not from incremental improvements in efficiency but from new and better approaches. The most powerful way to create social value, therefore, is by developing new means to address social problems and putting them into widespread practice.

The expertise, research capacity, and reach that companies bring to philanthropy can help nonprofits create new solutions that they could never afford to develop on their own. Since 1994, IBM has committed a total of $70 million to its Reinventing Education program, which now reaches 65,000 teachers and 6 million students. Working in partnership with urban school districts, state education departments, and colleges of education, IBM researched and developed a Web-based platform to support new instructional practices and strategies. The new curriculum is intended to redefine how teachers master their profession; it bridges the gap between teacher preparation and the classroom experience by providing a common platform that is used in the teachers' college courses and also supports their first years of teaching. Neither the colleges of education nor the school districts had the expertise or financial resources to develop such a program on their own. An independent evaluation in 2001 found that teachers in the Reinventing Education program were registering substantial gains in student performance.

Pfizer developed a cost-effective treatment for the prevention of trachoma, the leading cause of preventable blindness in developing countries. In addition to donating the drugs, Pfizer worked with the Edna McConnell Clark Foundation and world health organizations to create the infrastructure needed to prescribe and distribute them to populations that previously had little access to health care, much less modern pharmaceuticals. Within one year, the incidence of trachoma was reduced by 50% among target populations in Morocco and Tanzania. The program has since expanded aggressively, adding the Bill & Melinda Gates Foundation and the British government as partners, with the aim of reaching 30 million people worldwide. In addition to providing an important social benefit, Pfizer has enhanced its own long-term business prospects by helping build the infrastructure required to expand its markets.

Just as important as the creation of new knowledge is its adoption in practice. The know-how of corporate leaders, their clout and connections, and their presence in communities around the world create powerful networks for the dissemination of new ideas for addressing social problems. Corporations can facilitate global knowledge transfer and coordinated multisite implementation of new social initiatives with a proficiency that is unequaled by most other donors.

A Whole New Approach

When corporations support the right causes in the right ways—when they get the *where* and the *how* right—they set in motion a virtuous cycle. By focusing on the contextual conditions most important to their industries and strategies, companies ensure that their corporate capabilities will be particularly well suited to helping grantees create greater value. And by enhancing the value produced by philanthropic efforts in their fields, the companies gain a greater improvement in competitive context. Both the corporations and the causes they support reap important benefits.

Adopting a context-focused approach, however, goes against the grain of current philanthropic practice. Many companies actively distance their philanthropy from the business, believing this will lead to greater goodwill in local communities. While it is true that a growing number of companies aim to make their giving "strategic," few have connected giving to areas that improve their long-term competitive potential. And even fewer systematically apply their distinctive strengths to maximize the social and economic value created by their philanthropy. Instead, companies are often distracted by the desire to publicize how much money and effort they are contributing in order to foster an image of social responsibility and caring. Avon Products, for example, recently mobilized its 400,000 independent sales representatives in a high-profile door-to-door campaign to raise more than $32 million to fund breast cancer prevention. Fighting breast cancer is a worthy cause and one that is very meaningful to Avon's target market of female consumers. It is not, however, a material factor in Avon's competitive context or an area in which Avon has any inherent expertise. As a result, Avon may have greatly augmented its own cash contribution through effective fundraising—and generated favorable publicity—but it failed to realize the full potential of its philanthropy to create social and economic value. Avon has done much good, but it could do even better. As long as companies remain focused on the public relations benefit of their contributions instead of the impact achieved, they will sacrifice opportunities to create social value.

This does not mean that corporations cannot also gain goodwill and enhance their reputations through philanthropy. But goodwill alone is not a sufficient motivation. Given public skepticism about the ethics of business—skepticism that has intensified in the wake of the string of corporate scandals this year—corporations that can demonstrate a significant impact on a social problem will gain more credibility than those that are merely big givers. The acid test of good corporate philanthropy is whether the desired social change is so beneficial to the company that the organization would pursue the change even if no one ever knew about it. Cisco, for example, has achieved wide recognition for its good works, but it would have had sufficient reason to develop the Networking Academy even if no goodwill had been created.

Moving to context-focused philanthropy will require a far more rigorous approach than is prevalent today. It will mean tightly integrating the management of philanthropy with other company activities. Rather than delegating philanthropy entirely to a public relations department or the staff of a corporate foundation, the CEO must lead the entire management team through a disciplined process to identify and implement a corporate giving strategy focused on improving context. Business units, in particular, must play central roles in identifying areas for contextual investments.

The new process would involve five steps.

Examine the competitive context in each of the company's important geographic locations. Where could social investment improve the company's or cluster's competitive potential? What are the key constraints that limit productivity, innovation, growth, and competitiveness? A company should pay special attention to the particular constraints that have a disproportionate effect on its strategy relative to competitors; improvements in these areas of context will potentially reinforce competitive advantage. The more specifically a contextual initiative is defined, the more likely the company is to create value and achieve its objectives. A broad initiative such as Avon's efforts to improve the health of all women will not necessarily deliver contextual benefits, even if it helps some employees or customers. And a tightly targeted objective does not necessarily diminish the scale of impact. Narrowly focused initiatives, like Pfizer's trachoma program, IBM's Reinventing Education, or Cisco's Networking Academy, can potentially benefit millions of people or strengthen the global market for an entire industry.

Review the existing philanthropic portfolio to see how it fits this new paradigm. Current programs will likely fall into three categories:

- Communal obligation: support of civic, welfare, and educational organizations, motivated by the company's desire to be a good citizen.

- Goodwill building: contributions to support causes favored by employees, customers, or community leaders, often necessitated by the quid pro quo of business and the desire to improve the company's relationships.

- Strategic giving: philanthropy focused on enhancing competitive context, as outlined here.

Most corporate giving falls into the first two categories. While a certain percentage of giving in these categories may be necessary and desirable, the goal is to shift, as much as possible, a company's philanthropy into the third category. As for cause-related marketing, it is marketing, not philanthropy, and it must stand on its own merits.

Assess existing and potential corporate giving initiatives against the four forms of value creation. How can the company leverage its assets and expertise to select the most effective grantees, signal other funders, improve grantees' performance, and advance knowledge and practice?

Given its strategy, where can the company create the greatest value through giving in ways that no other company could match?

Seek opportunities for collective action within a cluster and with other partners. Collective action will often be more effective than a solo effort in addressing context and enhancing the value created, and it helps mitigate the free rider problem by distributing costs broadly. Few companies today work together to achieve social objectives. This may be the result of a general reluctance to work with competitors, but clusters encompass many related partners and industries that do not compete directly. More likely, the tendency to view philanthropy as a form of public relations leads companies to invent their own contributions campaigns, which are branded with their own identities and therefore discourage partners. Focusing on the social change to be achieved, rather than the publicity to be gained, will expand the potential for partnerships and collective action.

Once a company has identified opportunities to improve the competitive context and determined the ways in which it can contribute by adding unique value, the search for partners becomes straightforward: Who else stands to benefit from this change in competitive context? And who has complementary expertise or resources? Conversely, what philanthropic initiatives by others are worth joining? Where can the company be a good partner to others by contributing in ways that will enhance value?

Rigorously track and evaluate results. Monitoring achievements is essential to continually improving the philanthropic strategy and its implementation. As with any other corporate activity, consistent improvement over time brings the greatest value. The most successful programs will not be short-term campaigns but long-term commitments that continue to grow in scale and sophistication.

The context-focused approach to philanthropy is not simple. One size does not fit all. Companies will differ in their comfort levels and time horizons for philanthropic activity, and individual firms will make different choices about how to implement our ideas. Philanthropy will never become an exact science—it is inherently an act of judgment and faith in the pursuit of long-term goals. However, the perspective and tools presented here will help any company make its philanthropic activities far more effective.

Were this approach to be widely adopted, the pattern of corporate contributions would shift significantly. The overall level of contributions would likely increase, and the social and economic value created would go up even more sharply. Companies would be more confident about the value of their philanthropy and more committed to it. They would be able to communicate their philanthropic strategies more effectively to the communities in which they operate. Their choices of areas to support would be clearly understandable and would not seem unpredictable or idiosyncratic. Finally, there would be a better division of labor between corporate givers and other types of funders, with corporations tackling the areas where they are uniquely able to create value.

Charities too would benefit. They would see an increased and more predictable flow of corporate resources into the nonprofit sector. Just as important, they would develop close, long-term corporate partnerships that would better apply the expertise and assets of the for-profit sector to achieve social objectives. Just as companies can build on the nonprofit infrastructure to achieve their objectives more cost-effectively, nonprofits can benefit from using the commercial infrastructure.

To some corporate leaders, this new approach might seem too self-serving. They might argue that philanthropy is purely a matter of conscience and should not be adulterated by business objectives. In some industries, particularly those like petrochemicals and pharmaceuticals that are prone to public controversy, this view is so entrenched that many companies establish independent charitable foundations and entirely segregate giving from the business. In doing so, however, they give up tremendous opportunities to create greater value for society and themselves. Context-focused philanthropy does not just address a company's self-interest, it benefits many through broad social change. If a company's philanthropy only involved its own interests, after all, it would not qualify as a charitable deduction, and it might well threaten the company's reputation.

There is no inherent contradiction between improving competitive context and making a sincere commitment to bettering society. Indeed, as we've seen, the more closely a company's philanthropy is linked to its competitive context, the greater the company's contribution to society will be. Other areas, where the company neither creates added value nor derives benefit, should appropriately be left—as Friedman asserts—to individual donors following their own charitable impulses. If systematically pursued in a way that maximizes the value created, context-focused philanthropy can offer companies a new set of competitive tools that well justifies the investment of resources. At the same time, it can unlock a vastly more powerful way to make the world a better place.

CHAPTER 14

Strategy & Society

The Link Between Competitive Advantage and
Corporate Social Responsibility

Michael E. Porter

Mark R. Kramer

GOVERNMENTS, ACTIVISTS, AND THE MEDIA
have become adept at holding companies to account for the social consequences of their activities. Myriad organizations rank companies on the
performance of their corporate social responsibility (CSR), and, despite
sometimes questionable methodologies, these rankings attract considerable publicity. As a result, CSR has emerged as an inescapable priority
for business leaders in every country.

Many companies have already done much to improve the social and
environmental consequences of their activities, yet these efforts have
not been nearly as productive as they could be—for two reasons. First,
they pit business against society, when clearly the two are interdependent. Second, they pressure companies to think of corporate social responsibility in generic ways instead of in the way most appropriate to
each firm's strategy.

The fact is, the prevailing approaches to CSR are so fragmented and
so disconnected from business and strategy as to obscure many of the
greatest opportunities for companies to benefit society. If, instead, corporations were to analyze their prospects for social responsibility using
the same frameworks that guide their core business choices, they would
discover that CSR can be much more than a cost, a constraint, or a

December 2006

charitable deed—it can be a source of opportunity, innovation, and competitive advantage.

In this article, we propose a new way to look at the relationship between business and society that does not treat corporate success and social welfare as a zero-sum game. We introduce a framework companies can use to identify all of the effects, both positive and negative, they have on society; determine which ones to address; and suggest effective ways to do so. When looked at strategically, corporate social responsibility can become a source of tremendous social progress, as the business applies its considerable resources, expertise, and insights to activities that benefit society.

The Emergence of Corporate Social Responsibility

Heightened corporate attention to CSR has not been entirely voluntary. Many companies awoke to it only after being surprised by public responses to issues they had not previously thought were part of their business responsibilities. Nike, for example, faced an extensive consumer boycott after the *New York Times* and other media outlets reported abusive labor practices at some of its Indonesian suppliers in the early 1990s. Shell Oil's decision to sink the *Brent Spar,* an obsolete oil rig, in the North Sea led to Greenpeace protests in 1995 and to international headlines. Pharmaceutical companies discovered that they were expected to respond to the AIDS pandemic in Africa even though it was far removed from their primary product lines and markets. Fast-food and packaged food companies are now being held responsible for obesity and poor nutrition.

Activist organizations of all kinds, both on the right and the left, have grown much more aggressive and effective in bringing public pressure to bear on corporations. Activists may target the most visible or successful companies merely to draw attention to an issue, even if those corporations actually have had little impact on the problem at hand. Nestlé, for example, the world's largest purveyor of bottled water, has become a major target in the global debate about access to fresh water, despite the fact that Nestlé's bottled water sales consume just 0.0008% of the world's fresh water supply. The inefficiency of agricultural irrigation, which uses 70% of the world's supply annually, is a far more pressing issue, but it offers no equally convenient multinational corporation to target.

Debates about CSR have moved all the way into corporate board-rooms. In 2005, 360 different CSR-related shareholder resolutions were filed on issues ranging from labor conditions to global warming. Government regulation increasingly mandates social responsibility reporting. Pending legislation in the UK, for example, would require every publicly listed company to disclose ethical, social, and environmental risks in its annual report. These pressures clearly demonstrate the extent to which external stakeholders are seeking to hold companies accountable for social issues and highlight the potentially large financial risks for any firm whose conduct is deemed unacceptable.

While businesses have awakened to these risks, they are much less clear on what to do about them. In fact, the most common corporate response has been neither strategic nor operational but cosmetic: public relations and media campaigns, the centerpieces of which are often glossy CSR reports that showcase companies' social and environmental good deeds. Of the 250 largest multinational corporations, 64% published CSR reports in 2005, either within their annual report or, for most, in separate sustainability reports—supporting a new cottage industry of report writers.

Such publications rarely offer a coherent framework for CSR activities, let alone a strategic one. Instead, they aggregate anecdotes about uncoordinated initiatives to demonstrate a company's social sensitivity. What these reports leave out is often as telling as what they include. Reductions in pollution, waste, carbon emissions, or energy use, for example, may be documented for specific divisions or regions but not for the company as a whole. Philanthropic initiatives are typically described in terms of dollars or volunteer hours spent but almost never in terms of impact. Forward-looking commitments to reach explicit performance targets are even rarer.

This proliferation of CSR reports has been paralleled by growth in CSR ratings and rankings. While rigorous and reliable ratings might constructively influence corporate behavior, the existing cacophony of self-appointed scorekeepers does little more than add to the confusion. (See the insert "The Ratings Game.")

The Ratings Game

Measuring and publicizing social performance is a potentially powerful way to influence corporate behavior—assuming that the ratings are consistently measured and accurately reflect corporate social impact. Unfortunately, neither condition holds true in the current profusion of CSR checklists.

The criteria used in the rankings vary widely. The Dow Jones Sustainability Index, for example, includes aspects of economic performance in its evaluation. It weights customer service almost 50% more heavily than corporate citizenship. The equally prominent FTSE4Good Index, by contrast, contains no measures of economic performance or customer service at all. Even when criteria happen to be the same, they are invariably weighted differently in the final scoring.

Beyond the choice of criteria and their weightings lies the even more perplexing question of how to judge whether the criteria have been met. Most media, non-profits, and investment advisory organizations have too few resources to audit a universe of complicated global corporate activities. As a result, they tend to use measures for which data are readily and inexpensively available, even though they may not be good proxies for the social or environmental effects they are intended to reflect. The Dow Jones Sustainability Index, for example, uses the size of a company's board as a measure of community involvement, even though size and involvement may be entirely unrelated.[1]

Finally, even if the measures chosen accurately reflect social impact, the data are frequently unreliable. Most ratings rely on surveys whose response rates are statistically insignificant, as well as on self-reported company data that have not been verified externally. Companies with the most to hide are the least likely to respond. The result is a jumble of largely meaningless rankings, allowing almost any company to boast that it meets some measure of social responsibility—and most do.

1. For a fuller discussion of the problem of CSR ratings, see Aaron Chatterji and David Levine, "Breaking Down the Wall of Codes: Evaluating Non-Financial Performance Measurement," *California Management Review*, Winter 2006.

In an effort to move beyond this confusion, corporate leaders have turned for advice to a growing collection of increasingly sophisticated nonprofit organizations, consulting firms, and academic experts. A rich literature on CSR has emerged, though what practical guidance it offers corporate leaders is often unclear. Examining the primary schools of thought about CSR is an essential starting point in understanding why a new approach is needed to integrating social considerations more effectively into core business operations and strategy.

Four Prevailing Justifications for CSR

Broadly speaking, proponents of CSR have used four arguments to make their case: moral obligation, sustainability, license to operate, and reputation. The moral appeal—arguing that companies have a duty to be good citizens and to "do the right thing"—is prominent in the goal of Business for Social Responsibility, the leading nonprofit CSR business association in the United States. It asks that its members "achieve commercial success in ways that honor ethical values and respect people, communities, and the natural environment." Sustainability emphasizes environmental and community stewardship. An excellent definition was developed in the 1980s by Norwegian Prime Minister Gro Harlem Brundtland and used by the World Business Council for Sustainable Development: "Meeting the needs of the present without compromising the ability of future generations to meet their own needs." The notion of license to operate derives from the fact that every company needs tacit or explicit permission from governments, communities, and numerous other stakeholders to do business. Finally, reputation is used by many companies to justify CSR initiatives on the grounds that they will improve a company's image, strengthen its brand, enliven morale, and even raise the value of its stock. These justifications have advanced thinking in the field, but none offers sufficient guidance for the difficult choices corporate leaders must make. Consider the practical limitations of each approach.

The CSR field remains strongly imbued with a moral imperative. In some areas, such as honesty in filing financial statements and operating within the law, moral considerations are easy to understand and apply.

It is the nature of moral obligations to be absolute mandates, however, while most corporate social choices involve balancing competing values, interests, and costs. Google's recent entry into China, for example, has created an irreconcilable conflict between its U.S. customers' abhorrence of censorship and the legal constraints imposed by the Chinese government. The moral calculus needed to weigh one social benefit against another, or against its financial costs, has yet to be developed. Moral principles do not tell a pharmaceutical company how to allocate its revenues among subsidizing care for the indigent today, developing cures for the future, and providing dividends to its investors.

The principle of sustainability appeals to enlightened self-interest, often invoking the so-called triple bottom line of economic, social, and environmental performance. In other words, companies should operate in ways that secure long-term economic performance by avoiding short-term behavior that is socially detrimental or environmentally wasteful. The principle works best for issues that coincide with a company's economic or regulatory interests. DuPont, for example, has saved over $2 billion from reductions in energy use since 1990. Changes to the materials McDonald's uses to wrap its food have reduced its solid waste by 30%. These were smart business decisions entirely apart from their environmental benefits. In other areas, however, the notion of sustainability can become so vague as to be meaningless. Transparency may be said to be more "sustainable" than corruption. Good employment practices are more "sustainable" than sweatshops. Philanthropy may contribute to the "sustainability" of a society. However true these assertions are, they offer little basis for balancing long-term objectives against the short-term costs they incur. The sustainability school raises questions about these trade-offs without offering a framework to answer them. Managers without a strategic understanding of CSR are prone to postpone these costs, which can lead to far greater costs when the company is later judged to have violated its social obligation.

The license-to-operate approach, by contrast, is far more pragmatic. It offers a concrete way for a business to identify social issues that matter to its stakeholders and make decisions about them. This approach also fosters constructive dialogue with regulators, the local citizenry, and activists—one reason, perhaps, that it is especially prevalent among companies that depend on government consent, such as those in mining and other highly regulated and extractive industries. That is also why the approach is common at companies that rely on the forbearance of their neighbors, such as those, like chemical manufacturing, whose operations are noxious or environmentally hazardous. By seeking to satisfy stakeholders, however, companies cede primary control of their CSR agendas to outsiders. Stakeholders' views are obviously important, but these groups can never fully understand a corporation's capabilities, competitive positioning, or the trade-offs it must make. Nor does the vehemence of a stakeholder group necessarily signify the importance of an issue—either to the company or to the world. A firm that views CSR as a way to placate pressure groups often finds that its approach devolves into a series of short-term defensive reactions—a never-ending public relations palliative with minimal value to society and no strategic benefit for the business.

Finally, the reputation argument seeks that strategic benefit but rarely finds it. Concerns about reputation, like license to operate, focus on satisfying external audiences. In consumer-oriented companies, it often leads to high-profile cause-related marketing campaigns. In stigmatized industries, such as chemicals and energy, a company may instead pursue social responsibility initiatives as a form of insurance, in the hope that its reputation for social consciousness will temper public criticism in the event of a crisis. This rationale once again risks confusing public relations with social and business results.

A few corporations, such as Ben & Jerry's, Newman's Own, Patagonia, and the Body Shop, have distinguished themselves through an extraordinary long-term commitment to social responsibility. But even for these companies, the social impact achieved, much less the business benefit, is hard to determine. Studies of the effect of a company's social reputation on consumer purchasing preferences or on stock market performance have been inconclusive at best. As for the concept of CSR as insurance, the connection between the good deeds and consumer attitudes is so indirect as to be impossible to measure. Having no way to quantify the benefits of these investments puts such CSR programs on shaky ground, liable to be dislodged by a change of management or a swing in the business cycle.

All four schools of thought share the same weakness: They focus on the tension between business and society rather than on their interdependence. Each creates a generic rationale that is not tied to the strategy and operations of any specific company or the places in which it operates. Consequently, none of them is sufficient to help a company identify, prioritize, and address the social issues that matter most or the ones on which it can make the biggest impact. The result is oftentimes a hodgepodge of uncoordinated CSR and philanthropic activities disconnected from the company's strategy that neither make any meaningful social impact nor strengthen the firm's long-term competitiveness. Internally, CSR practices and initiatives are often isolated from operating units—and even separated from corporate philanthropy. Externally, the company's social impact becomes diffused among numerous unrelated efforts, each responding to a different stakeholder group or corporate pressure point.

The consequence of this fragmentation is a tremendous lost opportunity. The power of corporations to create social benefit is dissipated, and so is the potential of companies to take actions that would support both their communities and their business goals.

Integrating Business and Society

To advance CSR, we must root it in a broad understanding of the interrelationship between a corporation and society while at the same time anchoring it in the strategies and activities of specific companies. To say broadly that business and society need each other might seem like a cliché, but it is also the basic truth that will pull companies out of the muddle that their current corporate-responsibility thinking has created.

Successful corporations need a healthy society. Education, health care, and equal opportunity are essential to a productive workforce. Safe products and working conditions not only attract customers but lower the internal costs of accidents. Efficient utilization of land, water, energy, and other natural resources makes business more productive. Good government, the rule of law, and property rights are essential for efficiency and innovation. Strong regulatory standards protect both consumers and competitive companies from exploitation. Ultimately, a healthy society creates expanding demand for business, as more human needs are met and aspirations grow. Any business that pursues its ends at the expense of the society in which it operates will find its success to be illusory and ultimately temporary.

At the same time, a healthy society needs successful companies. No social program can rival the business sector when it comes to creating the jobs, wealth, and innovation that improve standards of living and social conditions over time. If governments, NGOs, and other participants in civil society weaken the ability of business to operate productively, they may win battles but will lose the war, as corporate and regional competitiveness fade, wages stagnate, jobs disappear, and the wealth that pays taxes and supports nonprofit contributions evaporates.

Leaders in both business and civil society have focused too much on the friction between them and not enough on the points of intersection. The mutual dependence of corporations and society implies that both business decisions and social policies must follow the principle of *shared value*. That is, choices must benefit both sides. If either a business or a society pursues policies that benefit its interests at the expense of the other, it will find itself on a dangerous path. A temporary gain to one will undermine the long-term prosperity of both.[1]

To put these broad principles into practice, a company must integrate a social perspective into the core frameworks it already uses to understand competition and guide its business strategy.

IDENTIFYING THE POINTS OF INTERSECTION

The interdependence between a company and society takes two forms. First, a company impinges upon society through its operations in the normal course of business: These are *inside-out linkages.*

Virtually every activity in a company's value chain touches on the communities in which the firm operates, creating either positive or negative social consequences. (For an example of this process, see the first figure in the insert "Mapping Social Opportunities" at the end of this article.) While companies are increasingly aware of the social impact of their activities (such as hiring practices, emissions, and waste disposal), these impacts can be more subtle and variable than many managers realize. For one thing, they depend on location. The same manufacturing operation will have very different social consequences in China than in the United States.

A company's impact on society also changes over time, as social standards evolve and science progresses. Asbestos, now understood as a serious health risk, was thought to be safe in the early 1900s, given the scientific knowledge then available. Evidence of its risks gradually mounted for more than 50 years before any company was held liable for the harms it can cause. Many firms that failed to anticipate the consequences of this evolving body of research have been bankrupted by the results. No longer can companies be content to monitor only the obvious social impacts of today. Without a careful process for identifying evolving social effects of tomorrow, firms may risk their very survival.

Not only does corporate activity affect society, but external social conditions also influence corporations, for better and for worse. These are *outside-in linkages.*

Every company operates within a competitive context, which significantly affects its ability to carry out its strategy, especially in the long run. Social conditions form a key part of this context. Competitive context garners far less attention than value chain impacts but can have far greater strategic importance for both companies and societies. Ensuring the health of the competitive context benefits both the company and the community.

Competitive context can be divided into four broad areas: first, the quantity and quality of available business inputs—human resources, for example, or transportation infrastructure; second, the rules and incentives that govern competition—such as policies that protect intellectual property, ensure transparency, safeguard against corruption, and encourage investment; third, the size and sophistication of local demand, influenced by such things as standards for product quality and safety, consumer rights, and fairness in government purchasing; fourth, the local availability of supporting industries, such as service providers and machinery producers. Any and all of these aspects of context can be opportunities for CSR initiatives. (See the second figure in the insert "Mapping Social Opportunities" at the end of this article.) The ability to recruit appropriate human resources, for example, may depend on a number of social factors that companies can influence, such as the local educational system, the availability of housing, the existence of discrimination (which limits the pool of workers), and the adequacy of the public health infrastructure.[2]

CHOOSING WHICH SOCIAL ISSUES TO ADDRESS

No business can solve all of society's problems or bear the cost of doing so. Instead, each company must select issues that intersect with its particular business. Other social agendas are best left to those companies in other industries, NGOs, or government institutions that are better positioned to address them. The essential test that should guide CSR is not whether a cause is worthy but whether it presents an opportunity to create shared value—that is, a meaningful benefit for society that is also valuable to the business.

Our framework suggests that the social issues affecting a company fall into three categories, which distinguish between the many worthy causes and the narrower set of social issues that are both important and strategic for the business.

Generic social issues may be important to society but are neither significantly affected by the company's operations nor influence the company's long-term competitiveness. *Value chain social impacts* are those that are significantly affected by the company's activities in the ordinary course of business. *Social dimensions of competitive context* are factors in the external environment that significantly affect the underlying drivers of competitiveness in those places where the company operates. (See figure 14.1.)

Every company will need to sort social issues into these three categories for each of its business units and primary locations, then rank them

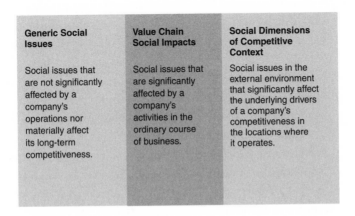

Generic Social Issues	Value Chain Social Impacts	Social Dimensions of Competitive Context
Social issues that are not significantly affected by a company's operations nor materially affect its long-term competitiveness.	Social issues that are significantly affected by a company's activities in the ordinary course of business.	Social issues in the external environment that significantly affect the underlying drivers of a company's competitiveness in the locations where it operates.

Figure 14.1   Prioritizing Social Issues

in terms of potential impact. Into which category a given social issue falls will vary from business unit to business unit, industry to industry, and place to place.

Supporting a dance company may be a generic social issue for a utility like Southern California Edison but an important part of the competitive context for a corporation like American Express, which depends on the high-end entertainment, hospitality, and tourism cluster. Carbon emissions may be a generic social issue for a financial services firm like Bank of America, a negative value chain impact for a transportation-based company like UPS, or both a value chain impact and a competitive context issue for a car manufacturer like Toyota. The AIDS pandemic in Africa may be a generic social issue for a U.S. retailer like Home Depot, a value chain impact for a pharmaceutical company like Glaxo-SmithKline, and a competitive context issue for a mining company like Anglo American that depends on local labor in Africa for its operations.

Even issues that apply widely in the economy, such as diversity in hiring or conservation of energy, can have greater significance for some industries than for others. Health care benefits, for example, will present fewer challenges for software development or biotechnology firms, where workforces tend to be small and well compensated, than for companies in a field like retailing, which is heavily dependent on large numbers of lower-wage workers.

Within an industry, a given social issue may cut differently for different companies, owing to differences in competitive positioning. In the auto industry, for example, Volvo has chosen to make safety a central element of its competitive positioning, while Toyota has built a competitive advantage from the environmental benefits of its hybrid technology. For an individual company, some issues will prove to be important for many of its business units and locations, offering opportunities for strategic corporatewide CSR initiatives.

Where a social issue is salient for many companies across multiple industries, it can often be addressed most effectively through cooperative models. The Extractive Industries Transparency Initiative, for example, includes 19 major oil, gas, and mining companies that have agreed to discourage corruption through full public disclosure and verification of all corporate payments to governments in the countries in which they operate. Collective action by all major corporations in these industries prevents corrupt governments from undermining social benefit by simply choosing not to deal with the firms that disclose their payments.

CREATING A CORPORATE SOCIAL AGENDA

Categorizing and ranking social issues is just the means to an end, which is to create an explicit and affirmative corporate social agenda. A corporate social agenda looks beyond community expectations to opportunities to achieve social and economic benefits simultaneously. It moves from mitigating harm to finding ways to reinforce corporate strategy by advancing social conditions.

Such a social agenda must be responsive to stakeholders, but it cannot stop there. A substantial portion of corporate resources and attention must migrate to truly strategic CSR. (See figure 14.2.) It is through strategic CSR that the company will make the most significant social impact and reap the greatest business benefits.

Responsive CSR. Responsive CSR comprises two elements: acting as a good corporate citizen, attuned to the evolving social concerns of stakeholders, and mitigating existing or anticipated adverse effects from business activities.

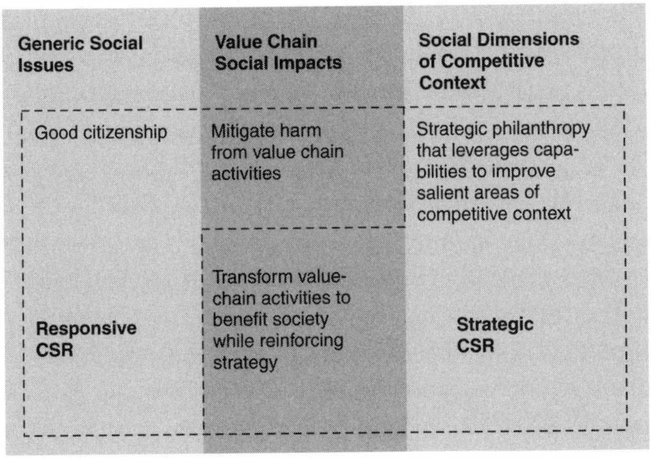

Generic Social Issues	Value Chain Social Impacts	Social Dimensions of Competitive Context
Good citizenship	Mitigate harm from value chain activities	Strategic philanthropy that leverages capabilities to improve salient areas of competitive context
Responsive CSR	Transform value-chain activities to benefit society while reinforcing strategy	**Strategic CSR**

Figure 14.2   Corporate Involvement in Society: A Strategic Approach

Good citizenship is a sine qua non of CSR, and companies need to do it well. Many worthy local organizations rely on corporate contributions, while employees derive justifiable pride from their company's positive involvement in the community.

The best corporate citizenship initiatives involve far more than writing a check: They specify clear, measurable goals and track results over time. A good example is GE's program to adopt underperforming public high schools near several of its major U.S. facilities. The company contributes between $250,000 and $1 million over a five-year period to each school and makes in-kind donations as well. GE managers and employees take an active role by working with school administrators to assess needs and mentor or tutor students. In an independent study of ten schools in the program between 1989 and 1999, nearly all showed significant improvement, while the graduation rate in four of the five worst-performing schools doubled from an average of 30% to 60%.

Effective corporate citizenship initiatives such as this one create goodwill and improve relations with local governments and other important constituencies. What's more, GE's employees feel great pride in their participation. Their effect is inherently limited, however. No matter how beneficial the program is, it remains incidental to the company's business, and the direct effect on GE's recruiting and retention is modest.

The second part of responsive CSR—mitigating the harm arising from a firm's value chain activities—is essentially an operational challenge. Because there are a myriad of possible value chain impacts for each business unit, many companies have adopted a checklist approach to CSR, using standardized sets of social and environmental risks. The Global Reporting Initiative, which is rapidly becoming a standard for CSR reporting, has enumerated a list of 141 CSR issues, supplemented by auxiliary lists for different industries.

These lists make for an excellent starting point, but companies need a more proactive and tailored internal process. Managers at each business unit can use the value chain as a tool to identify systematically the social impacts of the unit's activities in each location. Here operating management, which is closest to the work actually being done, is particularly helpful. Most challenging is to anticipate impacts that are not yet well recognized. Consider B&Q, an international chain of home supply centers based in England. The company has begun to analyze systematically tens of thousands of products in its hundreds of stores against a list of a dozen social issues—from climate change to working conditions at its suppliers' factories—to determine which products pose potential social responsibility risks and how the company might take action before any external pressure is brought to bear.

For most value chain impacts, there is no need to reinvent the wheel. The company should identify best practices for dealing with each one, with an eye toward how those practices are changing. Some companies will be more proactive and effective in mitigating the wide array of social problems that the value chain can create. These companies will gain an edge, but—just as for procurement and other operational improvements—any advantage is likely to be temporary.

Strategic CSR. For any company, strategy must go beyond best practices. It is about choosing a unique position—doing things differently from competitors in a way that lowers costs or better serves a particular set of customer needs. These principles apply to a company's relationship to society as readily as to its relationship to its customers and rivals.

Strategic CSR moves beyond good corporate citizenship and mitigating harmful value chain impacts to mount a small number of initiatives whose social and business benefits are large and distinctive. Strategic CSR involves both inside-out and outside-in dimensions working in tandem. It is here that the opportunities for shared value truly lie.

Many opportunities to pioneer innovations to benefit both society and a company's own competitiveness can arise in the product offering and the value chain. Toyota's response to concerns over automobile emissions is an example. Toyota's Prius, the hybrid electric/gasoline vehicle, is the first in a series of innovative car models that have produced competitive advantage and environmental benefits. Hybrid engines emit as little as 10% of the harmful pollutants conventional vehicles produce while consuming only half as much gas. Voted 2004 Car of the Year by *Motor Trend* magazine, Prius has given Toyota a lead so substantial that Ford and other car companies are licensing the technology. Toyota has created a unique position with customers and is well on its way to establishing its technology as the world standard.

Urbi, a Mexican construction company, has prospered by building housing for disadvantaged buyers using novel financing vehicles such as flexible mortgage payments made through payroll deductions. Crédit Agricole, France's largest bank, has differentiated itself by offering specialized financial products related to the environment, such as financing packages for energy-saving home improvements and for audits to certify farms as organic.

Strategic CSR also unlocks shared value by investing in social aspects of context that strengthen company competitiveness. A symbiotic relationship develops: The success of the company and the success of the community become mutually reinforcing. Typically, the more closely tied a social issue is to the company's business, the greater the opportunity to leverage the firm's resources and capabilities, and benefit society.

Microsoft's Working Connections partnership with the American Association of Community Colleges (AACC) is a good example of a shared-value opportunity arising from investments in context. The shortage of information technology workers is a significant constraint on Microsoft's growth; currently, there are more than 450,000 unfilled IT positions in the United States alone. Community colleges, with an enrollment of 11.6 million students, representing 45% of all U.S. undergraduates, could be a major solution. Microsoft recognizes, however, that community colleges face special challenges: IT curricula are not standardized, technology used in classrooms is often outdated, and there are no systematic professional development programs to keep faculty up to date.

Microsoft's $50 million five-year initiative was aimed at all three problems. In addition to contributing money and products, Microsoft sent employee volunteers to colleges to assess needs, contribute to curriculum development, and create faculty development institutes. Note that in this case, volunteers and assigned staff were able to use their core professional skills to address a social need, a far cry from typical volunteer programs. Microsoft has achieved results that have benefited many communities while having a direct—and potentially significant—impact on the company.

INTEGRATING INSIDE-OUT AND OUTSIDE-IN PRACTICES

Pioneering value chain innovations and addressing social constraints to competitiveness are each powerful tools for creating economic and social value. However, as our examples illustrate, the impact is even greater if they work together. Activities in the value chain can be performed in ways that reinforce improvements in the social dimensions of context. At the same time, investments in competitive context have the potential to reduce constraints on a company's value chain activities. Marriott, for example, provides 180 hours of paid classroom and on-the-job training to chronically unemployed job candidates. The company has combined this with support for local community service organizations, which identify, screen, and refer the candidates to Marriott. The net result is both a major benefit to communities and a reduction in Marriott's cost of recruiting entry-level employees. Ninety percent of those in the training program take jobs with Marriott. One year later, more than 65% are still in their jobs, a substantially higher retention rate than the norm.

When value chain practices and investments in competitive context are fully integrated, CSR becomes hard to distinguish from the day-to-day business of the company. Nestlé, for example, works directly with small farmers in developing countries to source the basic commodities, such as milk, coffee, and cocoa, on which much of its global business depends. (See the insert "Integrating Company Practice and Context: Nestlé's Milk District" at the end of this article.) The company's investment in local infrastructure and its transfer of world-class knowledge and technology over decades has produced enormous social benefits through improved health care, better education, and economic development, while giving Nestlé direct and reliable access to the commodities it needs to maintain a profitable global business. Nestlé's distinctive strategy is inseparable from its social impact.

CREATING A SOCIAL DIMENSION TO THE VALUE PROPOSITION

At the heart of any strategy is a unique value proposition: a set of needs a company can meet for its chosen customers that others cannot. The most strategic CSR occurs when a company adds a social dimension to its value proposition, making social impact integral to the overall strategy.

Consider Whole Foods Market, whose value proposition is to sell organic, natural, and healthy food products to customers who are passionate about food and the environment. Social issues are fundamental to what makes Whole Foods unique in food retailing and to its ability to command premium prices. The company's sourcing emphasizes purchases from local farmers through each store's procurement process. Buyers screen out foods containing any of nearly 100 common ingredients that the company considers unhealthy or environmentally damaging. The same standards apply to products made internally. Whole Foods' baked goods, for example, use only unbleached and unbromated flour.

Whole Foods' commitment to natural and environmentally friendly operating practices extends well beyond sourcing. Stores are constructed using a minimum of virgin raw materials. Recently, the company purchased renewable wind energy credits equal to 100% of its electricity use in all of its stores and facilities, the only *Fortune* 500 company to offset its electricity consumption entirely. Spoiled produce and biodegradable waste are trucked to regional centers for composting. Whole Foods' vehicles are being converted to run on biofuels. Even the cleaning products used in its stores are environmentally friendly. And through its philanthropy, the company has created the Animal Compassion Foundation to develop more natural and humane ways of raising farm animals. In short, nearly every aspect of the company's value chain reinforces the social dimensions of its value proposition, distinguishing Whole Foods from its competitors.

Not every company can build its entire value proposition around social issues as Whole Foods does, but adding a social dimension to the value proposition offers a new frontier in competitive positioning. Government regulation, exposure to criticism and liability, and consumers' attention to social issues are all persistently increasing. As a result, the number of industries and companies whose competitive advantage can involve social value propositions is constantly growing. Sysco, for example, the largest distributor of food products to restaurants and institutions in North America, has begun an initiative to preserve small, family-owned farms and offer locally grown produce to its customers as a source of competitive differentiation. Even large global multinationals—such as General Electric, with its "ecomagination" initiative that focuses on developing water purification technology and other "green" businesses, and Unilever, through its efforts to pioneer new products, packaging, and distribution systems to meet the needs of the poorest populations—have decided that major business opportunities lie in integrating business and society.

Organizing for CSR

Integrating business and social needs takes more than good intentions and strong leadership. It requires adjustments in organization, reporting relationships, and incentives. Few companies have engaged operating management in processes that identify and prioritize social issues based on their salience to business operations and their importance to the company's competitive context. Even fewer have unified their philanthropy with the management of their CSR efforts, much less sought to embed a social dimension into their core value proposition. Doing these things requires a far different approach to both CSR and philanthropy than the one prevalent today. Companies must shift from a fragmented, defensive posture to an integrated, affirmative approach. The focus must move away from an emphasis on image to an emphasis on substance.

The current preoccupation with measuring stakeholder satisfaction has it backwards. What needs to be measured is social impact. Operating managers must understand the importance of the outside-in influence of competitive context, while people with responsibility for CSR initiatives must have a granular understanding of every activity in the value chain. Value chain and competitive-context investments in CSR need to be incorporated into the performance measures of managers with P&L responsibility. These transformations require more than a broadening of job definition; they require overcoming a number of long-standing prejudices. Many operating managers have developed an ingrained us-versus-them mind-set that responds defensively to the discussion of any social issue, just as many NGOs view askance the pursuit of social value for profit. These attitudes must change if companies want to leverage the social dimension of corporate strategy.

Strategy is always about making choices, and success in corporate social responsibility is no different. It is about choosing which social issues to focus on. The short-term performance pressures companies face rule out indiscriminate investments in social value creation. They suggest, instead, that creating shared value should be viewed like research and development, as a long-term investment in a company's future competitiveness. The billions of dollars already being spent on CSR and corporate philanthropy would generate far more benefit to both business and society if consistently invested using the principles we have outlined.

While responsive CSR depends on being a good corporate citizen and addressing every social harm the business creates, strategic CSR is far more selective. Companies are called on to address hundreds of social issues, but only a few represent opportunities to make a real difference to society or to confer a competitive advantage. Organizations that make the right choices and build focused, proactive, and integrated social initiatives in concert with their core strategies will increasingly distance themselves from the pack.

The Moral Purpose of Business

By providing jobs, investing capital, purchasing goods, and doing business every day, corporations have a profound and positive influence on society. The most important thing a corporation can do for society, and for any community, is contribute to a prosperous economy. Governments and NGOs often forget this basic truth. When developing countries distort rules and incentives for business, for example, they penalize productive companies. Such countries are doomed to poverty, low wages, and selling off their natural resources. Corporations have the know-how and resources to change this state of affairs, not only in the developing world but also in economically disadvantaged communities in advanced economies.

This cannot excuse businesses that seek short-term profits deceptively or shirk the social and environmental consequences of their actions. But CSR should not be only about what businesses have done that is wrong—important as that is. Nor should it be only about making philanthropic contributions to local charities, lending a hand in time of disaster, or providing relief to society's needy—worthy though these contributions may be. Efforts to find shared value in operating practices and in the social dimensions of competitive context have the potential not only to foster economic and social development but to change the way companies and society think about each other. NGOs, governments, and companies must stop thinking in terms of "corporate social responsibility" and start thinking in terms of "corporate social integration."

Perceiving social responsibility as building shared value rather than as damage control or as a PR campaign will require dramatically different thinking in business. We are convinced, however, that CSR will become increasingly important to competitive success.

Corporations are not responsible for all the world's problems, nor do they have the resources to solve them all. Each company can identify the particular set of societal problems that it is best equipped to help resolve and from which it can gain the greatest competitive benefit. Addressing social issues by creating shared value will lead to self-sustaining solutions that do not depend on private or government subsidies. When a well-run business applies its vast resources, expertise, and management talent to problems that it understands and in which it has a stake, it can have a greater impact on social good than any other institution or philanthropic organization.

Mapping Social Opportunities

The interdependence of a company and society can be analyzed with the same tools used to analyze competitive position and develop strategy. In this way, the firm can focus its particular CSR activities to best effect. Rather than merely acting on well-intentioned impulses or reacting to outside pressure, the organization can set an affirmative CSR agenda that produces maximum social benefit as well as gains for the business.

These two tools should be used in different ways. When a company uses the value chain to chart all the social consequences of its activities, it has, in effect, created an inventory of problems and opportunities— mostly operational issues—that need to be investigated, prioritized, and addressed. In general, companies should attempt to clear away as many negative value-chain social impacts as possible. Some company activities will prove to offer opportunities for social and strategic distinction.

In addressing competitive context, companies cannot take on every area in the diamond. Therefore, the task is to identify those areas of social context with the greatest strategic value. A company should carefully choose from this menu one or a few social initiatives that will have the greatest shared value: benefit for both society and its own competitiveness.

Looking Inside Out: Mapping the Social Impact of the Value Chain

The *value chain* depicts all the activities a company engages in while doing business. It can be used as a framework to identify the positive and negative social impact of those activities. These "inside-out" linkages may range from hiring and layoff policies to greenhouse gas emissions, as the partial list of examples illustrated here demonstrates.

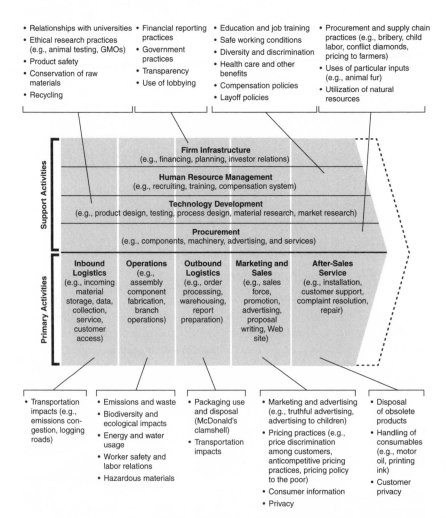

Source: Michael E. Porter, *Competitive Advantage: Creating and Sustaining Superior Performance*, 1985.

Looking Outside In: Social Influences on Competitiveness

In addition to understanding the social ramifications of the value chain, effective CSR requires an understanding of the social dimensions of the company's competitive context—the "outside-in" linkages that affect its ability to improve productivity and execute strategy. These can be understood using the *diamond framework*, which shows how the conditions at a company's locations (such as transportation infrastructure and honestly enforced regulatory policy) affect its ability to compete.

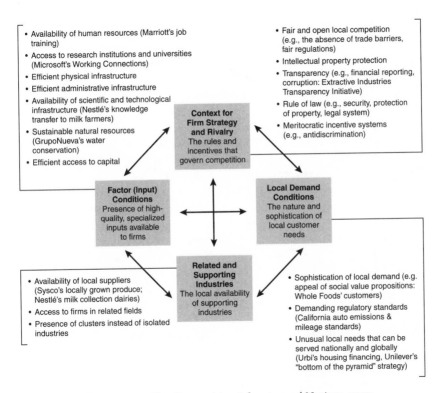

- Availability of human resources (Marriott's job training)
- Access to research institutions and universities (Microsoft's Working Connections)
- Efficient physical infrastructure
- Efficient administrative infrastructure
- Availability of scientific and technological infrastructure (Nestlé's knowledge transfer to milk farmers)
- Sustainable natural resources (GrupoNueva's water conservation)
- Efficient access to capital

Context for Firm Strategy and Rivalry
The rules and incentives that govern competition

- Fair and open local competition (e.g., the absence of trade barriers, fair regulations)
- Intellectual property protection
- Transparency (e.g., financial reporting, corruption: Extractive Industries Transparency Initiative)
- Rule of law (e.g., security, protection of property, legal system)
- Meritocratic incentive systems (e.g., antidiscrimination)

Factor (Input) Conditions
Presence of high-quality, specialized inputs available to firms

Local Demand Conditions
The nature and sophistication of local customer needs

Related and Supporting Industries
The local availability of supporting industries

- Availability of local suppliers (Sysco's locally grown produce; Nestlé's milk collection dairies)
- Access to firms in related fields
- Presence of clusters instead of isolated industries

- Sophistication of local demand (e.g. appeal of social value propositions: Whole Foods' customers)
- Demanding regulatory standards (California auto emissions & mileage standards)
- Unusual local needs that can be served nationally and globally (Urbi's housing financing, Unilever's "bottom of the pyramid" strategy)

Source: Michael E. Porter, *The Competitive Advantage of Nations,* 1990.

Integrating Company Practice and Context: Nestlé's Milk District

Nestlé's approach to working with small farmers exemplifies the symbiotic relationship between social progress and competitive advantage. Ironically, while the company's reputation remains marred by a 30-year-old controversy surrounding sales of infant formula in Africa, the corporation's impact in developing countries has often been profoundly positive.

Consider the history of Nestlé's milk business in India. In 1962, the company wanted to enter the Indian market, and it received government permission to build a dairy in the northern district of Moga. Poverty in the region was severe; people were without electricity, transportation, telephones, or medical care. A farmer typically owned less than five acres of poorly irrigated and infertile soil. Many kept a single buffalo cow that produced just enough milk for their own consumption. Sixty percent of calves died newborn. Because farmers lacked refrigeration, transportation, or any way to test for quality, milk could not travel far and was frequently contaminated or diluted.

Nestlé came to Moga to build a business, not to engage in CSR. But Nestlé's value chain, derived from the company's origins in Switzerland, depended on establishing local sources of milk from a large, diversi-

fied base of small farmers. Establishing that value chain in Moga required Nestlé to transform the competitive context in ways that created tremendous shared value for both the company and the region.

Nestlé built refrigerated dairies as collection points for milk in each town and sent its trucks out to the dairies to collect the milk. With the trucks went veterinarians, nutritionists, agronomists, and quality assurance experts. Medicines and nutritional supplements were provided for sick animals, and monthly training sessions were held for local farmers. Farmers learned that the milk quality depended on the cows' diet, which in turn depended on adequate feed crop irrigation. With financing and technical assistance from Nestlé, farmers began to dig previously unaffordable deep-bore wells. Improved irrigation not only fed cows but increased crop yields, producing surplus wheat and rice and raising the standard of living.

When Nestlé's milk factory first opened, only 180 local farmers supplied milk. Today, Nestlé buys milk from more than 75,000 farmers in the region, collecting it twice daily from more than 650 village dairies. The death rate of calves has dropped by 75%. Milk production has increased 50-fold. As the quality has improved, Nestlé has been able to pay higher prices to farmers than those set by the government, and its steady biweekly payments have enabled farmers to obtain credit. Competing dairies and milk factories have opened, and an industry cluster is beginning to develop.

Today, Moga has a significantly higher standard of living than other regions in the vicinity. Ninety percent of the homes have electricity, and most have telephones; all villages have primary schools, and many have secondary schools. Moga has five times the number of doctors as neighboring regions. The increased purchasing power of local farmers has also greatly expanded the market for Nestlé's products, further supporting the firm's economic success.

Nestlé's commitment to working with small farmers is central to its strategy. It enables the company to obtain a stable supply of high-quality commodities without paying middlemen. The corporation's other core products—coffee and cocoa—are often grown by small farmers in developing countries under similar conditions. Nestlé's experience in setting up collection points, training farmers, and introducing better technology in Moga has been repeated in Brazil, Thailand, and a dozen other countries, including, most recently, China. In each case, as Nestlé has prospered, so has the community.

NOTES

1. An early discussion of the idea of CSR as an opportunity rather than a cost can be found in David Grayson and Adrian Hodges, *Corporate Social Opportunity* (Greenleaf, 2004).

2. For a more complete discussion of the importance of competitive context and the diamond model, see Michael E. Porter and Mark R. Kramer, "The Competitive Advantage of Corporate Philanthropy," HBR December 2002. See also Michael Porter's book *The Competitive Advantage of Nations* (The Free Press, 1990) and his article "Locations, Clusters, and Company Strategy," in *The Oxford Handbook of Economic Geography*, edited by Gordon L. Clark, Maryann P. Feldman, and Meric S. Gertler (Oxford University Press, 2000).

Part V   Strategy and Leadership

CHAPTER 15

Seven Surprises for New CEOs

Michael E. Porter

Jay W. Lorsch

Nitin Nohria

BEARING FULL RESPONSIBILITY for a company's success or failure, but being unable to control most of what will determine it. Having more authority than anyone else in the organization, but being unable to wield it without unhappy consequences. Sound like a tough job? It is—ask a CEO. Surprised by the description? So are CEOs who are new to the role. Just when an executive feels he has reached the pinnacle of his career, capturing the coveted goal for which he has so long been striving, he begins to realize that the CEO's job is different and more complicated than he imagined.

Some of the surprises for new CEOs arise from time and knowledge limitations—there is so much to do in complex new areas, with imperfect information and never enough time. Others stem from unexpected and unfamiliar new roles and altered professional relationships. Still others crop up because of the paradox that the more power you have, the harder it is to use. While several of the challenges may appear familiar, we have discovered that nothing in a leader's background, even running a large business within his company, fully prepares him to be CEO.

Through our work with new chief executives of major companies, we have found seven surprises to be the most common. (See the insert "Learning the Ropes.") How well and how quickly new CEOs understand, accept, and confront them will have a lot to do with the executives' eventual success or failure. The seven surprises highlight realities

December 2004

about the nature of leadership that are important not just for CEOs but for executives at any level and in any size organization. (See the insert "The Seven Things You Need to Know" at the end of this article.)

Surprise One: You Can't Run the Company

Before becoming CEO, most executives are responsible for a major business or have been COO. They are skilled at running businesses and

---

Learning the Ropes

The New CEO Workshop at Harvard Business School is open only to newly appointed CEOs of companies with annual revenues of $1 billion or more. In keeping with the mission of HBS—to educate leaders who make a difference in the world—we introduced this workshop several years ago to address the distinctive challenges facing first-time chief executives in large, complex enterprises. We personally invite each participant, to ensure the appropriate size and composition of the group, which typically includes about ten CEOs whose organizations cover a broad cross section of industries. These CEOs run public companies based in advanced economies. They have been appointed and are either waiting to take office or within the first few months of tenure. Since the program's inception several years ago, about 50 new CEOs have participated, from world-leading companies such as Applied Materials, BellSouth, Cadbury Schweppes, Caterpillar, Lloyds TSB,

Lowe's, Novartis, Schlumberger, UPS, and Walgreens. Recently, a group of early workshop participants reconvened to review the first several years in their jobs and to recalibrate their agendas.

The workshop offers a unique perspective from which to explore both the predictable and the surprising aspects of becoming a CEO. We interview all participants in advance, using a structured set of questions about their strategy, their relationship with the board, and their immediate and longer-term challenges. Discussion sessions during the two-day program are built around these and other areas where new CEOs face unfamiliar challenges, and around peer and faculty dialogue.

We typically start by asking the CEOs to look ahead to the end of their tenure and give their retirement speech. The next day, we ask them to describe their immediate challenges. We then closely examine some of these challenges, such as crafting a strategy that creates lasting economic value, building a productive relationship with the board of directors, communicating effectively with inside and outside constituencies, and setting the proper tone and style to create a strong culture. The sessions are extremely interactive, and discussions involve in-depth sharing of personal experiences.

The seven surprises to new CEOs described in this article are challenges highlighted again and again in our workshop discussions. The stories we use to illustrate these lessons are drawn from the experiences of participants and from our own collective experiences working with CEOs. (We are grateful to Patia McGrath, our research associate, for her help in organizing these workshops and in preparing this article.)

relish the opportunity to run an entire organization. As new CEOs discover pretty quickly, however, running the business is but a small part of the job. On the second day of our New CEO Workshop at Harvard Business School, we go around the room and ask participants to describe what the job feels like to them. At a recent session, the CEO of a large midwestern manufacturer—an executive whose practiced, confident air bespoke decades of experience—revealed just how unsure he felt as he took his first steps on this new ground:

> Imagine serving the same company for 37 years. It is the only employer you have ever known, and this fact intensifies the tremendous loyalty you feel for the firm and the camaraderie you share with your colleagues. Your appointment to CEO was one of the proudest moments of your life. You have been training to run the business for your whole career, you think, and you are really looking forward to doing so.
>
> Now fast-forward a few months. Your calendar is booked solid with analyst meetings, business media interviews (which take ages to prepare for, since you never know where the shots will come from), and sessions in Washington (where you will attempt to explain to politicians the crucial and intricate details of your industry). You have also recently been elected to an outside directorship or two, and the charities that you have long supported are more eager than ever for you to join their boards and raise funds on their behalf. No one will accept a substitute—it has to be you.
>
> Not only do you have external pressures tugging you away from day-to-day business operations; the volume of internal demands is enormous. Before you became CEO, you prided yourself on visiting every unit in your region, you got to know the employees, you spoke directly with customers—you had your hands right on the pulse of the business. Since you have become CEO, you have not been able to do any of these things even for your old region—never mind the rest. You cannot shake the feeling that you have lost touch with the day-to-day workings of your company. To make matters worse, the unavoidable gaps in your own expertise loom larger than ever.

This type of response is typical; a new CEO's comfort and familiarity with internal operations quickly recede as demands on the executive mount. The sheer volume and intensity of external demands take many by surprise. Almost every new CEO struggles to manage the time drain of attending to shareholders, analysts, board members, industry groups, politicians, and other constituencies. CEOs hired from outside struggle to learn how their new company operates, but those promoted from within work equally hard to separate themselves from operations and learn the terrain of their outside constituencies. Some have told us quite frankly that they feel a sense of loss because they're no longer as close to the business as they once were. One participant in the New CEO Workshop who had come up through the ranks at his company told us that he felt as if he were starting all over again—he had to learn new management tools and build new relationships while reframing old ones. Workshop participants complete a forced-rank survey that asks how prepared they feel for their new responsibilities on a number of dimensions, such as dealing with the stock market, working with their board of directors, operating at the center of public scrutiny, building a senior management team, or being the company's chief spokesperson. It is clear from their responses that CEOs are apprehensive about, as one put it, managing the dual roles of Mr. Inside and Mr. Outside.

As the CEO learns how demanding it is to attend to the company's outside constituencies, he also discovers, often to his shock, that he has to let go of a lot of responsibility—not just for operating the company but even for knowing what's going on in it. The CEO can't monitor everyone. It's simply not possible for any one person to oversee every facet of a large company, even if he were willing to put in a 100-hour week. The new CEO may expect this to be true as he begins, but it still feels strange not to know what subordinates are up to, and many executives experience the change as a loss of control. One workshop participant recalled that he was stunned by the realization that he would have to rely on others in areas like operations, where he had previously thrived, and would have to master aspects of the company such as investor relations and regulatory affairs, where he had little experience. To be sure, the new CEO has the final say in hiring and firing, promotions, and compensation, but many of those decisions are, by necessity, in the hands of people closer to operations. Indeed, CEOs often end up knowing less about the operational details of their companies than they did in their previous positions.

While the CEO is responsible for the successful operation of the enterprise, then, he can no longer be personally involved in all the decisions needed to run a large, complex organization. The CEO's greatest influence shifts from direct to indirect means—articulating and communicating a clear, easily understood strategy; institutionalizing rigorous structures and processes to guide, inform, and reward; and setting values and tone. Equally important is selecting and managing the right senior management team to share the burden of running the company.

Surprise Two: Giving Orders Is Very Costly

The CEO is undoubtedly the most powerful person in any organization. Yet any CEO who tries to use this power to unilaterally issue orders or summarily reject proposals that have come up through the organization will pay a stiff price. Giving orders can trigger resentment and defensiveness in colleagues and subordinates. Second-guessing a senior manager can demoralize and demotivate not only that person but others around him, while eroding his authority and confidence. What's more, the need to overrule a proposal indicates that the strategic planning and other processes in place may be either inappropriate or insufficient. No proposal should reach the CEO for final approval unless he can ratify it with enthusiasm. Before then, everyone involved with the matter should have raised and resolved any potential deal breakers, bringing the CEO into the discussion only at strategically significant moments to obtain feedback and support. Ironically, by exercising his power to give orders, the CEO actually reduces his real power, saps his energy and his organization's, and slows down progress.

When CEOs wield direct power, they must do so very selectively and deliberately—and never without a broader plan of action in mind. Usually, power is best used indirectly, through the disciplined processes mentioned above (articulating strategy and so on). Together with tone and style, such processes enable the CEO to make effective decisions consistent with where he wants the company to go.

One of our new CEOs learned this the hard way. Soon after he became CEO, he was asked to approve a marketing campaign for the launch of a new product. The campaign was the result of more than a year's work by a division manager and his team. They had developed advertising, prepared promotional materials, crafted a sales and distribution plan, and assigned responsibilities for different parts of the plan. All that was needed was the new CEO's approval, which the executives assumed was largely a formality.

The CEO saw it differently. He felt that the company's advertising had become stale and that a makeover should start right away—and this would most likely mean hiring a new agency. He put the marketing campaign on hold until a new advertising plan could be developed—a decision that he hoped would send a strong signal about the changes he meant to introduce. Little did he realize that he had sent several other powerful signals as well.

Word of his order spread like wildfire. The CEO's calendar was soon filled with meetings with executives seeking approval of their plans. Some came to obtain consent for new capital expenditures, others for personnel decisions, and others on matters as mundane as whether to host a client conference. They had lost confidence that they understood the CEO's expectations, so they wanted to check with him before proceeding on anything. His calendar became a bottleneck, and organizational decision making virtually ground to a halt.

For a while, the CEO was oblivious to the high cost of his intrusive approach. As an outsider new to the company, he felt good about being part of all these conversations. He was now at the center of all the action. He viewed each meeting as an opportunity to communicate the new direction in which he hoped to take the company. But he began to recognize the impact of his actions when the division manager he had overruled came forward a month later with the news that he had decided to accept a job at another company. This came as a shock to the CEO, who, despite nixing the ad campaign, had been quite impressed with the other elements of the marketing program and the thoroughness with which they had been planned. What he had failed to understand was that he had undermined the manager's self-confidence as well as his authority with his subordinates and peers. As hard as the CEO tried to persuade him to reconsider and stay, the manager felt so demoralized that he was determined to leave.

Chastened, the CEO called a meeting of all his top managers the next week. He reassured them that they enjoyed his full confidence and that he had no intention of undermining their authority as he had done with the departing division manager. He candidly admitted that he might have been too precipitous in halting the marketing campaign, especially since he had not yet fully communicated his new strategy for the company. He identified the areas in which he wanted to make strategic changes, emphasizing that all this was a work in progress, to be completed with everyone's help. He clarified the issues on which he wanted to be consulted and those on which he would fully trust his managers. He created a task force to review some of the company's key management processes—planning, budgeting, performance evaluation, new product rollout, development of marketing campaigns, and recruitment of key employees—to ensure that there would be opportunities for early CEO input. Finally, he spent the next year working hard to make sure that his vision and agenda were clear to all employees, especially his senior management team. (We know this because he stayed in touch with us after the workshop, as many participants do.)

This CEO concluded, and we would agree, that it is rarely a good idea to unilaterally overrule a thoughtful decision that has cleared several other organizational hurdles. Indeed, a key indicator the CEO subsequently used to judge the health of the company's management processes was how enthusiastically he could approve the decisions that came his way. The need to overrule something is a sure sign of a broader organizational failure. Or, as hard as this is to admit, it may reflect the CEO's own failure to clearly communicate his strategy and operating principles. There are certainly some circumstances in which the harm done by moving forward with a major strategic decision that the CEO considers a serious mistake—a large acquisition, say—is greater than the harm done by issuing orders. But, as this CEO himself eventually acknowledged, the ad makeover could have waited.

A new CEO may need to put a stake in the ground to show that he's in charge and to let the organization know what he stands for. Giving a direct order (and especially undoing someone's work) is rarely the best way to do this, however. Instead, a CEO should look for ways to include senior managers and to promote agreement about decision-making criteria. At an off-site meeting, for example, the CEO can reveal his priorities and concerns by setting the agenda while giving his team a chance to participate and buy in. A new CEO must be willing to share power and trust others to make important decisions. The most powerful CEO is the one who expands the power of those around him.

Surprise Three: It Is Hard to Know What Is Really Going On

Even when CEOs understand that they cannot oversee every aspect of their companies, they nevertheless assume—wrongly—that they will be able to learn everything they need to know. Certainly, CEOs are flooded with information, but reliable information is surprisingly scarce. All information coming to the top is filtered, sometimes with good intentions, sometimes with not such good intentions. Receiving solid information becomes even more difficult because immediately upon appointment, the CEO's relationships change. Former peers and subordinates who used to constitute an informal channel—those who could read between the lines and who really knew what was happening at the ground level—go on their guard. Even those the CEO was closest to are wary of delivering bad news. Further, because the CEO can have so much impact on anyone's career, each individual's agenda colors the information the CEO receives.

Look at the experience of one workshop participant, whose organization was an equal partner in a poorly performing joint venture. As revenues failed to materialize and costs continued to rise, the CEO tried to better understand the lackluster performance by holding several reviews with key managers involved in the venture. Their explanations for the unimpressive results were not surprising: The managers placed the blame squarely on the JV partner. When it became clear to the CEO that he would not find out what was really going on simply by asking his own team for information, he approached senior managers from the other company—ones who, as it happened, were not directly involved in the JV's operations. Their understanding of the situation was different from what the CEO's own people had been telling him, and the partner's managers offered many constructive observations on the JV's operations.

In the end, the CEO recognized that the root cause of the problems was a lack of clarity—on both sides of the partnership—about the JV's objectives. His company eventually bought its way out of the venture, at a loss.

Looking back, the CEO did not feel that his team hid information with malicious intent. For one thing, he realized, his people had a natural instinct to protect themselves, especially in front of their leader. Others who knew how serious the problems were perhaps refrained from speaking up because they were concerned that the CEO would shoot the messenger. Also, it was inherently difficult for operating management to recognize the problem, which lay not in operational details but in the unclear and clashing goals with which the joint venture was established. For the CEO, the biggest surprise was having to seek external feedback to better assess what was really going on within his organization, because a clear picture was so hard to get from his own people.

It is a delicate challenge for a CEO to find reliable sources of information without undermining key reports, who might feel that the CEO is going around them. Many workshop participants recounted their efforts to engage in periodic face-to-face conversations with people at different levels and in various parts of the company. One CEO, for example, invited a group of ten to 12 employees to have lunch with him weekly. Employees volunteered to participate, and the group included people from all levels and divisions; managers were not allowed to attend with their direct reports. While the CEO recognized that not everyone in these lunches would speak frankly, he found that an informal setting reduced barriers to communication and provided an opportunity to hear the ideas and opinions of a cross section of employees. Other CEOs described using field visits and town-hall-type forums to pick up relatively unfiltered information.

Several new CEOs stressed the importance of continuing to seek information from deep within the organization—from employees closest to the front line—even though that approach might not sit well with managers in the middle. A CEO of a high-technology firm, for example, went several levels down to determine the status of technical projects by asking those directly involved how the work was progressing. He didn't tell the senior people overseeing the projects that he was taking these surprise "temperature checks." Another CEO took it as a warning sign if senior executives tried to discourage him from speaking directly to their subordinates. He underscored, however, that this sort of contact worked only if it was maintained regularly, so that it was not considered a big event—and if the people who spoke to the CEO felt confident that their candor would not come back to haunt them.

Many CEOs in the workshop find that unbiased information is available from external channels—for instance, through contact with customers, conversations with other CEOs, and affiliations with industry associations. Almost every workshop participant allocated time for such external discussions through a systematic process. Several CEOs also pointed to productive relationships they had with independent advisers who could tell the unabashed truth and had license to criticize the CEO's thinking.

Surprise Four: You Are Always Sending a Message

The typical new CEO knows that his actions will be noticed by those in his company. What he does not generally realize is the extent to which his every move—both inside and outside the organization—will be scrutinized and interpreted. His words and deeds, however small or off-the-cuff, are instantly spread and amplified, and sometimes drastically misinterpreted. (Remember the CEO who pulled the marketing campaign.) Even personal choices are subject to scrutiny. One CEO in our workshop joked that he had to choose the type of car he drove very carefully because the company parking lot would soon be full of the same model.

The first big message is in the CEO's appointment itself. People develop assumptions and expectations based on the CEO's background and previous experiences. This initial profile immediately takes on great significance. One CEO, the first American to take the helm of his major British company, reflected in our workshop that many constituencies expected the "barbaric American" to try to change the firm's centuries-old traditions and culture. A CEO with a legal background recounted how the markets reacted negatively to his appointment, on the assumption that the only reason to make a lawyer CEO was that the company was facing deeper asbestos-litigation problems than previously acknowledged. These sorts of messages are sent before the new CEO even does anything.

Once in the job, the new CEO can no longer afford to have speculative discussions with employees, because any half-baked idea he puts forth runs the risk of being latched onto as a good one. The CEO's microphone is always on, and his message can become distorted. Even an innocent question may be interpreted as a loss of confidence. The aura attached to the executive's words is illustrated in a story we heard from one CEO, who found, to his surprise, that too many people were invoking his name—hoping that simply starting a sentence with "Frank says. . ." would ensure action, even though, in most cases, Frank hadn't said anything of the sort.

And so new CEOs need to learn quickly what signals they are sending. They can then minimize inadvertent messages and maximize the impact of the messages they want to send, once they understand the multiplier effect of their words and actions. Consider, for example, the experience of one new CEO, whose organization is based in the southeastern United States. The company had avoided racially related class action lawsuits, even though other companies in the region had not. It had clear standards covering employee behavior, including a rule forbidding the display of the Confederate flag. When the local press revealed that one member of the executive team had publicly advocated that the company display the flag, the CEO immediately had that person terminated. As the CEO described it, he did this to signal that behavior inconsistent with company policy would not be tolerated at any level in the organization. No one had to guess the CEO's views on this topic—he sent a clear message.

To take another example, a new CEO of a transportation company wanted to signal the importance of customer and employee safety. While on a site visit, he noticed that a fire switch was disconnected on one rail car, so he shut down all trains in the system until every switch could be checked. He also launched an investigation into why the switch was disconnected, to prevent a reoccurrence. Although there were redundant systems in place, the CEO wanted his actions to send a message—both internally and externally—that nothing short of perfect safety compliance would be acceptable. He also hoped that employees would in turn feel empowered to do whatever was necessary to ensure safety.

A CEO's signals, already subject to misinterpretation, are further complicated by the fact that different constituencies will respond to the same news in different ways. It is particularly challenging when signals are sent to both internal and external groups. While Wall Street might delight in hearing a plan for a struggling unit's spin-off, for instance, employees may be shattered. The task of managing outside and inside constituencies, while keeping the message truthful and consistent to both, is never easy. The important lesson for new CEOs is to consider carefully how their actions and the way these are communicated will be interpreted by different audiences. An executive may be unable to avoid some negative impact on one group or another, but by thoughtfully framing his message, he can minimize the damage.

Finally, to the extent possible, CEOs must strive for consistency in their messages. A simple, clear message, repeated often and illustrated with memorable stories, is the best way for a new CEO to master the communication challenges of the job.

Surprise Five: You Are Not the Boss

Many new CEOs initially assume that they have finally reached a position where they have ultimate authority. They soon learn that the situation is much more complicated than that. Although the CEO may sit at the top of the management hierarchy, he still reports to the board of directors. The board hired him and can also fire him; it has the power to evaluate his performance, set his compensation, overturn his strategy, and make other major decisions. CEOs must attend to this relationship more today than ever before as new laws and regulations, court decisions, and shareholder activism have empowered and emboldened boards. As one new CEO told us, "We no longer have a clear picture of how to work with the board." Even if the relationship isn't contentious, it's become a bigger drain on the CEO's time and energy.

Just when new CEOs think they can finally stop managing upward, the need to do so grows in complexity. Instead of reporting to a single boss, the new CEO has ten or 12 bosses, one of whom is often a "lead director," who, by virtue of that position, is meant to balance the CEO's authority. And although the board is likely to comprise experienced and capable people, many members will have limited knowledge of the company's industry. This means the CEO (along with the management team) has to educate the board about what is happening in the company and the industry. While the CEO may have problems in getting information, the worst thing for his relationship with the board is for the directors to feel uninformed or surprised. Because board members have many demands on their time, information must be transmitted to them in a way that is easy to understand.

Moreover, most board members may have had little previous contact with the new CEO. Even if he was promoted from within and was previously on the board, their interaction with him was probably infrequent and brief. He has to spend time letting members get to know him and develop confidence in his ability and judgment. Should the new CEO's predecessor remain involved, in the chairman's seat or on the board, the challenge becomes even greater. The former CEO brings board relationships and a legacy of decisions that the new CEO may wish to reconsider. All of this creates awkwardness in the boardroom and makes it difficult for the successor to work with the board. In our experience, it is almost always a bad idea for a predecessor to remain on the board.

For one new CEO, the first few weeks in office were a trial by fire. The board had ousted his predecessor and the entire management team, and the company was undergoing an SEC investigation. The new CEO arrived amid falling employee morale, defecting customers, and media scrutiny. He resolved to quickly reinvent the company with new accounting policies, a new management team, and, eventually, a new strategic direction. But he soon realized that the company's directors, having been burned by the previous management, were keeping the company (and him) under much tighter control. It became evident that the board wanted to temper and closely monitor his actions. He immediately concluded he had to work carefully with the directors, trying his ideas on them early to get their support. Although this took more of his time than he had ever anticipated, he gradually earned their trust and was then able to move more quickly. While this example may be extreme, its lesson is applicable to all CEOs: At the end of the day, the board—not the CEO—is in charge.

As the CEO develops his boardroom relationships, he must view the directors as neither friends nor confidants (though some of them may eventually play those roles), but as bosses who hold him personally accountable for the success of the company. By actively investing in director knowledge and relationships—through one-on-one contacts, e-mail updates of corporate progress, and distribution of background material, for example—the best CEOs turn board meetings into partici-patory discussions rather than show-and-tell sessions by management. A new CEO who is open with—and creates the opportunity to collaborate with—his directors will be more likely to garner support from these bosses.

Surprise Six: Pleasing Shareholders Is Not the Goal

Upon taking office, new CEOs often mistakenly believe that their pri-mary responsibility is to keep the shareholders happy. After all, share-holder value is the mantra that has defined corporate goals for many years. Courting the favor of analysts and shareholders seems natural, and every CEO (especially a new one) likes an endorsement of his leadership through a higher share price.

The problem is that defining one's goal as shareholder approval may not be in the company's best interest. Actions and strategies favored by shareholders (and analysts) may not benefit the ultimate competitive position of the company. Shareholders come and go—the average share of stock in the United States is held for less than a year—and they care only about what happens to the stock during the period they expect to own it. Analysts are naturally concerned with moving in and out of a stock, not holding it. They tend to reinforce trends—and love deals—rather than reward a long-term focus. In fact, both shareholders and analysts are prone to take a short-term view. CEOs, however, need to concern themselves with creating sustainable economic value.

Sometimes the pressure from analysts and shareholders can get so strong that it becomes destructive. One CEO in our workshop said he'd felt compelled to spin off a major division—a dramatic step that appeased analysts in the short term. Unfortunately, it hurt the longer-term perfor-mance of the company because the sale of this division drove away some customers who were vital to the growth of other divisions.

An involved, informed board can be the CEO's best ally in staying focused on the long run. The CEO of a major retailer described the perfect storm he was stepping into when he took office: a mature industry, the seemingly unconquerable Wal-Mart, and a lackluster economy. As the CEO described it, the business was badly broken, and he needed time to restore it to its former success. He worked with the board to develop a new strategy focused on regaining market share. After two quarters of heavy lifting, results began to improve. The board was pleased and employees were energized, but the analysts remained conspicuously bearish. They saw the new strategy as being too slow and drawn out. After a number of time-consuming and fruitless meetings with them, the CEO came to understand that the analysts were interested only in immediate, dramatic change—regardless of the long-run effects on the company. As he told us, "There comes a time when you just don't give a damn what the analysts think." This CEO was able to keep the focus where it needed to be because he had worked hard to ensure that his board bought into the long-term merits of the turnaround strategy.

Rather than attempt to please all shareholders through the inevitable ups and downs, CEOs must recognize that, ultimately, it is only long-term profitability that matters, not today's growth expectations or even the stock price. A high stock price will eventually collapse without the underpinnings of fundamental competitive advantage. Instead of looking to shareholders for strategic direction, the CEO must develop and articulate a clear strategy to distinguish the company from others and address industry fundamentals. A key CEO role is to sell the strategy and shape how analysts and shareholders look at the company. CEOs should not expect that their strategies will be immediately understood or accepted; a constant stream of reiterations, explanations, and reminders will likely be necessary to affect analysts' perceptions. Success in this process may be slow. But a CEO with the courage to develop and articulate a sound strategy, even if it is currently unpopular on Wall Street, will eventually attract the right shareholders—those who buy and hold the stock because they believe in the big-picture strategy.

Surprise Seven: You Are Still Only Human

Too often, we view CEOs in the cinematic image of indefatigable superhero. Yet they remain bound by all-too-human hopes, fears, and limits. The attention and adulation that come with the job make introspection difficult and vulnerabilities inadmissible. Workshop participants told us again and again that they needed to make a conscious effort to resist the illusion of self-importance, omnipotence, and omniscience. The executives in our workshop have been remarkably forthcoming about the personal impact of being a CEO. Invariably, they have had to come to terms with the fact that they can't do everything well. They have found it difficult and ego-bruising to accept gaps in their expertise and admit that the job is more physically and emotionally taxing than any others they have held.

Maintaining some balance between the personal and the professional is another theme that comes up repeatedly in our workshop. It's easy for a new CEO to underestimate the number and magnitude of demands that will be placed upon him. Many new CEOs are confident that they can balance their new challenges with their personal lives without too much trouble—after all, they've managed to do so in other senior management positions. However, the CEO role, with all its demands and its public nature, can significantly intensify this tension. As one CEO concluded, "In the end, there is no such thing as balance. There are only trade-offs."

The difficulties don't arise solely from time constraints. Many aspects of a CEO's life become public that most of us would prefer to keep private. One CEO told us that his teenage daughter approached him after she read a high-profile newspaper article disclosing his compensation. He had never before discussed his income with his children. Even though his pay was quite modest compared with that of his peers, he had to explain to his family why he earned what he did. Another CEO said that he was dreading the first family holiday gathering after he'd become CEO and the reactions of his siblings now that his success was so public. Virtually every new CEO reports that relationships with friends and family have changed.

It surprised us that many new CEOs—even in the early days—were already thinking about their legacies. While this can lead to a long-term focus, which is desirable, it can also lead to bold (and even reckless) attempts to make a mark on the company by changing what should be left unchanged. With such goals, it is easy to be seduced by major deals and tempting to create an organization that is three times larger even if it is less profitable.

It is essential for new CEOs to make a disciplined effort to stay humble, to revisit their decisions and actions, to continue to listen to others, and to find people who will be honest and forthright. Otherwise, the rewards and praise bestowed upon a CEO can tempt him into acts of hubris. A capable and active board can also provide a check on such temptations.

Workshop participants recognized that they needed connections to the world outside their organizations, at home and in the community, to avoid being consumed by their corporate lives. Many found personally fulfilling outlets for their human needs through public service commitments. CEOs needed and wanted some relaxation too. Regular exercise, family vacations, and golf seemed to be the preferred avenues, though one CEO even took up race car driving as a hobby. He explained that he knew he would never be Mario Andretti, but he could occupy and challenge himself by trying.

The Seven Things You Need to Know

Most new chief executives are taken aback by the unexpected and unfamiliar new roles, the time and information limitations, and the altered professional relationships they run up against. Here are the common surprises new CEOs face, and here's how to tell when adjustments are necessary.

Surprise One: You Can't Run the Company

warning signs:

- You are in too many meetings and involved in too many tactical discussions.

- There are too many days when you feel as though you have lost control over your time.

Surprise Two: Giving Orders Is Very Costly

warning signs:

- You have become the bottleneck.

- Employees are overly inclined to consult you before they act.

- People start using your name to endorse things, as in, "Frank says. . ."

Surprise Three: It Is Hard to Know What Is Really Going On

warning signs:

- You keep hearing things that surprise you.

- You learn about events after the fact.

• You hear concerns and dissenting views through the grapevine rather than directly.

Surprise Four: You Are Always Sending a Message

warning signs:

• Employees circulate stories about your behavior that magnify or distort reality.

• People around you act in ways that indicate they're trying to anticipate your likes and dislikes.

Surprise Five: You Are Not the Boss

warning signs:

• You don't know where you stand with board members.

• Roles and responsibilities of the board members and of management are not clear.

• The discussions in board meetings are limited mostly to reporting on results and management's decisions.

Surprise Six: Pleasing Shareholders Is Not the Goal

warning signs:

• Executives and board members judge actions by their effect on stock price.

• Analysts who don't understand the business push for decisions that risk the health of the company.

• Management incentives are disproportionately tied to stock price.

Surprise Seven: You Are Still Only Human

warning signs:

• You give interviews about you rather than about the company.

• Your lifestyle is more lavish or privileged than that of other top executives in the company.

• You have few if any activities not connected to the company.

Implications for CEO Leadership

Taken together, the seven surprises carry some important and subtle implications for how a new CEO should define his job.

First, the CEO must learn to manage organizational context rather than focus on daily operations. Providing leadership in this way—and not diving into the details—can be a jarring transition. One CEO said that he initially felt like the company's "most useless executive," despite the power inherent in the job. The CEO needs to learn how to act in indirect ways—setting and communicating strategy, putting sound processes in place, selecting and mentoring key people—to create the conditions that will help others make the right choices. At the same time, he must set the tone and define the organization's culture and values through his words and actions—in other words, demonstrate how employees should behave.

Second, he must recognize that his position does not confer the right to lead, nor does it guarantee the organization's loyalty. He must perpetually earn and maintain the moral mandate to lead. CEOs can easily lose their legitimacy if their vision is unconvincing, if their actions are inconsistent with the values they espouse, or if their self-interest appears to trump the welfare of the organization. They must realize that success ultimately depends on their ability to enlist the voluntary commitment rather than the forced obedience of others. While mastering the conventional tools of management may have won the CEO his job, these tools alone will not keep him there.

Finally, the CEO must not get totally absorbed in the role. Even if others think he is omnipotent, he is still only human. Failing to recognize this will lead to arrogance, exhaustion, and a shortened tenure. Only by maintaining a personal balance and staying grounded can the CEO achieve the perspective required to make decisions in the interest of the company and its long-term prosperity.

Index

About the Contributors

Michael E. Porter is the Bishop William Lawrence University Professor at Harvard Business School. A leading authority on competitive strategy and the competitiveness of nations and regions, his work is recognized in governments, corporations, nonprofits, and academic circles across the globe. Professor Porter's core field is competition and strategy, and this remains the focus of his research. His ideas have also redefined thinking about competitiveness, economic development, economically distressed areas, and the role of corporations in society. He is the author of seventeen books and numerous articles. Professor Porter has recently devoted considerable attention to understanding and addressing the problems in health care evident in the United States and abroad. His book, *Redefining Health Care* (with Elizabeth Teisberg), develops a new framework for understanding how to transform the value delivered by the health care system. For more information, see the Web site of the Institute for Strategy and Competitiveness (www.isc.hbs.edu).

Mark R. Kramer is cofounder (with Professor Michael E. Porter) and Managing Director of FSG Social Impact Advisors, a nonprofit consulting firm focused on philanthropy and corporate social responsibility with offices in Boston, San Francisco, Seattle, and Geneva. Mr. Kramer is also a founder of the Center for Effective Philanthropy, and a Senior Fellow at Harvard's Kennedy School of Government. Mr. Kramer is a coauthor with Professor Porter of three influential *Harvard Business Review* articles on philanthropy and corporate responsibility. Previously, Mr. Kramer spent twelve years as a venture capital investor. He holds degrees from Brandeis University, The Wharton School, and the University of Pennsylvania Law School.

An associate at the Institute for International Management Research (FIM) of the St. Gallen Graduate School of Economics in Switzerland, **Claas van der Linde**'s research and consulting focuses on international and regional competitiveness and competition, as well as issues of international management. He is the author of the book *Deutsche Wettbewerbsvorteile* (German Competitive Advantage) and author or co-author of numerous articles in professional publications. He holds an MBA from the Columbia Business School in New York and a Ph.D. in business administration from the St. Gallen Graduate School of Economics.

Jay W. Lorsch is the Louis E. Kirstein Professor of Human Relations at the Harvard Business School. He is the author of over a dozen books, including *Back to the Drawing Board: Designing Corporate Boards for a Complex World* (October 2003) and *Aligning the Stars: How to Succeed When Professionals Drive Results* (2002). He has been elected as a Fellow of the American Academy of Arts and Sciences. Professor Lorsch has taught in all of Harvard Business School's educational programs and is currently Chairman of the Harvard Business School's Global Corporate Governance Initiative and Faculty Chairman of the Executive Education Leading Professional Service Firms Program. He has consulted with numerous large corporations in the United States and internationally, and is currently a Director of Computer Associates International, Inc. and a member of the *Antioch Review* National Advisory Board.

During his career with Arthur Andersen & Co. from 1958 to 1986, **Victor E. Millar** earned an international reputation in the management of professional services firms. He was the first in the profession to forecast the long-term growth potential of the IT services industry and to understand the correlation between investments in intellectual capital and increased profitability. Millar currently serves as chairman of The Columbus Group LLC, a consolidation of professional services firms, as well as a member of the boards of several professional services firms.

Nitin Nohria is Richard P. Chapman Professor of Business Administration and Senior Associate Dean and Director of Faculty Development at the Harvard Business School. His research centers on leadership and corporate transformation. Professor Nohria teaches courses across

Harvard Business School's MBA, PhD, and Executive Education programs. He also served as a visiting faculty member at the London Business School in 1996. He has coauthored more than ten books, most recently *Paths to Power: How Insiders and Outsiders Shaped American Business Leadership*, and is also the author of over seventy-five journal articles, book chapters, cases, working papers, and notes. Professor Nohria received his PhD in management from the Sloan School of Management, Massachusetts Institute of Technology, and a BTech in Chemical Engineering from the Indian Institute of Technology, Bombay. He joined the Harvard Business School faculty in July 1988.

Elizabeth Olmsted Teisberg is an associate professor at the Darden Graduate School of Business Administration, University of Virginia. Professor Teisberg's research and consulting focuses on the value of innovation and analysis of strategic opportunities in high technology and health care industries. She is coauthor of *The Portable MBA* (1997) and the author of numerous articles in professional publications. Prior to joining Darden, she was a professor at the Harvard Business School for eight years. She holds an MS and PhD in engineering from Stanford University.